England
in the 1670s

D1570149

A History of Early Modern England

General Editor: John Morrill

This series provides a detailed and vivid account of the history of early modern England. One of its principle aims is to capture the spirit of the time from the point of view of the people living through it. Each volume will be broad in scope covering the political, religious, social and cultural dimensions of the period.

Published

The Birth of the Elizabethan Age
England in the 1560s
Norman Jones

England in the 1670s
John Spurr

England in the 1690s
Craig Rose

The Birth of Britain
A New Nation 1700–1710
W. A. Speck

In Preparation

England in the 1590s
David Dean

England in the 1650s
Ann Hughes

England in the 1660s
N. H. Keeble

England
in the 1670s

'This Masquerading Age'

John Spurr

The right of John Spurr to be identified as author of this work has been asserted in accordance with the Copyright, Designs and Patents Act 1988.

First published 2000   DA

2 4 6 8 10 9 7 5 3 1   445

Blackwell Publishers Ltd   .S68
108 Cowley Road
Oxford OX4 1JF   2000
UK

Blackwell Publishers Inc.
350 Main Street
Malden, Massachusetts 02148
USA

British Library Cataloguing in Publication Data

A CIP catalogue record for this book is available from the British Library.

Library of Congress Cataloging-in-Publication Data

Spurr, John.
        England in the 1670s: this masquerading age / John Spurr.
            p.   cm. – (A history of early modern England)
        Includes bibliographical references and index.
        ISBN 0-631-19256-5 (alk. paper) – ISBN 0-631-22253-7 (pb : alk. paper)
        1. Great Britain–History–Charles II, 1660–1685.   2. England–Civilization–17th
    century.   I. Title.   II. Series.
    DA445 .S68 2000
    941.06′6–dc21   00-037897

Typeset in 10 on 11½ pt New Baskerville
by Best-set Typesetters Ltd., Hong Kong
Printed in Great Britain by Biddles Ltd, www.biddles.co.uk

This book is printed on acid-free paper

To
Henry, Alice and William

not to write at all is much the safer course of life: but if a man's fate or genius prompt him otherwise, 'tis necessary that he be copious in matter, solid in reason, methodical in the order of his work; and that the subject be well chosen, the season well fixed, and, to be short, that his whole production be matured to see the light by a just course of time, and judicious deliberation. Otherwise, though with some of these conditions he may perhaps attain commendation; yet without them all he cannot deserve pardon.

Andrew Marvell, *The Rehearsal Transpros'd: The Second Part* (1673)

It is not imaginable to such as have not tried, what labour an historian (that would be exact) is condemned to: he must read all, good, and bad, and remove a world of rubbish before he can lay the foundation . . .

John Evelyn to Samuel Pepys, 28 April 1682

I present not here what I would have chosen, but what I could find.

Robert Thoroton, *The Antiquities of Nottinghamshire* (1677), dedication to Charles II

Contents

Illustrations

The author and publishers gratefully acknowledge the following for permission to reproduce copyright material:

The publishers apologize for any errors or omissions in the above list
and would be grateful to be notified of any corrections that should be
incorporated in the next edition or reprint of this book.

Preface and Acknowledgements

On his thirty-third wedding anniversary, 5 April 1681, Sir Edward Dering, MP, administrator, and Kentish gentleman, sat down to review the 'great changes' in 'public affairs' during the course of his married life: 'in 1660 and then for twelve year more, we lived in peace, plenty and happiness above all nations of the world. But this blessing was too great to be continued long to those who deserved it so ill as we, and then the nation began to think that the court inclined to favour popery and France.' The grounds of popular suspicion of Charles II's government included the unjustified war against the Dutch and the Declaration of Indulgence in 1672, the Jesuits and priests who 'swarm in the kingdom, and even about the court', the employment of papists like Sir Thomas Clifford, and 'lastly to these and much more than all these put together was the Duke of York's being first suspected and afterwards universally believed to be a papist, which gave no unreasonable foundation to fear that the King having no children, when the Duke should come to the crown the protestant religion would be at least oppressed, if not extirpated.'[1] Here in a nutshell is the dominant interpretation of English history in the middle decade of Charles II's reign as 'the growth of popery and arbitrary government'. And here, too, is the reason for writing this book.

The 1670s is a decade overshadowed by the propaganda of the 'popish plot' and 'exclusion crisis' which darkened its last months. With hindsight Dering and many contemporaries, both tory and whig, were unable to look back and see much more than the gathering storm clouds. Less defensibly, historians too have looked for little else than the first signs of the tensions and developments of the exclusion crisis. Sandwiched between the 1660s' doomed attempt to resurrect the pre-civil war past and the turbulence of the years after 1678, the 1670s have been passed over too quickly in most accounts. The purpose of this book is simply to restore the richness and complexity of a crucial period of England's history.

We can never say how a period 'really was', but we can resuscitate some of the anxieties and aspirations, describe some of the culture, and explore some of the language of this exciting decade. This is imperative because even as the decade drew to a close, its history was being forced into a straitjacket. Although the master narrative of the 1670s is and will remain the 'growth of popery and arbitrary government', that is a constructed and partial story. While some of the English could recognize the danger of popery and authoritarian rule from the beginning of the decade, others still refused to see it in 1680. The growing threat from popery and absolutism was an account of the decade which had to establish its credibility in competition with other interpretations. During the 1670s the English had many different concerns. Were they and their King becoming 'effeminate'? Were 'luxury' and consumption sapping national economic vigour? Was the nation's true 'interest' agriculture, international trade or plantations? And how were these rival 'interests' to be melded into a single co-operative effort? Why were antiheroes so much more credible than the leaders who should have inspired the nation? Was religion fundamentally a matter of private conscience or of social stability? Why were women so uppity? And was marriage a trap for both sexes? These and related questions were just as profound as any suspicions about Charles II's authoritarian aspirations. And many of them were implicitly commenting on the direction of Charles's government.

We need to look afresh not only at the preoccupations of England in the 1670s, but also at the nature of its public life. The political culture of Restoration England was wide and pluralistic. Affairs still centred on Whitehall and Westminster, but new kinds of people were being sucked into their orbit: busy officials and men of affairs, men like Pepys, Harbord or Conway, who scurried around the City or the dockyards on the King's business; bankers, entrepreneurs and technological projectors; and those who serviced them by supplying information, newsletters, prices or coffee. Even more startling was the informed interest of ordinary London citizens or provincial yeomen in politics. A legacy of the religious and political upheaval of the mid-century, this political consciousness was promoted in Charles II's reign by the pamphlet press and the 'talk of the town'. Yet interest does not guarantee influence and, as we will see, in this decade English political life remained rooted in the royal court and its often squalid feuds. Faction counted for as much as principle at the palace of Whitehall. In an age of masquerade and double-dealing, opportunism and self-advancement flourished – as did delicious ironies like the payment of French bribes to the critics of Charles II's 'French' policies.

I hope that this book captures the flavour of these years. Five of its ten chapters are thematic discussions of issues which excited and worried the English, such as technical innovation, the acquisition of information, the dissemination of news, or the problems of religious pluralism and the economy. Here I draw on a wide range of materials including maps and sermons, diaries and tracts, but for other preoccupations, such as moral questions about heroism or sexual relations, literary sources have been most helpful. If literature seems to loom large in this book, it is because poetry, satire and drama were among the most significant ways in which the English reflected on and articulated their social, political and moral difficulties and aspirations. These are the most innovative chapters of this book and they are intended to enable readers to enter imaginatively the world of Charles II's England.

The brief for this book included the request that it should convey something of how this decade of English history was experienced. I have therefore designed the five narrative chapters to give a sense of what it was like to live through these years, to live from day to day, month to month, unsure of the next twist or turn in events. I hope that I have established the context for what did happen – that I have shown, for instance, why some people were ready to believe in a popish plot in 1678 – while also hinting at what *could* have happened. Or to put it another way, that I have described the sufficient, but not necessary, conditions for the events of this decade. Many other scenarios might have been played out from the conditions prevailing in the 1670s if individuals had made different choices. The political nation might have taken up other causes and slogans, against evil counsellors, the inhibition of trade or a luxurious court. Or the political nation might have traded parliamentary independence for economic growth and toleration for protestants. The arrangement of the book reflects this interpretation. The first three narrative chapters take readers to the point where they will appreciate the thematic chapters; chapters 9 and 10 narrate the descent into political crisis after 1678.

Nowadays historians are often enjoined to 'rethink' periods of the past, and increasingly historians of Restoration England are able and willing to do so. This book could not have been written without the findings and arguments of a generation of scholars.[2] To that extent, it is an exercise in reinterpretation. It is an invitation to dig deeper and wider, to be ever more imaginative in what we use to explore the world of Restoration England. Yet even a study of this sort has to omit much: some of the omissions will only be apparent to the author, but others will be glaring to all readers. Notably this book avoids substantial discussion of Scotland and Ireland – a heinous sin in these days of 'the British problem' – but not one for which I am overly repentant. After all, my focus is very much on what people thought was going on in England and how it affected them, not on the problems of ministers feuding and co-ordinating government over three kingdoms. The various radicals also command little attention here, principally because they have received so much elsewhere. It is more regrettable that lack of expertise and space has restricted what could be said here about printing, science, philosophy, drama, poetry or gender.

Wherever possible, and especially in constructing the narrative, I have drawn on and quoted manuscript newsletters, correspondence, contemporaneous diaries and documents (including those which flowed into Whitehall and are now State Papers), and printed works published in this decade. I have referred less often than might be expected to memoirs, such as those of Burnet, Baxter or Reresby, which were compiled or written at some remove from the events which they describe. I have sought to emphasize what the public knew or thought they knew at each moment, not least because the control of information and the power of rumour are major themes of this book. Consequently much less is made of the secret machinations of government – the discussions of the Foreign Affairs Committee or the reports of the French ambassador – than in some other studies. No historian would wish to tell the story without having used these materials, but in this book they do not achieve the prominence accorded to them in several notable studies of Charles II's reign. This is an appropriate point to mention that when writing this book four outstanding works of narrative political biography, John Miller's and Ronald Hutton's biographies of Charles II, Browning's life of Danby and Haley's biography of Shaftesbury, have rarely been off my desk. Although they occasionally conflict on points of interpretation and even detail, this quartet of biographies provides an indispensable political narrative of the decade, and my debt to them is great indeed.[3]

My understanding of the period is the product of many years' reading and there are too many fine historians of the period to acknowledge each individually. But among those who have recently enriched our view of the life and culture of Restoration England, Tim Harris has explored the political participation of the lower orders and shown the flexibility of 'anti-popery', while Jonathan Scott has revealed the complexity of at least one whig hero, and Steven Pincus has argued for an informed grasp of foreign politics among ordinary people and for a complex and dynamic process of foreign policy formulation. Those who have written on religion, portray a world of far greater theological and liturgical latitude than we had imagined. From Mark Goldie's contributions we have learned much about the way that political action shaded into political philosophy in this period and Alan Marshall has illuminated the murky world of Restoration espionage. Above all, Mark Knights has led the way towards a more plausible picture of what was at stake in the political crisis of 1678–81.[4] It is not only historians, however, who have cast light on the Restoration. Scholars working on the literature of the period continue to enlighten us. I have learned much from the work of those like Steven Zwicker, J. A. Winn, Philip Harth and Paul Hammond who have written on Dryden (among much else), and from Harold Love, Harold Weber, Frank Ellis, Rachel Weil, Susan Staves and many others who have written on the cultural history of the period.

Several institutions and their staff are to be thanked for their help. I am grateful for permission to consult the collections of and cite manuscripts held by the British Library, the Public Record Office, Lambeth Palace Library, Dr Williams's Library, Guildhall Library, the National Portrait Gallery, the Bodleian Library, Oxford, Bedfordshire Record Office and the Library of University of Wales Swansea. I am obliged to the British Academy for a grant towards the costs of research in London in the summer of 1997. On a more personal note, I have benefited from working with Stuart Clark, Hugh Dunthorne and Jon Walker in Swansea, from discussions with Blair Worden, Mark Goldie, Paul Seaward, John Miller and Mark Knights and from a probably long-forgotten query by Steven Zwicker. I am ever grateful to Eileen and Fred Spurr, Joanna Spurr and Eleanor, Edward and Ian Sisley, Ivor and Rene Colville and Edward Briffa for their generosity, hospitality and friendship. Anne makes everything possible and she and the three dedicatees of this book make it all worthwhile.

Abbreviations

AH	*The Agrarian History of England and Wales. V. II 1640–1750, Agrarian Change*, ed. J. Thirsk (Cambridge, 1985)
BL	British Library
Bod.	Bodleian Library, Oxford
Browning, *Danby*	A. Browning, *Thomas Osborne, Earl of Danby and Duke of Leeds 1632–1712* (Glasgow, 3 vols, 1951)
Buckingham	*Buckingham: Public and Private Man: The Prose, Poems, and Commonplace Book of George Villiers, second Duke of Buckingham (1628–87)*, ed. C. Phipps (New York, 1985)
Bulstrode	*The Bulstrode Papers*, [ed. A. W. Thibaudeau] (1897)
CSPD	*Calendar of State Papers Domestic*
CSPVen	*Calendar of State Papers Venetian*
Danchin	P. Danchin (ed.), *The Prologues and Epilogues of the Restoration 1660–1700*, Part I. 1660–76 (2 vols, Nancy, 1981), Part II. 1677–1700 (2 vols, Nancy, 1984)
Dering	*The Parliamentary Diary of Sir Edward Dering 1670–1673*, ed. B. D. Henning (New Haven, 1940)
Dering, *Diaries*	*The Diaries and Papers of Sir Edward Dering Second Baronet, 1644 to 1684*, ed. M. F. Bond (1976)
Dryden	*The Works of John Dryden*, ed. H. T. Swedenberg et al (Berkeley, California, 1956–)
Dryden, *Poems*	*The Poems of John Dryden: I 1649–1681*, ed. P. Hammond (1995)

Essex Papers	*Essex Papers*, ed. O. Airy (Camden Society, XLVII, 1890) and ed. C. E. Pike (Camden Society, 3rd series, XXIV, 1913)
Evelyn	*The Diary of John Evelyn*, ed. E. S. de Beer (5 vols, Oxford, 1955)
Grey	Anchitell Grey (ed.), *Debates of the House of Commons, From the Year 1667 to the Year 1694* (10 vols, 1763)
Haley	K. H. D. Haley, *The First Earl of Shaftesbury* (Oxford, 1968)
Henry, *Diaries*	M. H. Lee (ed.), *The Diaries and Letters of Philip Henry* (1882)
HM	*The Harleian Miscellany* (8 vols, 1746)
HMC	Historical Manuscripts Commission
HMC Ormonde	*HMC Marquess of Ormonde MSS, New Series, 8 vols*
HMC Verney	*HMC Seventh Report, Appendix, Part I*
Hooke	*The Diary of Robert Hooke MA MD FRS 1672–1680*, ed. H. W. Robinson and W. Adams (1935)
HOP	*The History of Parliament: The House of Commons 1660–1690*, ed. B. D. Henning (3 vols, 1983)
Josselin	*The Diary of Ralph Josselin 1616–1683*, ed. A. Macfarlane (1976)
Luttrell	Luttrell Broadside Ballad Collection in the British Library
Marvell, *Letters*	*The Poems and Letters of Andrew Marvell*, ed. H. M. Margoliouth; 3rd edn. revised by P. Legouis and E. E. Duncan-Jones (2 vols, Oxford, 1971), volume 2
Morrice P	Roger Morrice's MS Entering Book P, Dr Williams's Library
Pepys	*The Diary of Samuel Pepys*, ed. R. Latham and W. Matthews (11 vols, London, 1970–83)
PH	*The Parliamentary History of England*, ed. W. Cobbett (36 vols, 1806–20), vol 1, by column
POAS	*Poems on Affairs of State*, ed. G. deForest Lord et al (7 vols, New Haven, 1963–75)
PRO	Public Record Office
Reresby	*The Memoirs of Sir John Reresby*, ed. A. Browning; 2nd edn. by M. K. Geiter and W. A. Speck (1991)
Rochester	*John Wilmot, Earl of Rochester – The Complete Works*, ed. F. H. Ellis (1994)
Rochester, *Letters*	*The Letters of John Wilmot, Earl of Rochester*, ed. J. Treglown (Oxford, 1980)

Savile Correspondence	*Savile Correspondence*, ed. W. D. Cooper (Camden Society, LXXI, 1858)
T&C	J. Thirsk and J. P. Cooper (eds), *Seventeenth-Century Economic Documents* (Oxford, 1972)
Williamson	*Letters to Sir Joseph Williamson*, ed. W. D. Christie (2 vols, Camden Society, new series VIII and IX, 1874)
Wood	*The Life and Times of Anthony Wood*, ed. A. Clark (6 vols, Oxford, 1891–1900)
Wycherley	*The Plays of William Wycherley*, ed. P. Holland (Cambridge, 1981)

Note to the Reader

I have modernized the spelling, punctuation and capitalization of seventeenth-century material from all sources, except in the cases of titles and of some verse or dramatic prose. All works cited were published in London unless stated otherwise. I have assumed that the year began on 1 January.

Prologue: Masquerade and Interest

Mrs Caution: . . . I know you would be masquerading. But worse would
come on't, as it has done to others who have been in masquerade and
are now virgins but in masquerade . . . O, the fatal liberty of this masquerading age! When I was a young woman –

Hippolita: Come, come, do not blaspheme this masquerading age like an
ill-bred city dame . . . By what I've heard 'tis a pleasant, well-bred, complacent, free, frolic, good-natured, pretty age and if you do not like it,
leave it to us that do.

Wycherley, The Gentleman Dancing Master (1672)

Interest in all countries is changeable, that which was in one age, not being
always the same in the next . . .

[Slingsby Bethel], The Present Interest of England Stated (1670)

A verse prologue introduced every play of the 1670s with reflections on
the times, the audience, the playwright and the play. It was, suggests one
critic, 'a means of conversing' with the audience. Occasionally a prologue would capture a specific moment, as when in 1672 the poets
lamented 'how reformed and quiet we are grown, / Since all our braves
and all our wits are gone' to war. Now and again, a prologue would distil
the more general mood, as did these plaintive and anonymous verses
written for some now-forgotten play:

> this play was writ nine years ago,
> And how time alters, ladies you best know;
> Many then, fair and courted, I dare say,
> Act half as out of fashion, as our play.
> Besides if you consider't well, you'd find,
> Y'have altered since, ten thousand times, your mind;
> And if your humours do so often vary,
> These in our comedy must needs miscarry?
> For as you change, each poet moves his pen,

They take from you their characters of men.
The wit they write, the valour and the love,
Are all but copies, of what you approve . . .[1]

Wit, valour and love, the fickle taste of the audience, are all part of a wider sense of mutability. Change was in the air. Change precipitated by political crisis, but also brought about by the failure of an entire project based on social, religious and political values which were no longer sustainable. People were anxious, fearful of novelty and nostalgic for old certainties. Others, perhaps many others, were ready to embrace change, either to build a more pluralistic society in which religious minorities would enjoy greater freedom, trade, technology and information would flow more freely, and undreamt-of personal and national possibilities might be realized, or to explore the possibilities of government unhampered by the restrictions of parliaments and old prejudices. To outsiders it seemed 'the nature of this people to cherish nothing but change and confusion, which now reign here more than ever'.[2]

Two other characteristics of the age will weave their way through this book. One I have labelled 'masquerade'. Donning a mask for balls and frolics was popular among the elite in the 1670s: 'there's such perpetual masquerades and balls, that 'tis carnival all the year.' Every time this 'foppery' seemed to be going out of fashion, it was revived 'by some who find themselves the more acceptable the less they are known'; and although Hippolita asks Mrs Caution not to 'blaspheme this masquerading age', its 'fatal liberty' had a darker side, a side which symbolizes the dissimulation so characteristic of life in this decade. 'I am never in my element,' says one of Shadwell's characters, 'but when I am adventuring about an intriguo, or masquerading about business', and his friend replies that 'a masquerade's good for nothing else, but to hide blushes, and bring bashful people together, who are asham'd to sin barefac'd.'[3] An air of secrecy, deception and equivocation pervaded all manner of activities. Duplicity may, of course, be inherent to politics: dissimulation is often demanded by diplomacy or high politics; but not even the most prosaic political dispute of this period, over Irish cattle imports, say, or the customs duty on sugar, could be taken at face value. At times almost everyone seems to have been dissembling. Politicans, wits and criminals were as adept at assuming different identities as the celebrated actors of the day such as John Lacy (see plate 1). All hid behind or acted through masks: 'patriots' were in the pay of foreign governments; conforming Anglicans were covert papists or dissenters; highwaymen were government spies; men and women of exquisite sensibilities and gifts posed as gross libertines. Masquerade allows for irony and cynicism, just as it permits pragmatism and irresponsibility: 'why thus disguised and muzzled?' two masquers are asked; and they reply,

Plate 1 John Lacy, actor, in three of his most famous roles as Highlander, gallant and Presbyterian minister, by John Michael Wright. Lacy was apprenticed to John Ogilby, then a dancing master, in the 1630s and served in the royalist army in the civil war. A member of the King's Company after 1660, he specialized in comic roles and farce; he took the role of Mr Bayes, a caricature of Dryden, in Buckingham's The Rehearsal *(1671). He also wrote plays, adapted Shakespeare and Moliere, and may have been the author of a savage satire on Charles II of 1677. Lacy died in 1681.*

'because whatever extravagances we commit in these faces, our own may not be obliged to answer 'em'.[4] 'Counterfeit', 'wit', '[im]personation', 'masquerade', are all among the most resonant terms of this decade. But so too is the rather different word 'interest'.

A determination 'that the interest of England may be thoroughly searched out' was characteristic of the 1670s.[5] Interest, which, like masquerade, will be explored in a subsequent chapter, was regarded as the

key to national success. *The Present Interest of England Stated* was the goal
of writers be they republican or royalist, country landowner, nonconformist or overseas merchant. And there lay the rub. For the country's
true interest was open to debate and to change. No single recipe for
national improvement could command common assent. Interest and
masquerade are two of the figures around which the drama (a tragi-
comedy perhaps?) of change in the 1670s will revolve. But there are, of
course, many others, from piety to heroism, from luxury to the talk of
the town, which will shape the action to come. Before we lift the curtain,
however, this prologue must set the scene and introduce some of the
characters.

Pietro Mocenigo, the Venetian envoy who left England in December
1670, turned in his official report on the state of England some months
later.[6] 'As the sea causes wealth and arms to flourish in that island,' he
wrote, 'so the land blesses the country by its fertility, affording abundant
crops for sustenance.' He was impressed, too, by the speed of the
rebuilding of London after the Great Fire of 1666, by the strength of
England's navy, and by the prosperity of its merchants. The country had
clearly recovered quickly from the disastrous war with the Dutch republic in 1664–7: 'Holland is more respected than loved, and it may be said
that the friendship with that government is due to interest and not to
affection.' Mocenigo dutifully explained to his masters that Charles II
had no heirs by his Catholic Queen, Catherine of Braganza, and so next
in line to the throne were the King's brother, James, Duke of York, and
James's children by his duchess, Anne, and then followed William of
Orange, Charles's Dutch nephew. At court the great men included
Prince Rupert, the King's uncle, James Scott, Duke of Monmouth, the
King's illegitimate son, George Villiers, Duke of Buckingham, the King's
childhood companion, and Henry Bennet, Earl of Arlington and Secretary of State. 'The tranquillity of the country and the power of the
nation depend upon the perfect harmony' between King and parliament, observed Mocenigo, 'and this harmony is the sole remedy for
cutting off the seditious novelties which swarm, owing to the differences
in religion.' The official protestant church, the Church of England, was
in competition with a host of illegal rivals, including Roman Catholics
(colloquially known as recusants and papists), protestant nonconformists, such as presbyterians, baptists, congregationalists or Independents, and sects both large like the Quakers and small like the
millenarian Fifth Monarchy Men.
   The Venetian Senate could have learned much of this from a copy of
Edward Chamberlayne's recent *Angliae Notitia; or, the Present State of
England*, designed 'that the whole state of England might be seen at
once' and as 'a useful book for all Englishmen at all times: so every one

might without trouble, always carry it about with him as a companion to consult upon all occasions.' Chamberlayne catalogued the nobility, officers of state, the royal court, the legal profession, ecclesiastical dignities, military commands, the Corporation of London, the two universities, the Inns of Court, the College of Physicians and the Royal Society. But Chamberlayne's vade-mecum disguises its true nature. This is a sustained paean to a lost world masquerading as a reference book. Chamberlayne portrayed the England of the mid-1630s as a little Eden, peopled by valiant nobles, pious clergy, loyal commoners, honest men, chaste women, obedient infants, and then ruined by the 'children of Belial' who, resenting all authority, fomented the civil wars. These troublemakers managed to spoil church and state and, worse,

> to corrupt the minds, the humours, and very natures of so many English, that notwithstanding the late happy restoration of the King and bishops, the incessant joint endeavours and studies of all our governors to reduce this people to their pristine happiness, yet no man now living can reasonably hope to see in his time the like blessed days again; without a transplantation of all those sons of Belial . . . without an utter extirpation of those tares . . .[7]

This is a lament for the failed policies of the 1660s. Chamberlayne is describing here the attempt to put the clock back to the eve of the civil war. The 1662 Act of Uniformity excluded from the Church of England any protestant minister who would not conform and a series of punitive laws against dissenters opened them to prosecution for their private worship in 'conventicles'. Formulated by clergymen and MPs, and unfairly associated with the name of Lord Chancellor Clarendon, this was a policy of using conformity to the Church of England as a benchmark of political loyalty. In the hope of ensuring that towns were run by loyal men and of influencing the MPs returned from such towns, the Corporation Act imposed a series of oaths and the duty of receiving the Anglican sacrament on all members of urban corporations. 'These are the cornerstones which I hope I shall not see removed in my days,' wrote the old royalist Sir Leoline Jenkins in 1680.[8] What made Chamberlayne, never mind Jenkins, look so dated was that by 1670 this whole project of reconstructing the old regime of balanced monarchy and a single church with a uniform worship was faltering.

The nostalgic policy of the 1660s failed because too few individuals were prepared to see it through. At the grass roots few Justices of the Peace and constables would consistently enforce the laws against protestant dissenters, those purged from local government soon slipped back into office, and even the electorate, supposedly all those men with a substantial property stake in the community, 'trifle away the peace and security of the church and state . . . sometimes inconsiderately siding with imposing landlords, sometimes as rashly running with an unwary rabble, to depute insufficient, and many ill-principled persons to be their representatives in the great council of this kingdom'.[9] The government was half-hearted. Charles had no interest in religious persecution; he had quickly drawn a veil over the past and even taken his former opponents into his confidence and government; and, despite the help of Clarendon, he could not establish a happy relationship with the parliament which had been elected in 1661 and which would survive until 1679. The Anglican parliamentary majority of the 1660s could not be persuaded to provide Charles with sufficient money nor to relax the religious settlement. When a series of natural and man-made disasters, the Plague, Fire and humiliating naval defeat at the hands of the Dutch, culminated in Clarendon's fall from power in 1667, the business of the court – as the government was generally known – fell to Arlington, helped by Sir Thomas Clifford, and hindered by the rivalry of the wayward Buckingham. John Maitland, Earl of Lauderdale, ran Scotland, still a separate kingdom with its own parliament, law and church at this time, and Ireland was governed until 1669 by James Butler, Duke of Ormonde and leader of the remnants of Clarendon's followers. The former Cromwellian, Anthony Ashley Cooper, Lord Ashley, was Chancellor of the Exchequer, a second-rank portfolio; Sir Orlando Bridgeman was Lord Keeper of the Seals; Sir Thomas Littleton and Sir Thomas Osborne were joint Treasurers of the Navy; and much of the most significant business of government passed across the desk of Sir Joseph Williamson, clerk or 'under-secretary' to Arlington.

A new juncture in affairs had been reached by the end of the 1660s. Not only had Clarendon and his generation been supplanted, but the impetus behind the Clarendon Code had run out, the economy was in a slump, and people were asking what the nation's recent setbacks and escapes might mean: we 'have been exercised with such strange intermingled providences, as is a theme worthy the best historian['s] pen, and choicest Christian meditation'.[10] It was obvious to many that the nation had arrived at a turning point. New men and new methods were coming to the fore, practical, methodical men like Williamson, Sir George Downing or Samuel Pepys. And advice flooded in from all sides: an array of experts gave evidence to the House of Lords' committee on falling land prices and decaying trade; Sir William Coventry and Sir Edward Dering, who both possessed political experience and broad acres, drew up diagnoses of the economy's malaise. Moralists and clergymen proferred various remedies. Some were for 'comprehending' moderate dissenters within the established church by relaxing the Act of Uniformity and tolerating the rest. Their opponents wanted greater persecution and a new Conventicle Act to replace the one which lapsed in 1668. Most could agree, however, on the urgent need for action against the wits, atheists, Hobbists, libertines, and other sinners of this profane generation 'that have set heaven against us'.[11] Foreign policy was eagerly debated. The republican Dutch were commercial rivals and recent enemies, and yet also fellow-protestants and, since the Triple Alliance of 1668 between England, Holland and Sweden, part of the European balance of power against Louis XIV of France. In *The Present Interest of England Stated* (1670), Slingsby Bethel, member of the Merchant Adventurers and a republican, advocated closer links with the Dutch to offset growing French power. At much the same time Sir Thomas Clifford was preparing a secret paper for Charles II which argued that 'a war against Holland would in all respects suit with the interests of England' provided that the King could be sure of winning it.[12]

This deluge of analysis and advice was marked by a strong sense of the interrelatedness of policy options. Sir Daniel Fleming JP, a man who (unlike Chamberlayne) was actually struggling to make the intolerant policies of the 1660s work in his native Westmorland, wrote to his old friend Sir Joseph Williamson in February 1670. His letter ostensibly reported his progress in prosecuting conventicles, but it branched out into prescriptions for wholesale reform and improvement. He anxiously noticed the potential alliance of the Dutch and English dissenters; he suggested that the penalties for not attending church be enforced and the fines, instead of going to the poor 'who are little better for them', should be devoted to strengthening the navy, the herring fishing fleet and the local militias. Sir Daniel was just getting into his stride. He wanted lawyers' fees pegged, the payment of tithes and church dues to be enforced, and land banks and registries to be created in every county. A few months earlier an unknown memorialist had submitted a paper to the King on the realm's economic problems which extended its recommendations to include the toleration of dissenters, the naturalization of immigrants and the establishment of land registries.[13]

Unsurprisingly there emerged from these diagnoses common themes. Many analysts were preoccupied with disorder and disaffection, with those, especially JPs, civic officials and clergy, who failed in their duty, and with the insidious effects of gossip and murmuring. A report of about 1672 on 'the present state of the nonconformists' concluded that they were all censorious, frequenters of the coffee-houses and 'great improvers of any little matter that is but whispered against the court or the government', and that they were joined by hypocritical loyalists in spreading such news.[14] Commentators resented the preponderance of London and its commercial and banking communities and were quick to blame them for the economic problems of farmers in the counties. It was agreed that heedlessness to God's calls, especially his providential messages of war, disease and fire, had left the nation without a sense of moral direction. This was exacerbated by the eagerness of the English to 'import hither the air and carriage, and assurance of the French, therewith quitting their own staple native commodities of much greater value, the sincerity and generosity of the English disposition'.[15] With foreign manners came 'foreign softnesses', and this was the slippery slope to luxury, the sybaritic and heedless consumption of unearned delights, which sapped the native vigour of the people and drained the nation of money to pay for imported wines and silks.

If only all the remedies were as obvious. It was incontrovertible that ' 'tis state interest to countenance and encourage pure religion', but what was pure religion? To Edward Chamberlayne, for instance, it was the Church of England and so it was necessary to suppress all dissenters, those 'bastards', 'vermin' and lice who form 'the pudenda of the nation'.[16] Slingsby Bethel was outraged by Chamberlayne's book, and took particular exception to his suggestion that the younger sons of gentry should not go into trade; 'surely, it is the glory, and not shame of England (as our new pretenders to politics would have it) that by commerce, they have made themselves so formidable in the world?'[17] The Duke of Buckingham approved of Bethel's 'stating the true interest of England to be trade, of his observation of some of our customs which are useful to it, of his proposals of new laws to be made for the advance of it, and of the necessity of having some enlargement given to people in matters of religion'. But in his *Letter to Sir Thomas Osborne* (1672), Buckingham took the opposite line on England's foreign interest: France, he claimed, was England's natural ally and Holland her rival. Not that he pretended 'that all this is as plain, as that two and two make four, it being impossible to use that certainty of reasoning in things of this nature'. What none of Buckingham's readers could know for sure was that he was privy to secret diplomacy which had already committed England to war against Holland in alliance with France; indeed, Buckingham himself did not know all the details of the French alliance. Buckingham was dissimulating here, just as he would later in the decade when he turned into a critic of Charles II and his Francophile policies and simultaneously pocketed guineas from the French ambassador. As so often political masquerade obscured the present interest of England.

The scene is set, so the action can begin.

1

1670–2: So Bewitched a Time

In the spring of 1670 Charles II participated in two elaborate events, one a funeral, the other a family reunion. The funeral was the state obsequies of General George Monk, Duke of Albemarle, and the man whose intervention at the head of his regiment had ensured the restoration of monarchy in 1660. The reunion was with 'Minette' or Henriette, Charles's favourite sister and now wife to Louis XIV's brother. The funeral was a long-delayed affair: Monk had died on 3 January, and by March Andrew Marvell was commenting, 'it is almost three months, and he yet lies in the dark unburied, and no talk of him'; when, after Monk's lying-in-state in Somerset House, the state funeral did take place, it was, despite all the careful planning by the heralds and the estimated expenditure of £20,000, a dismal affair, 'base and sordid', and 'had not many volunteers come in to make up the train, it had been very pitiful'.[1] The reunion with Minette, however, was utterly different. Attended by the entire court, by the Queen and the Duke of York, by the Duke's company of actors, by ambassadors and by a French party of over two hundred, including many dignitaries and aristocrats, Minette and Charles revelled in each others company for ten days. The King pressed gifts of jewels on his sister; he exchanged news and, no doubt, confided worries; he admired her entourage and was struck by one young maid of honour, Louise de Quérouaille. Minette's visit was restricted to the port of Dover, a town which did not impress Charles, but plays and visits to the fleet and Canterbury were laid on, and some French nobles and clergymen ventured to London and Windsor. Dover itself saw 'the greatest gallantry and mirth imaginable', according to the newsletters, 'one day the French exceed in gallantry, another day the English, and such great feasting there is that barques go constantly to Flanders for provisions' and the cost to the King was estimated at £100,000. 29 May, the King's birthday and the official anniversary of his restoration, was celebrated with bells, bonfires, the militia parading on the beach, and salutes from the guns of the castle and men-of-war riding at anchor.[2] Both events, the funeral and the reunion, were rich in significance; they were intended to do public honour and to serve a secret purpose. No doubt the poor turnout at one and the flocking to the other simply reflect the preference of the fashionable world for the present rather than the past, but they also symbolize the turning point at which the country had arrived. Charles II, too, seems to have felt that the time was ripe for change; for the King both occasions were associated with drawing a line under the past and embarking on new projects.

I

At the beginning of the 1670s a long political process which had begun with the fall of Clarendon and the failure of the Dutch war was still in train. When parliament met in October 1669, it rapidly became a battlefield for the factions struggling to succeed to Clarendon's power, but after the Christmas recess Charles was determined to bring the assembly to heel. On 14 February he spoke imperiously to members, telling them that they must not revive the long-running jurisdictional dispute between Lords and Commons over Sir Thomas Skinner's case with the East India Company; he asserted that every penny had been spent on the Dutch war and the long post-mortem on its conduct was now over; he recommended a union with Scotland (where his viceroy Lauderdale had recently forced the parliament to concede to the King complete power in religious matters and over the militia). And Charles squarely placed the blame on parliament's shoulders for any consequences which might follow from their slowness in voting him money.

The trick seemed to work. During February and March, parliament co-operated with the King. Both houses accepted the erasure of all records of their clash over Skinner and, 'a pretty ridiculous thing!', the King threw open the doors of his wine cellar so that MPs could drink his health. Bells and bonfires celebrated 'the joy of the court and town' and 'the King was never observed to be so much pleased in his life.'[3] Before the Lords was a bill to allow Lord Roos to divorce his unfaithful wife and remarry. This innocent sounding measure was perceived as a kite being flown for a possible royal divorce: there was 'some curious talk among the commonalty' that the Roos divorce was aimed elsewhere, meaning the King. Anglesey and Lord Ashley supported the bill, Buckingham whispered of a new Queen, and Lauderdale of Monmouth's claims; while the Duke of York and his allies, the bishops, stoutly opposed it. Charles took a boat to Westminster and sat himself down next to the fire in the Lords' chamber to listen to the debates. 'At any other, but so bewitched a time, as this, it would have been looked on as an high usurpation, and breach of privilege,' claimed Marvell. However within a few days the house had voted him their humble thanks for renewing the ancient custom of his predecessors, and the King had been heard to say that the debates were better than a play. With a formal protest from the dissenting lords and bishops, Lord Roos's bill was passed by a narrow margin and received the royal assent on 11 April.[4] Roos's was one of 'the three notablest bills', the others being the supply bill and the bill to replace the 1664 Conventicle Act which had expired two years earlier. The new Conventicle Act was portrayed by many, including Charles, as the price extorted from the King by the Anglican Commons and the bishops for the vote of supply. In Shropshire they heard that it had been passed according to the vote but against the reason of the house. Marvell famously called this act 'the quintessence of arbitrary malice', and it was indeed an intolerant act in the mould of the persecuting 'Clarendon Code' of the early 1660s, designed to bring the weight of the law to bear not only on nonconformist ministers, but on negligent JPs, and to encourage informers to initiate prosecutions. Even so the King had been successful in inserting a 'Scotch' clause, clause seventeen, which reserved powers to the king including the power not to execute the law. Little wonder that on 31 March, Arlington was crowing that parliament had 'disposed themselves to do everything to his majesty's mind and satisfaction', while a few days before, Marvell stated that it is 'my opinion that the King was never since his coming in, nay, all things considered, no king since the Conquest, so absolutely powerful at home, as he is at present'. Nevertheless the innermost circle of government, the Committee for Foreign Affairs, decided that when the King spoke to MPs at the prorogation of parliament, he should not 'overthank them' for fear they would leave off the good work.[5] Overall, then, Charles II could bury the kingmaker of 1660 and regard his political debts to the past as paid. It was time to look to his French cousin and the future – a future of opportunism, experiment, mendacity and shifting alliances.

Only a handful knew the real reason for Minette's visit to Dover in May 1670. Marvell anticipated 'family counsels' and reported rumours of a royal divorce and a new marriage to a Frenchwoman, a Dane, or even 'a good virtuous protestant here at home'.[6] The true purpose of the meeting was to settle a treaty which had been under discussion for months. The terms of the treaty between Charles and Louis XIV of France, which was initialled in Dover on 22 May, were known on the English side only to Charles, York, Arlington, Arundel, Clifford and Belling. In brief, Charles committed himself to joining with Louis in a war against the Dutch republic. Charles would send sixty ships, although a further clause reduced this number to forty, and Louis would pay an annual subsidy of £230,000; Charles would supply 4000 infantry for the French army who would be paid by Louis. Louis was also to provide a

Plate 2   Charles II (artist unknown). A monarch who masked his intentions behind an easy-going charm? Or an irresolute and fickle ruler at the mercy of different 'interests' and his own lusts? Halifax commented that 'it would ruin all if his majesty continued to advise with those of one interest this day, and hearken to those of another tomorrow, nor could his ministers be safe under such uncertainties'.

subsidy of £150,000, and possibly some troops, to help Charles ride out any domestic squalls when he declared his conversion to Catholicism. Minette had been instructed to establish when Charles would be ready to declare himself a Catholic and launch a war, but even she could not pin her brother down. The secret treaty was vague about whether conversion or war was to come first. Minette sailed back to France with her copy on 2 June and Charles returned to London with his, and outside their immediate circle of advisors the secret treaty of Dover remained unknown until 1830 when John Lingard published Clifford's copy.

Although the population did not yet know it, England and Charles had just reached a watershed – for the rest of his life Charles II would be a French client and prey to constant anxiety that Louis would leak the details of their agreement.

The Duke of York, ever the man of action, had rushed back from Dover as the junketing continued so as to be on hand in London while the new Conventicle Act was enforced. The authorities were unsure of how to proceed and apprehensive about popular reaction. Reports were received of wild threats: for instance, Nicholas Cox, a baptist in St Giles, was alleged to have said that he would rather be hanged at his door than submit to the new act and that the King, who was worse than Nebuchadnezzar, would bring violence down upon his own head. The lieutenancy in London was overhauled, several notable citizens were relieved of their responsibilities for fear they would be too sympathetic to dissenters, and rumours spread of a national purge of JPs and the lieutenancy to guarantee the strict execution of the act. Some justices allegedly left of their own volition rather than impose the law, while London's Mayor and Aldermen went to Whitehall for advice on how to apply it. A show of force was judged necessary in the capital. As the Quaker George Fox arrived in 'the streets of London drums beat for every household to send forth a soldier into the trained bands, to be in readiness'. Sir John Robinson, Lieutenant of the Tower, took the lead, establishing a guard on the Exchange and searching for nonconformist ministers. 'This is a day of great gloominess and darkness, of fear and shaking, of doubt and disceptation [sic], in this great city and nation,' the nonconformists told the Lord Mayor, Sir Samuel Starling, and reminded him that he would be held responsible. 'God has (in a large degree) given us over to the power and lust of our enemies'. Yet, the nonconformist Philip Henry consoled himself, 'he that sits in heaven laughs, and even this also shall be for good.'[7]

Neither side backed down. In the City, the constables, aided by the trained bands, arrested ministers and some of their congregations, the Mayor imposed fines on the pastors, and meeting houses were smashed and boarded up: 'those in the suburbs and Westm[inste]r were more roughly dealt with, the Quakers at Westm[inste]r were beaten and had their coats and cloaks taken away, but at last restored. They are so numerous that it will be very hard to suppress them.'[8] Many conventicles went undisturbed or showed impressive resilience. If meetings were raided on Sunday mornings, it seemed that they were as full again in the afternoons; people refused to buy goods distrained from conventiclers; when the King ordered the seizure of nonconformist meeting houses, the conventicles simply met elsewhere. Dissenters claimed that their preaching was needed because of the lack of churches after the Fire, so the King ordered conforming clergy to preach in the seized meeting houses. In

Shropshire 'town and country [were] full of noise about distraints', but dissenters were braced. Nonconformists, admitted their opponents, 'are a stubborn people and seem to be armed with patience and perseverance'.[9]

Through the summer, the King, the Anglican clergy and the zealous justices all exhorted the various authorities to break up dissenters' meetings and suppress the sects and Quakers. In the counties enthusiasts for the act were convinced that military force, usually specified as 'a troop of horse', was the only effective way of suppressing conventicles: this was how Lord Frescheville, Governor of York, dealt with the 'stubborn and surly' conventiclers around Leeds and it was the fervent desire of the Wiltshire justice, John Eyre of Chadfield, who could get no help from local officials and encountered much animosity and even violence against 'informing rogues'. When John Hand of Culhorne refused to pay a fine for attending a conventicle, Eyre sent someone to take his mare in distraint, 'as he was going away with it, Hand's daughter remarked in a scoffing manner that it was a wise parliament that made such a law, to which her father replied, it was their time now, but it would not hold long.' The nonconformists of Hull were reported 'very bold', while those of Whitby built themselves a new meeting house to evade one of the terms of the act. Yarmouth remained a nonconformist stronghold, and although Coventry had fewer public meetings out of supposed deference to the act, it enjoyed many more undisturbed private meetings.[10]

For many contemporaries, the nonconformists, however deluded and disruptive, warranted neither such draconian persecution nor such dangerous invasions of the law and the subject's liberty. 'Two things of great remark' arose from the legal drive against nonconformity. The first occurred in the September 1670 trial of the Quakers William Penn and William Meade for conspiracy to commit a riot while witnessing for their faith in Gracechurch Street. The Quakers had developed some effective courtroom tactics and this trial like many others soon degenerated into chaotic argument about legal procedures. But what made it significant was the jury's repeated failure to find the pair guilty and the subsequent fining and imprisonment of the jurors. Led by Edward Bushell, the jurors took a legal stand and, thanks to a ruling from Lord Chief Justice Vaughan, ultimately established the legal precedent that judges could not punish juries for their verdict. The Quakers published a narrative of the case to ensure maximum publicity. In distant Shropshire the nonconformist Philip Henry carefully copied it into his diary.[11] The case of two London aldermen, Jekyll and Heyes, was even more tortuous. In the spring of 1670 the Mayor sought to neutralize these nonconformists by arresting them and demanding a bond in a huge sum for their good behaviour; they refused, went to gaol 'and at last (but it is a very long story) got free'. They then sued the Mayor for wrongful arrest. In order to ensure that he was indemnified, the Mayor brought the case before parliament in November 1670. After hearing both sides, and being reminded that 'there were thousands in the streets, like a rebellion' at the time the Conventicle Act came into force, the Commons gave the Mayor's actions grudging approval but also discharged the two aldermen. As William Denton remarked, 'all thinks he [Jekyll] times it ill, but I cannot hear that he is guilty of any crime.' Contemporary letters and the long account of the case in Sir Edward Dering's parliamentary diary make it plain that, even for those who accepted the Conventicle Act, this case touched the legal rights of the subject.[12]

The King meanwhile had suffered a personal blow. On 22 June, three weeks after he had said goodbye to his sister, news arrived of her sudden death. Struck down by 'extraordinary grief', Charles retreated into his bedchamber; 'the plays are silenced during this time of sadness and the whole court entering again into close mourning.' Arlington wrote to Temple that 'the embroilments that were in her domestics' – meaning her unhappy marriage – 'and the suddenness of her death, made the opinion easily take place with us that she was poisoned.' Such stories were not quelled by the post-mortem and the report that 'the stomach was free from all imaginable signs of poison, being clean and well-coloured.'[13] In July Buckingham was sent to France to offer condolences, although gossip alleged that there was 'some extraordinary business', perhaps England's withdrawal from the Triple Alliance, and 'others say it is upon a more secret affair which I dare not write.'[14] In fact Charles did ask Louis to offer Buckingham the secret treaty of Dover, shorn of Charles's promise to turn Catholic, and the Duke was duly flattered and misled.

Life, however, went on. The courtiers had, at least in the eyes of critics, soon regained their joie de vivre, frequenting Hyde Park at nights as before. The King arranged to pension off his mistress of the past decade, conferring on her the title of Duchess of Cleveland, a palace and other emoluments, before setting off on his summer tour of Richmond, Hampton Court, and later Newmarket and Windsor. In August the deserted palace of Whitehall was cleaned, the mourning taken down and other hangings put up. A tense London sweltered meanwhile. The crack-down against nonconformists simply added to the capital's usual atmosphere of hysteria and disorder. In June Charles had personally directed the fight against a fire in the Strand, caused by a careless maid but blamed on nonconformists. In July a fire in Southwark was attributed to 'malicious hands' and stories were heard of men being offered money to throw fireballs. Earlier in the year a group of apprentice tailors had planned a May day rising against the French who allegedly stole English trade and threatened war.[15] In the counties around London, masked men preyed on travellers: John Poole of Fenny Stratford was dragged from his horse and after they 'had taken away his money they did beat him and swore they would kick his guts out at his mouth'. The Bedfordshire justices had been on the trail of this gang of highwaymen led by John Fox for weeks; in separate encounters one highwayman was shot and killed, and a constable was shot in the face.[16] In Norfolk a suspected member of the notorious Claude Du Val's gang was taken and mounted men who could not account for themselves were arrested in Devon.[17] Not all criminals used force. Thomas Hill 'the great and notorious cheat' wheedled hundreds of pounds out of his victims; another scam involved false 'briefs', or letters authorizing charitable collections, taken around the countryside. Among the dozen malefactors condemned at the Old Bailey in September was Mary Carleton, 'the famous cheat, known by the name of the German princess' who was convicted of the theft of plate from a house where she lodged 'under the pretence of being a person of quality'.[18] Deception, it seems, was an art practised by the lowest and the highest in the land.

II

When parliament reconvened on 24 October the King and Lord Keeper Bridgeman 'spoke of nothing but to have money' – although neither of their speeches at the opening of the session was printed because, claimed the wags, Charles said too little and the uninformed Bridgeman too much, especially about Charles's intention to maintain the Triple Alliance. The gist of the King's appeal, however, was that he needed £800,000 for the navy and more to clear his debts, which were reported by the Lords of the Treasury to amount to £1.3 million. A 'thin and obsequious' Commons had agreed by 27 October to grant supply proportionate to royal needs; in mid-November MPs were 'so wholly intent on levying money for his majesty' that no other business was pursued.[19] Although the Committee for Foreign Affairs had discussed various proposals including an excise on beer before the session, Arlington's allies in the Commons now offered little guidance and the debates on supply floundered. MPs were uncertain how to raise the money they had voted the King. Would an excise on ale help? Could the goldsmith bankers be squeezed? Or why not impose a protectionist rate on imports and deal a blow to France? All manner of taxable goods were considered over the next weeks. Sir John Montagu suggested a levy on theatre tickets; Colonel Titus moved a tax on periwigs which provoked 'discourse no way becoming the gravity of that house'. But when Clifford, William Temple and Heneage Finch, speaking for the government, proposed a land tax, they were sharply rebuffed and told that such a tax only created enmity between a ruler and subjects. No one argued, however, when

Clifford estimated that the three taxes so far agreed only amounted to £400,000 a year. The next day, Charles sent for the Commons and told them that Louis XIV had sent a message to reassure him that Louis's planned visit to Dunkirk with 40,000 troops the next summer was simply a military exercise and not a threat to his neighbours. Perhaps, suggested Charles, parliament might like to help him 'so that we might owe our safety to our own strength' rather than Louis's 'courtesy'.[20] Parliament promptly decided to raise the remainder of the £800,000 through the old Tudor tax of a subsidy, in this case a rate on the value of all lands and offices and on all ready money and goods.

On 29 October the twenty-year-old William of Orange landed in England for a three-month visit. Long awaited and much delayed because of suspicions harboured by the Dutch republican government, the visit was a wild success. The King had, if only in public, an 'extraordinary kindness' for his nephew 'who wins much upon the affections of the whole court'. William was made much of, not least because 'the King owes him a great deal of money', as was repeatedly observed on the floor of the Commons. Along with a whirl of masquerades, balls, revels and ballets, the King, it was supposed, also hoped to sweep William off into a marriage, perhaps to York's nine year old daughter Mary or the even younger, but immensely wealthy, daughter of the Countess of Northumberland.[21] Although he did not mention them to the prince, Charles entertained hopes that William might somehow be involved in his plans for war against the Netherlands. While the court danced and winter closed in, events took a strange turn: 'an unruly spirit [was] let loose in London.'[22]

On the evening of 6 December, as Clarendon's old ally and viceroy in Ireland, the Duke of Ormonde, returned from an entertainment for the Prince of Orange, he was pulled from his coach in St James's Street by six horsemen and hoisted on to the saddle behind one of them. Spotting his abductor's hands were full with reins and pistol, the elderly peer, in his own words, 'wrested the pistol out of his hand and threw the fellow down, fell with him and upon him, and got his sword and got loose of them' in a hail of pistol shots, while the gang fled along Knightsbridge. Some said they were Irishmen or highwaymen, others that they planned to hang Ormonde at Tyburn, but although their identity was quickly established, their horses and weapons traced, informants interrogated, a watch put on ports and a £1000 reward proclaimed, the 'bold assassinates' had disappeared into thin air.[23] More violence on London's streets was to follow when Sir John Coventry, MP for Weymouth, made a cheap crack in parliament at the King's expense. During the debate on a theatre tax it was remarked that the playhouse was one of the King's pleasures, and so Coventry asked whether his pleasure lay among the actors or actresses. The following week as Coventry walked home in the early hours from a tavern near Haymarket, a group of Life Guards led by Sir Thomas Sandys and Captain O'Brien 'threw him down, and with a knife cut off almost all the end of his nose', a disfigurement intended to dishonour the MP. This cowardly attack by men of the Duke of Monmouth's troop caused outrage. The coffee-houses and taverns were full of it. On New Years' Eve the Coventry attack was 'still the only talk of the town' and it was feared that the issue might obstruct the passage of the supply bills 'for the country gentlemen seem to be very angry at his usage'.[24]

When parliament got down to work again in January 1671, the Commons first signaled their willingness to press on with the various bills for supply, but then, on 10 January, turned to Coventry's case and how 'to wreak our vengeance upon the assassins that had done this foul and horrid act'. A bill was agreed to banish the assailants unless they gave themselves up for trial and then the house 'entered into a great dispute' about whether all other business should cease in the meantime. Some wanted no business to proceed until the bill had passed both houses, but the compromise, based on the accurate prediction that the bill would take only a matter of days, was to put business on hold until it had passed the Commons. In what was doubtless an up-beat view, Arlington claimed that as soon as they had passed the bill, the Commons 'naturally and easily returned to their former good temper'.[25] Coming to the subsidy bill once more, MPs were surprised, however, by a pre-emptive bid by Sir Thomas Meres and William Garway for 'laying it aside till we might consider if some better way might be proposed'; a majority of 170 to 109 were for pressing on with the tedious business of deciding what rates should be imposed on bankers, mines, stock-in-trade and the like.[26] MPs like Meres and Garway formed a foot-dragging, awkward squad, giving a lead to those with vested interests in delay and voicing the widespread antipathy towards a land tax, but they did not form any sort of coherent opposition. When the house discussed a rebate to landowners of one third of their land tax bill 'for expenses', the concession was lost by 124 to 114 votes, largely, said the newsletters, because of carelessness: 'so negligent are the country gentlemen of their own concerns, as not to sit out a debate till it come [to] a question, there being then about one hundred out of the house that were in town.'[27] The subsidy bill progressed up to the Lords, as did other supply bills such as the excise on beer and ale, but they did not always find a welcome among the peers. 'Lord Lucas made a very smart speech,' according to reports. 'He said that the Common had sent up a bill for money wherein they had given they did not know what nor for what, that the Lords in this case ought to be a screen between the extravagancy of the Commons and the King's wants.'[28] When a version of this speech later appeared in print the Lords voted that it be burnt by the hangman.

Parliament was not simply there to vote taxes for the King, it also existed to express and address the concerns of the peers and the MPs and their constituents. In this session thirty private bills and twenty-seven public measures were enacted to remedy all kinds of problems. The Game Act, for instance, protected the game of the landed class against poachers by simply banning all those below the rank of esquire and a certain income from owning guns, traps, hunting dogs and other equipment, and it empowered gamekeepers to search private houses for these items. Religion was never far from MPs' minds. In February complaint was made 'of the growth of popery', and Sir Trevor Williams reported that there were more Catholic priests than orthodox ministers in Monmouth and Herefordshire and that the local papist community had mushroomed from four hundred to between four and five thousand. Tales of Catholic activity in Wales, Ireland, London and around the Court of St James, inflamed MPs. On 1 March the Commons read a bill to prevent any Catholic from holding civil or military office. By 11 March it had passed the house. Almost simultaneously parliament petitioned the King against the growth of popery and Charles replied that he would issue a proclamation against priests and those recently converted, 'but he must have respect for such as had been so educated, and merited in the service of himself and his father.' Protestant dissenters were also in the sights of some MPs. The issues thrown up by the Jekyll and Heyes case among others led parliament to consider the defects of the Conventicle Act; in December a bill was proposed which redefined conventicles as riots, and by April a complete bill, now deprived of the riot clause but giving indemnities to over-zealous officials, was brought forward to win approval in a very thinly attended Commons by 74 to 53 votes. As Witcombe points out, this was the last occasion on which Charles II's House of Commons voted for the persecution of protestant dissenters.[29] In the event neither this conventicle bill nor the anti-catholic 'test' bill became law because the Lords and Commons became locked into a dispute with each other which eventually prompted the King to prorogue parliament.

Disputes between the two chambers were a fact of parliamentary life. It seemed that Charles had no sooner resolved one, the squabble over Skinner's case, than another quarrel arose. Usually arcane, often farcical, these disputes generally arose over the House of Lords' jurisdiction as a court of appeal or over the proprieties of financial legislation. In 1671 the issue was the Lords' reduction of a proposed duty on imported white or refined sugar from a penny a pound to 'a halfpenny half farthing' or five eighths of a penny. This was done principally on the advice of Lord Sandwich, President of the Council of Plantations, who believed it best served the interests of English commerce and colonies. Sandwich, who left a full account in his manuscript journal, suspected that English sugar refiners, acting out of narrow self-interest, had swayed, perhaps even bribed, MPs to ignore the arguments of refiners in colonies like Barbados. As to the constitutional niceties of the House of Lords altering a tax voted by the Commons, 'I never had a thought exercised thereupon'. The Commons, however, lost no time in asserting that the Lords could not amend money bills, and the Lords as smartly rejected their assertion: Lord Holles wrote that this rule would render the Lords useless, reducing the peers to 'so many parish clerks only to say amen to what the House of Commons hath resolved'.[30] Beneath the claims of commerce and constitution, lay the realities of politics. And here Sandwich did have a view, albeit partisan. The problem, he claimed, lay in the rivalry of Buckingham and Arlington. The rights of the Lords were championed by Buckingham and accepted by 'the country party' in the Commons, but Arlington's 'court party' in the Commons were 'fierce against' the Lords (and Buckingham) and so agreement between the houses was prevented. The country MPs scented an opportunity in the rivalry of the two politicians:

> the country party, finding a difference at court, were glad to blow the coal. Besides that magnifying the House of Commons (whom Clifford and Arlington governs) did make those persons considerable and of great power with the King, which if the house of peers had been suffered to control them, the peerage would have lessened their power and interest, and Buckingham and Ashley and the nobles would have grown most in the King's esteem.

As the houses wrangled, swapped precedents and messages, held conferences, and got nowhere, Charles lost patience. 'There being no present medium of reconciliation to be found,' in Marvell's words, the King thought fit to prorogue parliament on 22 April until the following April.[31]

From the King's point of view this was at worst a disappointing end to a generally satisfactory session. Although the import duties bill had, like the conventicle and test bills, now been lost, parliament had already passed the subsidy and excise, and the Commons had shown itself well disposed. Charles may even, on Professor Miller's reading of events, have helped to sabotage the import duties bill to prevent offence to France.[32] Buckingham's disruptive role was an annoyance. But Arlington was clearly in the saddle; the Venetian ambassador reported that 'all the interests of the crown pass through his hands'.[33] And Arlington was privy to the King's most secret plans and alliances. Assessing the situation from the other end of the political spectrum, however, Andrew Marvell MP saw only corruption and conspiracy. Writing privately to William Popple, Marvell lamented that 'the court is at the highest pitch of want and luxury, and the people full of discontent.'[34] For Marvell, it all fitted together: the riotous masquerades and self-indulgence of the court; the depravity of the King and his avaricious mistresses; the violence of the King's bastard son, the Duke of Monmouth, who in February drunkenly murdered a beadle and was pardoned for it by his father; the physical attack on Coventry for daring to criticize the court and the burning of Lord Lucas's speech; and, of course, the pusillanimous behaviour of his fellow MPs, many of them in the pocket of Clifford and his master Arlington. There were so many strange episodes and unexplained turns of event that lent themselves to conspiracy theories. The attackers of Ormonde were not traced until May when the same gang made a curious attempt to steal the crown jewels. Thomas Blood 'a most bold, and yet sober, fellow, . . . seized the crown and sceptre in the Tower, took them away, and, if he had killed the keeper, might have carried them clear off. He being taken, astonished the King and court, with the generosity, and wisdom, of his answers', and so 'to the wonder of all', he and his accomplices were discharged later in the summer. It now seems likely that what astonished the government was Blood's potential as an informant on the republican and nonconformist underground of which he had been such an active member since the restoration; 'the man had not only a daring but a villainous look, a false countenance, but very well spoken and dangerously insinuating.'[35] Blood played a part in reconciling Cromwellian figures like Desborough and Kelsey to the regime, which naturally aroused comment – 'certainly some designs, more than ordinary, are on foot that such persons are received into favour.'[36] In so bewitched a time who knew where the court was veering?

III

The situation abroad also occupied the attention of newsmongers and politicians. In January 1671 it was confidently reported that 'the war between France and Holland in all probability will break out this spring'.[37] What the newsletters did not know, of course, was Charles's commitment to help France in this war. The Duke of Buckingham, who knew part of the plan, was now a keen advocate of a French alliance and a version of the secret Dover treaty without Charles's promise to convert was signed in December 1670. Charles's hopes of an English marriage or even an alliance with William of Orange had come to nothing when he found that young William was stubbornly independent minded. Nevertheless the prince returned to the Netherlands in February on a tide of English enthusiasm. MPs competed as to 'who should speak first and most in exaltation of his highness's person.'[38] Further diplomatic opportunities arose when Anne, Duchess of York, died on 31 March. The Duchess, who was widely believed to have died a Roman Catholic, was buried in Westminster Abbey, attended by the King and Queen, her widower, the nobility and MPs. Speculation was soon heard about the Duke's possible remarriage. Louis XIV sent an envoy to offer condolences, and then another with his compliments as he had arrived at Dunkirk. Courtesy visits between the French and English courts continued throughout the spring and summer. When the Marquis de Ragny arrived with a train of persons of quality, dukes and marquises, they were shown 'what is remarkable in these parts'. After a visit to Hampton Court, the French nobles were given a dinner at Clarendon House by the Earl of Ossory, and then entertained in turn by all the great officers of the household, including Ormonde, Arlington, Buckingham and Clifford, the last of whom laid on a memorable spread, 'one of the most noble and magnificent that has been known', not only were there 'infinite plenty and choice meats' and iced desserts, but 'after the old English fashion' a sideboard groaned under further dishes 'only for show'. Meanwhile the Duke of Monmouth was on a tour of inspection of the camps and fortifications at Dunkirk and a visit to Louis's court – followed soon after by Buckingham and the Earl of Carlisle. After being 'furiously treated by the French King with a supper of twelve courses', Monmouth returned clutching Louis's picture set with diamonds and a ring valued at £2000; when Ragny returned to France he took with him the English monarch's picture set in diamonds worth £1000.[39] Neither the fêting of William of Orange nor the treating of French nobles was more than convention required, but while all this was going on many felt that the threat of war must have receded. According to the Dutch informants of one newsletter of late May, the Dutch were satisfied there would be no war this summer.

The threat of domestic disorder had also receded. After the tensions of the previous year, the country seemed tranquil. There were the usual local problems with highwaymen, with the 'pranks' and knavery of 'nightwalkers' like the Worcestershire band of so-called 'Levellers' led by 'Robin Hood' or one Nicholas Fowler, but in general all was quiet. 'Yesterday being Shrove Tuesday (which commonly proves an unruly day in most corporations) the youth were very civil,' reported a correspondent from Bristol.[40] One explanation was that many authorities were simply avoiding confrontation with nonconformists. In places as far apart as Yarmouth, Taunton and London, the nonconformists enjoyed freedom. At Dover the mayor 'winks' at conventicles, and even when the baptists' meeting houses were boarded up, they simply forced their way in.[41] The 'insolencies' of nonconformists included evasion of the law by denying ownership of houses or removing their goods to another county and even turning the Conventicle Act against informers. In the summer it seemed to Londoners like Sir Thomas Player that 'the laws against conventicles have been laid asleep, and a moderate Lord Mayor has let the people do what they list.'[42] In fact the government was putting out feelers for even greater concessions. 'There were some overtures made not long since to some of the most considerable nonconforming parsons in the city about granting liberty of conscience to such as would pay so much a year for it, but the proposition was rejected,' claimed a newsletter in July.[43] Perhaps the government felt more secure about the loyalty of the moderate wing of dissent, and was reassured by the success of Blood in winning over radical leaders and informing on others. It was never safe to let down the guard completely: in June searches were made for Richard Cromwell and at the beginning of July Sir John Robinson raided a Fifth Monarchy meeting in Bell Lane, Spitalfields. Yet a fortnight later Sir John was in a high good humour as he mustered his men and marched them about the City, confidently asserting that 'all is in good order and quiet here.'[44]

The King was anything but calm. Charles roamed the country with a restlessness which Professor Hutton sees as a reflection of his energy, his newfound interest in government, and his mounting anxiety as his plans came to fruition. The death of the Duchess of York prevented his usual trip to Newmarket, but in May he visited Chatham and Sheerness, and from late May to early July he based himself at Windsor, where he oversaw the ceremonies of the Order of the Garter; occasionally business called him back to Whitehall as, for instance, on 28 June, when he spent the day dealing with yet another aristocratic duel. In July Charles went to Portsmouth and took out his new yacht the *Cleveland*: he sailed to Plymouth, landed, visited the sights, discomforted the local dignitaries, touched for the king's evil, and set sail once more. August and September were spent at Whitehall, enlivened when the rain allowed by hunting expeditions to Guildford, Windsor and Epping Forest. In mid-October, Charles decamped to Newmarket for the racing and spent some time at Euston, Arlington's Suffolk house, where he consummated his relationship with Louise, the pretty maid of honour first spotted in Minette's entourage (see plate 3). Louise had returned to England in November 1670 and had been dangled in front of Charles by Arlington and Croissy, the French ambassador – the fact that 'Madam Carwell' traveled to Newmarket with the French ambassador and her reception there did not escape popular notice or comment.[45]

As the court enjoyed itself and the country went about its business, military and diplomatic preparations were being made for war. Charles had sought and gained money from parliament to maintain his navy so that England could continue to represent a credible balance against France. During 1671 the routine business of maintaining the navy in good repair seamlessly became part of the building up of naval readiness for war, stockpiling, refitting, building new ships and pressing craftsmen into his majesty's service. Contracts were made for ash oars and handspikes, elm boards, oak planks and beech wedges; timber was

Plate 3   Louise de Quérouaille, Duchess of Portsmouth, by Pierre Mignard (1682). By the time of this portrait the young French maid of honour, who became Charles II's mistress in 1671, had matured into a powerful political figure at court and a hated symbol of French influence. Opponents cast her as Delilah to Charles II's Samson.

selected for knees, compasses, standards, masts; orders were placed for nails and bolts, sails, chains, cables, tar and tow for the rope-yards, cloth for the sailors' slops and victuals for the seamen. Yet behind the scenes all was not well in the naval administration or the shipyards. Contractors were kept waiting for their payments; wages were paid late to shipwrights and caulkers; officials had to use their own personal credit to raise cash to pay bills. In March the foreman at Deptford was roughed up by the shipwrights and suffered bruising, a broken finger and death threats. In November workers at the Chatham dockyard went on strike. The navy itself was riven by the rivalries of naval commanders and of the aristocratic factions to which they owed allegiance.[46]

If there was to be a war with the Dutch, then what was to be the cause? Several issues still rankled from the two earlier wars in 1652–4 and 1664–7, Dutch fishing off England's east coast was a grievance, and so was trade rivalry in the Indian Ocean and Indonesia, but none of these could be used to justify a war at this particular moment. In September 1670 the ambassador to the Hague, Sir William Temple, had been recalled and given a dressing down for his indulgence to the Dutch over the terms of the English surrender of Surinam in return for New York. By July 1671, it was widely believed that Temple, still in England, would be replaced and in August the yacht *Merlin* was sent to collect his wife from the Netherlands. Captain Crow had orders to pass through the Dutch fleet and demand from them the salute that was due according to the 1667 peace terms. When this salute was not immediately forthcoming, the English monarch took umbrage. England's honour and English sovereignty over the seas, it seemed, were to be the pretext for a breach with the Netherlands.

As a wet summer gave way to an unusually stormy autumn, the *Merlin* was out again cruising for trouble and Charles talked of visiting the sea towns of the east coast. On 22 September a proclamation announced that the parliament which already stood prorogued until April 1672 would be further postponed until 30 October 1672. 'Wise and not wise wonder at it,' remarked William Denton, and he guessed that the motive was 'very great intrigues between the crowns of England and France against Holland, which the French believe would not please the parliament'. Suspicions were strengthened when a few days later Sir George Downing, an uncompromising character and an inveterate enemy of the Dutch, was named the new ambassador to the Hague: 'our merchants are much troubled, fearing we shall fall out with Holland'. As Keith Feiling, the historian of foreign policy, observed, 'the secrecy of the secret treaties oozed away' as the new policy became ever more obvious to the public. Few seriously doubted that war was looming and the rumour mill naturally assumed that the hard-up English King was being subsidized by his French cousin. Stories had been current for some time, reported the Danish envoy in late October, of a secret treaty in which France paid England for a war against the Dutch so that Charles had no need to face parliament.[47]

Yet there were still loose ends for Charles to tie up. One was to ensure the nonconformists' quiescence. Through agents like Blood, the government obtained a mass of information on nonconformists, especially in London and in East Anglia. Most of it confirmed the general impres-

sion that while nonconformity was not bent on confrontation with government, neither had it given up its expectations. In September, for
instance, it was 'generally discoursed' among Yarmouth nonconformists
that 'there will suddenly be a dispensation' to presbyterians and Independents. Secretary Williamson, busily digesting the information from
Blood and others into his almost indecipherable personal memos,
worried that Blood might be painting too rosy a picture of nonconformist loyalty. 'They doing what they do now against the law without
licence, think it impotency in the government,' he reasoned. 'What will
they then do when they have the Dutch on the back?' On balance it
might be better to allow the Lord Mayor to connive at their meetings.
But the impression must not be given that the King is running scared.
On the other hand, were 'Dutch agents and partisans' encouraging 'this
running into meeting houses'? In September, November and December,
Williamson evaluated reports and opinions, logged rumours and sought
to square the circle. His notes of 11 November record that the King had
met nonconformist agents and replied to their request for liberty of
worship 'that he had all tenderness, but could not'. The notes go on,
apparently paraphrasing a mysterious intermediary, Dr Butler, to consider whether it might not be better to concede to nonconformists now
rather than later under duress, and to claim that 'in ecclesiasticals it is
apprehended the King has all power, he is supreme, the parliament has
no part in it. In civils it is otherwise.'[48] Within a matter of weeks the King
would be putting this claim to the test.

The other unresolved issue was the King's need for ready money.
Taxes did not produce immediate cash in the seventeenth century. The
1671 subsidy was slowly coming in, with the usual crop of disputes, evasions and under-assessments; in the view of one commentator, in some
places people did not pay more than 60 per cent of what they should
and in none did they pay more than 80 per cent.[49] The government
relied for cash on those who would lend against the proceeds of a tax.
In the late 1660s the bold step was taken of issuing orders for payment
to those who lent money or supplied goods which were guaranteed to
be repaid from a specific tax. These orders could be made over or
'assigned' to someone else, in other words they could effectively be
bought and sold. This was essential if the officials and tradesmen who
received them were to turn them into ready cash and in due course it
led to many of these orders being held by goldsmith bankers like
Colville, Backwell and Vyner. The other way of realizing cash from a
forthcoming tax was to sell the right to 'farm' or collect that tax to an
individual or consortium for so many years. The farmers paid the King
so much up front in the knowledge that the tax would actually bring in
far more over the term of their farm. In September 1671, for murky
reasons, the government failed to sign a contract for a farm of the

customs and proceeded to organize their direct collection by royal officials. Despite the undeniable long-term advantage of permanent royal
customs collections, this decision left a hole in Charles's ready cash at
the worst possible moment. City financiers refused him a further loan.
The books were not going to balance, never mind fund a war. And
so the King grabbed at an idea proposed by Clifford and opposed by
the rest of the council. On 2 January 1672 the King suspended repay-
ment of government debt with what became known as the 'Stop of the
Exchequer'.

The Stop 'will amaze all men and ruin thousands' and will be 'a snub
to trade'.[50] Arlington reported that it had led to 'a great outcry in the
City' and 'angry discourse', but 'we hope when those, who lent the
bankers money, shall reflect better upon it, and see their principal and
interest better secured, that they will appease themselves, and have no
cause to apprehend those ill consequences they have foretold upon it.'[51]
There was something to be said for the measure: it did not effect all
repayments, it was limited initially to twelve months and it promised
compensation. On 7 January the bankers were called to the Treasury
and persuaded to release those funds which they simply held for safe-
keeping; as merchants once again had access to their money 'the discontent is already visibly appeased; so that we do not doubt, but in a few
days, it will quite wear out.' Bankers and merchants were not the only
ones affected. Sir Thomas Osborne, busy trying to organize the navy,
was 'forced to go amongst the bankers all that day by reason of some
stop which was put upon payments in the Exchequer whereupon they
all refused to pay the notes which I had under their hand'. The notes
he had from Duncombe for £9000 and from Reeves for £6000 could
have been turned into cash in four days 'if the said stop had not been
then put'.[52] However, as far as we can judge from a later estimate of what
was owed to the bankers, the government's action released over a million
pounds to be spent on the war. There were many small-scale losers.
Richard Baxter and his wife claimed to have lost £1100. Sir John
Robinson complained that he had lost a promised £1900.[53] But it was
the unpopular goldsmith bankers, so clearly placed in the firing line
by the government, who paid the heaviest price as the Stop was repeatedly extended. It took several years, but eventually all the bankers of
1672 were driven into bankruptcy. The government, however, was concerned only with its immediate needs. Money was gratefully received
from any quarter. Late in January the first installment of the French
subsidy was landed at Rye and by 1 February £50,000 was sitting safely
in the Tower.

Diplomatic preparations for war were well in hand. The combative
Sir George Downing did not depart for the Netherlands until December 1671 and once he arrived he made peremptory demands of the

Dutch. The English monarch wanted satisfaction over the *Merlin* incident, saluting of English ships wherever they were encountered, redress
for insulting medals and prints issued in Holland in 1667, free access
to Dutch plantations in the East Indies and other such concessions.
Downing's task of provocation was made more difficult because the
Dutch were, with Louis XIV breathing down their necks, understandably conciliatory. Downing stepped up the pressure: when he received
no reply to his memorial about the salute, he submitted another 'requir-
ing speedy and positive answer which he therefore daily expects'.[54] He
quibbled about delay in replies, and when all failed he returned to
England before the Dutch could respond – and Charles sent him to the
Tower for six weeks for disobeying orders. As Arlington wrote to Sunderland on 25 January, the confused Dutch were certain that France
and England had combined against them and they saw the evidence in
the 'the coming of French money hither' and Monmouth's raising of a
regiment of 2400 men for French service, 'and the truth is, they are
not much deceived, for tomorrow we shall sign the treaty with France,
and a concert for joining our naval forces.' On 23 January Anglesey
had a long private meeting with the King 'who was very kind and free
telling me all his designs against the Dutch and for liberty'.[55] Gradually
everyone was being let into the secrets.

On Wednesday 6 March the Committee for Foreign Affairs met in
Arlington's lodgings and discussed the possibility of some kind of
religious liberty.[56] Clifford was the driving force, apparently assuring
the King that he had more power to change religious policy than was
thought and that 'you cannot alter [the Act of Uniformity], but you
may dispense with it'. Clifford proposed a proclamation suspending all
penalties for the present, but Charles also wanted to regulate the
nonconformists by authorizing their meetings and preachers. When
the committee reconvened on Saturday evening to hear a legal report
on the extent of royal power in ecclesiastical matters, Clifford seems
once again to have taken the lead, sketching out a scheme in which nonconformists had public worship and permitted preaching and Roman
Catholics were allowed private worship, and 'all penal laws to be
repealed, when the parliament meets, in the meantime suspended as
far as the King can do it'. Clifford's colleagues on the committee all
had their own reasons for relaxing the penalties against dissent, as did
Charles. Some historians see Charles as reluctantly giving way – he certainly thwarted Clifford's proposal to lift the penalties first and worry
about regulating the conventicles afterwards, on the grounds that it
would encourage more conventicles. On the other hand, as John Miller
suggests, there is something suspicious about the way Charles's and Clifford's arguments mesh, as if they had rehearsed the whole discussion.[57]
And these were, of course, arguments that Williamson had been brood-

ing over the previous November. Perhaps encouraged by Clifford's gung-ho approach not to worry too much over the legalities of such a move, and certainly conscious of the imminence of war, Charles grasped the opportunity to help dissenters and Catholics and to ensure their loyalty. On the Monday a draft declaration was ready, on Thursday it was approved, and on Friday 15 March the Declaration of Indulgence was published. The Declaration suspended all penal laws in matters ecclesiastical and allowed nonconformists freedom of worship if their preachers and meeting houses were licensed; Catholics were permitted to meet for worship only in private houses. All other kinds of meetings were illegal and would be punished. The existing position of the Church of England was guaranteed. The Declaration wasted little time explaining or justifying itself. It simply stated that a dozen years of persecution had not succeeded in creating religious harmony and that the King was exercising his inherent supreme power in ecclesiastical matters. No reference was made to the need for later parliamentary approval or legislation. Two days earlier the war had begun.

IV

On 13 March, 'Sir Robert Holmes being on the back side of the Isle of Wight with five men-of-war, the Dutch Smyrna fleet with several merchantmen and six convoys passing that way refused to pay their due respect – they would lower their topsails, but not strike – upon which an engagement began.'[58] Thus the first blows of war were struck as a consequence of the quarrel going back to the *Merlin*. In fact this was a transparent pretence. Monmouth's regiment had already departed for France; Williamson's spies in the Dutch ports were at the waterside counting vessels or pumping sailors for information; and Holmes had orders to intercept Dutch ships. John Evelyn had been given responsibility for dealing with the casualties and prisoners arriving in Kent and he soon had business to attend to. After the encounter with the Smyrna fleet, one hundred and twenty English casualties were landed, 'brave, courageous blades, but miserably mangled'. There were 'very grisly objects amongst the wounded of a no cheap victory', thought Evelyn, and it was better not to send them to London when the war had only just begun. Enthusiasm for the war seemed remarkably high among the people; several observers commented on the willingness of seamen to volunteer for the King's service.[59]

The Dutch fleet did not leave the safety of the Maas and Texel until the end of April, and the French fleet under D'Estrées only left Brest on 29 April and joined forces with the English under the Duke of York off Spithead early on 7 May. The English and French worked their way up the Channel against the wind, while the Dutch who had been off

Dover moved further north towards Harwich. At Dover on 16 May Evelyn saw the Anglo-French fleet of one hundred and seventy ships:

> Such a gallant and formidable navy never, I think, spread sail upon the seas. It was a goodly yet terrible sight, to behold them as I did, passing eastwards by the straits betwixt Dover and Calais in a glorious day. The wind was yet so high, that I could not well go aboard, and they were soon got out of sight.[60]

A game of hide-and-seek ensued: a squadron of ten English ships found the Dutch but were chased back into Sheerness; the Dutch withdrew, only to advance again towards the Anglo-French fleet which was by now off Sole Bay on the Suffolk coast. Once more they were chased back. The Anglo-French fleet rode at anchor in Sole Bay, taking on provisions, and letting seamen and officers go ashore.

At first light on 28 May, with the sun and a light wind behind them, the Dutch fleet of De Ruyter bore down on the Anglo-French fleet. Unprepared and ill-positioned, the English and French ships were too close to the shore to manoeuvre properly, while some of their seamen were still ashore in the pubs of Southwold and had to be drummed up, and some officers were even further afield dancing in Harwich. Northernmost, and therefore nearest the Dutch, was the blue squadron, led by the Earl of Sandwich in his flagship, *Royal James*, which carried a hundred guns and nearly a thousand seamen. So 'the brunt of the day lay on the blue squadron'. Before 7.00 a.m., Van Ghent's squadron had closed in and begun to subject the *Royal James* to withering cannonades. By 9.00 a.m. the *Groot Hollandia* was jammed beneath her figurehead and entangled in her rigging, and savage fighting had left 300 English seamen dead or wounded: now Van Ghent and Sandwich began exchanging broadsides. The confusion of battle meant that Sandwich had received no aid from his other ships and, with increasing casualties among the officers, his situation was becoming hopeless. Just as the *Royal James* was freed from the *Groot Hollandia*, a Dutch fireship grappled her and the flames took hold. By noon she was well ablaze and Sandwich ordered his men to abandon ship. The last man seen on board the *Royal James* was the Earl of Sandwich, dressed in the insignia of the Garter, with the star on his chest, and the jewelled collar and George around his neck. Those watching on the Suffolk cliffs saw the ship as a mass of fire which had burned to the hull by 4.00 p.m. (see plate 4).

Meanwhile De Ruyter's squadron had taken on the Duke of York's red squadron, and their ships fought a running battle over ten miles of sea. The Duke had to transfer from one flagship to another, as the *Prince* lost her maintopmast, then the *St Michael* proved leaky; and the engagement became a series of small clashes between little groups of two or three vessels. The white squadron, under French command, had taken

Plate 4   The Burning of the Royal James, Battle of Sole Bay, 1672, by Willem Van de Velde the Younger. This was how the Earl of Sandwich met his heroic death, 'flames over's head, his feet dabbling in blood . . . [he] did at last from death to death retire / Courting the water to avoid the fire'.

a different tack, and remained outside the battle, shadowed, but not engaged, by the Dutch admiral Bankert. The Dutch set out for their own coast, and the Anglo-English fleet rallied sufficiently to follow them, so that the next day they were 'ready in a most brave body to fall upon the Dutch, when a sudden and unusual fog fell'.[61] Cheated of this chance for revenge, the English and French limped home.

The battle of Sole Bay was probably a marginal Dutch victory on account of the loss of the *Royal James*, and of officers like Sandwich, Digby, Holles and Cox; in total the English and French lost 700 or so dead, and the same number wounded. But both sides were battered. The Dutch suffered 600 killed and 1200 wounded. Mourning the loss of Sandwich, 'that incomparable person and my particular friend, and divers more whom I loved', Evelyn rushed down to Rochester to see what could be done for the many wounded and sick survivors. His agents told him of the men put ashore 'in most unspeakable misery for want of clothes' and shelter. There were already more than 300 at Gravesend by 11 June, 'and before the fleet sail, God knows what a multitude of such miserable creatures they may be necessitated to impose and thrust upon us, to relieve the ships from the stench and taint of them abroad.' Evelyn was outfaced by the sheer numbers of sick men 'who are (many of them) put stark naked and mortified, on the shore'; there were no quarters for them, and the local people refused further help until they were paid some of what was already owed, which in Kent, where there were nearly 3000 sick seamen, amounted to £3000 by September.[62] When Charles II, Shaftesbury and Clifford went down to the fleet at the Nore on 4 June to decide on their next step, York was all for taking the fight to De Ruyter. But the argument that it would be better to intercept the Dutch East Indies fleet prevailed. The summer was spent fruitlessly patrolling the North Sea in search of the merchantmen, braving the stormy weather, failing to meet up with the victualling ships, and watching the chances of landing an army in Holland dwindle.

On 10 June the Earl of Sandwich's recognizable body was recovered from the sea off Harwich, thirty miles from the scene of the battle, and taken ashore. After embalming, the body was taken first to Deptford and then, on 3 July, up the Thames to the sound of trumpets and fifes, accompanied by the barges of the royal family, the Lord Mayor and the City Companies, past spectators on the banks and London Bridge, to Westminster, where it was taken in procession to the Abbey for burial in Henry VII's chapel. Sandwich, whose honour had been compromised by the capture of an East Indiaman in the 1660s, had suffered forebodings of his own death. He had told John Evelyn that 'he thought he should see me no more' and yet, he said, 'be as it pleases God, I must do something, I know not what, to save my reputation'.[63] His heroic death in the service of his monarch and nation had more than redeemed his honour. Yet even the most conventional and loyal of subjects might ask whether the cause was worth the sacrifice, or whether there was honour in the crooked path which Charles had followed from Dover to Sole Bay? And many Englishmen and women would have echoed Evelyn's piteous exclamation over the dead and wounded: 'Lord! What miseries are mortal men obnoxious to, and what confusion and mischief do the avarice, anger, and ambition of princes cause in the world.'[64]

2

1672–4: Affairs Begin to Alter

Rumours of peace began to circulate as early as June 1672: 'affairs begin to alter, and men talk of a peace with Holland,' wrote Andrew Marvell MP, while Ralph Josselin, an Essex vicar, recorded in his diary, 'sad with Holland, some speak of peace between us'. The Dutch 'desire peace at any rate' said the official newsletters.[1] What had brought the Dutch so low so soon was the astonishing success of Louis XIV's huge army which swept across the Netherlands, effectively seizing five of the republic's seven provinces, scores of strongholds and establishing an headquarters at Utrecht by mid-summer. Only Holland and Zealand remained unconquered and to prevent further French advances the Dutch opened the dykes and flooded the country. The Dutch were in danger of sinking beneath mutual recriminations and defeatism. Their situation was complicated by the bitter rivalry between the oligarchic republican government, led by Johan De Witt, and the supporters of William, Prince of Orange, whose dynasty had in the past supplied quasi-royal leadership to the struggling republic. At the beginning of the year William had been nominated as Captain General of all Dutch forces, and as the situation worsened, and Orangist propaganda against De Witt and his party intensified, the country turned increasingly to Orange. English newsletters reported that such dread had seized the Hollanders that the rich thought only of flight and the poor only of revenge on their governors. Orange became Stadholder of Holland and Zealand, and the people's 'mad fury' led to a wave of unrest, violence, purges and the murder of De Witt by a mob. By September 'drums beat everywhere in the Prince of Orange's name . . . never taking any notice of the States [General] at all.' English newsletters tended to portray this as Orange taking his rightful place as prince of his people; and they insinuated, too, that Orange would soon accede to the overwhelming popular demand for peace with England.[2]

The realities of diplomacy and politics were rather different. Charles was playing a complex game. In the peace terms that he hoped that he and Louis would offer the Dutch, Charles demanded territory in the Netherlands for himself and for William and the appointment of William as perpetual stadholder, along with the settlement of the ostensible causes of the war. In a nutshell the aim was to carve up the Netherlands and to substitute a petty principality for a powerful republic. William of Orange, however, was not about to join in the dismemberment of his country. The best that Charles could do was to agree with Louis that neither of them would make peace separately.

News management buttressed the English war-effort. Immediately after the battle of Sole Bay a proclamation was issued 'to restrain the spreading of false news, and licentious talking of matters of state and government'; in February 1673 the government took legal advice on ways of curbing the coffee-houses.[3] The official newsletters sent out from Williamson's paper office, meanwhile, were full of reassuring statements about the Dutch being on their knees and reports of crowds cheering for 'the King of England and the Prince of Orange' when English envoys passed through Rotterdam. But the government had little hope of controlling the free flow of information between England and the Netherlands: the English Gazette and the Dutch newspapers carried accurate information of the movements of each other's fleet, and were each available in the other country; 'the Haarlem and Amsterdam Gazettes are so public here, that sober men fear the truth of something they say, as indeed our killed and wounded men are 1000.'[4] The government resorted to propaganda. Henry Stubbe was commissioned to write *A Justification of the Present War against the United Netherlands*, a tedious rehearsal of all the Dutch insolence towards the English across the entire century and around the globe, which appeared in June 1672. Stubbe, who had some credibility among nonconformists, published a sequel defending Charles's Declaration of Indulgence and reassuring those worried by a war against fellow-protestants. The same arguments appeared in William de Britaine's *The Dutch Usurpation* (1672) which dwelt upon the rise of the Dutch at the expense of English trade and fishing, Dutch barbarity in Indonesia, notably in the torture and massacre of English merchants at Amboina in 1622, the sovereignty enjoyed by English kings over the British seas since Roman times, and the threat to European peace posed by the Dutch and their pretensions. Although these arguments satisfied Philip Henry in Shropshire, he remained troubled by a war against co-religionists. One response was to cast doubt on their protestantism: 'Interest's the God they worship,' declared Dryden. The less bookish audience might prefer the entertainment laid on in a booth in Charing Cross by Anthony Di Voto which portrayed 'the Dutch cruelties at Amboina', or the Lord Mayor's show which tarred the Dutch with the same brush as the Spanish plunderers of America. And, of course, a blizzard of ballads derided the 'Hogan Mogans' and called the English to arms: 'rouse then heroic Britons; 'tis not words, / But wounds must work with leather-apron-lords'.[5]

The government were not confident that any of this could overcome innate popular hostility towards France nor counter the powerful Dutch propaganda orchestrated by Peter Du Moulin and his agents. After long debates in the Committee for Foreign Affairs, it was decided to postpone the imminent meeting of parliament until February. Charles argued that a parliament would 'dog and rogue the French and the alliance' with the effect of driving Louis towards the Dutch and leaving England nothing to show for her war. Arlington put a more positive spin on the decision when he said it dashed Dutch hopes, 'having fancied to themselves that they should prevail with many of the members of it to make them clamorous upon his majesty for a separate treaty upon easy terms'.[6] This was also an opportune moment to make some political changes. Lord Keeper Bridgeman, who had displayed a marked lack of enthusiasm for recent policy decisions, surrendered the Great Seal which went to Shaftesbury who now became Lord Chancellor, Clifford was elevated to Lord Treasurer (despite the ambitions of his patron Arlington in that direction) and Duncombe became Chancellor of the Exchequer.

Ministers were also anxious about the reaction to the Declaration of Indulgence. When it was issued in March, 'many thoughts of heart there were about it; we being surprised with it,' admitted the presbyterian Henry Newcome; others judged it 'a thing diversely resented, as men's interest leads them, the conformists generally displeased at it, the presbyterians glad, the independents very glad, the papists triumph'.[7] Nonconformist pastors reacted according to their particular theological position. Among those, mainly presbyterians, who hankered after a single national church and who had been attending parish churches as worshippers, to take out a licence as a minister seemed a betrayal of their aspirations or even a schism. Others such as Independents or baptists believed in voluntary congregations rather then parishes and so eagerly applied to licence their pastors and meeting houses. The Quakers, one of the largest and most visible denominations, refused all licenses because they did not believe the state had the power to control religion. The presbyterian minister Philip Henry recorded in his diary for June 1672 the various doubts among nonconformists about taking licences:

> Some think by accepting of them we give the King a power above the laws, so we do above such bad laws as the act of uniformity. Others think 'twill end in a severe tax upon licensed meetings and persons distinct from others: others in a massacre, it being now known where such people may be met with, as if they all had but one neck.[8]

For many, a bigger issue loomed behind the question of whether a particular minister or congregation should accept a licence; did this indulgence favour papists? It worried not only presbyterians like Heywood that 'papists and atheists enjoy so much liberty' under the Declaration, but even politicians like Anglesey who had protested in the privy council 'that the papists are put thereby into a better and less jealoused state than the dissenting protestants.'[9] If the Declaration of Indulgence was a Trojan horse for popery then it should surely worry all English protestants. So too should the constitutional implications of the King's decision to suspend acts of parliament. In 1663 Charles II had been told unequivocally by parliament that he did not have this power, but here he was a decade later claiming and exercising this 'right'. Non-conformists and conformists alike were suspicious of Charles's motives. Few of them could have been immune to the arguments of anti-war propaganda pieces like *The English Ballance* (1672) which 'plainly laid out the insincerity, insufficiency, and uncertainty of this indulgence'.[10]

I

The King and the Foreign Affairs Committee did what they could to prepare the ground for parliament's meeting in February 1673. Eight new regiments were commissioned, Charles reaffirmed his devotion to the Church of England, after advice Sir Job Charlton was chosen as the new Speaker, Buckingham and his allies were sweetened, and Arlington and the other ministers sounded out MPs. The royal speech to parliament on 5 February was forthright. The war was in defence of the kingdom's honour and interest, but more money was needed. 'I will deal plainly with you, I am resolved to stick to my Declaration,' said Charles, while reassuring them that it was not a sop to papists; and he went on to dismiss the 'weak and frivolous' suggestion that the troops he had raised 'were designed to control law and property'.[11] Lord Chancellor Shaftesbury followed up with a tirade against the Dutch. Reputation was crucial in war and peace and the Dutch had been emboldened by their belief that the English parliament would never vote for a war against them – now was the moment to prove them wrong. He reminded MPs that in the 1660s the same parliament had believed in Cato's principle *Delenda est Carthago*, he asserted that the Dutch must be destroyed as they were England's 'eternal enemy, both by interest and inclination', and he concluded in ringing terms that thanks to God and our King, long may he reign, England's religion, church, parliament, properties and liberties were safe. On 7 February Sir Thomas Dolman's 'set oration' proposing a supply of £70,000 per month for eighteen months 'was well received by the House'.[12] Then, in a surprising move, a group of the government's leading critics, Garway, Strangway and Meres, the last of

Plate 5   Anthony Ashley Cooper, Earl of Shaftesbury (artist unknown, c.1673). A former Cromwellian, and a leading minister in the early 1670s, Shaftesbury later devoted himself to attempts to dissolve parliament, unseat Danby and thwart the Duke of York. He may have been a 'patriot' acting in defence of religion, liberty and property, or, as Charles II alleged, he may have been 'only angry in revenge, because he was not employed'.

whom had just made a speech attacking the whole drift of royal policy, proposed a grant of almost exactly what the government were asking. This may well have been the 'strange day in parliament' recorded by Anglesey in his diary.[13] It is likely that these critics, rather than being overcome by loyalty and patriotism, planned to use the pending supply to exert pressure on Charles.

After a hesitant start the Commons tore into the Declaration of Indulgence and its claims of royal authority: 'the debate quickly went off from justifying and maintaining the clause to the manner of laying it asleep', some wanted to ask Charles to withdraw the declaration, but more were keen to pronounce it illegal, and eventually the House resolved *nem. con.* 'that penal statutes in matters ecclesiastical cannot be suspended but by an act of parliament'. They then drew up an address to this effect which was presented to the King on 14 February, the same day that they decided to bring in a bill to give ease to dissenters in matters of religion 'to let him see that we did not dislike the matter of his Declaration but the manner, and did not doubt the prudence but only the legality of it'.[14] Charles received much advice on whether to withdraw the Declaration. York and Clifford were against withdrawing, as it seemed was Shaftesbury who feared a diminution of royal authority. But Rupert, Coventry and Arlington were concerned about the war and feared another 'Chatham'. Louis's view, too, was that supply for the war was paramount. The government played for time. Charlton fell ill and was replaced as Speaker by Edward Seymour. Charles sent a reply to the Commons which reasserted his rights, but also disclaimed any intention of suspending laws which touched the subject's rights or property, and he promised to concur with any bill they might offer which would achieve his only end of lifting penalties from dissenters. Politely, but firmly, the Commons replied that he was mistaken about his powers and the Declaration should be withdrawn. On 1 March the King consulted the House of Lords, but rather than endorse the Declaration, as Charles had expected, the peers debated for three days and then merely approved the notion of a bill to settle the issue – and when Clifford offered them a bill which gave Charles the powers he claimed, the Lords quietly shelved it. In the meantime the Commons had not only advanced their bill for ease for protestant dissenters, the heads of which were widely reported in newsletters, but they had drawn up an address against popery and received a bill to prevent Catholics from holding public office. There were effectively four interwoven initiatives afoot; supply, rescinding the Declaration, ease for protestant dissenters and anti-Catholic measures: progress was made on all fronts simultaneously.

The first to be achieved was the cancellation of the Declaration. Charles had decided that 'we must stand to what we can stand to' and the government had to stage-manage this humiliation as best they could.[15] On 8 March Charles made a gracious speech to parliament announcing that he had agreed to their request to banish popish priests and Jesuits and alluding to his late Declaration. He left it up to Secretary Coventry to tell the House how he had seen the great seal torn off the Declaration of Indulgence. But more was to be extorted from the King by the lever of money. 'We went forward with the bill of supply,' noted one MP, before turning to the test bill, the measure to weed out

Catholics from public offices. On 12 March the bill had been sent to the Lords where Clifford denounced it as the 'monstrum horrendum of Virgil' and where amendments were made 'to which the Commons will never submit'.[16] It came back to the lower house on the same day as the finished supply bill, and once again MPs agreed to let the supply lie on the table while they dealt with the test bill. Bitter reflections on Clifford followed, as did some hits at the Duke of York, but finally, having secured the withdrawal of most of the amendments, the Commons passed the Test Act which imposed the oaths of supremacy and allegiance, a declaration against transubstantiation, and the requirement of an annual communion in the Church of England on all office-holders. The session was now nearing its end – on 24 March the King sent a message that he would adjourn parliament before the 30th – but even at this late stage some MPs still hoped to bring up grievances such as the favour shown to Catholics in Ireland, pressing men for the fleet, martial law and billeting, before supply was finally passed on 26 March. And still outstanding was the bill for ease for protestant dissenters, which lifted the penalties against them and offered them freedom of worship provided they subscribed to the doctrine of the Thirty-nine Articles and the oaths of supremacy and allegiance, and informed the authorities of their public meetings. After much debate and not a little confusion, the bill went to the Lords from whence it returned at nearly the last moment with a series of amendments. One of these granted power to the King to dispense with penal statutes when parliament was in recess, a small concession, perhaps, but one too like the suspending power which had been denied so categorically by the Commons to be acceptable. In the last two days of the session MPs argued fruitlessly and the bill fell with the adjournment: 'the bill for dissenters is not passed,' wrote the puritan Sir Edward Harley MP to his wife, 'the lord be gracious to those who find few friends in this world.'[17]

Parliament was a forum for the nation's concerns and so MPs and peers brought to Westminster their anxieties about the war, the French alliance, taxes and the suspension of parliamentary statutes. But they were also open to persuasion and manipulation; their doubts could be played upon and enlarged or their fears could be laid to rest by reassurance and argument. MPs and the governing elite of Restoration England were assailed by propaganda in many guises. In February 1673 a spoof bill of sale was scattered about which offered to the highest bidder such choice items as the Chancellor's loyalty, Buckingham's religion, Nell Gwynn's virginity, and 'new fashioned paradoxes, the one to suppress popery by the suppression of the protestant interest abroad, the other to maintain liberty by the raising of a standing army at home'. Although aiming principally at 'a very fine cabal', such sweeping satire seemed to indict the entire political establishment, court, government and parliament, as corrupt and to offer few remedies.[18] Other propaganda pieces were more precisely targeted. *The English Ballance* opposed the French alliance and Dutch war because they were against the dictates of religion and national interest, but fundamentally because:

> It's plain his maj[esty] aimeth at being absolute and designeth to rule the nation independently from the advice of parliaments. . . . In plain English, the French government is affected by our English court, which we suppose can never be sufficiently illustrious, while there must be such an unbecoming dependence upon parliaments, for pitiful subsidies . . .[19]

Dutch propaganda harped on the dangers posed by France and the consequences at home and abroad if Charles and Louis succeeded in snuffing out the Netherlands. Peter Du Moulin's influential *Englands Appeal from a Private Cabal at Whitehall*, composed in January 1673, approved by William of Orange, smuggled over, and dispersed among MPs in mid-March, undertook to explain 'the surprising novelty and strangeness of these unexpected counsels' which had led England into war against its protestant neighbour. That explanation included a detour into the growth of Louis's power and the likely outcome of his Catholic crusade against European protestantism, before turning to the plot by corrupt counsellors to deceive Charles II. In April Joseph Hill's *The Interest of these United Provinces* (Amsterdam, 1672) appeared simultaneously in English in England and Dutch in the Netherlands. Its argument that the preservation of the Dutch, their religion and regime, depended on a peace with England, was couched in terms also designed to appeal to the English. Hill exposed the threat to both nations from Louis's self-aggrandizing Roman Catholicism and offered a defence of Charles II as a both a sincere protestant *and* a tolerationist. Of course, those writing in favour of the war, like Henry Stubbe or John Dryden whose propaganda play *Amboyna* was probably premiered that spring, took issue with this interpretation. On the contrary, they argued, the Dutch were not good protestants, but preferred gain before godliness and were ready to bow down before idols in Indonesia and Japan rather than sacrifice their commercial interest. This was, as Steven Pincus has shown, a well-worn theme in the propaganda accompanying England's seventeenth-century wars with the Netherlands.[20] Other than this, the defenders of the war could plausibly recount the episodes of Anglo-Dutch rivalry, they could exploit popular suspicion of republics, but they could do little to counter the most insinuating charge of their opponents, that there was a francophile and crypto-papist conspiracy in Whitehall.

The mud stuck because Roman Catholicism seemed to come so close to the royal family. The King's wife, his mistresses Cleveland and Quérouaille, and (or so many suspected) his brother were Catholics. James, Duke of York, had become convinced of Roman Catholicism by early 1669, but did not stop attending Anglican services and declare himself because he feared the opprobrium and confidently expected Charles to announce his own conversion at any moment. His wife, Anne, however, had no such compunctions and gave up the Church of England in 1669. In 1671 James did not take Easter communion, but he continued to attend prayer book services with Charles. At Easter 1672 James was away with the fleet, but apparently he had been received into the Catholic church just before leaving London.[21] As rumour spread, Charles begged his brother in vain to take the sacrament at Christmas 1672. The 1673 session of parliament ended on Easter Saturday and the following day John Evelyn heard the sermon at court and 'stayed to see whether, according to custom, the Duke of York received the communion with the King; but he did not, to the amazement of everybody'. Coming immediately after the Test Act, this 'gave exceeding grief and scandal to the whole nation, that the heir of it, and the son of a martyr for the Protestant religion, should apostatize. What the consequence of this will be, God only knows, and wise men dread.'[22]

The nation at large had become hypersensitive to popery as a result of the Test Act. In early summer Buckingham had gone recruiting for his regiment in Yorkshire:

> so jealous were the commonalty there of popery, that not a man scarce would come into his grace 'till he had gone and publicly with his officers took the sacrament at York. The whole town [London] do nothing but pretend to jealousies of the growth of popery, and have the strangest reports from diverse parts of Wales of their numerous meetings and nightly trainings, and furnishing themselves with arms, etc. and so superstitious some are to their own opinions that this touchstone of the oaths is not enough to root them out of command, because many of those that were formerly counted Roman Catholics have now swallowed the oaths . . .[23]

The Test Act gave office-holders until mid-summer to receive the sacrament and take the oaths, but there was an immediate rush to qualify during April. 'All people take the oath here lest they be snapt and lose £500,' Dr Denton told Sir Ralph Verney, 'and you (and I believe a thousand more) that little dream of taking it, must take it, or they'll be snapt.'[24] The great aristocrats and peers chose to take the sacrament at St Martins-in-the-Fields or St Margaret's Westminster and then take the oaths at King's Bench in Westminster Hall. Those taking the sacrament further afield could buy a blank printed certificate with the correct legal form for the witnesses' oaths. By May all eyes were on the only ministers who had not yet conformed, Lord Treasurer Clifford and the Duke of York. Clifford gave out that he was spending Saturday 17 May in retreat and most assumed he was preparing for the sacrament the next day. Unfortunately on 17 May the closed coach in which he and a Catholic priest were leaving Somerset House (where the Benedictines served the Queen's chapel) overturned in the Strand, exposing them 'to the view of the street'; as one bystander brought Clifford his hat and another his periwig, his secret was out: 'the whole town is no longer in doubt of my Lord Treasurer's being a Roman Catholic.' It was a foregone conclusion that Clifford would resign, but when? And who would succeed him?[25] York was equally slow to act, but in his case the government's legal officers were busy looking for ways in which he might retain his military commands. Eventually on 15 June York resigned his offices; and on 19 June Clifford followed suit. 'Great is the talk of the town upon these sudden alterations, especially of his royal highness's laying down,' Ball informed Williamson. 'The generality of people being so bold as to say he must not think to have the favour of England if he professes openly a Roman Catholic; nay, further, that his majesty must not make him commander of his forces, which is of great moment etc, with many other such rude and barbarous talk.'[26] Clifford and York were portrayed by their opponents – and sometimes by their friends like Croissy – as a pair of zealots, egging each other on with heroic delusions:

> He and his Duke each had too great a mind
> To be by justice or be law confin'd.
> Their boiling heads can hear no other sounds
> Than fleets and armies, battles, blood, and wounds;
> And to destroy our liberties they hope
> By Irish fools and by a doting pope.[27]

The fear of popery had implications for the fate of protestant dissent. It was after all one of the motives for forcing the cancellation of the Declaration of Indulgence. Many who were well disposed to dissenters were nevertheless glad to see the end of the indulgence 'if it was dangerous as to the growth of popery'. But they could not help fearing that 'an after reckoning must come for use of past liberty'.[28] Briefly they placed their faith in the abortive parliamentary measure for the ease of protestant nonconformists. Downhearted in March, nonconformists soon realized that they were not about to return to the situation of 1670 or 1671, to persecution and intolerance. The Declaration had been cancelled, but the licences held by preachers and congregations had not been withdrawn. In April Philip Henry of Shropshire received a letter from London which said 'it is supposed we are to take no notice of any th[ing] but may plead our licences till revoked'. Henry recognized that 'we are at great uncertainties' but gave himself up to God's will and was 'in this further confirmed by what the parl[iament] did, that 'tis now it seems their opinion, that 'tis fit we should have liberty to preach, at least for a year and if the quarter sessions grant it'. JPs in Oxfordshire and Leicestershire tried to prosecute dissenters and discount their licenses. At

Ashby-de-la-Zouche Sir Robert Shirley called a licence 'a silly thing' and found himself answering for it before the privy council. But the council sought compromise, claiming nothing could be done without parliament, urging forbearance on JPs, and reminding all parties of the continuing 'peaceable effects' of the late Indulgence. For all the labours of Lord Privy Seal Anglesey, the privy council found it impossible to draft an instruction 'with so much caution as neither to suspend the laws in force, nor give authority to the licences'. It was better to let sleeping dogs lie and resolve each case rather than formulate some general principle. When Philip Henry received this encouraging news, he observed 'Lord, thou keepest us at uncertainties that our hope might be in thee.'[29]

II

The second campaigning season of the war began with Louis laying siege to Maastricht. There was little hope of advancing in the Netherlands and a siege made a suitable stage for a warrior king. It also offered the Duke of Monmouth the chance to cover himself with glory by rallying dispirited French troops and leading a successful sally just days before the final capitulation of the city. Charles meanwhile was recruiting 10,000 troops for a descent on Zealand. Slowly the troops congregated at Blackheath where that summer's incessant rain 'very much incommodes' them, as did the Duke of Buckingham's 'frenchified' and incompetent attempts to put them through their paces.[30] Despite hopes that York might lead the army as 'generallissimo', his resignation as Admiral and legal opinions now rendered this impossible, and Prince Rupert, 'the only hero' in the people's thoughts, was given overall command with Frederick, Count Schomberg, as Lieutenant General of the army.[31] Schomberg was 'half English, half Palatinate, a stout protestant', but there was still 'some dissatisfaction' at the appointment of a foreigner who had served the French; not the least of the dissatisfied was Buckingham who withdrew from any further part in the campaign.[32] For all their grumbling, the people flocked to Blackheath: 'all persons travel thither to see the new and fine show, and various opinions there are of their being lodged so near London, and some persuade themselves it will not be long before they be disbanded.'[33] Finally, on 13 July, the army decamped, marching off towards the port of Gravesend where hired colliers awaited to transport them to Yarmouth. There they were to wait until the English and French fleet had established control over the seas.

The naval campaign was not going well however. The contending fleets were all at sea by May and the first action was a scrappy affair off Schooneveld in which ships were disabled and officers and men lost on both sides. One English account claimed that the Dutch 'played the poltroons more than ever', firing at a distance and running for home in the night; but Rupert admitted to the King that they were 'an enemy as strong and rather better seamen than we', while his second-in-command Admiral Spragge was caustic about 'our ill conduct and most notorious cowardice'.[34] Such disagreement between commanders was far from unusual. The Restoration navy was riddled with personal and professional rivalries, between experienced officers and gentlemen volunteers, former Cromwellians and Cavaliers, and this was now exacerbated by the Duke of York's attempt, even after his resignation as Lord High Admiral, to direct operations at one remove through his brother. The prickly Rupert, at odds with both Schomberg and D'Estrées, found his freedom of action hampered by a stream of royal advice and orders. A series of inconclusive encounters depleted the navy and wore down morale at home. It was said that things would have gone better with York in command, 'and all the ordinary people will have it that we were beaten, the roguish seamen writing so to their friends, which letters appear in some coffee-houses, and does much prejudice in dishearting the people'. The Dutch fleet 'brush about the coast and frighten the country', and to many it seemed that the Anglo-French fleet were avoiding a battle.[35]

This confusion and delay persisted even when Rupert encountered the Dutch off their own coast late in July; Rupert and De Ruyter finally closed for battle on the afternoon of Sunday 11 August. The Anglo-French fleet was organized in three squadrons, and the commander of each had distinct priorities, so as with many such battles, the action degenerated into three separate engagements. Spragge's ships lay side by side with Tromp's and exchanged gunfire for three hours. When Spragge's flagship lost her topmast, he decided to move to another. His boat 'had not rowed ten boats' length, but a bullet . . . broke his boat; they made back again as fast as they could on board, but before they came within throw of the ropes, the boat sunk and Sir Edward Spragge was drowned; being taken up dead, his head and shoulders above water, having taken so dead hold of the boat, they could hardly disengage him from it. Mr Littleton, Mr Smith and his page were drowned with him.'[36] Another heroic admiral had died at sea; and once more the chilling details seem to have touched a chord – many letters mention the dead Spragge's grip on his boat – and the admiral was accorded the same solemn funeral rites as Sandwich had received the previous summer. In the battle, meanwhile, Rupert sought to get De Ruyter further out to sea and engage with him, and the squadron commanded by D'Estrées got to the windward side of the enemy and then, curiously, held off from the fight. Eventually the fleets parted, 'both soundly torn', and with no decisive victor established; however, since the allied fleet was in no state to mount another attack that summer, the allies had failed to achieve mastery of the seas and consequently Dutch ports remained open and the threatened invasion was foiled. Certainly Prince Rupert felt the need to excuse and explain events. He rushed back to London 'very angry and raging' and issued an account which pinned the blame on the inaction of D'Estrées. He was adding fuel to a raging fire. Within days of the battle, 'it is whispered as if the French did not behave themselves well, as having the wind and yet not bearing upon the enemy' despite a signal to do so, although 'this may be but discourse, and proceed from the little inclination the English generally have for the French.' By 18 August, 'they now rail down right against the French, and say they are so far from assisting us, that they would willingly stand and look on, whilst our fleet are destroyed' and that parliament when it meets 'will take care that the nation is no longer abused in this manner'. This was 'in every ordinary man's mouth, every seaman's wife having an account from her husband of their having been betrayed, as they call it, by the French.' No explanations about confused signals or disagreements among the English versions could shake the conviction that the French aimed to ruin England.[37]

This xenophobic mood was not helped by the news that after months of deliberation York had finally chosen a new wife, an Italian Catholic no less. 'The town is now full of the news of the Duke of York's marriage with the young Duchess of Modena . . . sister to the present Duke . . . and great niece to the late Cardinal Mazarin,' wrote Henry Ball on 31 July; and a few days later it was reported to Sir Ralph Verney that 'we fear we shall have the daughter of Modena for our duchess.'[38] Mary of Modena was not yet fifteen, extremely pious, and presumably capable of bearing James many children. It took all summer to negotiate the details of the marriage, but it was common knowledge that Louis XIV supported the match, and it was said that he was to pay the duchess's dowry. News of the Modena match probably diverted attention from Charles's recent creation of Louise, his young French mistress, as the Duchess of Portsmouth. The 'undecent and extravagant' talk of the capital was all of Modena: 'a prince in Italy, to the thinking of the ordinary people, is too near the holy see of Rome, and a marriage proposed and concluded by the French cannot be good, but the conclusion of all is what will the P[arliament] say to these things.'[39] Some believed the marriage would be rushed through before the next scheduled meeting of parliament in October, others that parliament would not meet until after the wedding. Every hiccup in the negotiations was greeted with delight by the coffee-house crowd, but on 20 September the marriage was celebrated in Modena with the Earl of Peterborough standing proxy for York. As October arrived 'the town fills apace with parliament men' eager to censure this marriage; a report that Charles had suffered apoplectic fits 'sinks deeply into everyone's breast and it's all the talk': many must have wondered whether this was to be the moment when the papist James succeeded to the throne and set about fathering a Catholic dynasty with Mary. Gossip said Mary was 'not at all handsome' and named her 'deformities: as croaked [crooked?], red hair, thirteen, and very little'. There was talk of asking the King to forbid the consummation of the marriage. Meanwhile 'the hate and malice against the French continues as high as ever, every one taking a very great liberty of railing against them.'[40]

The Modena marriage convulsed parliament when it finally met. Technically the session had only been adjourned until 20 October, and to allow for a fresh appeal for money and, many suspected, to postpone the inevitable criticism of York's marriage, the court proposed to prorogue parliament at its first meeting and start a new session a week later. Although this is what happened, government plans were briefly disrupted on that first day by Mr Powle's dramatic speech claiming that their efforts to suppress popery were all in vain 'if it got footing so near the throne' and his motion for an address to the King that the intended match may not be consummated. Supported by Birch, Clarges and even Sir Robert Howard, the motion was passed and an address seems to have been drawn up and delivered: 'this seems a very ill beginning' wrote one correspondent, but many saw Howard's involvement as a sign of royal approval.[41] For a week MPs kicked their heels until the new session when they gathered in fractious mood. On the second day they received the King's reply to their address. The King's plea that he could do nothing, the marriage far from being 'intended' was already complete, and his honour was involved, cut no ice with members who responded with a new address stressing the 'dangerous consequences' which might follow from the Duke's marriage 'to the princess of Modena, or any other person of the popish religion'. They had received no reply when parliament was prorogued a week later.

The furore over the Modena marriage was stoked by propagandists and satirists. Manuscript verses circulated among the political elite and while some, like the song *Signior Dildo* attributed to Rochester, were scurrilous pieces with a subliminal political message, others were forthright statements of the threat of popery. *Advice to a Painter to Draw the Duke By* follows the conventions of the genre by offering sketches of York and his papist co-conspirators, including Peterborough, Clifford, Arundel, Bellasis and the Irish Talbot brothers, and concludes with an 'envoy' to 'Great Charles':

> Let not thy life and crown end together
> Betray'd by a false brother and false friend.
> Observe the dangers that appear so near
> And all your subjects do each minute fear:
> A drop of poison or a popish knife
> Ends all the joys of England with thy life.[42]

Indignation about French betrayal and the Modena marriage swirled around the streets and coffee-houses. It inspired calls for peace and prompted attacks on ministers. And in what seems a deliberate attempt to channel popular discontent, it found a focus in anti-popery demonstrations. On 5 November 'you might have seen the broad streets of London so thick with bonfires as of they had been but one hearth, and the fireworks flying in such numbers'; a great bonfire was held in the Poultry where 'the apprentices were resolved to make a new addition, which was a large effigy of the Whore of Babylon' and more than a thousand onlookers were treated to an elaborate mockery of Roman Catholicism and 'filled themselves with good liquor'. Evelyn attributed the apprentices' actions to their displeasure 'at the Duke for altering his religion, and marrying an Italian lady'. Thomas Derham was glad that the new Duchess of York had not arrived in London that night 'when madness has a licence' since 'she would certainly be martyred, for the common people here and even those of quality in the country believe she is the Pope's eldest daughter'. The Duchess landed at Dover on 20 November where her marriage was duly solemnized by Bishop Crew. When the Duke brought her to court, 'none wished him joy, nor would the city be brought to make bonfires.'[43]

III

Crisis seemed to be engulfing the government in 1673. The Test Act had made popery close to the crown a major issue – as had the Modena marriage. Never popular, the French alliance lost further support when Louis fostered Catholicism in captured Dutch towns in 1672, and marched off into the Rhineland in 1673. The French 'betrayal' at the battle of the Texel ruled out any further co-operation between the English and French fleets and virtually sabotaged the naval war. Moreover England had nothing to show for the war and by the autumn of 1673 Louis himself was forced to withdraw from the Netherlands. Nor was all well in Whitehall. According to rumour the 'cabinet' was 'quite broken' in July and 'strange reports as various as untrue' spread of who was to become Treasurer, Chancellor or Privy Seal.[44] The casualties from the Test Act, Buckingham's pique at not having a military command, and the failure to make headway in the naval war, undermined any cohesion between ministers. Arlington and Shaftesbury began to lose confidence in the whole idea of the war, other leading councillors had never been more than half-hearted, and the real enthusiasts, Clifford and York, were now out of office. Arlington, who 'seems weary of the fatigue of his place', was haggling with the Earl of St Albans for the less onerous office of Lord Chamberlain.[45] York and Shaftesbury were at daggers drawn and Shaftesbury was losing royal favour. Reports that Ormonde and 'the old honest party' would stage a come-back were ill-founded. Among the smaller fry, Anglesey became Lord Privy Seal in April and Sir Thomas Osborne became Lord Treasurer in May and was created Viscount Latimer in July. But everyone was running scared of the next session of parliament when heads would undoubtedly roll.

On 3 October 1673 Thomas Ross wrote from Whitehall that as parliament drew near, 'men of all sorts' condemned and acquitted politicians 'as if the next meeting of the parliament should be nothing but a High Court of Justice and a Gaol Delivery. The members begin to flock up to town, and are met at the very stirrup to be engaged in cabals against this or that great man.' On the eve of the session, Sir William Temple believed that one party 'would run up to the height and fall upon the ministers, especially Buckingham, Arlington, Lauderdale, and their carriage, particularly in the business of the war, so as absolutely to break all the present set both of men and business at court'. Arlington, claimed Temple, was one of the last believers in the war, which may do him 'very great wrong in parliament, since Buckingham pretends to have wholly left that seat, and will, they say, take an occasion to come into the House of Lords and clear himself, and throw it all upon Arlington.' The Venetian envoy also remarked on the other ministers' efforts to ruin Arlington through 'the violence of parliament' and observed that 'this parliamentary machine is a contrivance devised purposely, by intriguing ministers, to work it against each other; the King being of opinion that the custom will not prove prejudicial to him.'[46] Clifford's death, possibly by suicide, on 17 October was greeted by some cynics as a lucky escape from parliamentary inquiry; the other ministers took care to arm themselves with pardons for their past actions and Lauderdale took himself off to Scotland.

When parliament met on 27 October the King's speech attempted to steer members towards a vote of supply. He wanted peace but the insolence of the Dutch was proving a stumbling block and so he asked for the money to set out a fleet in 1674. He promised to help secure religion and property and recommended the case of the bankers to parliament's consideration. Unmentioned was the looming question of the Modena marriage and the vote of 20 October's meeting. Yet contemporaries were convinced, too, that 'discord in the court contributed much to the putting of the parliament out of tune, for some of the harshest notes were struck by their own hands' and Thomas Derham believed that Buckingham was content 'to lose an eye himself to leave his enemy none'.[47] The consequences were plain. Almost immediately the Commons saw an attack by Arlington's friends on Speaker Seymour for his closeness to the court. Neither Arlington's nor Buckingham's followers did anything to help the government gain supply. A day was spent debating *whether* to offer supply and which grievances should be redressed first: 'the war with Holland, the league with France, the dangers from popish counsels and counsellors, the standing army, and many others'. Sir William Coventry, who seemed to have imbibed Du Moulin's arguments, ferociously denounced the French and the war; and finally he came up with 'his subtle allay to make the vote pass in these words: not to grant any supply till the eighteen months tax were expired, unless the obstinacy of the Hollanders should make it necessary'.[48] Once agreed this meant that the King would get no further money unless he could demonstrate that the Dutch had refused reasonable terms; and that looked very like a potential invasion by parliament of the King's prerogative of making peace and war. Next day the house debated the grievance of a standing army, but Powle and Sacheverell gave the discussion a sharper point by referring to the summer's military manoeuvres and surreptitiously changing the final vote to read that *the* standing army was a grievance. Charles had no stomach for this – nor the planned assault on Lauderdale – and so prorogued the parliament after a session of only nine days.

The court was in disarray. On 9 November Shaftesbury was dismissed from office: Charles suspected him of deliberately allowing parliament to express its distaste for the Modena marriage on 20 October. But there were few other signs of royal decisiveness. When Latimer and Seymour urged Charles to appoint Finch as Lord Keeper, he changed his mind six times in six hours. York remained powerful, but Buckingham and his allies now seemed to be coming to the fore. Lord Conway described how he was swept off by Latimer to the Countess of Shrewsbury's where he found Nell Gwynn, Buckingham and Seymour; 'about three o'clock in the morning we went to supper, were very merry, and drank smartly.' Their dominance might be short-lived, warned Temple, 'for 'tis very transitory upon this scene'. Charles instructed his ministers 'to use all their skills to make his interest good in [the] House of Commons', but many of them were as concerned with their own interests.[49] The parliamentary storm against the ministers had been postponed, not averted. In January Sir Gilbert Talbot MP wrote to Williamson that since Buckingham had been named 'as a pernicious minister' in the last session, he had devoted himself to courting MPs, 'the debauchees by drinking with them, the sober by grave and serious discourses, the pious by receiving the sacrament at Westminster', but still the Duke believed that 'parliament must have a sacrifice to appease them' and so reserved his greatest efforts for portraying Arlington as the most dangerous minister. 'I hope we shall spoil his design,' continued Talbot, one of Arlington's faction, for we have prepared a petition against him in the Lords and an impeachment in 'our house'.[50]

While the principal ministers were at odds, Charles himself gave no clear leadership. In December the Venetian representative believed that government was so confused that 'the King calls a cabinet council for the purpose of not listening to it; and the ministers hold forth in it so as not to be understood.'[51] Charles refused to say whether he would give up the war. He was over a barrel. It was a matter of honour not to desert Louis, although commentators believed that the motive of this 'obstinacy' was 'not only the violence of [the] Duke, but the dread of having all that has passed between them and France published if they anger France'.[52] And if Charles went back to parliament cap in hand, he would undoubtedly be humiliated. Mixed signals emerged from the court. Charles was persuaded by Buckingham and Latimer to offer parliament sight of the 1672 treaty and so reassure them that liberty and protestantism were safe. Finch said that the King was going to let it be known informally that he would leave the French alliance by Michaelmas, and if this would not placate parliament, then the 'great men', Arlington, Anglesey, Buckingham, Lauderdale and possibly Ormonde, would be abandoned. Yet at the same time Charles summoned John Evelyn and asked him to write against the Dutch 'about the duty of the flag and fishing'.[53]

The government was in danger of falling apart and the contest for public opinion was hotting up. There was a real chance that Dutch propaganda could exploit public disenchantment with the war and parliamentary disaffection to force Charles into a separate peace: 'the Dutch libels swarm among us to sow the seeds of sedition,' complained Arlington. *A Relation of the most material matters handled in parliament, relating to religion, property, and the liberty of the subject* was 'a terrible new book' circulating among MPs at this time.[54] It reprinted from the Commons' Journals of 1673 the votes and addresses over the declaration of indulgence and other matters, but it wove these into a narrative of the dangers posed by the French alliance and by popery, and it included a bogus set of accounts detailing the pensions paid to courtiers and ministers. Another 'libel' addressed to MPs, *Verbum sapienti*, encouraged parliament to investigate 'this unchristian war . . . and imprudent league . . . the dark and mysterious contrivances of a small popish cabal' and demanded the removal of 'that great triumvirate of iniquity, Buckingham, Arlington and Lauderdale'.[55] The Dutch sent every MP and peer a copy of their peace terms 'thinking thereby to insinuate to the parliament their readiness to give all manner of satisfaction and compliance'.[56] Simultaneously parliamentarians were warned of the dangers of popish priests, permanent armies, massacres and dissolutions won by the foulest of methods:

> Before the meeting of the parliament Madame Carwell sat upon him [Charles] in the most efficacious manner with her coats up, for a dissolution, and he swore by Christ and her —— (his new sacrament) that it should be done. The next morning, she comes to him with an instru-

GEORGE VILLERS DUKE OF BUCKINGHAM.

Plate 6   George Villiers, second Duke of Buckingham (Lely, 1675). Charles II's boyhood companion and erratic minister; Charles's favour towards him was based on 'conversation and merriment' rather than trust or respect. Buckingham's vanity led him to assume many roles – soldier, politician, lover, writer and wit – but success ultimately eluded him in all of them.

ment ready drawn, which he refused to sign, alleging that he was drunk when he promised. But afterwards she came to him as he sat in his chair, took up her coats, and fell into his lap, and then again he swore to her as aforesaid to do it, but as before he was drunk with wine so now with lust, and they have not yet been able to screw him up.[57]

With such salacious rumours being spread by the Dutch and their allies, it was wise of Rochester to flee the court briefly when he inadvertently handed Charles 'a terrible lampoon' which not only repeated such accusations but roundly denounced all monarchs 'from the hector of France to the cully of Britain'.[58]

On 7 January the King opened the new session and spoke to a packed house. After promising his co-operation with any reasonable proposals to secure religion or property, Charles concentrated on the need for 'a speedy, a proportionable and above all a cheerful' grant of supply. Whether to wage effective war or to secure a good peace, money was indispensable. He concluded by offering a small parliamentary committee the chance to see existing treaties and by assuring them that there was no other treaty with France which would not be made known – Conway thought he 'fumbled' in delivering this last part of his speech. Nevertheless the King received more applause than had been heard for many years, reported Ruvigny; and even Du Moulin's correspondents agreed that he was 'hummed up'.[59] Having heard the King, the Commons adjourned for five days, but the Lords got straight to work on the 'great baiting' of the 'bears' which had been so long anticipated.[60] It was reported that the petition against Buckingham was on behalf of the young Earl of Shrewsbury and his family 'for the murder of his father and wicked and lewd conversations with his mother ever since'. In fact the petition only mentioned 'the deplorable death' of the Earl of Shrewsbury in 1668 which came some time after he had been wounded in a duel with Buckingham. Yet the central allegation of an adulterous affair between Buckingham and the Countess and 'the insolent and shameless manner of their cohabiting together since the death of the late Earl' was undeniable. Buckingham submitted himself to the Lords in a written answer a week later and on 6 February the House required him and the Countess to enter bonds of £10,000 each that they would no longer live together.[61] The Lords were also preoccupied in their first few meetings by rumours of papist plots. A boy of thirteen was interrogated by the peers about a paper he had found in the street warning of the danger to King and parliament from gunpowder or massacre. Shaftesbury made speeches about an imminent papist rising and proposed that every member of the Lords take the oath of allegiance, which included a repudiation of papal authority, before entering the house.

When the Commons reassembled on 12 January they fell straight into step with the peers – indeed York had no doubt that events were being orchestrated; as he told Ruvigny, there were meetings at Lord Holles's house where Carlisle, Shaftesbury, Salisbury and others 'concerted together the matters which were to be proposed in the lower house, where those lords had great influence'.[62] Both houses agreed on an address to the King for a day of fasting and prayer to lament 'intestine differences', chiefly raised by popish recusants, and to 'seek a reconciliation at the hands of almighty God'. Charles promptly agreed but jaundiced observers wondered 'how a debauched court and people relish this'.[63] The Commons then moved on to consider whether their griev-ances were more pressing than the usual vote of thanks for the King's speech, and found that they were. Many of these were resurrected from the previous session and included the pressing of men for the navy, 'martial law', heavy taxation, the disruption of trade, and the 'invasion' of property and religion; and beneath them all ran the conviction that 'we ought to find out the authors of our misfortunes,' in Russell's words, 'the ill ministers about the King' that had advised everything from the attack on the Smyrna fleet and the Stop of the Exchequer to the pro-rogation of parliament.[64] And so the Commons resolved that they would 'proceed, in the first place, to have grievances effectually redressed, the protestant religion, liberties and properties, effectually secured, to suppress popery, and to remove persons, and counsellors, popishly affected, or otherwise obnoxious, or dangerous, to the government'. Only now did they thank the King for his speech and ask him to put the metropolitan militias on one hour's stand-by to disperse tumultuous meetings of papists and other malcontents. The first evil counsellor was dealt with the following day. Lauderdale, who was safely out of reach in Charles's Scottish kingdom, was condemned on his record and reputa-tion and the Commons resolved *nem. con.* on an address to the King for his removal from all employments and from the royal presence and councils for ever.

Buckingham was a sitting target. This bear had already been baited in the Lords and on 13 January the Commons were presented with a long set of charges against him, ranging from encouraging popery, breaking the Triple Alliance and making the French alliance, to high-handed conduct as Yorkshire's Lord Lieutenant, exploiting his offices for financial gain, claiming the King was a knave and unfit to govern, his liaison with the Countess of Shrewsbury and even 'a horrid sin not to be named'. Just as the charges were being made, Buckingham sent a note asking to be heard – 'the Duke has good intelligence of what we do here,' one enemy wryly remarked. When he appeared, Buckingham, although armed with notes, spoke off the cuff and 'his discourse was full of distraction, and [he] said he was weary of the company he was joined with, and knew how to kill a hare with hounds but could not hunt with lobsters.' Next day he asked for another hearing and this time 'descended more to particulars', answering questions from the Speaker about alliances, the war, the indulgence and so on, and at almost every opportunity throwing the blame squarely on Arlington and 'one not now living' by which he meant Clifford. His performance 'did not answer expectation,' reported Sir John Musgrove MP, and 'many of our corner' seemed uneager to help him, 'nothing was said to justify him, and the question was put for his removal, and very few negatives.'[65] In fact

Buckingham's friends preferred to concentrate on delaying tactics, and managed to drag things out so that the address for his removal was only presented on the 7 February. Nevertheless Charles promptly stripped the Duke of his offices. The King's indignation was prompted by Buckingham's rash decision to go before the Commons (described by Waller as 'a great convulsion of state, a peer to come down to your house').[66] Even worse was Buckingham's readiness to lay before the Commons the details of foreign policy-making, which remained a royal prerogative as Charles had pointed out when just days before he had graciously allowed a small parliamentary committee to look at his treaties.

Arlington's turn came on 15 January. 'Nothing has passed for some years but through his hands, the army, the Declaration; he is the great conduit pipe,' claimed Gerrard. The supple secretary of state had taken care to ask permission of the King and the Lords before appearing in the Commons and, even more obviously, came prepared to answer his accusers. His 'modesty, clearness, and evenness of temper' helped Arlington to create a good impression. On 20 January, Sir Edward Harley wrote home that the 'Commons after several days debate, this evening resolved not to address the King to remove the Lord Arlington[;] possibly the other persons may escape.'[67] Now, confident of his acquittal, Arlington's friends in the Commons insisted that they proceed with his impeachment on charges of popery, profiteering and treason: 'although they turn every stone' his enemies could find no proof to build an impeachment; by early February the relevant committee 'are very slow in meeting, and when they do 'tis only to adjourn'; and at the end of the session, 'it is admired in public coffee houses and clubs how' Arlington 'that knew all things' should have passed through this parliamentary storm when the 'two dukes', Buckingham and Lauderdale were 'wrecked before the gale came to a height, and as a man may say neither of them pitied by any'.[68]

On 23 January Lord Aungier remarked on the King's goodness in permitting 'us to sit all this while and please our humours, without so much as hinting at supply or taking his condition into our thoughts'. Sir Robert Southwell believed that 'the temper of the house beats wonderfully towards a peace. The French alliance and the war sound equally ungrateful' to MPs.[69] But the Commons planned next to enquire 'into the grievance of the war and the sad condition of the kingdom thereupon'. Charles decided to intervene and on Saturday 24 January summoned parliament so that he could lay before them the most recent peace terms from the Dutch. Both houses postponed discussion of these until Monday, which allowed members to consult with, among others, the Dutch agents Trenchard and Medley, and yet when they came to consider the terms they could do little other than agree that the King should negotiate with the Dutch 'in order to a speedy peace'. Neither house wanted to comment on these articles, perhaps in case they were later seen as endorsing a defective peace; this was certainly why, in Sir Gilbert Talbot's view, the Commons had left it up to the Lords to read the earlier treaty. Conway commented that 'those who thought the French alliance a grievance, do now think that a peace, nay, a separate peace, to be the greater grievance, so that one may see they designed only to fetter the King and take their advantages.'[70] Arlington too believed that those who had railed most against the war now opposed a speedy peace because it allowed the King to escape 'those snares they had laid for him'.[71] Parliament's addresses for a speedy peace were made to the King on 3 February, the Spanish ambassador was empowered to negotiate for the Dutch by 5 February, the final treaty was signed on the 9th and Parliament informed on 11 February. The Treaty of Westminster, as it became known, saw the Dutch concede the English claim to a salute and pay 800,000 patacoons (which went straight to William of Orange in settlement of an earlier Stuart debt), English settlers were permitted to leave Surinam, and the Dutch East Indies monopoly was, at least for the moment, preserved.

Supply was still undecided. 'No-one knows whether parliament will give cash,' wrote a Dutch agent on 20 January, while William Sacheverell calculated a majority of just five for supply. Colonel Roger Whitley MP was still confident on 30 January 'that a little patience and good management will get the King money'; by 13 February Sir Gilbert Talbot reported only that 'the Commons pursue more grievances, and will not mention money till they have redressed all.'[72] The Commons managed to produce a substantial set of bills to remedy the grievances which they had identified at the beginning of the session. Measures were in hand to reform parliamentary elections and ensure better attendance by MPs; a bill was prepared 'to extend the benefit of habeas corpus to a degree beyond any possibility of hurting the subject's liberty by any warrants of state'; and two others were 'purposely intended to secure them against a successor in case of the King's mortality', by giving judges tenure of office and by prohibiting all taxation without parliamentary approval and limiting the grant of customs duties to the lifetime of the monarch.[73] The Commons petitioned the King to dismiss all troops raised since 1663 and asserted that any standing army was a grievance. 'Fear of the Duke makes them every day fetter the crown,' commented Lord Conway, and many MPs openly argued that 'this is the time to take care against our coming under a bad prince.'[74] The Commons had only to look to the other chamber to see how seriously the peers were treating the threat to protestantism from a popish successor.

A series of 'heads' to secure the protestant religion had emerged from the Lords' consideration of the King's speech. Salisbury introduced a proposal that children of the royal family should be educated as protestants, and Carlisle moved that none of the royal family should marry a Roman Catholic without parliament's consent. Throughout January and February these and other proposals were discussed and refined, sometimes with alarming modifications. The most notorious occurred on 10 February when the Lords were discussing the proposal that a prince should not marry a Catholic without parliamentary approval. Carlisle suddenly proposed that any prince who did should be excluded from the succession. Halifax seconded this and Shaftesbury urged historical precedents. But the bishops turned on this 'diabolical' suggestion to let parliament determine the succession, and 'finding it disgustful to the house' Carlisle let the matter drop.[75] The Lords discussed a Test Act, which was accompanied by another for the Commons, to ensure that both chambers were free of papists. Bills were planned to disarm papists, ban them from court, and impose even more explicit oaths on them. Another measure possibly designed to strengthen protestant unity in the face of the papist threat was the bill associated with Bishop Morley to make it easier for some moderate presbyterian clergymen to conform as ministers of the Church of England.

Informed observers believed that the ratification of the peace would prompt Charles to announce the date for the end of the session. On 24 February Charles appeared in parliament, announced that the treaty had been ratified, and unceremoniously prorogued parliament until 10 November. Lord Conway had never seen such consternation among members of both houses, 'every man amazed and reproaching one another that they had sat so long upon eggs and could hatch nothing', or as Lord Aungier put it, that the session had ended 'without the perfection of any one bill, or of effecting any other thing for the good of the nation than that peace which has been huddled up in haste'.[76]

The continuing threat to York, the progress of bills for which Charles had little sympathy, and the lack of supply, led the King to this decision. Verdicts on the session varied. To Talbot, the King had been pushed too far by the 'combination' between a group of turbulent MPs and 'some hotspurs' among the Lords, of whom Shaftesbury, Halifax, Salisbury and Clare were 'the most forward'. This group were largely to blame for the bills which 'pressed fiercely and avowedly against the Duke of Y[ork]' and for parliament misspending its time 'in ravelling too far into the government and plucking at all the feathers of his prerogative'. On news of the prorogation some of these MPs had even run to the City, cancelling a dinner in Covent Garden, 'suspecting themselves (I verily conceive without ground) unsecure in the suburbs'.[77] A Dutch agent took a different line. 'Good bills' had been lost, 'yet the same will be sweet as a history . . . For I had said to some, let us rather lose all the bills, and content ourselves with them as a history, than give money.'[78] The kind of 'history' he meant was *A Journal of the Proceedings of the House of Commons the Last Session of Parliament, Beginning Jan. 7 1673/4* (1674), a mixture of loaded political comment and accurate versions of the habeas corpus, illegal taxation, test and other bills and the proceedings about impressment. Despite the eloquent speech 'some of the cabal' had placed in the King's mouth at the prorogation, 'alas, poor men, they have deceived no body but themselves; their secret counsels have taken air, and those dark mines, which they have been so long a digging, are at length discovered; and for all their arts, the parliament had enough time to give the nation notice of their intentions and our dangers.' Parliament had been prorogued to prevent the passage of good bills and further investigation of Irish popery, York's 'obstinate temerity in marrying a papist', and English subjects serving in Louis XIV's armies. The King clearly preferred to lose the affections of his people than of 'that right trusty and well-beloved brace of cabalists Arlington and Lauderdale', and the pamphlet also pointed the finger of blame at York, Arundel, Finch, Danby, Anglesey and the Duchess of Portsmouth. In Essex the puritanical Ralph Josselin believed the prorogation was because parliament had 'touched Arlington', raised the issue of popery at home and in Ireland, refused money, and perhaps – for he is gnomic here – broached the notion of excluding Catholics from the succession, but he was grateful that 'God waited to be gracious by them to make peace with the Dutch'.[79]

The peace, the end of the French alliance and the baiting of the bears were all signs that things must change. A bold gamble which was sealed at Dover in 1670 had run its course by 1674. Naval failures, interference by French and Dutch agents, the marital and martial adventures of the Duke of York, the feuding of Buckingham and Arlington, made some MPs belligerent and much of the nation suspicious. With parliament unmanageable, the public mood antagonistic, ministers at one another's throats and the King dithering, the winter of 1673–4 must have seemed like the court's political nadir. 'Now there will be a new game played at court,' observed Conway, 'and the designs and interests of all men will be different from what they were.'[80]

3

1674–6: Nothing is to be Trusted to Good Nature

In 1674 parliament was so determined to protect 'the property, liberty, and religion of the subject, that nothing is to be trusted to good nature for the future'. Ministers were to be brought to heel, rights were to be safeguarded by statute, and Catholic heirs to the throne were to be monitored. The court, too, sought a new strategy. The options had all been laid out by Latimer. The use of force to improve the crown's position was unfeasible because the King could not afford an army and the use of French or Catholic troops would offend the whole nation 'as a total subversion of property'. The alternative was 'compliance' and that would be achieved either by 'infinite reduction of expenses' or by agreement with parliament. The present parliament could be gratified by enforcing the existing laws against popery and dissent; a new one would 'desire comprehension or toleration of all religions but popery': but any parliament, new or old, would require withdrawal 'from the French interest'.[1] The court's first instinct in 1674 was to contract its spending and meet a new parliament when the King was financially secure: Charles said that 'he had rather be a poor king than no king'. But there was still no decision on dissolving parliament: Josselin 'heard reports of a new parliament, all change' in March; a proclamation was issued to squash these rumours in April.[2] The ministers had been shaken by their mauling at the hands of parliament, and the tension was showing. 'A cruel dispute' occurred in council between Arlington and Anglesey. The weary Arlington was still bargaining to sell his own post to Williamson and use the proceeds to buy the office of Lord Chamberlain. Latimer had arranged for his former patron Buckingham to be compensated for his lost offices, but elsewhere had imposed 'retrenchments' on spending which had enraged courtiers. Now he was 'esteemed the great support of the crown' and even figures like the Duchess of Portsmouth had to come to terms with him. In June Latimer was created the Earl of Danby and, by September, it was claimed that 'he has greater

*Plate 7   Thomas Osborne, Earl of Danby (attributed to Lely). The secret of Danby's success
in the mid-1670s may have been sheer determination or even luck. His knowledge of parliament, financial experience and industry helped him maintain power, despite his
unimaginative policies and his reputation for financial greed. He fell from power thanks
to Charles II's secret dealings with France and his own alienation of too many talented
and ambitious politicians. Danby, however, was a survivor and returned to political
prominence after the Glorious Revolution.*

credit with the King than any man ever had.' Some said that Danby, Lauderdale and York 'govern all' and that 'thoughts of army and popery are still afoot', but others doubted the solidity of this alliance and suspected that the Duke of York 'governs absolutely' at court.[3]

I

In September Charles was persuaded to postpone parliament from November until the spring. This was a decision with several implications. William Harbord believed that 'the French have laboured in it'; Sir Robert Southwell wrote to Ormonde that it was thought 'the incitement of the Dutch and the discontence [sic] of the parliament would have pushed on a war against France'.[4] Danby was no friend of France, but James and Charles remained sympathetic to their French cousin. Louis was allowed to recruit troops in Scotland and Ireland even while the English government continued to rebuild relations with the Dutch. The amicable Temple was sent over to the Netherlands as envoy and Evelyn's hostile history of the Dutch war was suppressed. Yet 'things stand, as I hear, but ticklish and insincere betwixt us and Holland,' reported Marvell in November. This was the moment when Arlington embarked on a little freelance diplomacy designed to underline his political indispensability. He paid a private visit to the Netherlands during which, suggested 'prying rumour', he was negotiating a peace between France and Holland and a marriage between William of Orange and the Duke of York's daughter Mary. When he returned in the New Year, Arlington brought with him Admiral Van Tromp, who was lavishly entertained at court, but he had pulled off no diplomatic coup.[5] Lord Chamberlain Arlington's political credit continued its inexorable decline.

Whatever the state of relations with the Dutch, anti-French feeling was pronounced and growing. Popular animosity stemmed from the recent war, but interest groups also exerted political pressure. A 'scheme of trade' was produced in November 1674 by a group of fourteen prominent merchants to show the imbalance of English woollen exports to France and French luxury imports into England. Masterminded by Patience Ward as part of a long campaign to resurrect Anglo-French negotiations for a commercial treaty, this document became crucial evidence in the debate on the adverse imbalance of trade with France. The merchants 'bravely acquitted themselves' before the Council of Trade and established in the public mind the idea that England was losing over a million pounds every year to France. English cloth merchants protested repeatedly against French tariffs on their goods and encouraged talk of embargoes on imports from France.[6] Yet theirs was a partial perspective and trade in other areas was booming. While the Dutch were preoccupied by their war with Louis, England prospered: 'trade falling so unavoidably into our hands by the continuance of the war'. The growth of English shipping was noticed, as was the consequent growth in the customs revenue received by the King.[7]

Parliament's postponement was welcome to nonconformists because most were convinced that their present liberty was safe while MPs did not meet. Although the indulgence had been cancelled, many congregations and preachers held on to their licences and took heart from the government's obvious reluctance to curtail their worship. Archbishop Sheldon stressed to his clergy that all the laws governing religion were in force, and Arlington publicized the King's wish that unlicensed conventicles be suppressed, but for most nonconformists this was a period of freedom of worship when they took root in their communities, organized themselves and built chapels. Of course dissenters still faced the ingrained prejudice of their neighbours. Baptists and Quakers, in particular, were viewed with disdain. Ralph Josselin, the barely conforming minister at Earls Colne in Essex, claimed to be unconcerned when the local Quakers built a meeting house as he did 'not question the downfall of that sect under the feet of Christ and his servants'.[8] A general toleration began to seem a distinct possibility. Danby had pointed out that the tide of opinion suggested that a fresh parliament would expect toleration and in September 1674 the mere announcement of the postponement of parliament was enough to start rumours of a toleration for nonconformists. Recognizing 'the insupportable clamour of the people against the bishops', the Church of England had begun to explore the possibility of internal reform.[9]

The court had in fact decided to stick with the devil they knew and to pander to the Cavalier Parliament's distaste for dissent and popery. Danby initiated the policy in October by paying a visit to Bishop Morley at his palace in Farnham and telling him that the King wished the bishops to meet and 'to propose some things that might unite and best pacify the minds of people against the next session of parliament'. The subsequent meetings among the bishops and with the privy council baffled onlookers: no-one 'can guess what the mystery is of such a meeting,' wrote Marvell. Finch, Danby and Lauderdale 'spend yet whole days with the bishops at Lambeth: we shall at last know the bottom of it.' These were clearly difficult meetings: 'the bishops are upon their guard and are very jealous of being trepanned.'[10] What the bishops came up with was based on a wide conception of the nation's moral and spiritual problems and it was 'not upon the whole matter very satisfactory' in ministers' eyes. The bishops recommended 'the discountenancing of libertines, who make such mock at all religions', the enforcement of laws against nonconformists and papists, especially the revocation of the licenses and an end to the protection of papists from prosecution – in the last expression 'they seem to lay (as is suggested) some thing to his majesty's door.' The meetings at Lambeth Palace transformed this call for a moral crusade into a six-point plan to ban the mass, suppress priests, recusants and seminarians, prevent Catholics from waiting on the King, and to call in the licenses and suppress conventicles. All of this was wrapped up in a proclamation and trumpeted as 'more severity than has of late been expected from the court, against all sorts of recusants'; but to many who had expected something more 'momentous' this was simply the standard window dressing: Josselin heard the 'news of putting the laws in execution against papists and nonconformists' and predicted that 'the parliament shall sit in April, and be cajoled to give great tax.'[11]

In mid-February Mrs Beale, probably one of Thomas Manton's flock, anticipated that 'the country will smart for this late proclamation', but her congregation remained undisturbed and she had heard of none in London which had suffered. As usual the degree of persecution varied from place to place. Bishop Carleton of Bristol, inspired by the bishops' meetings, enthusiastically revived persecution in his city. On 10 February he led the raid on John Thompson's Independent meeting in person. Thompson was thrown in gaol for six months, ostensibly under the Five Mile Act (although he may also have refused fines under the Conventicle Act), but he died there three weeks later. Five thousand 'professors of all sorts, except Quakers' attended his funeral and accusations of his murder through mistreatment soon found their way into print.[12] By March informers were busy in many areas and meetings were being raided in London. Redcoats and JPs burst in on Manton's meeting and took the names of the congregation which included Lord Wharton. Yet time and time again these proceedings were thwarted on technicalities. Unwilling Justices and sympathetic aristocrats undermined the drive against nonconformity. Even the Duke of York earned Bristol dissenters' gratitude for his 'kindness in concerning himself so vigorously for liberty'. Secretary Coventry advised Bishop Carleton that 'being gentle to those that are modest and quiet (though dissenters) will greatly justify you in being severe against those that are insolent and presumptuous'.[13] Plainly the government still hoped to prise moderate dissenters away from their more dangerous co-religionists. Although the bishops offered some kind of 'coalition with the presbyterians', the terms were never defined and the church refused to relax its requirement on ceremonies, so by April the whole project had run out of whatever steam it had once possessed.[14]

Other preparations were necessary before meeting parliament. The Duke of York spoke 'to so many of the lords whom he thought of different sentiments, touching his indifferency and even his consent for any laws that might secure property and religion, for that he might be left to the freedom of his own thoughts'. Shaftesbury, who had been occupying himself with trade and plantations since losing office, was now perceived as a major threat and the court decided that 'it was expedient to have a better understanding with the little lord before the parliament met'. Lord Mordaunt was sent down to Wimborne St Giles to sound him out. There was talk of various ways in which he might 'return into grace and favour' including his appointment as Lord Lieutenant of Ireland or as Vicar-General, a position presumably akin to that held by Thomas Cromwell in the 1530s.[15] But in February Shaftesbury laid his cards on the table with a letter to the Earl of Carlisle which was intended for immediate copying and distribution among the political elite and in the coffee-houses. Couched in loyal terms, this letter refused office or 'place'. Shaftesbury stated that 'all their places put together, shall not buy me from my principles.' And his 'principle' was equally plain: 'to give the only advice I know truly serviceable to the King, affectionate to the Duke, or sincere unto the country, which is, a new parliament, which . . . is the clear interest of all three.'[16] Arlington was not yet a spent force. He and his friends portrayed the Lord Treasurer as pursuing Clifford's policies 'only in a more dangerous manner' and were rumoured to be preparing an impeachment. So Danby took countermeasures. Sir Thomas Meres, a professional politician and one of the busiest men in parliament, was summoned by the King and warned not to attack Danby.[17] The ailing Archbishop Sheldon summoned the bishops to the House of Lords with the news that the King has declared 'that religion (as it ought) shall have the priority in their debates, and the settlement thereof (if possible) concluded before anything else either of public or private consequence'. Letters went to the King's 'old friends of the loyal party' urging their attendance 'for the settling a good and lasting confidence betwixt his majesty and his people' and to ensure 'the disappointment of all foreign and intestine enemies'. The King wanted MPs like Colonel Sandys to help him 'to proceed in his resolution of restoring church and state to their natural and loyal condition'.[18] The court waited to see what other challenges would materialize once parliament had assembled.

II

'The town now begins to fill with parliament men and cabals grow hotter and hotter, but no man among them yet know what measures to take,' reported the newsletters in April 1675. 'There are preparations of all sorts, as articles against ministers, petitions of ease, and twenty other devices which will or will not be used as occasions offer themselves.'[19] At its first meeting Charles told parliament that he wanted only to content his subjects and he made no direct request for money. Parliament must advise him on how to secure religion and property and how to maintain the fleet, but it should resist the 'pernicious designs of ill men' who stir up misunderstanding between the King and his parliament and hope to bring about a new parliament.[20] Neither the Commons nor the Lords found it easy to return their customary thanks for the King's speech. There were 'bitter words' and 'cursed speeches' in the Commons when some MPs sought to pick and choose what they liked in the speech; thanking the King for his 'gracious expressions' without seeming to approve the present religious laws or ministers' recent policies. In response the King assured the Commons that 'he would always preserve them in the established religion, and in their liberties and properties.'[21] The querulous MPs wanted to continue where they had left off at the prorogation nearly fourteen months before: they revived measures like the habeas corpus bill and the test bill to rid both Lords and Commons of papists; and they returned to their pursuit of ministers. Neatly side-stepping what may have been a trap to make them appear 'as mutinous as the Long Parliament', 'the hunters of ministers' fell upon Lauderdale.[22] An assault on Danby was only a matter of time. So far as it could be the court was prepared. Each evening at 8.00 p.m. Danby met a trusted team of parliamentary managers at Hampden House to take stock. The best way of 'diverting' the Commons from Danby was to engage it in other business and 'the best business to be gone upon for the kingdom, and the likeliest also to engage the house warmly in it, was matter of religion.' So next day Sir Edward Dering encouraged MPs to review the laws against popery and consider means for the speedier conviction of popish recusants. The risk that this would allow members to renew earlier proposals like the bill for the education of royal children was preferable to an all-out attack on the chief minister. There were, agreed Danby's advisors, certain measures that it would be folly to resist. They anticipated a bill to make it treason to levy money without an act of parliament and a motion for the recall of the King's subjects serving in the French army. It was better to bow before the inevitable and to see what could be done to dilute or amend these measures later. Ever keen to identify likely diversions, Dering suggested that a bill against brandy imports and another to establish land registries would please the nation, occupy the Commons, and if they came from Danby's 'friends' it would show that 'they do mind the public good.'[23]

Concern for the public good of a rather different kind was demonstrated by the introduction in the Lords of a bill 'to prevent dangers which might arise from persons disaffected to the government' on 15 April. Danby had dusted off the oath used in the mid-1660s to weed out nonconformists and anti-royalists and now sought to apply it as a general test for all public office. Those taking the oath would swear that it was not lawful to take up arms against the King or his officers, that they abhorred 'that traitorous position', and that they would 'not at any time endeavour the alteration of the government either in church or state'. The oath was a blatant attempt to preserve power in the hands of Anglican royalists and it ignited a furious controversy. At the first opportunity 'there were very hot debates – the bishops and ministers of state for it, hoping to exclude some papists perhaps and puritans by it, but the generality of the rest against it, so that it is believed it will never pass.' Charles now sat in on debates as a matter of course; Danby managed the business in person; and inevitably when some debates lasted twelve hours there were occasional 'heats' and other 'marks of anger'. The bishops were the butt of much fury; some called this 'the bishops' bill; and others suggested that they should withdraw and not vote 'because it seemed to be in their own case'. The bill seemed very uncertain. 'They dispute it by inches,' commented Marvell. On 23 April it was saved by one vote, because a peer had gone to his dinner; the next day, the Lords got on with other work:

> Some conclude from thence that the great favourers of it are a little discouraged seeing their party decay from the odds of 61 to 27 to the equality almost of 39 to 38, many of which they were afraid, too, gave their votes against their judgment, because the King seemed to countenance the bill, and because they believed it would therefore pass without any great resistance; who now seeing the adverse side increase, would be content enough as they feared to unmask themselves and go over to their enemies, so that some think that bill will never be meddled with again, and others that if it be, it will go near to be lost.[24]

Danby was not ready to give up. His initial calculations of his majority may have taken a battering, but he was still able to push through the measure at each vote. His opponents, led by Buckingham, Shaftesbury, Winchester, Salisbury, Wharton and Holles, took to entering a 'protest', a written and signed dissent from the majority vote, in the journal of the house. The numbers signing the four protests against the test bill were twenty-four, twelve, twenty-one and sixteen. In some eyes, this was a defining moment for English politics in the 1670s. Shaftesbury and his allies would present this struggle between the minister and his aristocratic rivals as a constitutional battle and later commentators would find in this clash the genesis of a coherent opposition.

The battles in the upper chamber were matched by the endeavours of the Commons to bring first Lauderdale and then Danby to book. Fresh interest was added to the pursuit of Lauderdale by the new evidence of a Scots minister, Dr Gilbert Burnet, who told the Commons that in conversation in 1673 Lauderdale had talked of assisting Charles II to defend the Declaration of Indulgence by force and had associated himself with the policies of Clifford. The reports of Burnet's evidence before a Commons committee were more lurid: Lauderdale was alleged to have said 'that he wished the Scots presbyterians would stir, that he might bring the Irish papists to cut their throats'; when Burnet taxed him with joking, Lauderdale assured him that he was in earnest. After this no-one dissented from the address to the King for the removal of Lauderdale. The King's eventual reply was a robust defence of his minister; and a few days later he did Lauderdale the honour of driving with him in the royal coach through Hyde Park 'when there was more company and greater splendour in the park than there had been anytime this year.'[25] Danby's troubles turned out to be less severe. When Russell first launched the attack, Sir Samuel Barnardiston was ready with articles of impeachment which accused the Lord Treasurer of diverting revenues to enrich himself, imprisoning people, maintaining in council that a royal declaration had the same weight as a statute, and other misdemeanours. However Danby's friends gained the upper hand almost immediately when it was agreed that the Commons would hear the evidence for these charges before the impeachment was delivered to the House of Lords. On 27 April they began considering the evidence and had dismissed the lot by 3 May.

The other great grievance was the number of Charles's subjects still serving in the French army. In these debates MPs revealed not only their unease at the territorial strength of the French King, but also their inability to separate the issues of France and popery. 'We have fears of popery and fears of France,' said William Garway, 'for they draw on one another and are alike.' While for Sir Thomas Meres, it is Charles's greatest glory and interest to defend protestantism; 'the King of France is now the great patron of the popish interest . . . whoever will support the protestant religion must not support the French interest, and he lays that down for a principle.'[26] The King infuriated MPs by returning a bland refusal to interfere when they asked him to recall his subjects from Louis's army. On 10 May a 'very large' debate on this reply soon grew 'very hot' and degenerated into a fracas. After a whole day's debate, the house voted on whether to address the King again for the recall of his subjects, but a mistake among the tellers of the vote led to misunderstanding. The fiery Cavendish strode over to demand a new count, when Sir John Hanmer told him that was against the rules, 'my Lord Cavendish spit at him, which he returned, and my Lord Cavendish thrusting Sir Herbert Price from the table, Price laid hold upon his own sword, but did not draw it.' Seymour regained control and eventually every member in turn had to promise on his honour to harbour no resentments for what had passed.[27] The Commons had to debate the issue on another day and when the vote was tied at 94 on each side, Speaker Seymour voted for a new address, 'which is looked upon as against the King's interest and inclination, and yet he is, besides Speaker, Treasurer of the Navy, and the Lord Treasurer's particular friend,' observed a newsletter. 'Many men are posed with these mystical politics.' Yet to Sir Edward Dering, 'the true reason was popularity'; Seymour was becoming semi-detached from the government.[28]

On 29 April the house debated Sir William Coventry's bill to provide for automatic by-elections whenever an MP accepted any office under the crown. Although the former MP could stand for re-election, the aim was to reduce the number of officers in the Commons. Unsurprisingly there were few prepared to defend this bill and many ready to oppose it. It was an injustice to deprive members of royal favour and a restraint on the King's freedom of choice in his officials. This is 'a garbling [of] the parliament, and a new modeling [of] the government, from a monarchy into a commonwealth,' complained Sir Courtney Poole. Vaughan, on the other hand, was for committing the bill and observed that 'though we are loyal, yet there have been parties in the parliaments, court and country.' According to the newsletters, Coventry argued that there were forty pensioners in parliament in 1661, but now there were over two hundred, and unless this or a similar bill passed, or a new parliament was called and the triennial act revived, 'we should shortly be at the French lock, that an edict from the King would pass here for an act of parliament.'[29] MPs expected to serve their King and country in a variety of local and national offices. Some never rose beyond service as a JP, but others were plucked from the backbenches, just like Danby, and thrust into offices of honour and profit. Even several of the government's critics were also servants of the crown for at least some of their careers and were expected to toe the ministers' line on most occasions: William Garway was a Commissioner of Customs from 1671 to 1675 drawing an annual salary of £2000; William Harbord, who drew up the address against the Modena marriage, was helped by Arlington to the post of secretary to the Lord Lieutenant of Ireland at £500 a year; Sir Robert Carr rose to be chancellor of the Duchy of Lancaster thanks to his brother-in-law Arlington, and, although by 1676 he had turned against Danby, Carr retained his life patent on his office. Of course, no job is perfect. Harbord wrote to Essex on 1 May 1675 that 'I am e'en weary of my life to sit daily seven or eight hours in the house and at last be forced to vote against my reason or steal away, and if that be found out it gives offence also.'[30] If Harbord found parliament tedious, it was perhaps understandable that so many other, less ambitious, MPs stayed away. Absenteeism was a perennial problem: the Commons once again considered how it might compel better attendance by MPs; and Danby also began to turn his mind to the question.

At the beginning of May the Commons were asked to approve the appearance of Sir John Fagg MP in a legal appeal at the bar of the House of Lords. Dr Thomas Shirley, a royal physician, had lost a case against Fagg in Chancery and had now appealed to the House of Lords. The

Commons reminded the Lords in general terms to be tender of the privileges of the lower house. In response the Lords asserted their own privileges vigorously – but not forcefully enough for Shaftesbury who protested against their conciliatory tone. On 12 May the Commons attempted to arrest Dr Shirley but their order was intercepted by the hot-headed Lord Mohun who took it off to the Lords as evidence of the lower house's pretensions. The situation rapidly got out of hand. The Commons and Lords were soon at loggerheads over various infringements of each other's rights and privileges. Assertions and denials flew between the houses; contradictory votes were entered in their journals; conferences simply exacerbated the quarrel; other cases got sucked into the morass; officials and lawyers and even Sir John Fagg were taken into custody. 'The whole contest is too voluminous for letters,' wrote Marvell, who compared it to Skinner's Case. 'Much time slips away in this contest so that public acts cannot be so soon matured as were to be wished, nor are so secure of passing.' But then that may have been the point for some of those involved. The news-writers noticed that by 1 June the Lords had only a week's work left to complete Danby's test oath, 'but we fear they will not, for the House of Commons begin to come up close to them and to press them hard' over Shirley versus Fagg. On 3 June, one observer reckoned 'this cannot last long; two or three moves more must make it checkmate.'[31] On the 5th the King tried to conciliate, but he also bluntly stated that 'all these contrivances' were to achieve a dissolution: 'I look upon it as a most malicious design of those who are enemies to me and the Church of England.' It was no good: neither house would retract. Four days later, and complaining of 'the ill designs of our enemies', Charles reluctantly prorogued parliament until October.

The news-writers now had 'leave to breathe a little', and MPs were returning home 'dissatisfied enough, but with whom or what they can scarce tell'. All agree that the King had no alternative, but some think a prorogation is insufficient:

> The parliament must be dissolved, for no good can be expected from them. It is but lost labour to try them any longer, but the tests and the bishops bear the greater blame. The highest cavaliers and the best protestants are now convinced that persecution and English episcopacy is too narrow a foundation for our great monarchy to be built upon, considering the excessive odds between the numbers of the orthodox churchmen and dissenters, and therefore begin to be persuaded that a liberty of conscience so regulated as to secure the present government of church and state is ten times more likely to succeed as to the settlement of this kingdom in peace and plenty.[32]

This is a startling piece of political analysis to find in a newsletter. Yet it has the ring of authenticity. The weight of opinion seems to have been turning against the project of the 1660s, against the dream of one uniform religion, and against the Church of England, now cast as the villain of the piece. This is the view one would expect of Andrew Marvell: the bishops, he laughed to his nephew, were abused all session by Buckingham; 'and no men were ever grown so odiously ridiculous'. But Sir John Holland, the veteran Norfolk MP, in some ways the epitome of moderation, was also wary of the Anglican clergy's political pretensions: his 1675 letter to a Norfolk cleric urging him to support the community's candidate in the county's by-election circulated widely and indicates a real suspicion of the Church of England as Danby and Charles had presented it in the spring of 1675. William Sancroft heard that the candidates courted the nonconformists and aspersed 'many of our worthy clergymen with the opprobrious terms of drunken clergymen and high Church of England men'.[33] Such anti-clericalism and suspicion of the church was to be fertile ground for Shaftesbury's propaganda against 'iure divino' churchmen later in the year.

III

'Nothing is more necessary than the suppressing of atheism, profaneness and open and professed wickedness without the amendment or punishment of which nothing can avail to the preservation of a church which God has threatened for such sins, unrepented and unpunished, to destroy.' This was the conclusion reached by the bishops at their meetings in January 1675. They told the King that 'atheism and profaneness daily abound more and more' and drive people to take refuge in the superstition and idolatry of Rome or the 'destructive novelties' of the sects. In the spring *The Voice of the Nation* appealed to parliament 'for their just severity to repress the growing boldness of atheism and profaneness in the land'. Blasphemers should be indicted at the assizes. Action is required against those who deny the existence of God, or cast contempt upon the bible and Christ, 'men that bear themselves as the kings of wit among a company of fools; esteeming them no better that own piety and religion.' The tenor of this broadsheet, for all its quotations from a bishop, is nonconformist. So here we have Anglican bishops and nonconformists agreeing that something is very wrong with England in 1675.[34] There was a perception of a social crisis, rooted in godlessness and vice, but threatening a collapse of morality and order.

The evidence which led to such dramatic conclusions is not difficult to find. In January 1675 the King's Company first performed Wycherley's *The Country Wife* at the Theatre Royal, Drury Lane, and this comedy with its bawdy plot, salacious dialogue and cynical characters, represented another high-water mark in the 1670s fashion for sex comedies. A later chapter explores what connections, if any, existed between what made audiences laugh and their own sexual activity. Suffice it to say now that Londoners were no strangers to adultery, prostitution, drunkenness or other vices. It is possible that some were led astray by the bad example of their betters, especially by the example of the royal court and its hangers-on. The court was moderately accessible: there were criticisms when the King allowed his favourite Italian comedians to set up a public theatre in Whitehall 'so that now a papist may come to court for half a crown'. But courtiers lived in the public eye. In June 1675 Captain Kirke, courtier, soldier and brother to a maid of honour, forcibly abducted, with 'her own consent', a shoemaker's daughter, worth £1500, 'but not to marry her'. Kirke 'fought it through the streets to the waterside and lodged her in Whitehall'. A week later he defeated his sister's lover in a duel fought over her own recent disgrace at court. Then he left for service in the army of Louis XIV.[35]

Duelling was positively fashionable among soldiers and courtiers; violence, drunken and mindless, was rife. In August Sir Thomas Armstrong fought Gervaise Scroope at the Duke's Playhouse after Scroope initiated some drunken raillery, refused to desist and threw down a challenge. Another version of the story had it that they quarreled over Mrs Uphill, a masked actress, and that 'a ring was made wherein they fought.' All agreed that Scroope was in the wrong and that Armstrong killed him 'stark dead' at the first pass, but unfortunately this was the third man that Armstrong had killed and although he obviously had little choice in the circumstances 'yet this rubs up old stories and puts men upon making divers reflections.'[36] This same summer Rochester, the wit and courtier, drunkenly smashed up the King's sundial in the privy garden to general scandal. At the Surrey assizes Lord Colchester was convicted of murder, housebreaking and attacking women, and this was the second if not third time he had been caught 'in such sports': his only excuse was drunkenness, 'jest and frolic'. Londoners were also agog to hear that Lord Digby and Shaftesbury had come near to blows in sleepy Dorset. Digby told the Earl that 'you are against the King, and for seditions and factions, and for a commonwealth and I will prove it, and by God we will have your head next parliament': Shaftesbury took the wiser course and sued Digby for his words.[37] Later that year Sir Richard Sandford was murdered by two gentlemen after an alehouse quarrel and the culprits were hanged on specially erected gibbets in Fleet Street near the scene of the crime as a warning to 'the wild hectorian gentlemen wherewith this age and city too much abounds'.[38] Professional crime was a problem too. In January, Cusack 'alias Dixon alias Smith', an Irish pirate, escaped from prison before his trial, which rather tarnished the celebrations of his spectacular capture the previous year.[39] The streets were far from safe. In July Henry Killigrew's coach was attacked; late one August night Viscount Yarmouth was shot and wounded when highwaymen attacked his coach in Kensington; and in November shots were allegedly fired at Shaftesbury in his coach.[40]

Against such a disorderly background, one might expect mob violence to be common, but there was more talk than action. And where there was action, the connivance of local gentry was often suspected – as in the Somerset disorders against the excise in 1675.[41] The three days of rioting by London weavers in August 1675 was exceptional. Times were hard and this was a planned protest at the use of engine looms after earlier complaints had achieved nothing. The disorder spread from Moorfields through the suburbs to reach Westminster and Southwark; eighty-five looms were destroyed and much anger was vented against foreign immigrants and the French: calm returned to the streets only after the intervention of the Duke of Monmouth and 3000 redcoats of the royal guard. The King insisted that this 'insurrection' which had created such alarm, continued for so many days and in so many places, 'should find such a remarkable punishment as must hereafter let people know, they engaged no less than their lives, as well as goods and estates, in such frantic adventures'. Secretaries Coventry and Williamson were worried about 'the reflections which will arise to the government that a fantastical humour amongst one particular sort of workmen in London should continue a riot three days together without arms, and the military power at last obliged to assist' because the London militia failed to intervene effectively. As usual, the King's anger soon dissipated and eventually the ringleaders were sentenced to the pillory.[42]

Sex, violence and insubordination on the scale experienced in the mid-1670s troubled the devout and the respectable. The population had been taught for many years to expect divine punishments in this world for both personal and collective sins. The 1660s were a textbook example of the way God first extended mercies to a nation and then chastized that nation with plague, fire, and war for its backsliding. The 1670s now seemed to be heading in the same direction. On the night of 20 September 1675 a 'dismal' fire swept through three-quarters of the town of Northampton, destroying over six hundred houses, the market cross and All Saints church. 'Though people are apt upon such sad occasions to attribute the original to malice, revenge or some secondary cause, yet questionless God almighty was the superintendent, and next after him, possibly the neglect of some person or other.' A Latin elegy by one minister was translated as *The Fall and Funeral of Northampton* and compared the unfortunate town not only to London but to Sodom and Gomorrah. An account of a fire a few months later at Cottenham, Cambridgeshire, also encouraged sufferers not to grumble at providence but look to themselves as the authors under God of their own misfortune.[43] These authors treated these disasters with hard-headed practicality and as a prompt to moral improvement; in other cases, such accidents provoked a torrent of anti-popery from preachers and commentators. Perhaps the anxious mood of the autumn of 1675 is best captured by Ralph Josselin whose diary is peppered with fretful remarks on fires, mercifully escaped or not, on the 'great fears of our poor rising up and down our country', and on his own anxiety about 'our public peace'.[44]

IV

Just a few days after Charles II had angrily prorogued parliament in June, the Marquis of Winchester and the Earl of Shaftesbury were received at court and admitted to kiss the King's hand. This set the town talking that 'the Treasurer and all the present ministers are to be routed and removed, and the Earl of Shaftesbury and other protesting lords to be received into favour and employment.' It was the Duke of York who had engineered this little rapprochement and who now entertained Shaftesbury and Winchester at St James's Palace. Politics is a precarious business, as Danby's brother-in-law reminded him. So the Treasurer must remain firm to his plan 'to settle the church and state, to defend the one against schismatics and papists, the other against commonwealthsmen and rebels'. But this was precisely the policy which had impelled York to make overtures towards Shaftesbury. Danby quickly struck back, protesting at York's conduct and persuading Charles to send Shaftesbury a message that he was no longer welcome at court. York remained an unreliable ally to Danby and a patron of dissident parliamentarians, thanks in part to the funds which the French ambassador Ruvigny was channelling through York's former secretary Edward Coleman.[45]

As usual during the high summer months the King gave himself over to pleasure. 'We are here very barren of news,' reported a newsletter from Windsor in July 1675. 'Our country delights scarce leave us any room for business'. The Duke of York has been led a merry chase by a stag; the Duke of Monmouth has laid on a splendid entertainment; ambassadors have come and gone. Danby and Ormonde were taking the waters of Bath while Arlington was nursing his gout at Euston. Each Wednesday the King and Duke travelled to Hampton Court for desultory privy council meetings and the 'cabinet council' met after lunch. But the torpor was deceptive. As we have seen the weavers' riot caused a flurry of activity at court. Meanwhile Charles had agreed with Louis that if the October parliament failed to vote supply or showed itself hostile to France Charles would dissolve it and Louis would pay him £100,000 a year while parliament did not meet. Danby too was busy preparing for parliament.[46]

In September one hundred or more MPs received letters from the secretaries of state urging them to be in London at or before the opening of parliament on 13 October. Far more thorough than usual, this exercise had been prompted by Danby's review of the government's parliamentary management. Assuming, like most of their contemporaries, that a majority of members naturally supported the King's ministers, Danby and his lieutenant Sir Richard Wiseman had concluded that the problem lay in poor attendance and haphazard voting by the loyal majority which allowed a troublesome minority to endanger important votes. Hence the reminders of prompt attendance to those loyal MPs with a record of absenteeism. More reliable support for the government came from two directions. From the personal friends, relations and clients of ministers, which in Danby's case included his own 'interest' in Yorkshire, that of his wife's family, the Berties, in Lincolnshire, and Speaker Seymour's in the south-west. And from those in the pay of the government. 'The King's servants and dependents', officials of all degrees, assumed that it was perfectly legitimate to sit in parliament, as they had shown in the debates on Coventry's place bill in the previous session. Three separate lists of these officials drawn up in the autumn of 1675 contain the names of one hundred and thirty-seven individuals. In addition to this phalanx of government votes was a group of unidentified 'pensioners' who were perhaps the most politically useful of all the government's dependents. In the summer of 1675 Danby may have increased the number of these pensioners by up to fifteen to create a group of between twenty-three and thirty-four MPs who were paid unknown sums directly from the secret service money. As Browning pointed out, these pensions had their origin in justifiable compensation payments and it was Danby's revision of the excise tax farm on financial grounds in 1674 which left him with the power of allocating pensions. But whatever the cause, it was the political effect that mattered and in the autumn of 1675 it was widely assumed that Danby had mounted a campaign to buy loyalty and 'take off' opponents, that he had engaged in the naked 'corruption' of parliament.[47]

As parliament approached 'active men are very busy in preparing for it' and it was rumoured that Danby's test bill would be reintroduced in the Commons.[48] When they met, the King asked for supply and legislation to secure 'the protestant religion, as it is now established in the Church of England'; Finch assured members that the King had their liberty, property and religion at heart and urged them to ignore those who sowed dissension. Unimpressed by the request for money, the Commons sat in silence for an hour waiting for a copy of the King's speech. When it arrived some of 'the angry party' were for thanking the King only for his gracious care of religion, and the matter had to be adjourned for several days. Even then many MPs disputed the King's need for supply or they argued, like Sir John Holland, that the country could not bear further taxation. After 'many cursed speeches' the

Commons refused by 172 to 165 to vote supply to pay off the 'anticipations', the royal borrowing against future tax revenue which represented a substantial part of the £1,000,000 millstone of debt around the government's neck. However MPs would vote money for the navy. Having heard the case for forty ships, they agreed to provide twenty, and then laboriously considered how many and of what rate, before naming a figure of £300,000 on 4 November. Despite Danby's attempts to force this figure up, the Commons decided on 8 November that the £300,000 would be raised by a land tax and added 'that no other charge be laid upon the subject this session of parliament'. At several points MPs made it plain that they distrusted the government's handling of money. They decided, for example, to appropriate the customs to the use of the navy – ignoring the fact that the customs revenue was already spoken for – and they attempted to have the supply paid into the Chamber of London under the Lord Mayor's control rather than the Exchequer. It was the defeat of this proposal by 171 to 160 on 26 October which led to a storm of criticism of Danby's 'corruption' of parliament.

The 'angry Commons' had to find new ways 'to obstruct the money'. Sir John Hotham got into deep water with his colleagues when he suggested that several members had been 'taken off', but he was echoed by Sir Nicholas Carew and others who

> said plainly that they saw several members who had expressed themselves formerly very warmly as to the present management of affairs give their votes (as they had reason to believe) against their own judgements, without showing any cause to warrant their change, and therefore suspected that they had been dealt withal underhand, etc., upon which they moved that a test might be brought in for every member to purge himself by upon [sic] his honour that he had not taken any money or place, or any other reward or promise from the King or his ministers to bias his vote.[49]

Although this was quietly forgotten, there were many other expressions of disquiet and several measures designed to remedy grievances. Questions were asked about the letters sent out to MPs before the session began. Members admitted that fear of 'luxury', popery and a standing army were obstacles to their generosity. In a rambling debate on the state of the nation, which seemed to be preoccupied with the growth of atheism and debauchery, the aged former Speaker Sir Harbottle Grimston took the opportunity to propose the dissolution of parliament on the grounds that 'a standing parliament is as inconvenient as a standing army'. He was given short shrift by Meres and Speaker Seymour who talked of 'a strict conjunction between the fanatic and papist to dissolve this parliament'.[50] The Commons did make progress during these weeks with bills which dealt with habeas corpus, extra-parliamentary taxation, the exclusion of Catholics from the Lords, French trade and those Englishmen who persisted in service in the French army despite Charles's earlier proclamation for their return.

Two remarkable episodes in this session demonstrated parliament's penchant for play-acting. One was a piece of flummery which occupied the Commons for the first two weeks of the session, but the other was the revival of Shirley's appeal which precipitated the dramatic end of this session. The first stemmed from a chance remark and it shows the importance of libelous papers, honour and reputation as well as the machiavellian tactics of some members. In the summer of 1675 Colonel John Howard, youngest brother of the Earl of Carlisle, was killed in battle at Strasbourg while fighting for Louis XIV. When the news of his death along with other English troops was reported among the crowds promenading in St James's Park, Lord Cavendish and Sir Thomas Meres were heard to say that 'it was but a just end for such as went against any vote of parliament'. This comment reached the ears of Thomas Howard, Catholic older brother of the dead soldier, who responded with a letter, dated 30 August, to be copied and dispersed in St James's Park at the Mall in which he called Cavendish and Meres 'barbarous incendiaries' and mocked their pretensions as 'worthy patriots' and 'worthy and unbiased senators'. Strange to tell, it was only six weeks later, on the first day of parliament, that this erupted into controversy. Sir Trevor Williams rushed into the Chamber, claiming that the paper had been found by his servant in the park the previous evening, 'upon which Lord Cavendish, seeming never to have seen it before, went out of the house in a great heat, which was the beginning of the act' according to the newsletters. The affair, said some, was 'intended to be made bloody use of against the papists'. While Cavendish, 'who was very brave', postured, the Commons forbade him to issue any challenges over the letter and a deputation sought out Howard. Howard was offhand with the MPs and Cavendish said in the Commons that he was sorry John Howard had died fighting against the interest of his country, with which Meres concurred. Cavendish took matters into his own hands by posting a notice at Whitehall Gate and Westminster Hall which called Thomas Howard a poltroon and coward. The Commons took great exception, perhaps because it brought more publicity to the issue of Englishmen fighting abroad, and several of Cavendish's usual allies agreed that he should be sent to the Tower, where he languished for two days before gaining release. The affair rumbled on with reports of what one member had said to another in a coffee-house – about the bogus nature of the whole controversy – and with allegations that challenges had been made and duels were imminent. For his temerity in publishing this libelous paper, Howard spent two weeks in the Tower before he and Cavendish were summoned to the privy council for a formal reconciliation.[51]

The reintroduction of Dr Shirley's appeal to the House of Lords by Lord Mohun on 19 October was an equally transparent tactic. Other business immediately ground to a halt as peers considered whether they should sacrifice their rights and privileges to the Commons for the sake of a grant of money to the King. Mohun did not want the upper house to be duped any longer. But Danby claimed that Shirley had told the King that 'he was obliged by some persons of honour' to bring in his petition. Immediately some members began purging themselves of any association with this intrigue, while others protested at such heavy-handed royal interference. After six days of debate the Lords agreed to hear Shirley's appeal on 20 November. The Commons managed to take no official notice of this decision until the 15th when they ordered Fagg not to attend the hearing. The majority of MPs were probably eager to paper over the quarrel so that their bills could progress, but from the ministers' point of view there was little incentive to help them. When the Lords refused to postpone the hearing, the Commons unanimously resolved that anyone who appealed from a court of equity to the Lords was a betrayer of the rights and privileges of the Commons and ordered copies of this posted on the gate of Westminster Hall. The Lord's reply was to vote that paper 'illegal, unparliamentary, and tending to the dissolution of the government'. Mohun proposed that the only solution was to ask the King to dissolve parliament and Shaftesbury, with whom he was co-operating, made a long and detailed speech to second the motion. Since Danby could not be sure of winning the vote – York and the Catholic peers were likely to vote for the motion – the debate was spun out and when a vote was finally taken and all the proxies counted, the motion was hung with 48 on both sides. The Earl of Ailesbury then appeared and, although he had not heard the debate, he voted in his own right and with a proxy against the motion. Having lost by two votes, Shaftesbury entered into the journal a protest which denounced the evils of long-standing parliaments, and went home the moral victor. Despite the fact that his own brother had voted for a dissolution, Charles had decided, partly because of his agreement with Louis and partly no doubt because parliament was so refractory, on a prorogation. Parliament, it was announced, would meet in fifteen months time on 15 February 1677.

The prorogation left the country on edge. 'We talk much of a new parliament' in Yorkshire. In the country persons of quality told Sir George Reve that they would have cheerfully contributed to a tax of £500,000 for building ships and confirmed him in his fears of a rumoured dissolution of parliament.[52] Alarm was caused when an 'ugly distich' was pasted on the door to the King's bedchamber: 'in vain for help to your old friends you call / when you like pitied them must fall.' No sooner was it torn down than another copy appeared. 'I am sorry that they should have so

much effect as to make the King distrust his safety and walk with guards,'
commented Marvell. But 'among mean people' that winter there were
persistent rumours of the King's death.[53]

This was the atmosphere in which the English digested the latest propaganda emanating from Shaftesbury's circle. The famous anonymous
pamphlet, *A Letter from a Person of Quality to his Friend in the Country*, which
has been attributed to Shaftesbury himself and to John Locke, appeared
in the middle of the parliamentary session. On 8 November the Lords
were 'entertained with a little book called *A Letter to a Friend in the
Country*, which is a history of so much of the last sessions as concerned
the test in the House of Lords, with sharp reflections and remarks upon
several bishops and some great ministers of state; the book was brought
in by a bishop and ordered to be burned by the common hangman'.[54]
This substantial pamphlet not only reprinted the protests and summa-
rized the debates, it offered a conspiracy theory as a context for the proposed test. The 'churchmen' had at last found ministers bold enough
to achieve their long-cherished project to concentrate all power and
office in 'the high episcopal men' and the old cavaliers. The government of church and state is to be declared unalterable or 'of divine right'
thus rendering episcopacy and monarchy free of human law, 'absolute
and arbitrary'. To secure this, parliament is to be reduced to 'an instru-
ment to raise money and to pass such laws as the church shall have a
mind to' and the King is to have a standing army. The final goal is 'that
priest and prince may, like Castor and Pollux, be worshipped together
as divine, in the same temple, by us poor lay subjects; and that sense and
reason, laws, properties, rights, and liberties' shall be defined by 'those
deities'. The origin of this conspiracy is traced back to the attempts by
Archbishop Laud and the canons of 1640 to overturn Magna Carta and
subvert the rights and liberties of the people. Its later manifestations
include the Clarendon code and the Declaration of Indulgence which
was, and here the pamphlet supposedly quotes Clifford, a chance for
the King to 'settle what religion he pleased, and carry the government
to what height he would'. The account of 1675 gave prominence to
the bishops' arguments and to Shaftesbury's attack on the Church of
England's doctrinal confusion, and it made much of the constitutional
stance of 'the country lords', men like learned Wharton, acute Halifax,
courageous Mohun, Salisbury 'who stood like a rock of nobility and
English principles', Buckingham 'the general of the party' and many
others who supported 'the English interest'.[55]

This masterful piece of propaganda tapped into two great streams of
sentiment, one religious, the other constitutional. It exploited a prevalent cynicism about the clerical profession and religion. It appealed,
often simultaneously, to those, whether conformist or dissenter, who
disliked the pretensions of the bishops and the persecuting Church of

England, to those whose suspicion of popery was aroused by any reference to the Arminianism of Laud, and to those cynics who believed that
the clergy really would use any means to acquire power for themselves
and to flatter weak monarchs with delusions of absolutism. The *Letter*
concluded that the clerical advocates of divine right monarchy 'are the
most dangerous sort of men alive to our English government'. But the
defenders of the English constitution, with its balance of aristocracy,
commons and king, are the stalwart 'country lords' led by Shaftesbury
and Buckingham. Inconvenient facts of history, such as Shaftesbury's
defence of the Declaration of Indulgence in 1673 or the censure of
Buckingham by both houses in 1674, are explained away or ignored.
The lords are presented as the constitutional backstop. 'The power of
peerage and a standing army are like two buckets, the proportion that
one goes down, the other exactly goes up.'[56] There were many reasons
for this insistence on the role of the peers and for the virtual absence
of the lower chamber from the pamphlet. One lies in the immediate
context of the publication of the tract in November. Shirley versus Fagg
had just begun to cast its shadow again over parliament. And in his
speech on 20 October, encouraging the Lords to defend their privileges
in this appeal, Shaftesbury made precisely the same points, often in
similar language, that the *Letter* had made about the Lords' constitutional significance and the Laudian plot. After the session finished, this
speech was printed along with Buckingham's speech on 16 November
when he asked for permission to bring in a bill of indulgence for protestant dissenters. A cheap, even cynical, bid for popularity, Buckingham's
brief speech stressed the irrationality of persecution by 'those that have
power in the church that's in fashion'.[57] The underlying reason for the
emphasis on the role of the Lords was, of course, the conviction that the
Commons were corrupt and parliament must be dissolved.

Two Seasonable Discourses concerning the Present Parliament (1675) publicized the arguments used in the Lords on 20 November for a dissolution. It was in the interest of the three estates, king, commons and peers,
of the church, of the great ministers, of dissent, and even of papists, to
choose a fresh assembly. A Commons which sits so long 'must necessar-
ily produce cabals and parties, and the carrying on of private interests
and court factions, rather than the public good'. A standing parliament
and a standing army were compared to Siamese twins. And the dispute
over Shirley's appeal made parliament's continuance impractical: 'it is
very well known that many of the ablest and most worthy patriots
amongst them have carried this difference to the greatest height, with
this only design, that by this means they might deliver the nation from
the danger and the pressure of a long continued parliament.'[58] Another
analysis of the autumn session, *A Letter from a Parliament Man*, was slanted
towards a nonconformist audience, but amplified the theme of the 'cor-

ruption' of the Commons and their 'dread of dissolution' while claiming that the old cavalier minority, having grown 'damnable godly', was content 'to pare the nails' of civil government if they could 'sharpen the ecclesiastical talons'. The 'true country gentlemen' were exhorted to think calmly and to resist the hysterical demands of these misguided zealots: if the threat is from an 'encroaching prerogative' then the bishops and their allies were part of the danger rather than a defence.[59]

This propaganda was an attempt to redraw the political landscape. The notion of a 'country party' was emphasized, but almost by default. Its only representatives appeared to be a small band of heterogenous peers, while by this account supposedly 'country' MPs lamentably failed to assert 'country' principles. Danby's efforts to bring more discipline to government support in the Commons had played into the hands of those who were already disposed to see 'corruption' in parliament. There is little evidence of well-drilled rival blocks of MPs voting consistently, but people had begun to believe that members fell into 'court' and 'country' groups. Similarly, by the end of 1675, the seeds had been sown in the public mind of a powerful, but ill-founded, suspicion that the Anglican clergy harboured long-term political pretensions. This canard was an immediate response to the way that Charles and Danby had wrapped themselves in the colours of the Church of England – somewhat to the discomfort of the bishops. It is a measure of just how infuriating these insinuations were that Danby tried to intimidate the coffee-house keepers from spreading these tracts and that country gentlemen like Sir Peter Leicester and Anglican divines like Dr Francis Turner were so quick to rebut them.[60]

V

In January 1676 the Church of England undertook a census of religious conformity which asked every minister to say how many inhabitants there were in his parish, how many real or suspected popish recusants, and 'what number of other dissenters . . . (of what sect soever) which either obstinately refuse or wholly absent themselves from the communion of the Church of England at such times as by law they are required.' Archbishop Sheldon was nominally in charge, but as the administrative impetus came from Bishop Compton of London this survey is still known as the Compton Census. Its political impetus lay in the need to 'unmask and lay open' misapprehensions about the strength of dissenters so as to show that they could and should be suppressed, that conformity was an attainable goal, and so that 'the increase of schism and superstition will no longer be imputed to our easiness or inadvertency' – although these motives were not spelled out in public. Sheldon's correspondence hinted that Danby had reported the King's enthusiasm for the project and the church's leaders obviously hoped that the information they gleaned would cement the government's new-found devotion to the church. The final figures did indeed show that papists and dissenters were a small proportion of the population. They also revealed that there was a hazy middleground of partial or semi-conformity to the church, some of which was dangerously close to apathy or irreligion. Many returns suggested that the growing numbers of the 'profane and unstable' were the greatest threat to the Anglican interest.[61]

This internal enemy was difficult to confront, and it was predictable that both the laity and the authorities found it easier to concentrate on the threat from outside, from alien popery with its foreign associations and its well attested subversion of England's religion and government. A furore arose late in 1675 over the alleged attack on M. de Luzancy, a French priest recently converted to protestantism, by St Germain, a Jesuit attached to the Duchess of York's household. Luzancy, reputed to be an actor's son and a man with an unsavoury past, may well have lied about how St Germain and his toughs forced him to sign a recantation of protestantism at knifepoint. Yet the allegation was political dynamite. Russell introduced it to the Commons on the day that they were to give a third reading to a bill to purge parliament of Catholics. Holles brought it to the King's attention and Luzancy told the privy council that St Germain had claimed that Charles was 'a Catholic in his heart' and that they were working to establish liberty of conscience. The Commons asked for the arrest of not just St Germain, but all priests and Jesuits, and remonstrated that the ministers had allowed St Germain to escape. Whatever the truth, this was one more 'fact' confirming the reputation of the Jesuits among English protestants.[62] Popery at court was further underlined in March 1676 when, not content with refusing to receive Easter communion in the Church of England, the Duke of York apparently declared that 'he would never more come under the roof of Whitehall chapel, which makes everyone say he is a perfect papist'. This was followed by a rumour of a proclamation to make it punishable to say that York is a papist.[63] The danger from popery seemed very real. A terrible fire at Southwark in May led Josselin, among others, to conclude 'there was treachery and firing'. During the summer there was a stream of reports about 'Frenchmen', strangers, incendiaries and mysterious blazes from towns as far apart as Bristol and York, Marlborough and Nottingham, or Derby and Dover.[64]

'Firing is now become such a trade' that not only the capital but all the country's towns are in perpetual danger, remarked Francis Jenks in a speech at London's Guildhall on 24 June. Jenks, a Cornhill linen draper, went on to blame the French for the decay of English trade and to say that 'worse than all the rest . . . is the just apprehension that is upon the minds of good men, of danger to his majesty's person and the protestant religion'. The remedy was to ask the Lord Mayor and aldermen to hold a common council so as to petition the King for a new parliament under the statutes of Edward III which stipulated that a parliament should be held every year. 'There was a great "well moved"'; the Mayor 'gave an insignificant plausible answer'; and Jenks was hauled before the privy council, where he gave nothing away – although Charles was justifiably convinced that this was all the work of Buckingham. Jenks was committed to gaol where this 'single brave fellow' basked in the support of grandees like Sir Robert Peyton. There was a history of civic politics and economic grievances to his stance and he gained further support from addresses circulating in the city on the sufferings of weavers and other artisans due to French 'incroachments'. Jenks courted publicity. Rather than expunging his contempt by begging for pardon, he combatively sought his release through habeas corpus. His speech was published along with another, 'intended' for a common council, which stressed the dangers to the rights, liberties and estates of Englishmen if the rights to speech and petition were to be trampled on in this way. This speech also asserted that 'the papists among us lift up their heads, and say their day is near.' Between us and the return of popery lies nothing but 'the breath of our King (which may pass before morning)'. If the heir to the throne is a papist, how safe is the King? And if the King is a papist, how secure is protestantism?[65] Sir Robert Carr accused Sir Philip Monckton of 'the same kind of attempts in the country'. Called before the King on the same day as Jenks, Monckton admitted that he was for a new parliament and 'talked with the liberty of an old cavalier and his own peculiar folly' of the danger from popery. Although Monckton, an eccentric figure, said enough to turn the tables on his accuser and implicate Carr in efforts to stir up the Lincolnshire gentry and clergy in favour of a dissolution, this could not save him from several weeks confinement in the Tower for writing a seditious letter.[66]

In the same month that Jenks and Monckton were getting into trouble, two incidents further blackened the court's reputation. One was the trial of Lord Cornwallis for the murder of a young page at Whitehall. The House of Lords acquitted Cornwallis – it was his companion who rushed the boy and precipitated the fall which broke his neck – but six peers wanted to convict him of manslaughter. What was so repugnant was the evidence of drunken courtiers roaming Whitehall late at night, swearing obscenely and picking fights with the guards and innocent passers-by.[67] Even worse was the affray at Epsom on 17 June when Rochester and his companions provoked a fight with the watch. Rochester was 'said to have first engaged and first fled and abjectly hid himself' while his friends were beaten so severely by the outraged locals that one of them, George

Downes, later died. Rochester, an intimate of the King's, now had a reputation for cowardice as well as degeneracy.[68] Another striking example of
aristocratic violence and popular insubordination occurred in October,
when two 'exchange women' and four 'braves', one a soldier and the
other three Irish, all drunk on brandy, called on Lady Mohun about some
overdue bills. 'The women went up, spit in my lady's face, etc, and the men
stayed below and cried where is my lord the son of a [whore] and swore
they would do his business for him.' Lord Mohun came out swinging a
sword and shooting and the braves soon took to their heels. Mohun, an
intemperate young man, an inveterate duellist, possibly a wife-beater, and
a veteran of Shaftesbury's recent parliamentary campaign against Danby,
was slightly injured in the hand. A year later he was to die from wounds
received in a duel.

   An obsession with honour, an addiction to violence and a disdain for
conventional constraints were part of the ethos of many English gentlemen in the 1670s. Clearly this outlook led them into dangerous
escapades. One wonders whether it also led some into political adventures and confrontations? The behaviour of this swaggering minority
certainly convinced many of their contemporaries that the royal court
was a degenerate place, full of depraved characters, and a poor example
to the nation.

   The final months of 1676 were far from uneventful. The drums were
soon beating for volunteers to join the force to be sent to Virginia where
a group of settlers under Nathaniel Bacon had rebelled against the
negligent Governor Berkeley. The English possession of Tangier also
needed urgent help to defend itself against local warlords and pirates.
More ominously, during the summer France had not only enjoyed military successes in the Netherlands, but had also begun to cut a more convincing figure as a naval power. Domestic politics were a shade less frantic
than usual, as parliament's next meeting was still some months away, but
Danby and Wiseman were already hard at work in preparing the ground
for a productive session. At the end of the year Harbord thought that
Charles would listen 'to any reasonable thing' from parliament in return
for money: but no-one knew what Danby and York designed, other than
'in general to keep their power at any rate'.[69]

Politics in these middle years of the decade really can be described as
kaleidoscopic. From one perspective the picture was dominated,
whether for good or ill, by the Church of England; from another, by the
fate of this aged and 'corrupt' parliament; and from a third, by the commercial and military might of France. Observers of parliamentary politics in 1675 easily identified Shaftesbury as a factious, self-seeking,
politician attempting to force his way back into office and surrounded
by a mediocre bunch of men who were either on their last legs, like

Holles, or hotheads, like Cavendish or Mohun. Others traced all ills to the pre-eminence of Danby and his lacklustre clique or to the malign influence of the Duke of York. All too often parliament looked like the arena for struggles which had their origin elsewhere. Orchestrated from the Lords, these feuds had been fought out as much between the two chambers as on the floor of the Commons. Shaftesbury and the 'protesting lords' had adopted the dangerous tactic of promoting a dissolution which inevitably alienated many in the Commons. The 'country' did not as yet command much credibility as a political rallying call, although Shaftesbury and his propagandists worked hard to invest it with significance. The 'court', on the other hand, was already a metonym not just for the ministers, Danby and York, but for Charles and his mistresses, courtiers, foreign contacts and dependents. The court inspired little confidence among the parliamentary class or the people.

VI

The narrative of the first three chapters has largely been driven by the high politics of court and parliament. These chapters have told a story of constant political change against a background of contending interests, public debate and the fear of violence. Charles II had tried a new tack with the French alliance and Dutch war and the concomitant change of religious policy. His failure reaped its rewards – and some of his ministers defended themselves by encouraging parliament to turn on their own colleagues. The next change of direction, Danby's attempt to placate parliament by espousing the old Cavalier and Church interest, only provoked more criticism. Danby's methods were crass and his touch clumsy; and more importantly the Church of England was no longer a winning political ticket. Throughout these years the brute facts of political life were simple. England was a client of France and France terrified the English. Most diplomacy and any war meant trusting Charles with money and troops that he might misuse. England was a society of several religions. The Duke of York was a Catholic. And, finally, Charles II's dissembling and reversals of policy, never mind his private life, had eroded his subjects' trust in him. It is a short list. However the significance of each of these factors and the ways in which they interacted are only to be judged adequately if we know something of English attitudes to dissimulation and principle, war and heroism, national interest and destiny, news and information, and a host of other issues. To concentrate on the immediate, as our narrative has required, is to overlook these larger questions about Charles II's England, but they can be ignored no longer.

4

Great Souls: Heroism, Wit and Masquerade

1   In Search of Heroism

No age abounded more with heroical poetry, and yet there was never any wherein fewer heroical actions were performed.

Samuel Butler, Prose Observations

> The greatest heros by historians pen'd,
> Have for their mighty labours found an end;
> The greatest victor underneath the sun,
> Dy'd ere his aimed-at Conquest he'd begun;
> Yet their great names still to the world do stay;
> And mayst thou have as great a name as they;
> But this poor age is with the old at odds,
> As men stove then to make 'em demy-Gods
> We silence fame, which is to honour sin,
> And think on men as if they ne're had been;
> Deeds now, though ne're so arduous and high,
> Scarce reach the life of one mens memory.
> That mighty soul whom all the world admir'd
> Seems like a dream when once the breath's expir'd;
> And ev'ry act though ne're so good or brave,
> Sinks with the corps in the forgotten grave.

On the death of that brave and worthy hero, Edward,
Earl of Sandwich in C. F., Wit at a Venture (1674)

We have taken the boldness to approach the heroes, and to examine their genius; which in many of them, we find not only the most wild and extravagant, but the most idle and trifling that ever bestrid an age. And certainly either historians have been much to blame in recommending to us a pompous name of virtue, glory and renown, acquired by our ancestors, making that appear noble and useful to mankind, which was dull and rude, or else their children have nothing in them worthy of their fathers . . .

S. L., Remarques on the Humours and Conversations of the Gallants of the Town (1673)

In the 1670s England badly needed heroes and yet the English could not bring themselves to trust heroism. It was not simply that all heroes seemed flawed, nor that recent heroism had too often served dubious or false causes; these, after all, are age-old paradoxes. No, it was rather that the English had lost their bearings as to what counted as heroic. Dramatists produced subtle accounts of the disparity between heroic aspiration and human reality, clerics promoted role models of Christian fortitude, and the popular press dangled seductively amoral rogues before the public. Confronted by competing accounts of the heroic, it was all too easy to descend into confusion.

Physical heroism, bravery in battle, existed in this as in every other age. But courage can rarely be isolated from cultural influences: Captain Haddock's incontestable composure at the battle of Sole Bay, when he continued to command the ship while 'one of our chirurgeons was cutting off the shattered flesh and tendons of my toe', bespeaks a certain view of how an old salt, a professional sailor, conducts himself; so too does the 'stout and gallant' seaman who endured an amputation 'hardly making a face or crying oh'.[1] Other acts of valour were even more obviously indebted to an heroic ideal. In the same battle, the Earl of Sandwich, dressed in full insignia, remained on board his flagship, the *Royal James*, as it burned down to the waterline. The elegists made the most of this gesture:

> And Death in several vizards did appear;
> The cruel elements seeming at strife,
> Which of them first should rob him of his life:
> Had you but seen how unconcern'd he stood,
> Flames over's head, his feet dabbling in blood;
> In what a fearless and compos'd estate
> He brav'd the approach of the severest fate;
> And did at last from death to death retire
> Courting the water to avoid the fire . . .

Fate betrayed the hero 'and let in Death in gloomy masquerade', but 'fate did this civil'ty with him use / That of two deaths she gave him leave to chuse.'[2] Sandwich had experienced premonitions of death and may have been seeking to expiate a personal dishonour. Others too died that day: 'noble Worden, Fowler, Finch and the rest . . . that hero-troop ne'er to be praised enough'; 'Finch' was William Finch, Lord Maidstone, who 'fell, and as he fell, the seamen cry, / Here is true valour, true nobility'.[3] Yet even as the poetasters apostrophized the dead – 'Blest Sandwich! Earth's envy! Heaven's delight! / Whom the Gods honoured to die in fight!' – they worried too that the English did not know how to recognize and commemorate their heroes.[4]

Commanders, princes and rulers were courageous by convention in both senses of the term. They were bred to leadership: Charles and the

Duke of York had fought the Great Fire in person, and York had a long
and distinguished military record on the continent before cementing
his reputation with a naval victory at Lowestoft in June 1665. Just
as dramatists and critics could equate virtue with status – 'though it
is not necessary that all heroes should be kings, yet undoubtedly all
crowned heads by poetical right are heroes' – the panegyrists assumed
their subjects were heroic.[5] In 1672 'Mrs E. P.' warned the Dutch that
York was about to vanquish them; 'that glorious hero, never arms put
on / But he made victory herself his own'.[6] The Duke of Monmouth's
martial prowess on behalf of his father and Louis XIV was equally
celebrated:

> When he at Mons so terrible appear'd
> Like Mars, all o'r with blood and dust besmear'd
> When he, like the great Trojan Hector fought,
> And wheresoe'r he came such wonders wrought.[7]

'Heaven has already taken care to form you for an hero,' Monmouth
was told. 'You have all the advantages of mind and body, and an illustrious birth, conspiring to render you an extraordinary person.'[8] Sometimes, however, those designed for heroes by rank or poetry could not
live up to the role. Monmouth, for instance, was notoriously belligerent
when off-duty and references to him as 'Hector' may have raised a
wry smile from contemporaries who knew him to be one of the 'town
hectors' or drunken bully boys of Restoration London. And once he was
an acknowledged Catholic, the Duke of York's military record was a
cause of anxiety rather than admiration for many of his future subjects.
General Monk, the Duke of Albemarle, a man of great military experience, but with no particular reputation for personal bravery, was
made a hero when the King ordered that he be buried 'with all the circumstances of honour' and when his funeral preacher praised him as
'that glorious performer of heroic actions'. For some Monk was a 'generous hero' who in 1660 had refused to bring in a king fettered like
a royal slave – 'heroes are such by birth'; but for others this ex-
Cromwellian was a perjured, self-serving turncoat: 'His valour hath been
very much / Against both cavaliers and Dutch / . . . Now he is dead let
him rot.'[9]

   Heroism was a contested quality, even in times of war. An apparently
straightforward appeal to arms, *Honour's Invitation, or a Call to the Camp*
(1673), extols the glorious arts of war from which all honour and power
flow and to which nations owe their safety and greatness. The poem pits
the call of the camp against 'all the luxuries of wanton peace' as experienced by young men about town. A vision of Charles II appears and
exhorts the narrator:

Then rouse at last from this lethargic dream,
And let heroic actions be thy theme.
No more to base effeminate follies yield,
Thy country's genius calls thee to the field![10]

War, even war in alliance with Louis XIV, could be invoked as the
nation's destiny. 'A liberty' had been established by the alliance 'to
uncage the mighty English souls, and to give them elbow room, in order
to the great and popular designs now abroad in the world.' Since the
reformation there had been no opportunity 'of training up our youth
in martial activities . . . which brought our nation to some effeminacy'.
But now Charles had provided the chance 'to join with the most
Christian king in order to the redeeming of the ancient gallantry, which
used to attend the subjects of monarchy, and has been a long time
fettered and almost stifled'.[11] Other pamphleteers took up these claims
and a joust ensued over the nature of true heroism which also managed
to glance at the playwrights (for these were simultaneously literary
wars) and allude to the Dutch war. The contest is between 'those, Sir,
who celebrate perpetual action, and reproach study, with drowsiness and
idle sloth' and those who advocate country virtues, a roster of political
and social ideals with political resonance in the midst of a war.[12] 'Whom
have all ages allowed for heroes? . . . not the lazy and the speculative, not
the boisterous and injurious, but those who have applied themselves to
court [the] human race with kindnesses and benefits.'[13] In this 'too too
active age', a false notion of honour and nobility was abroad. Playwrights
'have made the three great characters of a hero, to be love, honour
and friendship.' Audiences were presented with heroes whose 'honour
consists in an obstinacy to combat necessity and time; in maintaining
the feiry [sic] ground of fame; to vanquish reason and generosity in
contempt of life; gathering the spreading glory of a hero into a single
punctilio.'[14]

Whether life imitated art or vice versa, adherents of this debased
notion of heroism stalked the streets of London. 'Our Westminster
heroes', as contemporaries ironically referred to them, were either
boisterous and debauched courtiers, or even worse the dull, affected,
drunken louts who tried to emulate them.[15] The self-deluding hectors
who assaulted whores, broke windows or fought with the watch were
often ridiculed by those they aped. Rochester, the acme of debauchery,
satirized them in *Timon*, when the narrator is dragged off to dinner by
a ludicrous gallant who is as happy in the company of 'Halfwit and
Huff', men who 'will both write and fight', as Sedley and Buckhurst.[16]
But not everyone was as discerning as Rochester. If they had been
the gallants would presumably not have found drinking pals and the

tellers of tall stories in the taverns and coffee-houses would not have found a ready audience. A guide to the tricks and stratagems of the 'wheedle' or conman lets us eavesdrop on the braggadocio of the town hector:

> to make himself more observed, he urges how frequently he has duelled, and not a Dutch fight in which he has not been engaged; that, being Captain, he was forced to shift his ship twice, that De Ruyter coming up, he made him with a warm reception loof and stand another way; that when the prince hearing of his eminent service in the fleet etc, here he stops, and cries, but no matter, I scorn to trumpet out my own praise, though upon this very ground I was desired to attend his grace against Maastricht, that I was the next man that entered after him, etc.[17]

If this worked for the trickster, it must have answered to at least some expectations of what heroes were like.

Some curious alchemy even managed to turn a few of the era's rogues and rakes into popular heroes. This, of course, was a product of their representation not of reality. Picaresque fictions of the highwayman and 'rogue' transmuted louse-ridden, sweat-stained horse-thieves into something far more alluring (see plate 8). The highwayman Francis Jackson, alias 'Dixie', and his gang wrote their own story as they waited for their appointment with the gallows. One day in March 1674, after robbing coaches on the Staines road, they had been chased from Acton to Harrow, Paddington, Kilburn, Hendon and, finally, to Hampstead Heath, where they held off two hundred men with nothing but their swords 'for near about an hour'. The gang did not glory in the action, 'and yet if the cause had been good there could not have been a nobler defence' – it seems they could not resist a little bravado.[18] They wrote principally, however, to thwart 'false pamphlets' appearing after their deaths. But it was to no avail: even as their bodies were still hanging, Richard Head, a major author of rogue literature, published *Jackson's Recantation, or, the Life and Death of the Notorious High-way-man now hanging in chains at Hampstead. Delivered to a friend a little before execution; wherein is truly discovered the whole mystery of that wicked and fatal profession of padding on the road* (1674). In 1679 two highwaymen fought their way through Islington until they were unhorsed and their swords were broken in their hands; ''tis great pity such men should be hanged,' sighed John Verney.[19]

A different allure was represented by Claude Du Val, a highwayman hanged at Tyburn on 21 January 1670. The exploits and gallantry of this mundane young Frenchmen were glorified by the hacks who wrote his life in ballad and in pamphlet form. Stress was laid upon his birth at Domfront in Normandy, 'a place very famous . . . for the production of mercurial wits', and upon his Gallic charms. During one robbery he

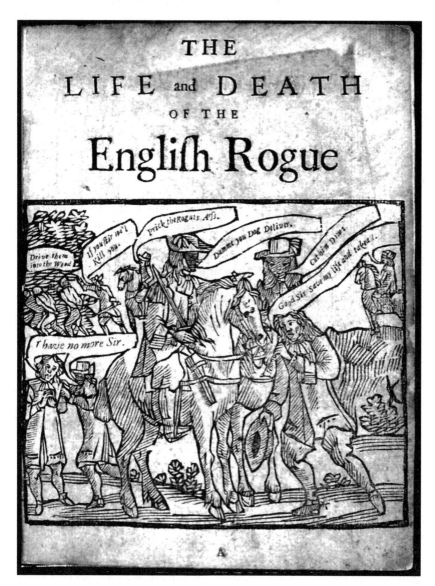

Plate 8 The Life and Death of the English Rogue *(1679). 'You must, when you are on the pad, have your masks, and chin clothes to disguise your face'. The popular 'rogue literature' thrilled and terrified readers with its supposed insights into the picaresque world of highwaymen, cheats and thieves. Thanks to the pamphleteers, some of these highway robbers, like the notorious Claude Du Val, came to embody all that was glamorous. Yet highwaymen were a serious problem on England's increasingly busy roads.*

invited a lady to descend from her coach and dance with him 'upon the heath' and he amazed all with his elegant 'footing'. Much was made of his fondness for the English ladies and theirs for him: he spent his earnings on women; and masked ladies visited him in Newgate and accompanied him to the gallows. His supposed epitaph ran

> Here lies Du Val, reader, if male thou art,
> Look to thy purse; if female, to thy heart.
> Much havoc has he made of both; for all
> Men he made stand, and women he made fall.
> The second conqueror of the Norman race.[20]

Even after Du Val's execution, the authorities remained on the lookout for members of his gang, and some criminals claimed an affinity with him.[21] When twenty 'heroes of the road' or highwaymen ambushed fifteen York butchers riding to North Allerton fair, the pamphlet account claimed that two of the culprits acknowledged 'that they were first initiated in the discipline of the road, by that famous artist Du Val, who brought out of his own country into England the most gentile methods of following the high-pack, taking a purse alamode, mustering his savage Arabians, and exercising them to perform their parts on all occasion with the most obliging dexterity.'[22] Du Val was a literary type: when a ballad writer decided to celebrate the thief Thomas Sadler, hanged in 1677 after a record fifteen spells in Newgate, he invoked the precedents of 'brisk Du Val that French Latroon (who put the ladies in a swoon)' and Mary Carleton, 'the German Princess'.[23] And in Thomas Duffett's burlesque play, *Psyche Debauched* (1675), Bruine, 'the White Bear of Norwich' reveals his true identity: 'I am Du Val, that French prince of the padders, that was thought to be hang'd, I have lived ever since in this disguise, because I would not quite break the kind ladies' hearts to see me hanged twice.'[24] The glamorous, bold, gallant Du Val, 'that embodiment of eros', as Derek Hughes has called him, is a hero woven from the stuff of reality by those answering the demand for romances with a spice of sex and danger.[25]

An overt fabrication, *The French Rogue* (1672), purporting to be the autobiography of a Calais-born adventurer, played knowingly upon the appeal of this rogue literature. Its hero was 'a pretty rogue, not guilty of murder, and those heinous ballad crimes that are as miserably sang every day in the street, as committed, if they were true. Yet this I'll tell you; he lives by his wit, and perhaps it shall cost thee a shilling or two before thou get him.' To readers who had already purchased a copy of Meriton Latroon's *The English Rogue*, the publisher recommended the French rogue with the 'common' answer, 'it is the fashion, and he's better company for ladies.'[26] English rogues like Captain James Hind, executed for treason in 1651 but the subject in 1674 of *No Jest Like a True Jest*, 'a compendious record' of his 'merry life and mad exploits', might have 'a running pate' or fertile criminal mind, but they clearly lacked the sexual allure of those from across the Channel. Even Hind seems to have been caught in the coils of his own myth – in reply to crimes alleged against him, he averred 'upon the word of a Christian, they are fictions'.[27] A fiction like *The Lives of Sundry Notorious Villains* (1678) included several exemplary lives of French villains and 'a novel as it really happened in Roan [Rouen]'. While dwelling upon the swindles, abuses and scrapes of his villains, the author hedged his bets, referring to the courage of one rogue 'if a man may term that courage which is in such persons', and ensuring that all his villains eventually suffered for their crimes.[28] Whatever the realities behind the fictions, there was a healthy market for the adventures of bold bad individuals like Jackson, Du Val and Hind. The anti-hero – for that, surely, is what we should call them – was a recognizable literary type and one rooted in the possibility that there might really be such people in the world.

A similar slippage between reality and myth occurred in the case of the debauched courtiers and rakes who surrounded Charles II. These drunkards, adulterers, duellists and scoffers at conventional morality and piety were the subject of prurient public interest as much for who they were as what they did. Gossip and rumour, dramatic and literary representations, even prejudice about the nature of royal courts and their denizens, all helped to create an image of the 'court wits'. Although Monmouth, Buckingham or Sedley could all be used to illustrate the point, it is Rochester who most completely and glaringly demonstrates both the interplay between reality and myth and the rake as archetypal anti-hero.

There was a kind of symbiosis between the alcoholic, depraved, courtier-poet, John Wilmot, Earl of Rochester, and the literary representation of 'Rochester', who may be disguised as Horner in *The Country Wife* or Dorimant in *The Man of Mode* or Aphra Behn's Willmore or Nathaniel Lee's Rosidore and Nemours (see plate 9). Gossip created an even worse caricature. In 1670 rumour credited Rochester with the murder of a watchman who had dared to remark on the Earl's extreme handsomeness; in 1677 when a French chef was stabbed at an inn where Rochester was dining, 'the good nature of the town has reported it all this day that his lordship was the stabber' and if the tale gets as far as York 'the truth will not be believed under two or three years.' The world is not 'only apt to believe but very ready to make lies concerning you,' Savile told him; and Rochester claimed that his mistress must believe his protestations 'its being notorious that I mind nothing but my own satisfaction'.[29]

Rochester was a 'famous hero', according to his elegists, 'truly heroic more than can be told' fighting with sword and pen; but his 'heroic

Plate 9   John Wilmot, Earl of Rochester, crowns his monkey (unknown artist, mid-1670s?). This painting alludes to Rochester's disdain for human vanity and pretensions, and reflects the libertine commonplace that man is as much at the mercy of his passions and his body as are brute animals.

virtues' were far from clear: his youthful courage had certainly been tested at the naval battle of Bergen, but thereafter his physical bravery was demonstrated principally in destroying sundials and fighting constables and his intellectual courage by a series of corruscatingly cynical or nihilistic poems.[30] As so often, Rochester himself both raised and subverted the question. In the poem *To the Post-boy*, the 'peerless peer' recounts his debauchery and blasphemy, and alludes to his cowardice during the 1676 affray at Epsom when his companion was abandoned to his fate; then the poet asks the postboy which is 'the readiest way to hell', and receives the reply, 'Ne'er stir:/ the readiest way, my Lord, 's by Rochester.'[31] If this was written by Rochester, it is a striking example of the propagation of his own myth as both a debauchee and a wit. The effrontery of the final pun, its brazen assertion that the poet will go to hell his own way, and the poet's refusal to flinch from the consequences of his actions, are brave indeed. The fact that John Wilmot does not seem to have lived up to them is neither here nor there, for our purposes what matters is how such portrayals made 'Rochester' into an anti-hero. Even his elegist contributed to this; 'Heroic virtues shin'd in him so bright, / That thy oft daz'd the sharpest eagle's sight.' Is this poor couplet perhaps hinting that few could discern Rochester's heroic virtues? Or that only those of superior feeling and talent could appreciate them? After all 'the famous hero writ / Such mysteries as puzzled dull mankind.'[32] This is heroism beyond our comprehension, even if we admit to a sneaking admiration.

We are beginning to move away from anti-heroes who thrill simply because of their glamour and exuberance into deeper and darker waters. In the lives of villains, 'you have in these persons the character of a grand debauchee or daring villain, abolishing and enervating, as much as in them lay, all laws and rules, without which it is impossible to suppose a society.'[33] In a figure like Rochester – for all his claims to be 'the wildest and most fantastical odd man alive' – we encounter the stock figure of the libertine, the man brave and mad enough to defy not only social conventions but even God.[34] The anti-hero is a rebel against constraint; his determination to gratify his appetites, to sate his senses, and live by his own rules, may excite readers, but how is it to be compared with the heroism of young William Finch or the sacrifice of the Earl of Sandwich? Little wonder that heroism seemed such an uncertain quality in Restoration England.

I

Heroism had its theorists, and most of them traced their thinking back to Aristotle's teaching that human beings were capable both of 'heroic virtue', which was a special non-moral form of virtue, inspiring great actions and compelling awe, and of the profoundly ethical 'magnanimity'.[35] Heroic virtue is a topic to which we will return in a moment, but let us first consider how magnanimity was understood in seventeenth-century England. Christianity and the Renaissance produced an ideal of 'Christian magnanimity', a notion which was described by Thomas Traherne as 'an infinite hope, and a vast desire, a divine, profound, uncontrollable sense of one's own capacity, a generous confidence, and a great inclination to heroical deeds'. Or even more simply, in the title of the pertinent chapter, 'magnanimity or greatness of soul'.[36] How did this greatness of soul manifest itself?

'God is pleased in all ages to raise up Christian heroes for a testimony to the energy of his eternal gospel,' preached Seth Ward at Monk's funeral. The 'foundation of great and heroical performances' is the absolute contempt of death which 'is only derived from the Christian principle. This inspires passive valour in the hearts of men, and furnishes invincible martyrs for the stake; this excites active courage and equips and furnishes heroical soldiers and generals for the field.'[37] As Milton put it in *Paradise Lost*, the 'better fortitude of patience and heroic martyrdom' outweighed the 'tinsel trappings' of chivalry and 'wars, hitherto the only argument / Heroic deemed'. This fortitude was displayed in the figure of Christ in Milton's *Paradise Regained*. The contemplative Christ withstands Satan's temptations and repudiates all the means by which he could win his own kingdom. His time is not yet come, and if God has 'decreed that I shall first / Be tried in humble state', then he will accept his lot: 'Who best / Can suffer, best can do; best reign, who first / Well hath obeyed.'[38] Milton's Christ may be an exemplar to all, and especially to English nonconformists, of the duty of suffering for the truth, but in *Samson Agonistes* (1671) Milton presented a human hero and a more ambiguous message about activism. Obviously Samson is a flawed hero and even his final act in destroying the Philistines and himself has been seen as vengeful, but to most readers he is a man chosen by God, a man whose self-sacrifice is a response to a divine call to action. In the poem the Chorus presents Samson with the stark contrast: God either raises up an agent of his justice to defeat the wicked 'with plain heroic magnitude of mind / And celestial vigour armed': or

> patience is more oft the exercise
> Of saints, the trial of their fortitude,
> Making them each his own deliverer,
> And victor over all
> That tyranny or fortune can inflict,
> Either of these is in thy lot,
> Samson, with might endued
> Above the sons of men; but sight bereaved
> May chance to number thee with those
> Whom patience finally must crown.[39]

Such a choice lies within the potential experience of all Christians, but it was particularly pertinent to the English nonconformist community of which Milton was a member.

The heroes of Restoration nonconformity may have been those who accepted 'martyrdom': the Quakers whom Pepys saw going off to gaol 'like lambs', perhaps with Penn's words, 'the bearing of thy daily cross is the only true testimony,' ringing in their ears.[40] Or they may have been those who kept out of trouble in order to maintain the gospel. But all serious Christians had to acknowledge, like Pilgrim confronting the lions on the hill of difficulty, that 'to go back is nothing but death, to go forward is fear of death, and life everlasting beyond it.' Bunyan vividly describes Pilgrim's struggle to pass through the river of death which lies before the Celestial City and observes in the margin that 'death is not welcome to nature, though by it we pass out of this world into glory.'[41] For Bunyan and his co-religionists, struggle against temptation, fear, doubt and oneself were the common experience: Christian heroism lay as much in running this race as in braving the persecution of the authorities. But it was not Christian magnanimity, especially in its guise as passive fortitude, which captured the Restoration imagination, nor was it the puritan authors who set the tone; the poets and dramatists of 'heroic virtue' were in the ascendant.

Poetry has always been concerned with heroism, and heroism of an active kind; when, in 1674, Thomas Rymer, perhaps one of England's first literary critics, reviewed the history of English attempts at epic poetry, he observed that Cowley's *Davideis*, an epic on the troubles of the Biblical King David, was based on fundamentally unsuitable material for an heroic poem, 'it is rather the actions, than his sufferings, that make an hero.'[42] This highly prescriptive tone was not uncommon among critics and poets who were struggling to find a new form for a new generation of artists. In mid-century the exchanges of Davenant and Hobbes, and Cowley's writings, enunciated a theory of literature which encouraged poets to aspire to epic, the highest literary form, and to pattern heroic dramas after epic poetry. Another fillip in the same direction came from contemporary French criticism which laid down rigid aesthetic rules about such things as the unities of space, time and place, propriety, decorum and probability, and, of course, these technical formalities were to be seen at work in the great French tragedies of Racine and Corneille. The dramatists also sought themes relevant to their own society and audience. Hobbes had argued that there were literary forms suitable to each of 'the three regions of mankind, court, city and country' and in the case of the court (a metonym for a hierarchical society and monarchy), it was the heroic, either in the form of the epic poem or the dramatic tragedy: 'for there is in princes and men of conspicuous power, anciently called heroes, a lustre and influence upon the rest of men resembling that of the heavens.'[43] Aesthetically and thematically, heroic drama was the obvious step; but it also suited the particular talents and moral and intellectual aspirations of several writers and, above all, of the Poet Laureate, John Dryden, who believed 'heroic poetry . . . has ever been esteemed, and ever will be, the greatest work of human nature.'[44]

Heroic tragedy, initiated by Sir Robert Howard and John Dryden's *The Indian Queen* in 1664, was the dominant dramatic form of the 1670s. Written in rhymed couplets of decorous language, located in remote or exotic locations such as Africa, Ancient Rome, China, Troy, Babylon, Mughal India, Peru or Central America, and ranging across history for their plots, these dramas concerned the vicissitudes of noble figures, usually kings and queens, princes and generals (among the roll call are Hannibal, Alexander, Herod, Nero, Montezuma, St Catherine and Cleopatra), caught up in conquests, wars, sieges or rebellions. Heroic tragedies often place personal dilemmas, such as divided allegiance or thwarted love, in the context of a broader cultural clash, such as those between Spaniards and Muslims, Conquistadores and Indians, Christians and pagans, or Rome and Egypt. The twists and turns of the plots are driven by the caprice of ungrateful rulers, the fortunes of war, the intrigue of courtiers and the elaborate codes of honour espoused by the heroes: women are almost always placed on a pedestal and heroes are often men of mysterious background and super-human valour. The central characters have to wrestle with the conflicts between love and honour, between private inclinations and public roles: when Dryden's Antony turns his back on Cleopatra and faces his duty, his friend marvels, 'Methinks you breathe / Another soul; your looks are more divine; / You speak a hero, and you move a god.'[45] But in general, the hero does not die; however corpse-strewn the stage, those struggling with duty are rewarded. These plays make much of redemptive suffering and of the power of love; several of the heroes are civilized or tamed by female love.

Dryden set the mark, perhaps above all in *The Conquest of Granada* and in *Aurungzebe*, but he had competitors aplenty in the 1670s: Elkanah Settle's *Cambyses*, *The Empress of Morocco* and *Ibrahim the Illustrious Pasha* were in this genre, as were Nathaniel Lee's *The Rival Queens* and *Mithridates*, Thomas Otway's *Alcibiades* and *Don Carlos*, John Crowne's *The Destruction of Jerusalem by Titus Vespasian* and Edward Ravenscroft's *King Edgar and Alfreda*. To list titles does little more than illustrate the diversity of settings; and even this selection represents a range of styles and success. Modern analyses of the new dramas produced in the two London theatres suggests that fierce competition and the eagerness of professional playwrights to experiment with their writing had diverse results. In the 1676–7 season, for example, there were several heroic dramas on the same stories: two versions of the Titus and Berenice story, two of Antony and Cleopatra, and three on Alexander the Great. In other ways the serious dramas diverged. Some plays were reminiscent of Jacobean tragedies and their amoral villainy, others were tortuous examinations of virtue under stress, and yet others pandered to the audience's delight in spectacular scenery and effects; there was a marked tendency towards what one modern critic has called 'horror' plays replete with gory atrocities; and even those playwrights attempting to write full heroic tragedy had to absorb the implications of Dryden's renunciation of rhyme after *Aurungzebe* in 1675.[46]

The avowed aim of the dramatists was to move the audience to pity and terror and to bring them to love virtue; 'the end of tragedies or serious plays,' says one of Dryden's spokesmen, 'is to beget admiration, compassion, or concernment.'[47] In the character of Almanzor, 'I have formed a hero, I confess, not absolutely perfect, but of an excessive and overboiling courage: but Homer and Tasso are my precedents,' explained Dryden in his dedication of *The Conquest of Granada* to the Duke of York. 'I designed in him a roughness of character, impatient of injuries; and a confidence of himself, almost approaching to an arrogance. But these errors are incident only to great spirits.' In the mould of Achilles or Tasso's Rinaldo, Almanzor has a frank, open, noble nature – 'vast is his courage; boundless is his mind' – he is passionate but lives by the code of honour, and his frailties are open to correction or reformation in the course of the play.[48] A less lenient gloss of Almanzor is offered by Derek Hughes for whom he is 'a dangerously flawed hero whose extravagant illusions are consistently contradicted by the realities of life and frailties of his own nature'.[49] Certainly by the time Dryden created his next study of heroism, in the figure of Aurungzebe, he injected more introspection, restraint, and fortitude into the character of his hero and set off these characteristics by providing Aurungzebe with a foil in the shape of his impetuous, violent, half-brother Morat. And two years later, in the preface to *All for Love*, his reworking of the story of Antony and Cleopatra, Dryden claimed that 'the hero of the poem ought not to be a character of perfect virtue, for, then, he could not without injustice, be made unhappy; nor yet altogether wicked, because he could not then be pitied.' Accordingly Antony is presented as a man torn – as is said of him, 'virtue's his path; but sometimes 'tis too narrow / For his vast soul.'[50] Dryden's concern was to make all of his heroes plausible in the sense of making them a 'more exact image of human life', combining failings with their great virtues, so that they engaged the admiration and pity of his audience. In offering *The Conquest of Granada* to his patron York 'as these faint representations of your own worth and valour in heroic poetry', and claiming that 'the feign'd hero inflames the true: and the dead virtue animates the living,' Dryden was doing more than making the conventional noises to his dedicatee.[51] He was drawing attention to the poet's role in creating heroism. At one point Charles II and his brother had set Dryden on writing an heroic poem about England's recent history in which they would both be heroes, but nothing came of it. Dryden certainly acknowledged a different kind of heroism in his fulsome dedication of *Amboyna* to Lord

Clifford, his patron who had relinquished office rather than take the new test. He noted 'with how much magnanimity you quitted these honours'.[52]

For all this self-conscious theorizing and practice, it may be that Dryden and the other poets failed to create a meaningful version of heroism for their audience. After watching *The Conquest of Granada*, Mrs Evelyn reported that it contained more ideas than the most refined romance she had ever read and that 'love is made so pure, and valour so nice, that one would imagine it designed for Utopia rather than our stage.'[53] Although outside the moral remit of the dramatist, the disparity between Restoration England's quotidian heroes and figures like Almanzor and Aurungzebe was striking. Some of Dryden's critics were less than forgiving: 'those who take upon them to form the genius of an age, are to consider what is useful, and like to occur, and they ought to decline ideas, that fly too high for practice and experience.'[54] Critics feared that the heroes were *too* super-human, that they would overawe the audience rather than move them. Of course, much depended, too, upon the casting and acting. Charles Hart played most of the great heroes and one courtier allegedly commented that his portrayal of Alexander the Great in Lee's *The Rival Queens* 'might teach any king on earth how to comport himself'; on the other hand, the dramatist Settle was thrown into 'a fret' when Mr Jevons, appearing in *The Conquest of China* (May 1675) in a scene of mass suicide, lay his sword still in its scabbard on the stage 'and fell upon it, saying, now I am dead'.[55]

Contemporaries recognized that heroic tragedies had other appeals besides the moral grandeur of their protagonists: 'the great heroes now / In plays of rhyme and noise with wondrous show./ Then shall the house (to see these hectors kill and slay, / That bravely fight out the whole plot of th' play,) / Be for at least six months full ev'ry day.'[56] The spectacle, the scenery, the violence and the passion made these tragedies seem almost melodramatic at times. Of course, some found them simply laughable. In 1671 the Duke of Buckingham's play *The Rehearsal* mocked Dryden as 'Mr Bayes' and ridiculed Almanzor and his ilk:

> *Johnson*: Pray, Mr Bayes, who is that Drawcansir?
> *Bayes*: Why, sir, a fierce hero, that frights his mistress, snubs up kings, baffles armies, and does what he will without regard to numbers, good manners, or justice. . . .
> *Johnson*: But, Mr Bayes, I thought your heroes had ever been men of great humanity and justice.
> *Bayes*: Yes, they have been so; but, for my part, I prefer that one quality of singly beating of whole armies, above all your moral virtues put together, 'egad.

The rants of Almanzor are easy meat for the satirist: 'Spite of myself I'll stay, fight, love, despair: / And I can do all this because I dare' is transmuted into Drawcansir's 'I drink, I huff, I strut, look big and stare; / And all this I can do, because I dare.'[57] The language of heroic tragedy is one of Rochester's targets in *Timon*: when the witless Huff praises Settle's *Empress of Morocco*, he

> Said rumbling words, like drums, his courage raised:
> *Whose broad-built bulks the boist'rous billows bear,*
> *Safi and Sale, Mogador, Oran*
> *The famed Arzile, Alcazar, Tetuan.*
> 'Was ever braver language writ by man?'[58]

And in Joseph Arrowsmith's comedy *The Reformation*, the whole edifice of heroic tragedy is cruelly exposed when an expert gives away the secrets of the genre:

> Take a subject, as suppose the siege of Candy, or the conquest of Flanders . . . let it always be some war-like action: you can't imagine what grace a drum and trumpet give a play. Then sir I take you some three or four or half a dozen kings . . . you must always have two ladies in love with one man, or two men in love with one woman: if you make them the father and the son, or two brothers, or two friends 'twill do the better. There you know is opportunity for love and honour and fighting, and all that . . . Then sir you must have a hero that shall fight with all the world; yes i'gad, and beat them too, and half the gods into the bargain . . . In all you write reflect upon religion and the clergy . . . be sure to raise a dancing, singing ghost or two, court the players for half a dozen new scenes and fine cloths . . . put your story into rhyme, and kill enough at the end of the play, and probatum est your business is done for tragedy.[59]

It would be impertinent to ask satirists for their own definitions of heroism. This mockery was not meant to be constructive. What remains a matter of judgement is how far it was motivated by an aesthetic distaste for the plays themselves, by literary opportunism and personal animus, especially against the Laureate, and by an unease that those with pretensions to dictate the genius of the age really believed that their 'poetic fictions' would be 'instructive' about virtue, duty, love and heroism: 'where are the heroes they have fashioned by their precepts?'[60]

II

Restoration England had no simple formula for a hero. However several notions recur in different contexts; magnanimity is one, fortitude another, and self-mastery a third. Heroes, true heroes, were always in charge of their emotions. The Earl of Ossory's panegyrist knew he 'must write/ With the same equal temper that you fight; / As free from passion and as clear from rage.'[61] While Captain Thomas Harmon had taken inspiration from Admiral Sir John Harmon 'who cou'd his passions, as his men, control'.[62] But how is self-mastery achieved? Is it through submission to external forces and events or through the realization of some inner strength? Does the hero who has mastered himself really need law, morality or religion to guide him? The ranting Almanzor proclaims his indifference to death, but disputes Boabdelin's authority to order his execution, 'know that I alone am king of me. / I am as free as nature first made man / Ere the base laws of servitude began / When wild in woods the noble savage ran.'[63] There are echoes here of Hobbesian and libertine ideas about the natural order where humans followed their internal dictates and not some imposed authority. But brave and bold as he may be, Almanzor at this point in the drama still has much to learn, and his thrilling rant is not a recommendation for the virtuous life.

The free agent, the self-fashioned, autonomous, defiant being is a Restoration preoccupation, but not one to be taken too seriously. Often the libertine free spirit is a device to explore the paradoxes of the human condition. The speaker in Rochester's *A Satyr against Mankind*, printed in 1675, argues that if he could choose, he would be an animal, governed by animal sense, rather than a human being supposedly governed by 'reason, an ignis fatuus in the mind, / Which leaves the light of nature, sense, behind'. Animals kill only of necessity, but humans through 'wantonness'; man is a pitiful vainglorious creature:

> For fear he arms and is of arms afraid,
> From fear to fear successively betrayed,
> Base fear, the source whence his best actions came,
> His boasted honour and his dear-bought fame,
> The lust of power to which he's such a slave
> And for which alone he dares be brave . . .

And the speaker goes on, 'all men would be cowards if they durst.'[64] The paradox which this poem explores so wittily, was often handled more roughly in satires designed to expose the mindless libertinism of the rake.

Ramble, a rake figure in one of Crowne's comedies, parodied Rochester's *Satyr*, when he declaimed 'the order of nature is to follow my appetite: am I to eat at noon, because it is noon, or because I am hungry . . . I will pay no homage to the sun, and time, which are things below me'.[65] John Oldham's poem *Aude aliquid*, which is 'suppos'd to be spoken by a court hector at the breaking of the [sun] dial in the privy garden' at Whitehall – one of Rochester's more notorious japes – is just as boisterous. The 'court hector' rails against the 'virtuous fools / Who think to fetter free-born souls, / And tie 'em up to dull morality and rules'; he lauds the 'happy brutes' who observe 'the great rule of sense', confined by nothing but their own power and will, and undisturbed by the 'stings of sin'.[66] Crowne and Oldham are engaging with a literary voice, that of the speaker of Rochester's poem, and they are savage in their exposure of the vacuous, egotistical, quasi-philosophical libertinism which it enunciates – indeed many would read Rochester's poem itself as a paradoxical attack upon this libertinism. Libertinism does not make heroes, it creates monsters: the author of a stinging satire, *Upon the Beadle*, makes this crystal clear when he places in the mouth of the Duke of Monmouth a full-blown libertine speech:

> Curs'd be their politic heads that first began
> To circumscribe the liberties of man,
> Man that was truli'st happy when of old,
> His actions, like his will, were uncontroll'd,
> Till he suffer'd fear to fetter him with law . . .

And what is this bold speech in defence of? Monmouth's murderous attack on 'one saucy watchman' who dared to question a drunken, aristocratic party late one night outside a Holborn brothel and paid for his temerity with his life.[67]

True heroism required mastery over oneself and that required magnanimity, 'a great soul', the nobility of soul and mind which Milton's Christ shared with Dryden's Aurungzebe, and the youthful Lord Maidstone may have shared with the French rogue: this was how the dead Earl of Sandwich was addressed, 'Thou hero of so large and free a soul, / A judgment clear, a courage uncontrol; / So wisely noble, and so brave a mind.'[68] 'Plain heroic magnitude of mind' is a phrase which echoes in places in Restoration England where John Milton would have feared to tread. Dryden saw magnanimity in the Catholic suicide, Lord Clifford. Its echo can be heard in descriptions of Mary Carleton, the 'German princess', whose 'tow'ring spirit was too large for her narrow fortunes' and whose location, socially and geographically, was 'too narrow for her spacious soul to act in'.[69] Rochester's spirit and mind were praised in similar terms: 'nor is this vast wit crowded together in a little soul, where it wants freedom, and is uneasy, but fills up the spaces of a large and generous mind.'[70] A 'great' soul, spirit or mind was at the centre of whatever it was to be heroic, and perhaps this was why poets were held to be so good at identifying and evoking some of the ineffable aspects of 'heroism': 'the hero and poet were inspired with the same enthusiasm, acted with the same heat, and both were crowned with the same laurel,' claimed Rymer. 'Wit and valour have always gone together, and poetry been the companion of camps.'[71] The perplexing search for heroism has led us to that maddening term, so crucial to social and artistic life in the 1670s, 'wit'.

2   A Monstrous Witty Age

> About this wit such dreadful wars befall,
> That wiser men suspect, they ha' none at all,
> Or that 'tis grown the philosophers stone
> Which all pretend, yet is produc'd by none.
>
> *News from the Press* (1673)

'Oh, Sirs, this is a monstrous witty age,' begins the prologue to John Crowne's *The Country Wit*, first performed in 1675. Wit was prized in Restoration England and consequently it was much claimed and much disputed, especially among poets and dramatists. Of course, wit was a wonderfully self-confirming quality; just as 'heroes shou'd onely be judg'd by heroes', so only wits can judge wit.[72] The scene was set for endless debate. 'And for wit, there is such a stir amongst you, who has it and who has it not,' runs an exchange in Shadwell's *Epsom Wells*. 'The wits are as bad as the divines, and have made such civil wars, that the little nation is almost undone.' It was certainly true that the little nation of the wits had formed into 'parties and factions'.[73] The 'sessions of the poets' called 'severely to punish the abuses of wit' were given over to the quarrels of poets and playwrights, Howard, Rochester, Dryden, Shadwell, Scroope and Buckingham, and on.[74] The contest between 'truewits' and 'witwoulds', those who had the elusive quality and those who simply thought they had, was pursued in the prologues, dedications, characters and raillery of the comedies. Prologues and epilogues either lamented the critical tyranny of the wits of the pit or threw the playwright upon the mercy of his or her judges. So, in the first instance, this was a contest over wit in writing.

Wit had shared in the critical elevation of epic and the heroic during the 1650s. In the field of poetics, as Steven Zwicker has argued, wit was promoted as a rebuttal of prophecy and inspiration, that 'spiritual fit' which had been tarnished by association with the religious and political cause of puritanism. Davenant and Hobbes, he suggests, offered wit as 'a political, social and cultural stance that would replace the fury of zeal and the destructiveness and moral absolutism of divine politics with propriety, reason and nature'.[75] Wit became a hallmark of the professional writer, a figure who was becoming increasingly defined by notions of authorship and originality. It was the great defence of the literary 'profession', especially when writers were criticized for their dependence upon earlier plays, to argue that it was their 'wit' which they brought to their materials: as Aphra Behn famously retorted when charged with having rewritten Killigrew's *Thomaso*, she was a pen for hire; 'I make verses, and others have the fame.'[76] The literary war over wit owed much to Dryden's taste for laying down the poetic law; he quarrelled with

Howard, Settle and Shadwell about rhyme and comedy, and he was criticized and mocked by Buckingham, Rochester, and their acolytes at
court and in the universities for his adaptations and borrowings from
French, Spanish and earlier English comedies. No doubt he exasperated
many by pronouncing airily that 'the definition of wit (which has been
so often attempted, and ever unsuccessfully by many poets) is only this:
that it is a propriety of thoughts and words; or, in other terms, thoughts
and words, elegantly adapted to the subject.'[77] This less than helpful definition of written wit perhaps simply shows that we must look at practice
rather than definitions.

At its simplest, yet most elusive, the wit about which the poets quarrelled was enshrined in the couplet of neoclassical verse. Here the two
lines, end-stopped in both sense and rhythm, and balanced around a
strong pause, create the 'witty turn', that inversion, paradox, antithesis
or contradiction, which gives the thought the quality of an epigram, suc-
cinct but patterned, surprising yet logically compelling. This is an effect
which is very difficult to pull off; the combination of sense, rhythm and
image is demanding. One striking example of how wit in this sense could
operate on language is Dryden's rewriting of Milton's *Paradise Lost* as an
opera, *The State of Innocence*, in 1677: over 10,000 lines of blank verse
became 1400 lines of rhyme; Satan's convoluted and rhetorical explanation to Gabriel of his motives for leaving hell becomes the snappy
couplet, 'Lives there who would not seek to force his way / From pain
to ease; from darkness, to the day?'[78] Ultimately wit of this kind is a question of poetic technique; it is about the verbal facility, the artistic skills
and the quality of imagination displayed by writers; and it will always be
open to question or doubt. Many Restoration critics complained that the
rhythm or the rhyme carried the reader over some strange imagery or
peculiar diction. Rochester poked fun at one of Dryden's images:

> Mine host, who had said nothing in an hour,
> Rose up and praised *The Indian Emperor:*
> *As if our old world modestly withdrew,*
> *And here in private had brought forth a new.*
> 'Twere but two *lines*! Who but he durst presume
> To make th' old world a new withdrawing room,
> Where of another world she's brought to bed!
> What a brave midwife is a laureate's head!'[79]

Much else that passed for 'wit' like versifying, 'clenches' or puns, raillery
or repartee, was equally open to argument.

The dexterity in writing which was wit drew upon a second and distinct sense of 'wit', wit as a quality of mind. Walter Charleton admitted
that in the English language wit 'is not altogether exempt from ambiguity' since it is used both of understanding – as in a man has great wit

– and of the product of the understanding – such as a jest or a pleasant conceit. Charleton was interested in wit as a mental quality and distinguished such aspects as celerity of imagination, ingenuity, acumen and perspicacity.[80] Wit is 'a perfection of our faculties, chiefly in the understanding and the imagination,' argued Joseph Glanvil. 'Wit in the understanding is a sagacity to find out the nature, relations and consequences of things; wit in the imagination is a quickness in the fancy, to give things proper images.'[81] There was a growing tendency to separate wit and judgement and to associate wit solely with fancy or the imagination. In 1675 Hobbes claimed that 'men more generally affect and admire fancy, than they do either judgment, or reason, or memory, or any other intellectual virtue; and for the pleasantness of it, give it alone the name of wit, accounting reason and judgment but for a dull entertainment.'[82] For Obadiah Walker, wit 'differs very much from judgment . . . that [wit] chiefly considers appearances, this reality; that produceth admiration and popular applause, this profit and real advantage.'[83] And for an artist like Dryden, wit 'is no other than the faculty of imagination in the writer which, like a nimble spaniel, beats over and ranges through the field of memory, till it springs the quarry it hunted after'.[84]

There was a danger that wit would be debased; the separation of imagination from judgement, the equation of wit with abuse, the aspiration of every ink-spattered youth to write wittily, and the growing association of wit with comedy, worried commentators. Sir Thomas Culpeper thought that 'to have the reputation of a wit, as this denomination is generally taken amongst us, signifies little to its repute, because it is rather applied to railleries and satire, than pregnancy and beauty of conceit.'[85] 'Wit, of late,' complained another pamphleteer, 'is grown so wanton, and the humour of affecting it, become so common, that each little fop, whose spongy brain can but coin a small drossy joke or two, presently thinks himself privileged to asperse every thing that comes in his way.'[86] Everyone had pretensions to wit, but few had the ability or the 'original stock by nature'. 'True wit is a severe and manly thing,' said Robert South the preacher; 'wit is a very commendable quality,' agreed John Tillotson, 'but then a wise man should always have the keeping of it.'[87] If 'real wit' was esteemed, wrote Crowne, 'Men wou'd not foolishly then take in hand, / To judge, or write, but first wou'd understand; / Then he, who has but little wit, wou'd know it, / And not presume to be a judge, or poet.'[88]

Wit was associated with satire and comedy. Some of the satire was personal, especially that of the 'court wits'. Many had reason to fear the Earl of Dorset's 'censorious wit' or Etherege's 'sharp, mercurial wit': as Scroope observed 'what you call harmless mirth the world calls spite . . . Consider, pray, that dang'rous weapon, wit, / Frightens a million where a few you hit.'[89] The malicious edge of personal satire might be dulled in the popular comedies of the playhouse: here satire was combined with humour – the portrayal of folly so as to render it ridiculous – and with wit. Note that wit is only an ingredient. The Restoration undeniably saw the association between wit and the comedic become closer, but it never became an exclusive relationship: in comedy 'the business of the poet is to make you laugh,' explained Dryden, 'when he writes humour [i.e., a specific type of comedy] he makes folly ridiculous; when wit, he moves you, if not always to laughter, yet to a pleasure that is more noble'.[90]

The association of wit and satire stems from a third aspect of Restoration wit, that it was lived, it was a quality of behaviour and conversation, individuals not only had wit they were wits. This wit was manufactured in the space between life and art. Neither 'reality' nor literature enjoyed precedence. It was a convention that wit on the stage or page reflected the world in which it was nurtured, honed and appreciated, the 'language, wit and conversation' of Restoration England. ''Tis not the poet, but the age is prais'd.' For by comparison with the days of Ben Jonson, 'Wit's now arriv'd to a more high degree; Our native language more refin'd and free. / Our Ladies and our men now speak more wit / In conversation, than those poets writ.'[91] Wit was at home in company; it was a child of conversation. The affability, loquacity and quick apprehension of Charles II's 'wit was not acquired by reading,' explained Halifax; 'that which he had above his original stock by nature, was from company, in which he was very capable to observe.'[92] Indeed, when Isaac Barrow attempted a definition, he described wit as 'manner of speaking out of the simple and plain way (such as reason teacheth and proveth things by) which by a pretty surprising uncouthness in conceit of expression doth affect and amuse the fancy, stirring in it some wonder, and breeding some delight thereto.'[93]

It was repeatedly claimed that the model for dramatic wit was the conversation and behaviour of Rochester and his cronies. 'The best comic writers of our age,' Dryden told Rochester before they fell out, 'will join with me to acknowledge, that they have copied the gallantries of the court, the delicacy of expression, and the decencies of behaviour, from your lordship.'[94] During his short honeymoon with the Rochester set, Dryden was quick to defend them. He 'laughed at the ignorant and ridiculous descriptions which some pedants have given of the wits (as they are pleased to call them) ... those wretches paint lewdness, atheism, folly, ill-reasoning, and all manner of extravagances amongst us for want of understanding what we are.' The 'genial nights' Dryden spent with Sedley and Rochester were given over to pleasant, often instructive, discourse, moderate drinking and 'raillery neither too sharp upon the present, nor too censorious on the absent'. 'The wits' described by his critics 'are the fops we banish.'[95] Dryden's whitewash will not do. These wits were capable of 'all manner of extravagances', and their cynicism, dissipation and flouting of convention have done much to create even today's image of the court wit of Charles II's England. Contemporaries were wary of them – the pious John Evelyn did not enjoying dining with the Lord Treasurer and 'the Earl of Rochester, a very profane wit' – but they were fascinated too. There is surely a hint of indulgence in Evelyn's description of Catherine Sedley as 'none of the most virtuous, but a wit'.[96] 'The mad bawdy talk' of Harry Killigrew and other blades one night made Pepys's 'heart ache': 'Lord, what loose cursed company was this that I was in tonight; though full of wit and worth a man's being in for once, to know the nature of it and their manner of talk and lives.'[97]

What the wits talked about so wittily was other people. Wit was frequently at the expense of others. The wit of the merry monarch himself 'consisted chiefly in the quickness of his apprehension. His apprehension made him find faults, and that led him to short sayings upon them, not always equal, but often very good.'[98] 'He that can abuse another handsomely is presently applauded for a shrewd wit': the wits' addiction to what was called 'raillery' began in banter and repartee, but soon acquired a more judgemental and malicious edge of mockery and ridicule, which the age called 'detraction'.[99] Detraction was rife at court, claimed Dryden: 'few men there have that assurance of a friend, as not to be made ridiculous by him, when they are absent.' Courtiers compensated for their own lack of wit 'by an excess of malice to those who have it.'[100] Raillery was constantly paired with flattery. 'Railing now is so common,' says Eliza in *The Plain Dealer*, 'that 'tis no more but the fashion, and the absent think they are no more the worse for being railed at than the present think they are the better for being flattered.'[101] Raillery had a respectable French pedigree and a noble purpose. Whether it was being used to complement, to reproach, or to expose, the aim was always to set off the mockery with a show of outward geniality.[102] But in practice raillery had become the playground of a wit that was quick and careless, sharp and often cruel: it was neither considered nor just. The barb was the point, and no opportunity for wit was to be passed up, whatever the damage, whatever the cost. 'I have observed among these witty men, that nothing must stop a jest when it is coming, nor friend nor danger, but out it must, though their bloods follow after.' Alithea recognizes Harcourt as one 'of the society of the wits and railleurs, since you cannot spare your friend, even when he is but too civil to you'.[103]

Other people were not the only target for wit: the 'two poles' on which the wit's 'discourses turn, are atheism and bawdy'.[104] The critics of wit insisted that it was the idiom of atheists, in which the most sacred things were held up to mockery and blasphemy, and a 'fashion of customary swearing, and atheistic drollery'.[105] The wits spared neither virtue, nor religion, nor even God, for atheism was 'esteemed a piece of gallantry, and an effect of that extraordinary wit in which we pretend to excel our ancestors'. Where once only the fool had denied God, now the wit rushed to follow him.[106] Quite what it meant to be an atheist is unclear, but it is undeniable that scoffing, especially at the clergy and the sanctimonious, was all the rage.

The preoccupation with 'bawdy', with sex, was another characteristic. 'The pursuing variety of amours, is the peculiar gusto of a great wit': the sexual activity, the seductions, the adulteries, the orgies, are presented as a compulsive behaviour; and these exploits are glorified into a quest for what James Grantham Turner has called 'sexual heroism'.[107] Heroic perhaps, but the wits did not deceive themselves; 'drinking, to engender wit' was a common enough theme of witty literature, as was the priority of Bacchus over Cupid. Cupid's bow often remained undrawn: the wits were no strangers to the 'disappointment' or 'imperfect enjoyment', the premature ejaculation or the 'dry bob'; the disabled debauchee was brought to 'impotence' by way of wine and pox.

Women and their appetites were a subject of fascination and revulsion in wit literature: 'make the women more modest, more sound, or less fair,' pleaded Rochester. Their diseases were to be feared and their appetites belittled as love of 'fools', 'morophilia', the preference for lusty carmen, porters or fops as partners before the wits. If 'heroic' was applied to women, it was usually in mocking reference to the ability of a Nell Gwynn or Cleveland to accommodate so many lovers. Rochester admired the 'greatness' of his mistress's 'spirit' in loving him, but thought heroism generally an impertinent virtue in a woman.[108] The female body was not the only attraction; lovers were brought together by their wit: 'Let us, since wit instructs us how, / Raise pleasure to the top: / If rival bottle you'll allow, / I'll suffer rival fop.'[109] Catherine Sedley is said to have wondered what her appeal was for James, Duke of York, since she had no beauty, 'and it cannot be for my wit, [since] he has not enough to know that I have any.'[110] Was this the sad reality behind the equally-matched gay or witty couples of the comedies? The illusion of equality of wit was, however, more compelling for Restoration audiences. It was the ability of playwrights to provide scenes of witty repartee – along with Charles Hart and Nell Gwynn's acting – which sustained the craze. The notion of a pair of equal wits was also significant because it accords with ideas about wit in conversation. As the Duchess of Newcastle observed, 'the greatest wits . . . cannot discourse wittily, unless they either imagine or have a real witty opposite to discourse to'.[111]

This deeply frivolous wit was occasionally turned to weightier matters. Wit was certainly a political weapon, even though the court wits were 'errant fumblers', in their own and in historians' eyes, when it came to playing the political game.[112] We know that their satires and lampoons were politically effective, both at the popular level, witness the success of *Absalom and Achitophel*, and at the factional level, where Buckingham could undermine Coventry by his 'personation' in *The Country Gentleman* or thwart Ossory by turning 'all his wit and humour' to make the Earl's plans 'appear ridiculous and impracticable' to the King.[113] Buckingham's malign influence on the King and the court, especially in ridiculing the clergy and their sermons, was deplored by Clarendon.[114] Buckingham's ability to be 'infinitely pleasant' upon the bishops in the Lords or to use his wit and reason to make 'a speech late at night of eloquent and well-placed nonsense' in the hope that it might achieve what sense had not, earned him enemies.[115] His levity, along with his other vices, was a target for attacks in Parliament in 1674. The Lords chastized him for his adultery with the Countess of Shrewsbury; but the Commons charged him with, among much else, a lack of seriousness and a love of wit. The King and nation were in danger, said William Russell, 'from a knot of persons that meet at the Duke's, who love neither morality nor Christianity, who turn our saviour and parliaments into ridicule, and contrive prorogations.' Robert Sawyer thundered against 'this new light, a thing called wit, [which] is little less than fanaticism, one degree below madness: of Democritus's family, he laughs always at all religion and true wisdom.'[116] 'I am represented,' complained Buckingham, 'as a constant companion of drolls and lampoons and as one that abuses all serious things.' His defence was that the only 'grave things' he had deliberately ridiculed were 'grave follies' in the belief 'that some follies are more foolish for being grave.' He wished that his enemies had turned only his own weapons of 'mirth' and 'innocent laughter' against him.[117]

Rather like heroes, wits were more widely represented than experienced by the late seventeenth-century English: few actually got to meet them, but many felt they could recognize them. Whether it was gossip about the latest scandal at court or escapade in Covent Garden, or a comedy in which the wit trounced all the pretenders, or a pamphlet which debated some ephemeral issue wittily, wit was appreciated. The 'character of a wit' was constructed through wit.[118] The prose, poetry and comedies which celebrate *or expose* wit are in themselves exercises in literary wit. And so wit is more often to be found on the page or stage than in life. When asked to describe a wit, or to define wit itself, it was common to answer by saying what a wit was not; thus one 'character' of the 'town gallant' ridicules the youth 'posted to town for genteeler breeding, where three or four wild companions, half a dozen bottles of burgundy, two leaves of *Leviathan*, a brisk encounter with his landlord's glass windows, the charms of a little miss, and the sight of a new play, dubbed him at once both a wit and a hero'.[119]

Wit in the Restoration is the imagination and intellect at work, it is manifest in conversation and literature, and it is increasingly, but not exclusively, applied to satires, raillery and comedy. In all these forms it is mercurial – fluid and evasive – and it is contentious. But what was its significance? Wit was a language of social, artistic, and possibly political evaluation which, like the vogue for politeness later in the century, was bound up with aristocratic self-esteem and the search by newly emergent elites for a social code. What was it saying? Robert Markley has claimed that dramatic wit is a displacement of radical political energies, a natural style for the many diverse voices of the period, and a manifestation of the ideological tensions just beneath the surface. But wit also debunks itself. Wit poses as elitist, but constantly prostitutes itself before the masses; obviously, it was simply a fact that the playhouse was more public than a salon, but the plays, prologues and epilogues, very self-consciously worry at this question of who is to judge and appreciate wit. We have heard Dryden – a leading culprit – claim to have siphoned off aristocratic wit and piped it into the London theatres, and yet all the time wit was being held up as an elite quality. Wit perhaps shares with satire a desire to undermine the fictions of authority without feeling any need to offer substitutes. Or, as Rose Zimbardo has suggested, in its self-reflexive refusal to be pinned down, the wit of this period, and especially of its literature, is engaged on deconstructing all that purports to be true and solid.[120] Restoration wit was a slippery quality, perhaps even more evasive than heroism, certainly more eager to disguise whatever moral outlook it may have possessed.

Wit revelled in irony and deception. And those who lived by wit were endlessly duplicitous, never coming clean about who they were, never owning up to what they had done, and never choosing between reality and myth. Wits played with personal identity and responsibility. The famous Mary Carleton, imposter, thief and wit, paid for her crimes at Tyburn, but her reputation lived on: ' 'twas a cruel fate / Should make her wit the object of its hate . . . she whose beauty lay within her pate.'

> Here lieth one was hurried hence,
> To make the world a recompence
> For actions wrought by wit and lust,
> Whose closet now is in the dust
> Then let her sleep, for she has wit
> Will give disturbers hit for hit.[121]

Carleton's genius for deceit, her inability to remain confined within narrow horizons, was part of her wit. And wit was the great spur to the criminal mind. With his inventive biographer speaking for him, Francis

Jackson, the highwayman, was carried away by 'my disordered fancy' and the eloquence of his own vanity until '[I] persuaded myself that the machinations of my brain were able to unhinge the poles.'[122] Elsewhere the same author explained that every 'wheedler' required 'a good genius': 'wit alone though natural, yet if active, and acute, can apparel itself with more variable delightful colours, and suit itself with more pleasant resemblances, than the Polypus.'[123] The wit of Rochester writing *To the Post-boy* and manipulating his own image; the claims that his 'vast wit' roamed 'a large and generous mind' and yet that much of what this hero wrote puzzled dull mankind: all of this suggests that wit was part of 'magnitude of mind'. But it also alerts us to danger that great wits tended to disguise themselves, and to the fact that this was an age given to masquerade.

3 Masquerades and Counterfeits

> last night was a great ball at the French ambassador's where most of the court were in masquerade, on Friday will be one at the Temple, on Saturday at Lincoln's Inn, and on Candlemas night a great one at court.
>
> *Newsletter, 4 January 1671*

> Masquerading! A lewd custom to debauch our youth.
>
> Aphra Behn, *The Rover* (1677)

The vizard, a mask of black velvet, 'which is of late become a great fashion among the ladies, and which hides their whole face', was worn at the theatre, in the park, or at masquerade balls.[124] Mrs Pepys bought a mask the very day that her husband had seen Lady Fauconberg wearing one at the theatre. It was a vogue at which dramatists and poets endlessly poked fun:

> You meet in masquerade to pass your time
> Without the help of reason or of rhyme,
> You talk, and cheat each other in disguise,
> And draw ten blanks of beauty for one prize[.][125]

The King and court led the fashion, especially in the early 1670s, by attending the usual round of winter balls 'disguised in cloths and vizards' or 'in strange antick masking habits': the newsletters were full of such reports as 'their majesties, accompanied by the Prince of Orange and most of the nobility and ladies about the court in masquerade were pleased to be present at the revels at Lincoln's Inn.' The court also indulged in other adventures. The Queen and the Duchesses of Portsmouth, Richmond, Monmouth and Buckingham were rumoured to have ventured out 'incognito' to visit the Bartholomew Fair, and some maids of honour attended the theatre in the guise of orange girls. Bishop Burnet later alleged that the court was addicted to masquerade and 'people were so disguised, that without being [in] on the secret none could distinguish them'.[126]

The potential frisson of assuming a mask and setting off into the night is enormous. As Rodophil explains when donning his mask, ' 'tis extremely pleasant; for to go unknown, is the next degree to going invisible.'[127] And those who go unknown can also go unquestioned. 'So poets sure, though ill, may be allow'd / Among the best in masquerade to crowd';

> But now hee's in, pray use him civilly,
> Let him, what e're he sayes, unquestion'd be,
> According to the laws of masquerade,
> Those sacred laws by dancing nations made,
> Which the young gallants sure will ne're invade.[128]

For all the 'laws', for all the assurances that it was a 'good-natured, pretty age', masquerade was far from innocent, and it could sanction all kinds of intrigue, irresponsibility and even subversion. Domestic disorders, and worse, might follow on parties in masquerade. Lady Castlemaine was accosted one dark night by three men in masks. Mr Newport was involved in a duel 'upon a quarrel begun at a masquerading [on] Saturday night'.[129] After the masked revels at Lincoln's Inn on 26 February 1671, the Dukes of Monmouth and Albemarle and Viscount Dunbar attacked and murdered Peter Vernell, a beadle, which was soon 'all the talk of the town'. It was widely rumoured that the King, 'considering the many mischiefs that may arise and have lately by persons under pretence of masquerade', was on the verge of banning the practice.[130] In other circumstances, disguises and masks spelled danger: the vizard mask was a sure sign of a highwayman – 'you must, when you are on the pad, have your masks and chin clothes to disguise your face'; plotters and Jesuits were imagined as shrouded in masks.[131] Even in the haunts of fashionable London, the masked woman was an unknown quantity.

Masks were a troubling sign. A vizard disguised identity but what did it signify? Was it a sign of modesty? Or of availability? Allegedly first worn by women at the theatre to save their blushes should the play prove smutty, the mask was a wonderful device for flirtation. One night at the theatre, Pepys observed Sir Charles Sedley's encounter with a woman who sat

> with her mask on all the play; and being exceeding witty as ever I heard woman, did talk most pleasantly with him; but was, I believe, a virtuous woman and of quality. He would fain know who she was, but she would not tell. Yet did give him many pleasant hints of her knowledge of him, by that means setting his brains at work to find out who she was; and did

give him leave to use all means to find out who she was but pulling off
her mask. He was mighty witty; and she also making sport with him very
inoffensively, that a more pleasant rencontre I never heard.[132]

Too often, joshed the poets, the vizard was there 'to soothe and tickle
sweet imagination', or as Pinchwife put it, 'a woman masked, like a
covered dish, gives a man curiosity and appetite, when, it may be, uncovered, 'twould turn his stomach': when Woodly chased one 'vizor mask'
for a furlong, 'I thought I had a got a prize beyond my hopes, proved
an old lady of three-score, with a wrinkled pimpled face, but one eye,
and no teeth; but which was ten times a worse disappointment, the next
that I followed proved to be my own wife.'[133] The fashion had become
hateful, says one of Etherege's characters, because 'the proper use is
wickedly perverted' and the whores all sported masks. Indeed the popularity of the mask seems to have suffered from its association with prostitutes and the fear of respectable women that they would be mistaken
for whores.[134] Wycherley plays on this tension between masked and bare
faces when a group of ladies reveal their sexual rapacity or 'kindness' to
Horner: Lady Squeamish assures him 'that demureness, coyness and
modesty that you see in our faces in the boxes at plays is as much a sign
of a kind woman as a vizard-mask in the pit'; Dainty Fidget discloses that
'women are least masked when they have the velvet vizard on'.[135] This
was Charles II's England at its wittiest.

Masking and masquerade were particularly suited to such a culture,
absorbed by the problems of dissembling and illusion, troubled by the
ease with which roles and identities could be assumed and then dis-
carded – whores passing for ladies, fops for wits and rakes for heroes –
and taking a perverse delight in irony and paradox. The refinements
of polite society, for instance, were available to any who cared to buy
and study *The New Academy of Compliments* (1671), 'compiled by L. B., Sir
C. S., Sir W. D. and others, the most refined wits of the age'. Or were
they? Was politeness open to all social groups? And were complaints
about falling social barriers even valid? When Mr Courtage plays up to
Lady Woodvill's conviction that the world has gone to pot, telling her
among much else that 'all people mingle nowadays' and that 'forms and
ceremonies, the only things that uphold quality and greatness, are now
shamefully laid aside and neglected', the other characters and the audience know all too well that Courtage is none other than 'that wicked
Dorimant', the debauched embodiment of all that Lady Woodvill
believes wrong with the age.[136] The instability of appearances and the
uncertainty about standards of behaviour and morality were accentuated
by the stories emanating from court of the wild extravagances of some
courtiers and the indulgence of the monarch towards such dissipation.
Even the routine life of the court must have seemed caught up in play-
acting: two days after they had revelled in masquerade at Lincoln's Inn,

the court appeared 'in their blacks at chapel' to mark the solemn fast day anniversary of the execution of Charles I.

The theatre was the natural place to play with identity. Both comedy and tragedy revelled in mistaken identities, disguises and deceptions, and, for the first time in England, the Restoration stage was able to exploit to the full the possibilities of confusion between the sexes on stage. Male actors had often been called on to play women disguised as men, but now real women dressed up for breeches roles.[137] The leading actors and actresses had to display their virtuosity in their roles, and some became famous for their portrayals of certain characters or certain types, as can be seen in the triple portrait of the comedian John Lacy. Charles Hart was described by Flecknoe as 'a delightful Proteus' and after his death in 1683 the elegists lamented: 'With thee the glory of the stage is fled, / The hero, lover, both with Hart lie dead.'[138] But like modern stars, to whom they bear a more than passing resemblance, these actors were also famous as themselves and for their off-stage liaisons: Hart, who played Horner, Manly, Almanzor and Aurungzebe, was Castlemaine's lover; Edward Kynaston, who played Leonidas, was alleged to be Buckingham's catamite. Actresses such as Becky Marshall, Nell Gwynn, Elizabeth Barry 'and chestnut-maned Boutell, whom all the town fucks', were notoriously promiscuous. Appearances could be deceptive; the actress Margaret Hughes 'seems, but is not, modest,' observed Pepys.[139]

The confusion between off-stage lives and on-stage performances was fertile ground for writers. Speeches were written for Nell Gwynn which played on her closeness to Charles. The vogue for 'personation', the deliberate impersonation by playwrights or actors of real people, was another example. Much of this was inspired by literary infighting, Shadwell's personation of the Howard brothers in *The Sullen Lovers*, Buckingham's of Dryden in *The Rehearsal*. Other instances stemmed from political and court rivalries: the lampooning of Sir William Coventry in Buckingham and Howard's *The Country Gentleman* was enough to get the play banned before performance and to contribute to Coventry's political downfall. Actors could also suffer as a result of personation; Kynaston was beaten up by hired ruffians after impersonating Sir Charles Sedley on stage. Katherine Corey offended Lady Hervey by her 'acting of Sempronia [in Jonson's *Cataline*] to imitate her'; when Hervey had her cousin, the Lord Chamberlain, arrest and interview Corey, Lady Castlemaine persuaded the King to order her release and encouraged 'her to act it again worse than ever the other day where the King himself was. And since it was acted again, and my Lady Hervey provided people to hiss her and fling oranges at her. But it seems the heat is come to a great height, and real troubles at court about it.'[140] Potentially even more serious was the performance in November 1677 of *Sir Popular Wisdom or the Politician* in which 'my Lord Shaftesbury and all his gang are sufficiently personated,' reported Marvell; 'I conceive the King will be there.'[141] Even when there was no obvious attempt at personation, audiences were tempted to look for disguised portraits of real people. Three days after the first performance of *The Man of Mode*, 'general opinion will have Sir Fopling to be Mr Villers, Lord Grandison's eldest son. Mr Betterton under the name of Dorimant means the Duke of Monmouth and his intrigue with Moll Kirke, Mrs Needham, and Lady Harriet Wentworth.'[142] Note the casual elision of the differences between Betterton the actor, Dorimant the character and Monmouth the man.

Impersonation could not be confined to the stage. There are hints here and there of how the actors continued to perform once off-stage. A 1675 agreement regulating the much troubled King's Company specified that none of the actresses were to wear the company's costumes outside the theatre. Is this to save wear and tear or to avoid deception? Joseph Haines, the famous comedian, allegedly used his skills to pass as a count in France and a physician, lord and duke at home.[143] The rogues, wheedles, cheats and quacks who thronged seventeenth-century England, and especially London, could apparently slip into disguise and into another persona at will. They were as adept at faking 'counterfeit sores' or 'counterfeit patents to beg for hospitals', as at playing the gent or the dissenter: 'being naturally addicted to ill practices,' confessed *The English Rogue*, 'I soon became an open actor upon the stage of the world.' Near Windsor in December 1677 a woman was captured who for six months had 'acted all the parts of an highwaymen, in clothes and accoutrements suitable to the rest'. The adventures of highwaymen and rogues, as retailed to the public, were punctuated by the heroes' assumption of airs and graces, of a gentility, which was not theirs by birth. In *The Lives of Sundry Notorious Villains*, Arpalin could 'change himself into as many shapes as Proteus, being a man that so well understood the world'. He changed 'continually his post and fashion . . . today he was a merchant, tomorrow a soldier, the next day a gentleman, the next day after a beggar'.[144]

Major Clancy, a self-fashioned gentleman who fetched up at Tyburn, was another such Proteus, or at least that is how he is presented in *The Life and Death of Major Clancie, the Grandest Cheat of this Age* (1680), sometimes ascribed to Elkanah Settle. Dennis Clancy was an Irish adventurer whose 'pranks' began as a page when he tried on his master's clothes and could not at first recognize himself in the mirror. There then followed a series of assumed identities, including 'a great man' in Wexford, 'the only gallant of all the town' in Limerick, a Franciscan novice, and even the disguised Duke of Ormonde on a clandestine visit to London. When a gentleman whose daughter he is chasing warns her against marrying 'a man that for ought he knew would prove a counterfeit', Clancy took violent exception against 'the word counterfeit . . . as the greatest term of reflection in the world'.[145] But counterfeit he was. Nor was he the only one. Mary Carleton was a counterfeit lady, a notorious thief and conwoman who had passed herself off as a German princess, had been tried and acquitted for bigamy, and who was finally hanged in January 1673. Carleton was the subject of at least twenty-five publications, including Francis Kirkman's *The Counterfeit Lady Unveiled* (1673) in which she was presented 'as a looking glass, wherein we may see the vices of this age epitomized'. Kirkman maintained that had 'she been exposed to show for public profit' after her 1663 bigamy acquittal, she might have earned £500, since her unparalleled career 'was the only talk of all the coffee-houses in and near London'. But in fact she had been exposed, the counterfeit lady had impersonated herself in the Duke of York's theatre; Pepys 'saw *The German Princess* acted – by the woman herself. But never was anything, so well done in earnest, worse performed in jest upon the stage'.[146]

In the summer of 1675 Alexander Bendo, physician of Tower Hill, protested that he was the victim of the cheats and deceivers:

> if I appear to anyone like a counterfeit, even for the sake of that chiefly ought I to be construed a true man. Who is the counterfeit's example, his original, and that which he employs his industry and pains to imitate and copy? Is it therefore my fault if the cheat by his wits and endeavours makes himself so like me that consequently I cannot avoid resembling of him?[147]

Here Rochester – for the wit was now impersonating a foreign quack and treating the maidservants of Tower Hill – is once again holding up a mirror to his readers and dazzling them with paradoxes. While this supposed handbill advertising Dr Bendo's services accurately captures the tone of the quack, of men like George Jones of Hatton Gardens, whose own advertising dwelt on how his cordial pill 'was counterfeited by so many cheats', Rochester is not just an impersonator.[148] This 'handbill' is an artful exploration of the part of role-playing, deception and even hypocrisy in our lives and in our politics. 'Dr Bendo' offers a defence of mountebanks – 'in case you discover me to be one' – as using 'craft' to achieve some unattainable ability or work some miraculous cure. Then he makes a striking comparison.

> The politician (by his [the mountebank's] example no doubt) finding how the people are taken with specious miraculous impossibilities, plays the same game, protests, declares, promises I know not what things which he is sure can never be brought about. The people believe, are deluded, and pleased. The expectation of a future good, which shall never befall them, draws their eyes off a present evil. Thus are *they* kept and established in subjection, peace, and obedience, *he* in greatness, wealth, and power. So you see the politician is and must be a mountebank in state affairs . . .[149]

Tempting as it is to consider the mountebanks and counterfeits in politics, the secret agents like Thomas Blood, the informers, the bribes and the secret treaties, never mind the duplicitous Charles ('whose word no man relies on . . .'), Rochester is addressing a larger question. We all collude, he says, with deception; we all condone illusion; and we all want the impossible to be true.

'To go unknown', to be 'invisible', to slough off personal identity and be what you want to be, is a deeply attractive and profoundly frightening proposition. Some, like Dennis Clancy failing to recognize his own reflection, leapt at the opportunity, but more feared that they would be cheated out of the very sight of themselves.[150] Rochester, who may well have lost sight of himself during the 'five years together he was continually drunk', certainly wrote of this desire to shed identity: 'were I . . . a spirit free to choose' my physical shape . . . ; 'Cupid and Bacchus my saints are . . . with wine I wash away my cares . . .'; 'humanity's our worst disease'.[151] This is self-abnegation of a very different sort from conventional military heroism or Christian magnanimity.

The Restoration was fascinated with heroes and anti-heroes, wits and rakes, rogues and counterfeits because of their ambiguity and instability. Later chapters will describe much more solid and reliable heroes, men and women with plans to 'improve' the nation, to 'redeem' sinners, and to turn people into better workers, parents and subjects. But this chapter has offered a glimpse of other possibilities. It is only a glimpse because we are dealing with something which was never an articulated programme, nor an agenda to be achieved, but simply a handful of inarticulate or semi-conscious longings. Such yearnings are only to be seen fleetingly in what moves people, in what people laugh at or admire despite themselves, or take a secret guilty pleasure in, and the traces of these sentiments survive only in ephemeral literature, ballads and plays. The suggestions that criminals are free spirits, that dissipated courtiers have great souls, that wit is almost sublime, that a mask will liberate an individual, may be ridiculous escapism, but they appealed. What they amounted to, is another question. However tempting it might be to point out the relevance of magnanimity to an issue like religious tolerance, or to underline the political campaigns of a wit like Buckingham, it is not possible to connect such attitudes to political positions. After all, these were dreams about escaping from politics, from responsibility, perhaps even from oneself.

5

England's Interest and Improvement

In 1673 Samuel Fortrey reprinted *Englands Interest and Improvement*, his tract dealing with trade and agriculture, enclosure, cattle-rearing, mining, immigration and liberty of conscience, the balance of trade and much else. No copies of the first, 1663, edition were available to meet the demand of 'such friends as seemed very desirous of them', and it is easy to see why such a book might find a ready market. Its very title spoke to its time.[1] 'Interest' and 'improvement' are words which fired seventeenth-century imaginations: the 'projectors' and 'virtuosi' of Cromwellian and Restoration England were full of schemes to 'improve' the country's land, economic performance, social conditions, and legal and commercial arrangements. 'Improvement' was a flexible term, as readily applied to draining a fen or disseminating a new crop as to the wholesale revision of commerce envisaged by Fortrey. Roger Coke's prescription for *Englands Improvement* (1675) was even more grandiose: part one was designed to increase the value of land and the revenues of church and crown, and establish peace with foreign nations, and so improve the kingdom in strength, employment, wealth and trade; part two aimed to increase the 'navigation' of England and to secure the sovereignty of the British seas. 'Improvement' could be both absolute and relative; improving the country from the distressed state of the mid-1660s, and advancing beyond neighbours such as France and the Netherlands. The English should not throw away the fruits of war, as Thomas Sprat had optimistically insisted:

> The arts of peace, and their improvements, must proceed in equal steps with the success of [English] arms: the works of our citizens, our plough-men, our gardeners, our woodmen, our fishers, our diggers in mines, must be equally advanced with the triumphs of our fleets: or else their blood will be shed in vain: they will soon return to the same poverty, and want of trade, which they strove to avoid.[2]

In linking improvement, trade and war, Sprat was playing, as we shall see, on deep notions of national 'interest'.

'Interest' was, for all its fashionableness, 'a word of several definitions'. An anti-French pamphlet of 1677 simply stated any nation's interests as 'religion, reputation, peace and trade'. But the more theoretically sophisticated took 'interest' to mean that which serves 'the preservation and propagation' of creatures or states.[3] Their cue came from the work of the Duc de Rohan, first translated into English in the 1640s, and Pieter de la Court's *The True Interest and Political Maxims of the Republic of Holland*, which was available in Dutch and then French in the 1660s. 'Interest' was a means of describing the political calculations of rulers and of nations in their dealings with other nations. This was how the term was used by Buckingham, Slingsby Bethel, Joseph Hill, Thomas Manley and others in their pamphlets on English foreign policy in 1671–2. It was used in a broader way by Sprat of the Royal Society's contribution to 'the universal interest of the English nation' by increasing the country's advantages and correcting its imperfections;[4] this was how William Carter formulated his case for *Englands Interest by Trade Asserted* (1671, second edn) and how Carew Reynell advocated the agricultural, technological, educational and colonial improvements which were *The True English Interest* (1674). Whether applied to individuals or states, 'interest' was the surest guide to success. The maxim that 'interest will not lie' evoked the ineluctable force of self-interest and hinted too at a universe of amoral, even Machiavellian, political calculation.[5] Discussing during the Dutch war the family relationship of the Prince of Orange to the English King, Joseph Hill concluded that 'it must be power as well as policy that can relieve us; and that in the affairs of the world, interest is preferred above all relations; the whole world turning upon the hinge of self interest: and all princes, states, families, and persons eagerly pursuing that which they apprehend their interest.'[6]

As debated in the 1670s, the 'interest' of England was taken to be 'trade', but what that implied was less certain. For some it underwrote assumptions about a fixed volume of world commerce, the balance of trade and the consequences of domestic consumption; for many it raised disturbing questions about the social and economic clout of the agricultural and the commercial sectors: and it prompted thought on the role of government regulation, and the relationship of individual and public interests. Fortrey asserted that 'private advantages are often impediments of public profit' and 'interest more than reason commonly sways most men's affections. Whereby it may appear, how necessary it is that the public profits should be in a single power to direct, whose interest is only the benefit of the whole.' Or as William Petyt put it, 'private interest is that many-headed monster.' The English were held back, Sprat lamented, by 'a want of union of interests and affection'.[7] There was a powerful assumption abroad in England that diverse 'interests' could, should, and, if necessary, must be made to work together in harmony.

Yet all this talk of 'interests' and 'improvement' took place in the absence of hard information about England's resources and economy. When, for instance, MPs debated the land tax in 1670, they were all at sea. 'For a long time the discussion went upon the quantity of acres or of value of England,' recorded Dering. 'Some saying it was 18, some 12, some but 9 millions yearly; some that it was 50, some 46, some 30, some but 24 millions of acres.' The lack of figures for the acreage under cultivation or its rental value led MPs like Dering to accept 'the most probable calculation I could hear', in this case that the kingdom's rents were 'about £12 millions per annum'.[8] Nor was trade any better recorded. The Customs Farmers replied to a House of Lords' request for an account of imports and exports that 'it is a weighty business and for a long time they understand not what is meant by the balance of trade'. Eventually figures were produced for 1662–3 and 1668–9, but no system was established even after the Customs were taken under government control, so that in 1679 the Committee of Trade had to ask the Customs Commissioners to repeat the exercise and in 1681 the Commissioners were still bitterly complaining that it took their clerks three months to compile these returns.[9] And even had the figures been available, there was no theoretical consensus among the experts and lobbyists about how the various components of the economy interacted.

What there was, however, was a depth of practical experience. Samuel Fortrey, for example, may only have been a minor official, but he had experience in the Great Level in the Fens and in the Ordnance at the Tower, and he was of mercantile and immigrant stock. Many of the other commentators were men with years of experience as farmers, clothiers, merchants, bankers and administrators. The practical bent of so many of these individuals can hardly be overstated. There was nothing abstract about the challenges and achievements of those who rebuilt the City of London after the Fire; or mounted two naval wars against the Dutch; or drove the maritime trade not just within Europe, but to America, Africa and Asia: 'their brave and wandring fleets, and boundless trade / Has more geographers and learned made, / Than many universities have done.'[10] While this chapter celebrates their heroic achievements and applauds their dreams, it also describes the obstacles facing them, and it therefore begins with economic crisis.

1 Our Decayed Condition

So general and loud, for divers years past, have been the complaints for want of trade and money throughout this nation, and so pressing are the necessities of most men, that there is scarce any person can be insensible of it.

R[ichard] H[aines], *The Prevention of Poverty* (1674)

whilst everyone hath eagerly pursued his private interest, a kind of common consumption hath crawled upon us: since our land rents are generally much fallen, and our home commodities sunk from their late price and value; our poor are vastly increased, and the rest of our people generally more and more feel the want of money.

[William Petyt], *Britannia Languens, or a Discourse of Trade* (1680)

The widespread sense that England's economy was in crisis was exactly that, a sense or feeling. Contemporaries felt the pinch, they sensed the distress, but they had no precise information to confirm or deny their alarm. No measures existed of national production, coin in circulation, volume of trade or even the population: interest rates were fixed by statute and the prices of stock in the few joint-stock companies were of little help. Some, it is true, suggested that 'the wages of a labourer [are] the certainest pulse of a nation's poverty or riches'; others paid heed to 'the tradesmen daily breaking in the city', or, in other words, to the frequency of bankruptcies; but most looked to the price of land and its rentable value as the best index of prosperity. And no one disputed that land values were falling: 'that rents decay every landlord feels,' observed Sir William Coventry in about 1670.[11] Their land agents wrote to tell landlords of rent arrears, requests for rent abatements, tenancies thrown up and a lack of tenants at any rent. In June 1679 one agent wrote 'that the markets here are so quite down that I am in despair of any rent for you. There was but one drover at the last Newtown fair who brought scarce twenty cattle.' In Glamorgan the livestock market was sluggish 'land being a very drug, and no tenants that will pay honestly are to be had in the country'. On Mr Hungate's Norfolk estate meadow land and pasture were being let in 1674 at rents 10 per cent or 20 per cent less than fifteen years before.[12] Land was conventionally priced at a nominal twenty years' purchase. So land which brought in a yearly rent of £100 should command a price of £2000. But it was claimed that land which would have produced £100 a year rent in 1640 would by 1677 only fetch two-thirds of that value if it could be sold.[13] No wonder that those trying to raise mortgages on their estates frequently found that the lender or their agent doubted whether the rents would be maintained in the difficult circumstances of the 1670s.[14]

Although all land differs in its agricultural potential and therefore its value, in general terms land values in Restoration England were closely associated with the price of the two agricultural staples; grain which fed the population and wool which 'is like the water to the mill that driveth all other trades'.[15] Grain production was one of the seventeenth century's success stories. Since mid-century the cereal farmers had regularly been producing too much grain to maintain the prices which they had been used to or even to make it worth their while. But government could not allow farmers to abandon this vital crop and so in 1656 they were allowed to export surplus grain once domestic prices had dropped to 5 shillings a bushel. In 1670 legislation permitted export regardless of domestic prices and from 1674, in direct imitation of French practice towards the cloth industry, bounties were paid to farmers to export their bumper crops of wheat, rye, oats and barley. The result seems to have been a steady supply to English consumers and stable prices: farmers grumbled – Sir John Lowther said he grew corn simply to employ the poor and never made a profit – but continued to sow grain in their fields.[16]

Wool prices did not enjoy the same protection however. George Clarke claimed that wool which fetched 7 pence a pound in 1677 would have fetched 12 pence a few years earlier and 16 or 18 pence in time of war. The collapse of the price of this one commodity had, he asserted, wiped a third off the real value of the kingdom in recent years. John Aubrey blamed the fall of wool prices for the fall of rents and stated that 'by these means my farm at Chalke is worse by £60 per annum than it was before the civil wars.'[17] Matters were complicated by the wool trade's connection with the struggling English cloth trade. The export of raw wool had long been banned so that domestic wool could be spun, woven and finished in England. To help the sale of English cloth abroad, export dues, which were 5 per cent on most goods, were reduced on the 'old draperies' which made up half of England's cloth production; meanwhile customs duties were levied on imported foreign cloth. Nevertheless English cloth production was falling. As Sir Patience Ward lamented in 1674, a weaving town like Kendal was sending only 300 pieces a year to London rather than the 6000 or 8000 of a dozen or so years before, and the same precipitous decline was true of Lancashire bayes and Yorkshire kerseys.[18] The interests of the clothier predominated and the wool-producing sheep farmers received neither encouragement from government to export their wool nor help in raising its domestic price.

After the fall of rents, the second great complaint of the age was the decay of trade. This was felt 'by many working, and especially by all ancient shop-keeping tradesmen, as the woollen draper, the linen draper, the mercer, the grocer, and others' in the market towns. In the city tradesmen were 'daily breaking'. It was alleged that an excessive number of shops was the cause of these bankruptcies. And there were too many shops because commerce was disordered. Anyone and everyone seemed to think that they had a right to set up as shopkeepers. The easy life enticed young people and the legal restrictions and requirements of apprenticeship were blithely ignored. Nor were the boundaries between the different retail trades respected. In London, for example, the most common type of shop, after those selling food and drink, was the haberdashery. But metropolitan haberdashers sold a promiscuous range of goods. To quote Peter Earle,

Thomas Oldham, a member of the Girdlers' Company, sold whips, canes, sticks, spurs, powder and drinking horns, knives, forks, scissors, combs, chess and backgammon men, leashes, hawking bags and other equipment for hawking and cock-fighting such as collars, swives and heel spurs . . . as well, surprisingly, as girdles. It was, perhaps, too varied a stock to bode well for, when he died in 1672 aged thirty, he was insolvent.[19]

The shopkeepers' spokesmen complained that they were undercut by 'petty shopkeepers', 'for now in every country village' men set up 'that never served an apprenticeship to any shop-keeping trade', and these proceed to deal in substantial commodities without paying taxes. Even more heinous were the 'petty chapmen' or pedlars who hawked goods from door to door and supplied the village shopkeepers. These small dealers were trading on borrowed capital, using credit to acquire stock which might be worth twice their capital, and in turn extending long credit to their customers. 'These breaking times will make all men cautious,' prophesied one merchant in 1675. But he was wrong. Small shopkeepers continued to trade with liabilities far beyond their assets. Richard Grassby believes that while the whole century suffered a febrile business climate, the 1670s saw the credit financing of small scale business at a height.[20]

Yet for all the problems of farmers, landlords and shopkeepers, this was not an economic situation to everyone's detriment. Those who actually tilled the soil and tended the beasts may have felt slightly better off in the 1670s. Overall higher cash wages and falling prices, especially for food and clothing, should have left the labouring population with a little more money in their pockets. Modern economic historians disagree about the proportion of the average budget devoted to food and fuel and therefore about what might have been to spare for comforts. But the evidence of their personal property, and of the production and retail trades, suggests that from the 1670s the labouring population were beginning to buy more of the modest niceties of life such as knitted stockings and linen sheets, earthenware dishes and brass cooking pots. The returns of the excise, a sales tax levied on beer, ale, cider, spirits, tea and coffee, rose dramatically after the peace of 1674 and this too implies that ordinary people were consuming more.[21] Not that economic commentators were overjoyed to see this improvement in the people's lot. It was claimed by many theorists that while the poor needed to be kept at work and fed lest they rebel, higher wages would lead to greater idleness since it was well known that the workers would down tools once they had earned enough to survive. Unconvincing though this analysis may be, it reveals a perception of the labouring population as one of the mainsprings of the economy. And that is significant because of the common belief that there was 'nothing so much wanting in England as people';[22] as the population fell and labour became scarce, the great danger was that the lower orders would exploit the situation.

Tenant farmers were another group that was believed, by landlords at least, to profit from the economic situation. Tenants could pick and choose tenancies: haggling for the right terms as Henry Baker did in Monmouthshire in 1670, requesting a tenement 'at such reasonable terms as shall fit (farms being fallen these late years by reason of the cheapness of corn and scarcity of money)'.[23] As landlords saw it, this was naked self-interest by tenants: 'there are more farms than tenants, which the country fellows perceiving have not so little wit as to make use of the advantage, and therefore unless their old landlords will let them fall in their rent they will leave them and go to a better pennyworth.'[24] No doubt some did take advantage, but for many tenant farmers scratching together the rent must have been a struggle. Asking for rent abatements or surrendering tenancies were hardly the actions of prosperous tenants: in 1672 a tenant on a Henley estate decided to give up his farm even if the rent was reduced 'in respect of the hardness of the times'.[25]

Generalizations about the whole of the kingdom may, however, be misleading. Agriculture, markets and economic conditions were regional, not national, in the seventeenth century. The corn specialists, for example, who profited from the bounties were located close to ports, in Lincolnshire, the East Riding, East Anglia, the Kentish North Downs and the South Downs. Those farmers close to cities such as Bristol, Norwich and above all London, could do well out of supplying the townsfolk with dairy produce, vegetables, fruit and other food. Where favoured by land and location, landed gentlemen might diversify into mining, the iron industry or even ship-owning. The regional differences were pronounced in the livestock industry. Cattle were bred in the north, west, Wales and Ireland, and then sold on to be fattened by grazing the permanent pastures of East Anglia, the midlands and the south-east. In the 1660s legislation had first limited and then banned the import of cattle from Ireland. This would help the English and Welsh cattle breeders, but push up the prices of the lean cattle for the graziers of southern and eastern England. In Kent 'we are forced to buy at dear rates and sometimes cannot get wherewith to stock our land unless we will buy lean cattle as dear as we can sell them when fat'. Whenever parliament debated the issue it reached deadlock: in the discussions of 1677 members' opinions varied 'according to the different interests of their counties'.[26] Where it was possible, as in the midlands, a mixed farming regime of alternate grazing and grain-growing was the most successful strategy. This often went hand in hand with the adoption of the agricultural improvements recommended by the pundits. The overall effect, according to Sir William Coventry, was an increase in productivity which 'cannot be denied by any who considers not only the draining the fens, grubbing up woods, enclosing common fields and commons, parks, chases, etc, but also the great improvements made upon the lands of private men by watering, marling, liming, clover, grass, sainfoin, etc'.[27]

In brief, the economic circumstances of the 1670s were a mixed blessing. What a landlord like Coventry perceived as 'this evil of abundance' may have saved rural workers from going hungry or challenged an enterprising farmer to find new markets, but it probably drove upland sheep farmers to the wall and bankrupted rash shopkeepers. There were no disinterested observers of the economic scene. The Kentish gentleman and courtier Sir Edward Dering offered a full analysis. He attributed the fall of local rents to specifically Kentish causes such as the shrinking overseas market for the county's 'course rough cloth', excessive taxation of the county, the ban on Irish cattle, competition from Herefordshire hops, and the malign influence of London and its brewing and banking cartels. But he prefaced this with a catalogue of more general woes:

> the general decay of trade, especially of exportation, the neglect and disesteem of our native commodities and fondness of foreign, the extraordinary resort to London, the general decay of hospitality, the draining of the fens, the ploughing up of parks by the nobility and the gentry, the want of people by resort to the plantations, the goodness of our coin in comparison to the standard of some foreign states, [and] the great consumption of French wine and brandy.[28]

This long list encapsulates the traditional concerns of the gentry and reveals the confusion of moral issues, such as a fondness for London or luxuries, with economic problems.

Each of Dering's complaints was a seventeenth-century commonplace. And they were all of a piece. For instance, the 'extraordinary resort to London' of the gentry and their servants had been going on for decades, and so had the consequent decline of good housekeeping and hospitality in the country and the spending on 'rich coaches, fine liveries, and a house à la mode' in the city. But in the difficult conditions of the 1670s, the laments had an added edge and were more explicit about the moral failings which underlay the rural crisis. London stood for the espousal of luxury in many ways. The rejection of honest English fare; 'good beef, mutton, veal, and lamb are as good meat as combs, gills, pallets, frogs, mushrooms and such like French kickshaws.'[29] Or opting after a life as a servant to open an alehouse or baker's shop rather than returning to the country as a tenant farmer: just like their masters, 'so many servants are by living in London grown so expensive that the profit of a farm cannot satisfy their expense so that luxury cannot live but upon luxury which must be met with in London.'[30] This was a betrayal of the countryside. Just as it was when the grazier sold his stock at Smithfield and left his money with the London bankers and then bought further stock in the country on credit. The values and interests of landed society were under threat.

So too were urban and commercial values. A broadsheet on *The Art of Thriving or the Way to Get and Keep Money* (1674) expatiated on such virtues as frugality and diligence while lambasting conspicuous consumption: 'can our best-studied fashion mongers tell us what use there is of lace bands at six, seven or eight pounds . . . Nor is it any other than a foolish vanity to treat any women often at extraordinary expenses.' The next year, *The Art of Husbandry* lectured its readers 'upon that inestimable jewel, time, which most people slight, like the cock in the fable, if they cannot make use of it, to satisfy their lascivious appetites' in the alehouse or coffee-houses.[31]

What lay behind all this anxiety was the fear of 'luxury' or consumption without production. The unproductive city devoured what the countryside grew and England absorbed the commodities of other nations without exporting any of her own. In the late seventeenth century, 'luxury' took the tangible form of all that imported silk and linen, brandy and wine, and the English gold which went abroad to pay for these goods: 'our wealth becomes a prey to other nations,' while 'all that our goods and money bring in is soon consumed, and comes as it were to the dunghill.' Temple drew unflattering comparisons between the 'voluntary poverty' of the Dutch and English luxury, a 'humour' which could never be curtailed.[32]

This analysis assumed that a favourable balance of trade was the key to domestic prosperity. It was obvious to many that England had grown great on wool and could do so again if only the government would intervene. First, English wool had to be retained in England to be worked up into cloth. English wool had no equal in the world: Leominster produced the finest and 'in every shire there is variety according to pasture, fit to make all sorts of stuffs'.[33] But despite the ban, raw wool was exported. Customs officials on the south coast admitted that they were helpless to stop the blatant smuggling: and one clothier, William Carter, became so obsessed with the wool smugglers of Romney Marsh that he spent four years lobbying for legislation and then mounted his own prosecution of the smugglers.[34] The law against the export of wool 'cannot be too strict', Colonel Titus of the Council of Trade told the Lords Committee; and parliament frequently debated the problem.[35]

If the wool was made into cloth at home, England, claimed Joseph Trevers, could become 'the general market for the whole universe for matter of clothing'.[36] Why was it then that English woollen cloth was not in fact finding a ready market either at home or abroad? The textile industry blamed unfair competition from the Dutch weavers; the 'intolerable impositions laid on English manufactures by the French king and others'; the English East Indies and Guinea Companies for selling cloth too dearly abroad; and the discouragement of excessive customs dues levied in England.[37] Last but not least of the culprits was the fickle English consumer who no longer wore good English cloth, but imported textiles, linens or calicoes.[38] The clothiers' propagandists proposed that the English should be compelled to wear more native cloth, and that this should apply to subjects in the American plantations, and even beyond the grave – the resulting 1677 Burial in Woollen Act required all corpses to be buried in a woollen shroud and one estimate was that at 4lb of wool per shroud this annually consumed nearly half a million pounds weight of wool. Naturally, the cloth industry's calls for government regulation and further protection against foreign competition were always couched in terms of the public interest: 'the profit gained by working up our wool by our own poor people is almost unspeakable and influential to all degrees of persons in this kingdom.'[39] Whereas if the wool went abroad, 'neighbouring nations thereby employ in the manufactures thereof their own poor, supply foreign markets, and reap a great advantage. Our wool being exported, our trade is also exported and thousands of our manufacturers have followed and more will follow, which will tend much to the unpeopling of our nation, the great abatement of rents and the loss of the nobility and gentry.'[40] Here, as in virtually every analysis of the country's malaise, the great factors in the economic equation are money, land and people.

2 Money, Land and People

> If we were once full of people and full of trade, rent of lands would quickly raise, the king's revenue would be greater, the nobility and gentry richer, the commonalty more substantial, and the poor be all employed to advantage.
>
> Carew Reynell, *The True English Interest* (1674)

> People and plenty are commonly the begetters the one of the other, if rightly ordered.
>
> Samuel Fortrey, *Englands Interest and Improvement* (1663)

Money was scarce. The 'want of money in the country to stock the grounds and keep the markets quick' was only part of a larger problem, the lack of coin and capital for investment.[41] Money aroused ambivalent attitudes: while it was widely appreciated as a tool of trade, serving both as a token of security while goods were exchanged and a form of stored wealth, many people simultaneously assumed that it possessed an intrinsic value. The gold and silver content of coins mesmerized some individuals and encouraged others to think in terms of a quick fix to the money supply. Richard Haines proposed that the King simply call all his coinage to the Tower, and 'three pence taken out of every twelve pence, and then new coined for a shilling' would give his majesty 'five shillings out of every pound'. This 25 per cent devaluation would see off foreign imports, allow English manufacturers to compete at home, 'and for as much as nine pence in weight is made twelve pence in value, no subject may complain that he us hereby a penny the worse.'[42] Indeed the people would have more money to spend. And increasing the money supply, thought Robert Verney, 'will probably make a greater and quicker trade by increase of consumption'. Others took a more subtle view. 'Money is that by which all commodities are valued; and is of no other use,' asserted Roger Coke; 'the most profitable use of money is so to buy, as to sell to profit.' Robert Ferguson argued against measuring the national wealth in money, 'nor ought gold and silver to be excluded from being merchandise, to be traded with, as well as any other sort of goods.'[43] This presentation of money as a commodity was far from theoretical, as both authors wrote in defence of the East India Company which exported millions of pounds worth of English money to India in return for silks and calicoes: this haemorrhaging of specie was a constant worry for many commentators.

The lack of money for investment made borrowing expensive. But this was not a market mechanism: interest rates had been set by law since 1545 and presently stood at 6 per cent. In 1669 Josiah Child, later Sir Josiah, Director of the East India Company, advocated a reduction of the interest rate as a general panacea: 'while interest goes up, land must go down,' he argued; and if the rate was lowered to 4 per cent bankers would soon get used to it and land would soon be at twenty-five years' purchase.[44] Experts like Child, Sir Thomas Culpeper Jnr, Thomas Manley, Benjamin Worsley and Aldermen Love, thrashed out the issues in print, in the Council of Trade and before the Lords' Committee. Even if a lower interest rate was desirable in principle, argued Worsley and Love, it was not prudent to legislate. Holland enjoyed low interest rates and was rich, but it was because Holland was rich that her rates were low. Money, as Waller put it in a parliamentary debate, is, like any other commodity, cheapest when most plentiful, 'so make money plentiful and the interest will be low'.[45] Only a prosperous economy, not governmental fiat, could provide low interest rates.

Waller also sought to distinguish between the high interest rate and scarce money by asserting that 'it is scarcity of money that makes land at so low a rate and not the height of interest.' His contemporaries believed that there was less spare cash about, especially among landlords in the early 1670s, but they were also convinced that what investment there was was going to the wrong places. The convention that land was the most attractive investment available led pundits like Manley (an opponent of lower interest rates) to claim that the 'dignity and stability of land' made it the best bet; so £6 invested in good rents was equal in value to £8 or £9 lent out at interest. But rents, of course, were no longer so good as they had been and there were new and arcane opportunities for hard-pressed investors. Sir William Coventry claimed that 'the great reason for want of money in the country is the banker in London' and he was not alone in his suspicions of what Child called 'the late innovated trade by the bankers in London'.[46]

London's merchants, goldsmiths and scriveners offered several long established financial services, among them, money-lending, pawnbroking, inland bills of exchange, safe-deposits and secured lending to others. By the 1670s, however, more sophisticated banking services were offered by the thirty-odd banks concentrated in Cornhill and Lombard Street. At houses like Edward Backwell's or Sir Robert Vyner's, those with spare cash could deposit their money for safe-keeping and draw upon it as necessary or they could agree to leave it on deposit for a fixed term and a specified rate of interest. These bankers began to run current accounts, cash their clients' cheques against the client's deposit, and issue notes serving as a receipt for the depositor and a promise by the banker to repay. It was accepted by the bankers that these notes would pass from hand to hand as a form of paper currency; indeed Sir William Coventry recognized the public benefit, 'if there be a want of the species of money, as many think there is, by banks it is supplied, paper many times supplying the place of money.'[47]

What did the bankers do with the money on deposit? The short answer is that they lent it to the King at a princely 10 per cent. So the great goldsmith bankers – Vyner, Backwell, Colville, Snow and the Meynell brothers – made a handsome profit even if they paid depositors the full 6 per cent interest rate. The Stop of the Exchequer effectively destroyed this generation of bankers, but not the lucrative operation. Their successors were men even more closely associated with government, such as Sir Stephen Fox, Paymaster of the Navy, who by mid-decade had become a major channel of funds to the government, and Charles Duncombe, Backwell's former apprentice, creditor to Fox, and Receiver-General of the Customs, who was responsible with his partner for advancing forty per cent of the government's revenues by 1680. These financiers were drawing on a wide circle of investors – modern research shows that investors came from the country as well as the capital and that they were regularly receiving 5 or 6 per cent interest.[48] As Coventry complained, the root of the 'problem' lay with the exorbitant interest paid by the King. If he were to give the statutory 6 per cent, then bankers could offer their depositors no more than 3 or 4 per cent and the surplus money of the countryside would once again be invested in buying or stocking land.[49] Such thinking prompted Edward Seymour to argue in parliament that paying the King's debts off would suppress the London bankers and solve the scarcity of money.[50]

At least one banking house, that of Clayton and Morris of Old Jewry, steered clear of government finances and successfully specialized in investing their clients' money in the land market. Their brokering service allowed impecunious landed gentlemen, or those who wished to buy more land, to borrow money from the bank's clients on the security of the land, in other words to take out a form of mortgage on land. Dryden's observation of how the 'needy gallants in their scrivener's hands / Court the rich knave that gripes their mortgaged lands' is a jaundiced view.[51] Clayton was more than a scrivener or broker. He made his clients' money work for him while on deposit and he prospered. When Clayton became Sheriff in 1672, Evelyn marvelled at his house 'where we had a great feast; it is built indeed for a great magistrate, at excessive cost' with a cedarwood dining room decorated by Streeter's paintings of the giants' war; later Evelyn admired the 'extraordinary expense' lavished on the banker's country seat; and in 1679 when Clayton became Lord Mayor, Evelyn was once again a witness to 'the pomp and ceremony of the Prince of Citizens, there never having been any, who for the stateliness of his palace, prodigious feasting, and magnificence, exceeded him'.[52] Clayton and his agents, with their deep expertise in local land values and the law of mortgages, and their knowledge of their clients' needs, were fulfilling an essential role in servicing the land market. Not that Clayton's indispensability guaranteed universal appreciation. His correspondence files and ledgers show that his practices were sometimes beyond the ken of his clients; and his interest charges over the legal 6 per cent presumably did not endear him to his clients. But Clayton and Morris came to monopolize the large-scale loan business simply thanks to their unprecedentedly thorough and scientific assessments of landed estates and their meticulous analyses of their acreage, legal security, potential and value.

The economic relationship between land and money was presented in another light by the theorist Philpot who claimed that 'the difficulty to borrow money proceeds not from its scarcity but the diffidence of good security.'[53] If lending against land had been straightforward Clayton and Morris would have been out of work. Clayton's agents not only steered their clients' business through the shoals of the law and secured accurate and acceptable valuation of their lands, they also took on the arduous task of searching through the Close Rolls and other records for all titles and encumbrances upon the lands. Unless title to land was clear and all claims against the estate known, an inheritance or mortgage could be thwarted or tied up in court for years by the sudden appearance of a long-lost document. One solution was to establish a register or even county registers of land titles which would be easy of access and use. Strongly urged in the 1650s and recommended in 1669 by the Lords as 'a principal remedy' for uncertainty of title, a register was seen by its many advocates as giving security to purchasers and lenders. The economic benefits would be immense. A register 'in a natural way, will abate the interest of money, and make purchases certain,' opined Bethel. Europe and Scotland had registers, and so too did the Somerset manor of 'Taunton Dean (o happy Taunton Dean!)' which abounded in trade and riches, and where lands were worth twenty-three years' purchase while elsewhere they were valued at only sixteen years.[54]

Neither money nor land could enrich a nation without the people to work, earn, spend and consume. One memorialist told Charles II that

> I take it for granted, that the strength and glory of your Majesty, and the wealth of your kingdoms, depend not so much on anything as on the multitude of your subjects, by whose mouths and backs the fruits and commodities of your lands may have a liberal consumption in proportion to their growth, and by whose hands both your Majesty's crown may be defended on all occasions, and also the manufactures of both your native and foreign commodities improved; by which trade and your Majesty's revenue must necessarily be increased.[55]

The concern with England's apparent depopulation is in part explained by the psychological impact of the Civil Wars and Great Plague; contemporaries also believed that 'the young and prolific people' were fleeing abroad to the continent, Ireland and above all the plantations of North America;[56] and they may also have somehow sensed what modern demographic historians have shown, that the rate of population increase was falling.

The remedy was two-fold: encourage marriage and breeding at home and entice foreigners to settle. But encouraging the English to breed raised the spectre of a larger horde of the dependent poor, and so most commentators preferred to concentrate on the prospect of skilled, industrious, ambitious immigrants. It would be necessary to lift the disabilities suffered by such 'aliens', to remove the extra duties they paid, to give them political rights, and, especially important to merchants, extend full legal and property rights to them. And to introduce a general, cheap and easy process of naturalization as an English subject in place of the limited status offered by letters patent of denization or the protracted business of an individual seeking naturalization through a private act of parliament. A general naturalization 'would make us thrive infinitely, and bring in all the arts, manufactures and ingenuity of Europe'. Many believed that religious freedom would also be required: Thomas Sheridan claimed the 'restraint' of liberty of conscience 'has been the greatest cause at first of un-peopling England, and of its not being since re-peopled'. Reynell, that admirer of all things Dutch, asserted that 'free naturalization, and some kind of general indulgence, the bugbear of former ages, is now by statists found to be the great security and cement of society, as well as the aggrandizing of them, to vastness of trade, riches, and populousness.'[57]

In November 1669 the Lords Committee was unequivocal – 'the want of people in England is a cause of the decay of rents and one chief remedy for this is to have a bill of naturalization.'[58] The issue was discussed time and time again. Bills for a general naturalization were considered in 1664, 1667, 1670, 1673, 1677, 1678 and 1680. But nothing was achieved. Some MPs suspected that dissenters exploited the question to press for a liberty of conscience; interested parties such as the Dutch and French protestant communities in London sponsored their own more narrowly defined initiatives for trading freedom and the like; and, as always, other political issues intervened.

3   Navigation and Commerce

Trading is the life of all the habitable world.
John Smith, *England's Improvement Reviv'd* (1670)

The chief end of trade is riches and power which beget each other.
John Locke, 'Notes on Trade' (*c.*1674)

All trade [is] a kind of warfare.
Josiah Child's evidence to the Lords' Committee, 4 November 1669

The decay of England's foreign trade was apparent from the startling decline in cloth exports. 'We do not now send forth a third, scarce a fifth, of the cloth we did forty years since,' Worsley told the Lords' Committee in 1669, and we have lost woollen cloth production to the value of £900,000. Two years later, a submission to the Council of Trade agreed that English cloth exports to Hamburg, the Hanse, Holland, Spain, Portugal, Italy and Turkey had declined by two-thirds in the last forty years.[59] To make matters worse, the English continued to import and consume. The 'French trade', imports of wine, brandy and mum, coffee and chocolate, silks, linen, paper, salt, saltpetre, iron and timber, was particularly damaging, although its scale was rather hazily grasped. Fortrey conjured up a figure of £1.6 million as the imbalance in France's favour, which Reynell echoed in 1674; Richard Haines, however, suggested in the same year that 'we can guess' the imbalance might be 'twenty or thirty hundred thousand' pounds; and a group of leading merchants came up with an adverse balance of £965, 128.[60] Nevertheless these estimates lent credence to the lament that the trade 'doth much exhaust our money'; the lack of commodities to export in return for all these French luxuries or German linens or Dutch herring meant that gold and silver was flooding out of England and, in the eyes of pundits, ruinous poverty would inevitably follow.[61]

Indeed a ruin worse than poverty awaited the profligate English. Roger Coke gloomily prophesied that the loss of trade would lead to the loss of 'navigation' or shipping and then the forfeiture of sovereignty over the seas; 'then read the condition of the nation in the Danish invasion, and remember it not long since.' A man of an utterly different political complexion, Slingsby Bethel, took a similar view. Beginning with the fact that Britain is an island, and 'as self defence is the chief interest of every creature, natural or politic, and as without trade, no nation can be formidable, especially at sea, nor able to maintain a sufficient naval guard, or defend themselves against their powerful neighbours; so trade must be the principal interest of England.' The Duke of Buckingham concurred that 'the undoubted interest of England is trade, since it is that only which can make us either rich or safe; for without a powerful navy, we should be a prey to our neighbours, and without trade, we could neither have seamen nor ships.'[62]

Such arguments were chilling in their implications. National strength was tied directly to 'navigation', the state of the merchant navy and naval power, and then to commerce since the balance of trade theorists equated national wealth with a surplus of exports over imports. Commerce was a contest, a battle, in which exports were the weapon: 'the only way to be rich,' proclaimed Fortrey, 'is to have plenty of that commodity to vent [i.e. sell], that is of the greatest value abroad; for what the price of any thing is among ourselves, whether dear or cheap, it matters not; for as we pay, so we receive, and the country is nothing damnified by it; but the art is when we deal with strangers, to sell dear and buy cheap; and this will increase our wealth.'[63] Profit only comes from foreign trade: 'increase and wealth of all states is evermore made upon the foreigner.'[64] As if this was not enough to fuel commercial aggression, it was a commonplace that trade was a 'lady' now 'more courted and celebrated that in any former [age] by all the princes and potentates of the world'; in *Navigation and Commerce* (1674), Evelyn wrote of the English and Dutch 'courting the good graces of the same mistress, the trade of the world'. Their critics jeered at the 'toyish sophism, when men will compare commerce to a mistress, that only one can marry'.[65] But it was a metaphor men believed. Lady Commerce was not to be shared. And if interest was trade, then interest compelled the English to enmity. As Buckingham put it, 'rivals are the things in this world, which men commonly do, and ought most to hate.'[66] The ease with which such pronouncements were translated into political action can be seen in Charles II's assurances to Louis XIV that he can never lack a reason to quarrel with the Dutch 'such is and ever will be the competition and emulation in trade between this and that nation.'[67]

The belief that England was and had to be locked into a fight to the death for trade, and that she was in mortal danger without commercial pre-eminence, was all very well for posturing pamphleteers or even declarations of war, but it was not borne out by the underlying economic facts. As Josiah Child observed in 1669, 'the trade of England [has] not decayed in gross but increased.'[68] Although the trade of other nations might have outstripped that of England and despite short-term fluctuations, foreign trade was growing. Take for example the much lamented trade with France which has been analysed by Priestley.[69] Perturbed by French tariffs, English merchants spent years lobbying for a commercial treaty with France and as part of their campaign drew up the 1674 'Scheme of Trade' which showed the adverse balance as £965,128. Designed as propaganda and calculated on figures for 1668–9, the scheme painted a very unfavourable picture of English cloth exports to France, overestimated the effect of French tariffs and grossly exaggerated imports. Over Charles II's reign the French cloth trade did shrink. It reached a low point in 1675–6, but then grew so that by 1682–3 the volume of trade was 136 per cent of that of 1675–6. The French were buying different kinds of English cloth, abandoning the coarse kerseys for the lighter worsted serges or the Wiltshire cloth made from dyed Spanish wool. Important as they are, such changes within existing markets pale in comparison with the impact of the new and expanding markets for English traders in the West Indies and North America.

Trade with the colonialists of the West Indies and America was regarded as domestic trade. These were 'plantations' which existed solely for the benefit of the mother country and so were seen as an integral part of Charles II's dominions: the West Indies were (in Jackson's phrase) no different from the West Riding.[70] The implications of this were spelled out by the colonialists' friends. The plantations annually furnished £800,000 worth 'of native commodities produced from the earth by the labour of its people, without costing one penny of this nation's bullion' and since all agreed that 'the decay of our woollen manufactures' had left England's balance of trade precarious, it was the plantations' 'treasure [which] keeps the great wheel of trade going without which it must stop and decay'. The plantations sent valuable commodities – sugar, tobacco, cotton, drugs and the dyestuffs indigo and logwood – 'whereas in our trade to the plantations we carry not only all sorts of iron, brass, tin, and leaden manufactures with several others of leather, silk and woollen, but all sorts of provisions and drink and all other necessaries, which we cannot with any profit carry into other countries.' This author neglects to mention the substantial trade in slaves driven by the monopolist Royal African Company which, for example, shipped 2000 'negroes' to Barbados in 1674 and 3000 the next year and sold them at about £15 a head. But he does put his finger on the paradox that while imports from other countries consumed England's wealth, imports from the plantations 'ease' English bullion and 'by exporting the commodities abroad into foreign parts again, we do further increase the balance of our trade, and make a recompense for that consumption of foreign commodity which . . . would . . . otherwise be a ruin to us.' It seemed undeniable that the plantations 'do not more, if so much, depend upon the interest of England as the interest of England does now depend upon them'.[71]

The Atlantic trade was underpinned by a series of strong statutory requirements known as the Navigation Acts. Legislation in 1660, 1663 and 1673 created a system which, at its simplest, ensured that all goods destined for and coming from English plantations had to be shipped in English vessels and to go via England. Evasions and disputes plagued the system, but it held: and some like Christopher Jeaffreson, a planter in St Christopher's Island, took a patriotic pride in seeing the islanders buy English commodities while 'their sugar or indigo etc, are shipped in English bottoms for England, to the increase of his majesty's customs, and the encouragement of navigation.'[72] Since the first formulation of the Navigation Acts, it had been recognized that such a system would develop England's role as a European entrepôt. In emulation of Amsterdam, London would become the great centre for re-export of goods and materials brought from East and West. This is what occurred. The customs paid at London on imports from the plantations show a steady growth; dues of £46,767 were paid in 1671–2 and of £114,883 in 1682–3. Even more telling is the proportion of these dues paid back because the goods were re-exported; in 1671–2 the repayments totalled 14 per cent and in 1682–3 37 per cent. The story of the East India Company was similar. The company bought commodities like pepper and saltpetre and manufactures such as calico, but paid in bullion since there was little demand for European goods in Madras or Bombay. Once back in England, however, these oriental commodities were swiftly re-exported to the richer countries of continental Europe: calicoes came second only to sugar in the list of England's re-exports.[73]

These commercial realities may have helped to temper the belligerent tone of those who wrote and theorized about international commerce. Indeed, even as they asserted the need to lift all restraint on trade and compared commerce to war, the pundits admitted the benign and beneficial dimension of trade. Every country, like every individual, 'stands in need of being supplied by another', observed Roger Coke, when dismissing the idea that nations should trade only with those of the same religion: 'to restrain therefore the society and commerce of nations to those of the same religion, is to violate an institution of God in the conversations of humane society, and to deny the benefits which places mutually receive from one another.' John Evelyn, writing from a different perspective, nevertheless took up many of Coke's hints about the tangible benefits of commerce, and then took the defence of 'the miracle of commerce' to a higher plane: 'yet we have said nothing of the most illustrious product of it; that it has taught us religion, instructed us in polity, cultivated our manners, and furnished us with all the delicacies of virtuous and happy living.'[74] Trade was England's interest, not only because it guaranteed national survival and prosperity, but because it contributed to the 'improvement' of the nation.

4 Improvers and Improvement

> Many offers have been made of late years for England's improvement, which show that we are sufficiently sensible of our decaying condition, if we could but tell how to help ourselves.
>
> George Clarke, *Treatise of Wool and Cattel* (1677)

Robert Hooke spent the evening of 26 December 1673 at Garraway's coffee-house deep in conversation 'with one Yarrington with Cap[tain]n Hamden who had seen the latten-making works near Leipzig'. Andrew Yarranton had been commissioned by Midland ironmasters to visit Saxony and learn the secret of tin-plating or 'latten-making'. Clearly what this ingenious gentleman had to say excited the imagination of Hooke, Surveyor for the City of London, Gresham Professor of Geometry and Curator of Experiments to the Royal Society. There was 'much discourse' over the coffee cups about 'the great cast iron rolls softened, turned and graven for shafts', about hammers, pillars, hardening of iron and pressing of cloth.[75] And this conversation encapsulates the omnivorous interests of both the professional scientist and the amateur, their concern with practical problems and applied science, with technique and technology, all in the service of improvement. Improvement had been a vogue since the Hartlib circle and others began collating and disseminating scientific and practical information on almost every aspect of agriculture, technology and science in the late 1640s and 1650s. Some of those at the forefront of Interregnum discussions remained active two decades later: Benjamin Worsley, the assiduous commercial propagandist of the 1640s was on the Council of Trade in the 1670s; Petty the surveyor of Cromwellian Ireland was now Sir William Petty; and, of course, many like Hooke who had been students in the Interregnum were now leading virtuosi. The books of the 1650s were still being reprinted, bought and read; in 1673 Hooke bought seven books on husbandry including works by Ralph Austen and Gabriel Plattes.[76] But things had inevitably moved on. 'Improvement' had lost some of its Utopian and religious associations, it had been taken up by the Royal Society in the 1660s and gained from the society's researches, and for some it had become a weapon in the pursuit of England's interest. Yet for all this, 'improvement' remained a slogan of those generously committed to pooling knowledge, husbanding and exploiting the nation's resources, and advancing the well-being and prosperity of the people.

The improvers of the 1670s were a motley bunch. Some were windbags and armchair theorists, others monomaniacs peddling a pet cure-all, and many simply indefatigable meddlers and scribblers who offered their opinions on anything from arboriculture to workhouses. Their readiness to go into print often betrayed their partisan affiliations – writing for the East India Company or the cloth interest – or it reflected an indiscriminate approach to the nation's problems – Yarranton's own recipe for *England's Improvement* included 'reasonable proposals' on land registers, canals, shipping, ports, fire prevention, the wool trade and the tin, iron and linen industries. Beneath the vagueness of detail, the vanity and self-publicity, several of these authors had serious suggestions to make. Perhaps predictably, they often harked after old methods even as they trumpeted innovations and so some of their prescriptions included a dizzying mixture of bans and incentives, prohibitions and liberalization. Many of them were essentially compilers of information and recyclers of ideas. For instance, John Worlidge, a Hampshire gentleman, produced two influential handbooks, *Systema Agriculturae* (1669) and *Systema Horti-culturae* (1677), which built upon earlier books by Samuel Hartlib and Walter Blyth; John Houghton, apothecary and FRS, synthesized a great deal of diverse practical information in his *Collection of Letters for the Improvement of Husbandry and Trade* (1681–3). All this endeavour also generated genuine works of scholarship such as Robert Plot's *Natural History of Oxfordshire* (Oxford, 1676) and Robert Thoroton's *The Antiquities of Nottinghamshire* (1677).

The hands-on approach was valued by improvers. They wanted solid information and practical advice. The Royal Society set up committees to gather information on past and present techniques and materials from the country's craftsmen and traders. The 'Georgical Committee' aimed to compose 'a good history of agriculture and gardening in order to improve the practice thereof'. The improvers constantly present their views as the fruits of experience. Yarranton offered his book as the 'choicest observations after twenty-five years in trade'; Joseph Trevers was 'experientially enabled to speak' on the wool trade after his years as a clothier and customs house surveyor; and 'Captain John Smith, late of London, merchant', based his *Englands Improvement reviv'd: digested into six bookes* (1670) on thirty years' experience of forestry in England and Ireland.[77] These authors strove to be scientific, to explain and record their information and techniques in an objective manner, to offer figures and calculations, diagrams and examples: some of them were a little absurd in their addiction to an orderly exposition through 'petitions', 'propositions', 'theorems', 'corollaries', 'annotations upon corollaries' and much more.[78] Several had unfulfilled aspirations of public service. Mathematician and minor functionary John Collins pleaded in vain in 1670 for a sinecure which would allow him the time to produce a full comparative analysis of England's foreign trade, including her balance of trade with each partner, the dues and tariffs levied and an assessment of rival economic theories. Sir William Petty, on the other hand, had the chance to set down his thinking, but he was an exceptional figure. John Evelyn never knew 'such a genius' as Petty, mathematician, statistician, surveyor, inventor, mimic, self-made Irish landowner and more, who 'outwitted all other projectors'.[79]

Petty's posthumous *Political Arithmetick* (1690) gave a name to a quasi-statistical approach to questions of state. 'You know my virtue and vanity lies in prating of numbers, weight and measure, not sticking to talk even of the proportions of kingdoms and states,' he told his friend Southwell. But this book began in the early 1670s as a riposte to Roger Coke's dire predictions of catastrophe for trade, church and state. Petty was determined to show the situation in a more positive light and circulated manuscript drafts of his work widely; his statistical calculations were always part of a larger political equation, and he appears to have taken a remarkably relaxed approach to the status of his data: 'now the observations or positions expressed by number, weight and measure, upon which I bottom the ensuing discourses, are either true or not apparently false . . . and if they are false, not so false as to destroy the argument they are brought for.' William Letwin has argued that while Petty's numbers are often simply illustrative, he did pioneer a new method of persuasion in economic matters through the logical chain of his arithmetical manipulations of the figures. Whatever Petty's claims to innovation, the airy assumptions about values and figures were characteristic of most of his contemporaries. Yarranton blithely claimed that his proposals would enrich the country by £10 million a year; the backers of a 1677 petition for an act to build 500 herring busses argued that it would save £300,000 a year presently spent on Dutch fish and would eventually produce a return of £2,644,003.

Improvers were just as obsessed as everyone else with the success of the Dutch. But they did not simply want to seize trade and fisheries from the Dutch, they wanted to learn from them. Much had already been gained – the engine loom, floating water meadows, sugar-boiling – but there was more to be learned; Josiah Child, echoing an earlier writer, proposed fifteen specific practices for emulation. Some proposals, like concentrating certain trades and manufactures (Reynell suggested lace at Manchester, knives at Sheffield, sails at Ipswich and tobacco at Winchcombe), would be feasible. Other obvious Dutch precedents were difficult and expensive to follow: Dutch sea-borne trade rested on a large fleet of cheaply built and crewed merchant ships, and so, as Downing remarked, 'if England were brought to navigation as cheap, [then] Goodnight Amsterdam.'[80] And yet other Dutch practices, like general naturalizations or the imposition of sales taxes rather than customs, would involve major issues of state.

Whatever the provenance of their ideas, the improvers sought ways to help England produce more at home. There was a flood of bright ideas to establish or expand the domestic production of tapestries, fine silk, cider, salt, wine, paper, gilded leather, iron, saltpetre, 'Normandy toys', and 'curious earthenware of all sorts, china and the like'.[81] Too much trust was often placed in new or unusual crops. Around 1670 Eustace Burnaby gained a patent to grow the dyeplant safflower – a skill he had picked up in Alsace – but despite confident predictions of £20 or £30 an acre profit, he never grew enough to make a dent in German imports. Tobacco was a crop much praised by improvers, but the Virginia merchants defended their interests, and not only had parliament outlaw the crop in 1660 and 1671, but even ensured the ban was enforced each summer by troops of horse sent to trample down fields of tobacco in Gloucestershire, Worcestershire, Herefordshire and elsewhere.[82] A native linen industry offered a single cure for several ills. First, England could grow the raw material rather than import it: 'our English ground will produce hemp and flax in such abundance, as may make linen cloth sufficient for all occasions.' Secondly, weaving the flax and hemp into linen cloth would employ the poor, curb vagrancy and ease poor relief. Then, home-produced linen would save the several hundred thousand pounds currently spent abroad on all those Osnabrucks, Munsters, Polonias, Hanovers and other linens named after their place of manufacture. Downing rhetorically asserted that £500,000 a year was spent on French linen alone. But the necessary measures were unconcerted. In 1663 legislation sought to entice foreign linen weavers to settle in England. In the 1660s and 1670s parliament debated measures to oblige every farmer to set aside a certain acreage for hemp and flax, but MPs and their constituents gibed at such blanket compulsion. In 1682 John Houghton reviewed all the incentives and initiatives, including 'the mighty things' done by Thomas Firmin in London to build and equip a workhouse, train children and others, and support their weaving, and he concluded that while all 'these attempters' were laudable and 'time may make a little of everyone's project useful', the only practical step was to make coarse linens at home more cheaply than they could be imported and to this end import duties should be lifted from foreign yarns and doubled on imported linens. As he put it, 'I wish we may drive that nail which will go easiest.'[83]

Technological innovation was to be the handmaiden of industry. The Dutch loom (also known as the inckle or engine loom) with which, it was claimed, one man could produce the same length of ribbon that four men could make on a narrow loom, was established in workshops in Manchester and London. The hand-operated stocking frame also spread to middle-sized towns like Nottingham and Leicester and allowed mass production of worsted stockings. Applied science was an obsession of the virtuosi: Petty invented a double-hulled boat; Sir Samuel Morland, producer of numerous gadgets including a calculator, invented a new style of pump and trialed it in the naval dockyards; engines, pumps, mining, ship-building, salt-extraction, metallurgy, gunnery, navigation, dyeing, tanning and brewing presented men like Boyle, Hooke and Ray with a fascinating array of practical scientific problems. Sir Jonas Moore, Surveyor of Ordnance, inspired the foundation of the Royal Observatory at Greenwich in 1675, which was explicitly designed 'to the finding out of the longitude of places for perfecting navigation and astronomy' and for the use of English seamen.[84]

Agricultural improvement had a slower rhythm. John Aubrey was told that in the fifty years since 1630 Wiltshire's 'fashion of husbandry . . . had been altered three times over: still refining.' The 'earliest improvers' were Devon's farmers, those of Wiltshire 'are very late and very unwilling to learn or be brought to new improvements'. Yet improvement was in its stride in many areas by the 1670s and in 1682 Houghton could confidently look back at the progress made since 1660:

> parks have been disparked, commons enclosed, woods turned into arable, and pasture land, improved by clover, sainfoin, turnips, coleseed, parsley and many other good husbandries, so that the food of cattle is increased as fast, if not faster, than the consumption, and by these means, although some particular lands may fall, I strongly persuade myself that altogether the rent of the kingdom is far greater than ever it was.[85]

As a Fellow of the Royal Society, Houghton naturally attributed much of this to the Society's 'profitable hints'. The Society's work was continued by scholars like Robert Plot who in about 1670 printed 'enquiries to be propounded to the most ingenious of each county in my travels through England and Wales, in order to the history of nature and arts', a questionnaire on everything from the area's water supply, soil and minerals to its crops and vegetation, and even asking whether there were any notable local echoes. The publications of Plot, Houghton and others were aimed at provincial gentlemen who, in increasing numbers, were bitten by the improving bug. Several Glamorgan gentlemen were 'wholly addicted to husbandry', among them Martin Button of Dyffryn, 'improving his estate being his greatest study'; another was Drayner Massingberd of South Ormsby in the Lincolnshire Wolds, who introduced sainfoin on his home farm in 1672 and slowly spread it among his tenants.[86] Dramatic improvements were reported: Herefordshire land that had been worth 10 groats an acre under rye was, after liming, worth 10 shillings an acre under wheat, and other grounds leapt in value from 10 groats an acre to 20 shillings when sown with clover 'and nothing better to feed pigs that that'.[87] Not that improvement always worked to the advantage of landlords or others with a claim. In 1673 the owner of tithes in Hadlow, Kent, sued William Norman for unpaid tithes after Norman had spent £8 an acre manuring and improving 'very barren, poor, heathy ground' so that it produced good crops of wheat, peas, beans and oats.[88] Other improvements risked the long-term for immediate gain: high-yielding industrial crops such as flax, hemp, liquorice, saffron, madder or tobacco were thought to exhaust the land. It was not unreasonable therefore for landlords to lay down restrictions. In 1680 Daniel Finch told his Essex steward as 'a standing rule' to ensure that all tenants agreed 'not to sow coleseed or [w]oad, etc, nor indeed anything save only wheat, barley, rye, oats and peas, etc.'[89]

Protecting the fertility of the land was vital, and contemporaries felt just as strongly about conserving the country's timber. Forestry preoccupied Restoration England. 'That great foundation of all shipping; timber, chiefly the oak' was an obsession: their oak was 'deservedly accounted the best in the world and a great strength and ornament'.[90] The nation lamented the loss and waste of wood within living memory and especially since the civil wars. Coke believed that Henry VIII's England had five times more timber than Charles II's; John Smith blamed the voracious demands of the iron industry for fuel. The King and Council, the Royal Society, and the Navy Commissioners were all exercised by the problem.[91] The King contemplated taking the management of the royal forests in hand to ensure proper planning of planting, thinning and felling; and he undertook plantations like the 11,000 acres of the Forest of Dean enclosed under an act of 1668. The Royal Society asked Evelyn to look into the problem and he produced *Sylva: a Discourse of Forest Trees, and the Propagation of Forest Timber in his Majesty's Dominions* in 1664, of which there were further editions in 1670 and 1679. Joseph Glanvil later wrote to Evelyn that the local gentlemen to whom he had lent a copy of this book had been inspired to plant thousands of trees. Popular myth attributes millions of trees to Evelyn's books – the elder Disraeli claimed that Nelson's fleets were built from oaks planted at Evelyn's behest. Gentlemen were not only motivated to plant by pious, patriotic and elegant discourses – timber fetched a good price. Desperate for timber the Navy Commissioners had purveyors scouring Ireland and elsewhere; back at home they exploited a network of local dealers, or even negotiated directly with landowners. Robert Mayors, the principal purveyor in 1670, reported that he had visited 'Reading and Newbury, chose the timber for the new ship at Woolwich, and proferred £4 a load; but they refuse to sell and deliver it under £4 5 shillings', and so the commissioners ordered him to make the best deal he could.[92] The improvers recognized that timber was a slow-growing crop, but did their best to propose safeguards, including restricting the rights of commoners and of the iron industry. But English forests continued to suffer depredations. And occasionally, if we listen to the scholar-antiquaries, it seems that something more than a natural resource was being squandered. There is a hint of lost sylvan charm in Thoroton's elegiac remark that the Duke of Newcastle's officials allow so many claims to cut wood in Sherwood Forest 'that there will not very shortly be wood enough left to cover the bilberries, which every summer were wont to be an extraordinary great profit and pleasure to poor people, who gathered them and carried them all about the county to sell. I shall therefore at this time say no more, May 24 1675.'[93]

5 Resurgam

> When the surveyor in person had set out, upon the place, the dimensions of the great dome, and fixed upon the centres, a common labourer was ordered to bring a flat stone from the heaps of rubbish . . . to be laid for a mark and direction to the masons; the stone happened to be a piece of gravestone with nothing of the inscription but this single word in large capitals, RESURGAM.
>
> Account of Wren laying the first stone of the new St Paul's Cathedral in 1675

The resurrection of the City of London after the Great Fire says much about the myth and the reality of 'improvement' and not a little about the power of interest. The rebuilt city was a 'phoenix', a 'new Troy', a testimony to the virtues of its citizens and the leadership of its King. When the Monument to the Great Fire was raised in 1676 its west side was adorned by Cibber's allegorical sculpture which celebrated civic fortitude and industry, the natural sciences and manual arts, architecture, liberty and justice, all under the gaze of Charles II, who supervised the restoration of peace and plenty to the languishing city (see plate 10). London was a symbol of all the abundant possibilities of 'improvement' in the 1670s: every virtuosi seemed to have a design for the new city; the Royal Society and the Court of Common Council were taken with Hooke's 'exquisite model or draught for rebuilding of the city' on a chessboard layout. The legislation for rebuilding the city stipulated dimensions, materials and designs. Uniform, wide streets were to be created, lined with buildings of stone and tile rather than the old timber and thatch; traffic was to be improved and new market places laid out; plans were made to build London a proper waterfront, the Thames quay, and to canalize the Fleet. Yet this great vision of metropolitan improvement was never achieved.

Plate 10   Engraving of C. G. Cibber's relief on the Monument to the Fire of London (1676). Civic industry, using all the arts, sciences and virtues, restores London under the supervision of Charles II. Some contemporaries questioned the contribution of government and regulation to the recovery of the City. Others were more concerned to lay the blame for the Great Fire on popish incendiaries.

But what was achieved still impressed contemporaries. The huge diversion of labour, materials, especially timber, and finance amazed onlookers: Philip Henry remarked on 'the strange and wonderful rebuilding of it in so short a time, which but that my eyes saw, I could hardly have believed'. 'Nay what is more miraculous I'll tell / It rose almost as quickly as it fell,' marvelled the author of *Troia Redeviva* (1674).[94] In October 1667 the first stone was laid for the new Royal Exchange; Guildhall was underway in December; by 1670 Sion College had been rebuilt; by 1671 Blackwell Hall, Customs House and the Old Bailey Sessions House, soon followed by Wood Street Compter and Newgate prisons; by the mid-1670s most of the forty-one Livery Company halls were in use again. And meanwhile 9000 houses had been rebuilt.

What is perhaps most striking about all this was the energy and finance coming from the mercantile community and the Corporation – as one might expect given the opportunities here for making money. Take the rebuilding of the Royal Exchange at a cost of over £50,000, half of which was put up by the Company of Mercers and half by the City Corporation: on the ground floor of the new Exchange were one hundred and ninety shops each to be let out at a premium rent, 'so that it will be the richest piece of ground, perhaps in the whole world,' believed Edward Chamberlayne, 'it is but very little more than three quarters of an acre of ground, and will produce above £4000 yearly rent.'[95] The speculative builders moved in and got rich: the flamboyant and notorious Dr Nicholas Barbon built houses in the City, the suburbs and the expanding West End; Joshua Marshall, who succeeded his father as the King's master-mason in 1675, built houses and shops as well as the Monument and worked on St Paul's and other churches. Meanwhile many of the more grandiose civic projects remained unexecuted, and even the reconstruction of parish churches lagged behind the rebuilding of homes and shops. We may suspect that improvement, even at this fundamental level of rebuilding the ravaged city, required independent initiative, private enterprise and self-interest to succeed.

The same lesson writ large may well apply to England in the 1670s. England was 'improving'. It did not always feel like that in every part of the kingdom. Agricultural and industrial 'improvement' was often patchy in effect; hardship was common to several sectors of the English economy in the early 1670s; many were convinced that the nation was being outstripped by France and the Netherlands. Yet the English were undoubtedly consuming more than they had before. One problem was that they were told so often and so loudly that consumption was not a sign of improvement. As Joyce Appleby has pointed out, the argument that the balance of trade must be helped by protecting English manufactures and depressing domestic consumption to maximize exports was all very well, but it was unable 'to explain the prosperity and development that had become conspicuous by the 1670s'.[96] Voices were occasionally raised in praise of consumption: John Houghton wrote in 1677 in defence of 'all our supernecessary trades' and luxuries and argued that if they were to be removed the English would all return to being plowmen 'and our City of London will in short time be like an Irish hut.'[97] The underlying assumptions here about economic growth and the reciprocity of markets remained largely alien to economic theorists – 'I meet but with very few of your mind' remarks 'Complaint' in this dialogue. It was only after the Glorious Revolution that consumption came to be more widely promoted as an economic good. So it seems that many of those who preached the various gospels of 'improvement' in Restoration England did so within a framework of economic theory which both undermined their own arguments and lagged behind economic realities.

There was a similar difficulty with the notion of 'interest'. Improvers, like William Petyt, author of *Britannia Languens, Or a Discourse of Trade* (1680), would frequently convince themselves that they discerned 'a concatenation and sympathy between the interest of land and trade, and between these and that of the government'. In other words, there was a convergence of particular interests in a single national interest; that 'general amity and mutual assistance' of these interests 'render a nation happy and secure'. And as we noted at the outset of this chapter, for many such theorists, the national or the public interest *must* take priority over private interests. This attitude appeals to minds keen on regulation and governmental control or, as we have seen, to those speaking for monopolist or privileged interests. But it simply does not equate with the realities of the cut-throat competition between different economic interests in later seventeenth-century England. Other observers were much more clear-sighted about the power of self-interest and the very limited role of regulation or well-meant schemes of improvement. Sir William Temple, for instance, argued that Dutch trade was not the 'effect of common contrivances, of dispositions or situations, or of trivial accident; but of a great concurrence of circumstances'.[98] Robert Thoroton castigated landlords who depopulated their lands by converting them to pasture, but recognized they did it because they profited 'by this false-named improvement of their lands'. Since these landlords also controlled parliament, there would be no legislative restraint, no 'self-denying act in this particular', and so 'we cannot expect a stop for this great evil till it stay itself, that is, till depopulating a lordship will not improve or increase the owner's rent; some examples whereof I have seen already, and more may do, because pasture already begins to exceed the vent for the commodities which it yields.'[99] The final witness is another improver, virtuosi and member of the Council of Trade between 1672 and 1674, John Evelyn, who wrote of his inquiry into commerce to his friend Samuel Pepys:

I concluded it a very vain thing to make any probable, certain, or necessary proposal about trade, not but that it might be infinitely improved, if princes and people did steadily, unanimously, and with a public spirit (and as our advantages, of situation etc, prompts) set themselves honestly, and with industry about it; but for that as things go, and are hitherto managed (since Queen Elizabeth's time) the whole advantage this nation receives thereby, is evidently carried on more by ancient methods, and the sedulity of private persons, than by any real public encouragement.[100]

6

Surveying and Communication

John Ogilby, sometime dancer, impressario, translator and poet, knew what he was about when, on bended knee, he presented Charles II and his Queen with a proposal to prepare an accurate map of England and Wales (see plate 11). Restoration England was hungry for cartography in every form – maps, atlases, globes or even playing cards; for instance, in 1676 the public were tempted with both *The 52 Counties of England and Wales, Geographically described in a pack of Cards* and William Redmayne's pack which were 'geographical, chronological, and historiographical . . . showing the commodities and rarities of each county. Very useful for all travellers'.[1] People wanted to know where they were in the world: they wanted maps of their own localities and country, of their colonies and plantations, of the places they traded with and of the territories of their enemies. In 1670 the Council of Plantations was instructed 'to procure exact maps, plats or charts of all and every [of] our said plantations abroad, together with the maps and descriptions of their respective ports, forts, bays, rivers with the depth of their respective channels coming in or going up'. Once the Dutch war was underway, several maps of the seventeen provinces were advertised, some distinctly elderly, but others newly prepared. At his shops in Wapping and Cornhill, John Seller, the King's Hydrographer, offered maps of the Netherlands and of Maastricht; and by August 1673 he was advertising *A New Map of the French Conquest in the Netherlands, in the years 1672 and 1673*.[2] At the time at least six chart and print sellers in London serviced the market, offering maps as a 'very pleasant and delightful ornament for houses, studies or closets'.[3]

Ogilby's proposal to survey England was then, to say the least, opportune. The Restoration was busy mapping the world, the oceans and, from the new Observatory at Greenwich, the stars as well. Geographical metaphors came naturally to contemporaries: observing that 'maps of [the Netherlands] grow so much in request,' William Temple 'thought

Plate 11 John Ogilby presents the King and Queen with the subscription book to Britannia, in which he proposed to survey England and Wales. Charles subscribed £500 in his own name and £500 in the Queen's. Ogilby's first maps of England appeared in 1675.

a map of their state and government would not be unwelcome to the world, since it is full as necessary as the others, to understand the late revolutions and changes among them'; while in Edward Chamberlayne's *Angliae Notitia*, 'the whole state of England might be seen at once . . . as in a map'.[4] Thomas Hardcastle envisaged a yet larger picture when he entitled his 1674 volume of sermons *Christian Geography and Arithmetick; or a True Survey of the World*. Closer to home, virtuosi like John Aubrey were already surveying the English counties and recommending 'a register general of [the] people, plantations and trade of England'.[5] When Robert Plot dedicated his *Natural History of Oxfordshire* (1676) to the King, he implored Charles to consider 'whether if England and Wales were thus surveyed, it would not be both for the honour and profit of the nation'.

This hunger for geographical knowledge was symptomatic of a wider desire for information. As an inquisitive, 'improving' and competitive society, Restoration England valued reliable information both for itself and for its practical uses. Hard information was crucial whether one was buying an estate, lending money or voting for a parliamentary candidate. It was as necessary to those who wished to argue for legislation or the dissolution of parliament, as it was for the government who monitored dissidents and plotters. An interest in gathering statistics, in standardizing, enumerating and tabulating anything from French imports to the number of dissenters and papists in each parish, was characteristic of the age. It was the interest, rather than the skills, which was most developed. But however unsophisticated the techniques used to collect and analyse data, the sheer energy put into these enterprises commands respect, as does the relentless enthusiasm for practical applications. Sir Jonas Moore, who rose through the ranks of the surveying profession to eminence in the Ordnance Office, published his *Mathematical Compendium* in 1674 with the breathless promise on its titlepage of 'useful practices in arithmetic, geometry and astronomy, geography and navigation, embattling, and quartering of armies, fortification and gunnery, gauging and dialling. Explaining the logarithms, with new indices; Napier's rods or bones; making of movements, and the application of pendulums; with the projection of the sphere for a universal dial, etc.' That 'etcetera' covered a diary, tide tables and a perpetual calendar.[6]

This chapter describes the Restoration's quest for information. It surveys the surveyors of Charles II's realm and attempts to evoke the various ways in which such information was disseminated. The circulation of information about their physical environment encouraged the English themselves to circulate; they travelled around the country and above all to London. The metropolis was the hub of the nation: it was the lynchpin of the networks through which information, ideas and culture were disseminated. London was the great talking shop of Restoration England and it is in the buzz of the coffee-houses that deals were done, information exchanged, gossip spread and subversive thoughts unleashed. So while this chapter begins with maps and roads, with coaches and waggons, it ends with conversation, rumours and the ephemeral talk of the town.

1 Surveying, Mapping and Travel

Booted and spurred, these horsemen survey the prospect before them (see plate 12). One of them holds a scale map of the road in front of them, with roadside hedges, woods, hills, stone and wooden bridges, villages and manor houses all depicted. Their map shows them the terrain through which they will shortly ride, the cornfields, the deer parks, the 'moor with a great many coal pits'. If the Elizabethan map makers had first given the English visual and imaginative possession of their own country, it was Restoration surveyors and map makers, along with coach

Plate 12 Frontispiece to John Ogilby, Britannia *(1675). A horseman holds one of Ogilby's accurate inch-to-a-mile strip maps of the road ahead. These were first published as* Itinerarium Angliae, or Book of Roads *(1675) and set a new standard in practical route-finding.*

drivers and postboys, who made that possession real, who allowed the population access to each other and to their country on an unprecedented scale. These horsemen are equipped with one of John Ogilby's strip maps, a detailed, accurately surveyed, map of the road between one town and another. There had been other such maps before, but none so thorough, and none which were part of such a large scale project as Ogilby's *English Atlas.* This was to be an English-made five volume world atlas; in his own words, Ogilby was 'girding himself courageously for no less than the conquest of the whole world, making the territorial globe his quarry, by a new and accurate description of its four quarters, viz. Europe, Asia, Affrick and America, and teaching them English, bring [sic] them home in triumph illustrated with large maps and embellished with various sculptures of their several concerns, adorning with their most famous cities, and other rarieties and new remarks, the product of our later discoveries.'[7]

Such bravado was characteristic of the man and of the business of map-making and map-selling in Restoration England. The market for maps was booming, but it was not new. Indeed, many old and out-of-date maps were revived and refurbished to satisfy the demand for atlases and wall maps to adorn the libraries of country gentlemen. Edward Phillips's 1676 edition of John Speed's *The Theatre of the Empire of Great Britain,* decorated with the arms of dukes and earls and descriptions of his majesty's dominions abroad, was a steady seller, even though Speed's maps had first appeared in 1611. Enterprising stationers offered maps in various bindings and colours, in pocket book form or backed with satin to be hung at windows, and they imported them from overseas, above all from the Netherlands, the acknowledged centre of contemporary cartography. A correspondent told Sir Daniel Fleming in 1678 that 'Swarts, a Dutch bookseller' had arrived in London with the plates of Jansen's atlas, first produced in competition with Bleau, and had persuaded Moses Pitt, a London bookseller, to republish it: 'my thoughts are that the whole atlas will come short of Bleau's, yet if it have the advantage of new maps and be well printed at the theatre in Ox[ford], as is promised the whole atlas will be well worth £22'.[8]

The entrepreneurial Ogilby brought innovation to map-selling. He pioneered the advertising of maps in the London *Gazette,* the only newspaper of the day, and the raising of funds through pre-publication subscription and book lotteries held at Garraways and other coffee-houses. In 1669 he had announced, in bombastic style, his intention to publish his five volume atlas: by November 1671 he could advertise the appearance of volume two, on America; the same summer he had persuaded the King to grant him the title of Cosmographer Royal and had then proceeded to seek royal backing for his mapping of England and Wales. The original single volume on England and Wales was now to be several volumes, some of geographical and historical description illustrated with county maps, a volume describing and mapping London, and a volume of all the principal roads of the country. In the midst of preparations for the war in February 1672, Charles appointed five peers (Holles, Bridge, Essex, Sandwich and Anglesey) to report on Ogilby's proposal and after their approval he subscribed £500 in his own name and £500 in the Queen's.[9]

Not all geographical projects enjoyed such munificent support from the court, and Ogilby was undoubtedly a persuasive salesman, but what made his maps of Great Britain so significant when they finally began to appear in 1675 – and what no doubt helped him earn his titles as Cosmographer and 'Geographic Printer to His Majesty' and his twenty marks salary – was the accuracy of the surveying and the attention to practical needs.[10] Ogilby gathered information from diverse sources, including churchwardens and members of the public, but he also sent out teams of surveyors; Gregory King and Robert Felgate surveyed Essex and then in 'very severe cold weather' surveyed Ipswich and Maldon. Others commissioned for the work were more dilatory: John Aubrey, who described Ogilby as 'a cunning Scot', was sacked from the job of surveying Surrey after producing only a sheaf of monumental inscriptions, and he acidly reported that Ogilby would now get 'what scraps he can out of books or by hearsay'.[11] The whole surveying process was estimated to have cost £14,000, and for all the generosity of the court and others, Ogilby had only raised about £1900 in subscriptions. The first volume of what was now called *Britannia* appeared in November 1675 and included both text and maps; it was followed a few weeks later by his *Itinerarium Angliae, or Book of Roads*, a forty-shilling volume containing strip maps or route maps with precise distances between each place on the road. These inch-to-a-mile strip maps were more thorough than anything seen so far in English map-making: topographical features were included and precise distances were given between each place on the road. Mileages were offered in three forms: the 'direct horizontal' distance as the crow flies; the 'vulgar computed' distance in customary miles along the road; and the 'dimensurated' distance as measured by Ogilby's surveyors with a wheel dimensurator. Contemporaries often commented on the lack of a standardized measure of distance. Robert Plot claimed that in Oxfordshire 'as almost everywhere else' there were three different 'miles' and while he had taken the 'middle' measure of nine and a quarter furlongs, he recognized the usual English mile was only eight furlongs.[12] No wonder that Ogilby's tables of distances were to be widely pirated by his rivals.

Yet Ogilby faced serious competition. John Adams, a Shrewsbury-born lawyer of the Inner Temple, was a far more sophisticated geographer. For his great map of England and Wales of 1677, Adams computed

a projection and grid which would permit him to map the curved
surface of the country on to the flat surface of his map. He then plotted
on to this map the available data, which came from earlier maps, from
lists of the latitudes of ports, havens, and the entrances to seaways, and
from his own or others' observations. His informant in the north-west,
Sir Daniel Fleming, told him of the places omitted from Speed's map,
and Adams then asked Fleming to mark their position on a map and so
'you will give me a certain method in putting places very near their due
latitude and longitude'. Adams did not know the location of Acorn
Bank, 'for though you say it is near Temple Sowerby I cannot tell how
near, neither whether it lies north, south, e[ast] or w[est]. Your pregnant fancy will readily find what I aim at.'[13] Adams, like his peers, found
distances a thorny problem. He sent out a 'paper of columns', or questionnaire, in which local correspondents entered the distances between
specified places. The information they gave was, as they recognized, far
from precise: 'many of the ways are so rough as a man can scarce meet
with two persons who agree exactly in their distances; besides there
being several ways from many places, one often fancy[ing] one, another
person another way, to be nearer.'[14] The distances Adams gave on his
map are not always reliable, but then his was not a route map. He did
not map the course of roads, but drew straight lines radiating out from
each local centre to the surrounding settlements and printed distances
alongside these lines. In some cases there were not even roads between
these places. Apart from a few rivers and some symbols standing for hills,
there was little on Adams's map to aid the traveller on the ground.
Adams later published *Index Villaris* (1680), a gazetteer of 24,000 places
listed with their geographical coordinates of latitude and longitude. As
these coordinates were 'fitted to the parallels and meridians' of his 1677
map, the reader could now locate all the villages which it had been
impossible to include on that map. But in the same book, Adams
announced his dissatisfaction with his earlier procedures and his determination to embark upon a proper survey of England and Wales. He
packed his bags and set out for the country, and had soon established
a twelve-mile base-line on Sedgmoor.

Surveying in seventeenth-century England was a practical as well as a
scientific procedure. Land surveyors were a no-nonsense breed, out in
all weathers with their field-book and their measuring rods, and little
influenced by technological and mathematical developments. It is true
that some of the century's most successful surveyors such as Petty, Moore
or Worsley were sophisticated mathematicians, and the growing professional literature for surveyors stressed the benefits of trigonometry and
geometry as well as the advantages of tools like the plane table, the 'cir-
cumferentor' and theodolite. Enthusiastic amateurs saw the point. John
Aubrey surveyed Avebury 'with a plane table and afterward took a review

of Stonehenge' with royal encouragement.[15] When Thomas Manley added a section on 'the legal part of surveying' to the third edition of William Leybourn's *Compleat Surveyor* (1674), he stressed the need to standardize the measurements and recommended the use of the statutory mile.[16] But many estate surveys were still carried out by men with little theoretical knowledge or working from books like Adam Martindale's *The Country-Survey-Book* (1682) which recommended measuring by chain rather than angle-measuring instruments.[17] This was very different from the work that Ogilby and his surveyors were carrying out in London during the early 1670s. Leybourn, Holwell, King and others were measuring every house and garden, lane and street to produce an accurate ground plot of the city at 100 feet per inch. Set on by the city authorities and in close contact with scientists like Robert Hooke and Christopher Wren, these surveyors worked methodically through the City and Westminster. They published detailed accounts of their surveying methods, the use of the theodolite, measuring wheel, and chain poles: John Holwell, who measured and plotted over 200 acres of London for Ogilby, offered a complex account of his procedures in the *Sure Guide to the Practical Surveyor* (1678), and yet concluded with a typical appeal to practical experience; 'this is the best and most accurate way that I can find out in all my practice; one day's experience will confirm anyone in my opinion.'[18]

For all their defects, the new maps drawn up in Restoration England helped people to grasp their own country. But maps also reveal how that world is already envisaged by the map-makers and their customers. And Restoration maps exhibit a clear tension between different ways of imagining and representing the geographical space of England and Wales. This tension is exemplified by the different modes of representation on John Ogilby's maps. As he explained, 'capital towns are described ichnographically, according to their form and extent; but the lesser towns and villages, with the mansion houses, castles, churches, mills, beacons, woods, etc scenographically, or in prospect.'[19] In other words, some of the major towns and cities were represented by linear ground plans or 'plots' of the sort drawn up for the Cities of London and Westminster. Such ground plans have to be based on precise measurement and seem to promise the most objective representation of reality. On the other hand, 'prospects' or views of villages and mansions, towns and churches, are a prey to artistic licence. Yet some might ask whether one could more easily recognize a place from a prospect or from a ground plan, whether a picture postcard or a street-plan is a better guide to a visitor?[20] There were, of course, very practical reasons for retaining this mixture of conventions: maps were too small and printing too poor to offer an Ordnance Survey style ground plan for every settlement on a map, never mind the fact that few places had as yet been properly surveyed. On his

maps (which offered neither prospect nor ground plans), John Adams
was troubled by the difficulty of distinguishing cities, shire towns, market
towns and villages and came up with a cumbersome mixture of different fonts and symbols:

> The greatest inconvenience I lie under is that some villages have seats of
> noblemen, baronets, knights and gentlemen and by consequence should
> have four symbols or more. Dover has a right to four symbols. First it sends
> two barons to parliament; second, it is a seaport town; thirdly, 'tis a post
> town; and fourth [it] has several seats of gent[ry].[21]

County historians like Dugdale and Thoroton decorated their road maps
with views of great houses or towns. Plot's map of Oxfordshire makes
qualitative judgements: any village with less than ten houses is not
included on the map; but the map does key the county seats of the gentry
to their coats of arms which decorate the borders of the map.

Restoration maps bear the marks of their own production: the people
who paid for them, those who subscribed to the ventures of an Ogilby
or an Adams, expected to see not only their name in the list of subscribers at the front of the atlas or book, but also their house promi-
nently marked, possibly depicted, and identified by their name on the
map itself. When Sir Daniel Fleming of Rydal Hall, Cumbria, found that
he and his house had been missed off Moses Pitt's new map, he hit the
roof. He was soon assured that 'Mr Pitt has been severely chidden for
omitting your quality and dwelling house and, though "Hall" is omitted,
in all other things it is in the book as you direct.'[22] Even the map of
Ogilby's exact survey of London included identifications not only of
public buildings but also of the private homes of several aldermen
who had helped fund the work. Geometry and precision could not be
allowed to outweigh the claims of patronage, status and pride when it
came to mapping the world of Restoration England.

This was also an intensely provincial world, and since identity and
status were primarily local, it was expected that cartography should
reflect this order of priorities. The chorography of Tudor and early
Stuart England had done, but by the later seventeenth century this tradition of delineating a particular region was on the wane. Not everyone
would go so far as Professor Chambers who suggests that Ogilby established a new sense of place, 'the old chorography attached to the new
geometry of surveyed maps', but his maps certainly exhibit a tension
between different procedures – the figurative and the qualitative – and
different concerns – the national and the provincial.[23] The national perspective seemed dominated by the capital.

The centrality of London is unmistakeable on Restoration maps. The
roads radiate out from the metropolis on Adams's map and the major

routes of Ogilby's strip maps begin in London. On the maps, and perhaps in people's imaginations, London looks like the hub of a great spoked wheel. Along the great roads flowed goods, material, people and information. On 14 August 1671 Philip Henry and friends set out on horseback from Shropshire and arrived in London on the 18th, having travelled via Wolverhampton, Coventry, Stony Stratford and Barnet, 'the ways fair and the weather favourable beyond expectation'. The ways were not always so fair: the year before Sir Robert Southwell's coach had 'sailed to Newark through a sea of waters' and then became stranded with a broken axle at Stamford.[24] Land carriage from London to the counties grew remarkably from the 1630s to 1680 and even more in the next thirty years. During the Restoration much of this growth can be attributed to the rise in the carrying trade between London and its adjacent counties. Contemporaries were particularly struck by the advent of the stage coach. It was claimed in 1672 that stages coaches from London to all the principal towns of the kingdom had been established in the last thirty years and many very recently: 'now all the great towns have set up stage coaches, and every little town within twenty miles of London swarms with them.'[25] In 1680 Philip Henry rode down to London from Shropshire, but returned on the Chester coach at a cost of £1 15 shillings and 12 shillings travelling charges. There were four coaches a day from London to Windsor and Reading, ten to St Albans; a one day service between London and Oxford was introduced in 1670. In 1678 a four-day stage coach between York and London was advertised: it set out from each terminus three times a week; leaving York at 6.00 a.m., it reached Doncaster on the first morning, Newark by lunchtime of the second day, Stamford that evening and London two days later. By 1681 London was linked to eighty-eight towns by stage coach. Fares to Exeter, Chester or York were 40 shillings in summer and 45 in winter, plus tips and the cost of subsistence; the fare to Bristol was 25 shillings, to Bath and Salisbury 20, to Northampton 16, and to Reading 7.[26]

Not everyone welcomed the stage coach. John Cresset, like John Adams a member of the Inner Temple, waged a paper war against stage coaches in the early 1670s.[27] He petitioned parliament, published tracts and lobbied for their suppression, especially in the immediate neighbourhood of the capital. What seems to have begun as a campaign in concert with the innkeepers who were losing trade, became in some of his petitions a full scale diagnosis of the country's economic malaise and the contribution of the stage coach to the crisis of English agriculture, horse-breeding, horsemanship, livery, the farrier's calling and much else. Cresset's message was amplified by other authors, including George Clarke, who claimed the growth of coaches 'is so injurious and destructive both to our breed[ing] of horses, and to all inns upon the roads, and at London too, that it may well be reckoned among the public griev-ances of the nation, and bears a considerable part in the fall and great abatements of our rents'.[28]

Cresset circulated his letters against stage coaches to the provincial postmasters, who were often also innkeepers, in the hope of enlisting their support. He claimed that since the coaches carried 'multitudes' of private letters they undermined the post office and its profits. It is true that many private routes and informal networks were used to send letters: the banker Clayton sent letters out to Windsor and Staines on the Egham coach from the White Hart in the Strand, and entrusted his Kent letters to the water carriers at the Queen's Head in Billingsgate. Lord Thanet was convinced that most letters sent by the Canterbury post 'miscarry' and so urged his correspondents to use the more reliable carrier whose porter 'may be found at the May Pole in the Strand' every Thursday about seven o'clock. There was no guarantee that any letter would arrive: in 1670 Aubrey lamented that he had sent a letter to Wood in Oxford 'by the coachman; I never heard from you since and there-fore suspect that he being then drunk, lost it.'[29] Yet, in general, the post office, first established in the 1630s, offered by our period an efficient national service, with letters leaving London on Tuesday, Thursday and Saturday night, and arriving at the London letter office on Monday, Wednesday and Friday. Mail cost 2 pence if sent to a destination within a radius of eighty miles, 3 pence if sent further, 4 pence to Scotland and 6 pence to Ireland; and this could be either prepaid or paid by the re-cipient when the letter was collected from the postmaster. The mail was carried by postboys riding on a relay of horses along the six great roads, to Holyhead, Bristol, Plymouth, Edinburgh, Yarmouth and Dover, at a stipulated rate of one hundred and twenty miles a day, which ensured that a letter from London reached Plymouth in three days and Edin-burgh in five. Post to European destinations left the London letter office twice weekly.[30]

The traffic in letters and people and goods between London and the provinces is not easily quantified, but it can be judged from the very fact of so many postboys, coaches and waggons making their way across Restoration England. Stuck in London during the parliamentary session, Sir Edward Harley kept up a regular correspondence with his wife in Herefordshire, sending three or more letters each week 'to be left with the postmaster at Ludlow'; when Sir Edward missed the post, it cost him 18 pence to have the letter sent on.[31] The bill for letters received at Swarthmoor Hall in Lancashire during one year was £7. And it was not only letters, of course, which circulated as far as remote Swarth-moor. Casks of wine arrived there on the carrier's wagon from the port of Newcastle via Kendal; other shopping was carried from Lancaster across two estuaries; in 1677 George Fox sent cheese and, significantly,

maps from Holland.[32] Sir Daniel Fleming had atlases sent from London
up to Cumbria by the carrier, because 'the box being so very large both
as to breadth and length and so extraordinary heavy' that it could not
be managed by a man on horseback.[33] At a much humbler level, the
spread of small luxuries like linen, haberdashery and ready-made goods,
such as gloves, stockings or handkerchiefs, among working people in the
later seventeenth century is evidence of more economic transactions
and more traffic on the lanes and roads. These domestic and personal
items were hawked from door to door by petty chapmen who usually
travelled on foot or horseback.[34] Nor is it fanciful to see the boom in
highway robbery as evidence of a sort for increased mobility among
England's population.

All of this suggests a well-developed road system with wagons and
coaches, horsemen and pedestrians thronging the king's highway, and
moving ceaselessly along the roads which lead to and from London. We
should not forget the cross-country traffic, the many local journeys and
errands which presumably made up the vast majority of movements.
Ogilby's volume of strip maps may have given pride of place to the thirty-
two roads radiating out from London, but it included another thirty-one
'cross independent' roads running, for example, between Bristol and
Chester or Gloucester and Coventry, and twenty 'accidental' roads like
that between Chelmsford and Maldon. Perhaps the road map of Restoration England was more reminiscent of a spider's web than a spoked
wheel. Yet the pull of the metropolis was powerful; it dragged people
down the rolling roads and into its maw, growing at the expense of the
rest of the country. Roads did begin and end in London for many of
Charles II's subjects: the fabulous City enticed them; for some it was their
only hope of bettering themselves; for others the 'Town' was always the
centre to which their minds returned when 'imprisoned' in the country
or provinces.

2 Metropolis: City, Town and Country

> If your lordship had been in town, and I in the country, I durst not have
> entertained you, with three pages of a letter; but I know they are very ill
> things which can be tedious to a man who is fourscore miles from Covent
> Garden.
>
> John Dryden to the Earl of Rochester, 1673

> The Worlds Chief Mart, Rich Christendoms Rare Inn,
> From which all Cities doth the Garland win:
> . . . Nor on Earths Globe, is there a City can
> Compare to Brittains Metropolitan.
>
> George Eliott, *Great Brittains Beauty;*
> *or Londons Delight* (1671)

That place of sin and seal coal . . . there's pride, popery, folly, lust, prodigality, cheating knave and jilting whores . . .

Thomas Shadwell, Epsom Wells (1672)

London's fascination lay in the fact that it was more than a city, it was a
one-off, a wonder, a phoenix, a metropolis, an imperial capital. 'London
the great Emporeum of the World' brought together all the fruits of the
globe and bounteously redistributed them to the English and to other
nations. The poets talked of the City of London as a land flowing with
milk and honey. In the 1673 Lord Mayor's pageant for the grocer Sir
William Hooker, 'a Negro-boy, beautifully black' sat atop a figure of a
camel 'betwixt two silver panniers that are fraught with several sorts of
fruits, as raisins, almonds, figs, dates, prunes' which he scattered among
the people.[35] Not only was London a commercial entrepôt, it was also
the centre of legal, medical, scientific, financial and artistic expertise.
Every service was for sale in the capital. It is an historical truism that the
most administratively decentralized state in Europe was also one in
which the capital monopolized much of the country's political, legal,
financial and cultural life. London was the clearing house for information of all kinds and the nation's employment bureau. Since it dwarfed
all other English cities, the metropolis sucked in immigrants: the population had grown by perhaps a hundred thousand during the 1660s until
it had topped the half million mark. The capital distorted the economies
of the satellite towns which supplied it with food, fuel and people. It
drew the very water out of the hills to its north to feed the conduits at
New River Head and Jack Straw's Castle in Islington.

London was a diverse, shimmering, contradictory place; as Henry
Savile wrote to his friend Rochester in the country, 'the noble variety of
this town, which stands just where it did, is full as foolish, and full as
wise, full as formal, and full as impertinent as you left it, there is no one
contradiction you left in it but you will find again at your return.'[36] The
sheer magnificence of the metropolis, the grandeur of its public buildings, the speed of its rebuilding after the Fire, the opulence of its merchants, had to be set against its dark allies, its teeming suburbs, its
violence and its poverty; the style of its leisured inhabitants, the ingenuity of its virtuosi, the prevalence of piety and preaching, were all to
be weighed against the debauchery, vice and ignorance of the city's
underworld.

Unique and various, then, but London was also strangely familiar to
the rest of the country. Numerous individuals had lived or worked there
temporarily as servants or apprentices or visited in pursuit of some
private business; others had gone to make their fortune or simply to
experience the city. Many a latter-day Dick Whittington must have
gawped at the sights of the crowded streets. 'Walking in London differs

much from doing so in the country,' explained the well-travelled John Verney to his father. 'The roughness of the treading, the rubbing by people, and the bustle of 'em wearies the body and giddies . . . the head.' London's spell was also a product of its reputation. Its gold-paved streets, its Tower and port and Lord Mayor, the notorious dangers of its cheats and hectors, 'those that do live and prey without pretence / On boyish and on country innocence', were the stuff of ballad, rogue literature and folk tale.[37] If they listened to their preachers the English would also have learned to see London as a moral representative of the nation, a sinful Sodom divinely punished by fire and pestilence.

London was known, too, because it had been endlessly 'surveyed'. Each of its twenty-six wards had been surveyed in prose by John Stow at the beginning of the century; the city was anatomized in verse by Dryden and in more hackneyed works like *Troia Rediviva, or, the Glories of London Surveyed in an Heroic Poem* (1674) or *The Renowned City of London Surveyed and Illustrated* (1670); and, of course, the city was portrayed in views, prospects, panoramas and maps. Map- and print-sellers happily recycled earlier works: Dankaerts's map dating from the 1630s was reissued in 1675 and 1716. Maps of London were generally map views such as those executed by Wenceslas Hollar or Richard Newcourt in the 1650s. The Fire gave new impetus to the mapping of the city: some commercially-minded individuals, usually based in Amsterdam, published maps of the extent of the devastation; others were set to work on producing 'an exact survey of the streets, lanes and churches contained within the ruins of the city of London'; and in due course maps were offered of the rebuilt city, such as *Englands Glory* (1676), intended as 'a guide for strangers and such as are not well acquainted herein to direct them from place to place'.[38] But it was, predictably, John Ogilby who offered 'the most accurate survey of the City of London and the Liberties thereof than has hitherto been done' and who promised an ichnographic map of the City's twenty-six wards, a scenography of eminent buildings and a prose description.[39] The common council gave him its support and urged the companies and citizens to back the project too. Led by Leybourn, Ogilby's team had produced their accurate survey at one hundred feet per inch by 1674, but it was not until 26 October 1676 that the finished engraved map on twenty sheets was displayed to the aldermen.

Surveys, maps and 'prospects' only captured the changing city momentarily. The protean metropolis never stood still. From the ashes of the Fire arose a new City of stone and brick, of wider, cleaner streets. As a ballad *Upon Sight of Londons Stately New Buildings* (1672) asked,

> O Thrice Illustrious Famous City London
> What Tongue can say that ere thou yet were undon!
> Or who can think that thou ever so shalt be,
> Since Fire, which All Consume, Increaseth Thee. . . .

Inferiour unto None, before thou wert,
But now the Glory of the World thou art:
That far transcends that Phoenix which of old
In Antient stories to us have been told.

But the city's contradictions were never to be denied. It remained a dark, dirty, industrial city: the smoke of the sea coal burnt in its hearths and workshops blackened the stately new buildings; its labouring poor crowded into tenements behind the rebuilt houses. More than 40 per cent of the city's labour force was engaged in manufacturing; they worked in textiles and clothing, in silk-throwing, in the docks, in clock-making, brewing, baking, metalwork, tanning, soap-making or in one of the fifty or more sugar refineries. These industries and their noisome and dangerous by-products spilled out into the teeming suburbs beyond the walls like St Giles Cripplegate. Even getting around the crowded city was difficult and dangerous. There were four hundred hackney coaches for hire, but at 18 pence for the shortest journey, they were beyond most Londoners' pockets, as were the few equally expensive sedan chairs, so most people simply walked.[40] In the day, the crowds and dirt were the main obstacle; at night the streets could be dark and dangerous, and one hired a 'link boy' to light the way. The Thames remained the city's main artery: there were a thousand two-oared skiffs plying for hire which could take people up or down river or, since there was still only one bridge linking the City and Southwark, to the south bank.

While the City of London was rebuilt a second and very different city was created to the west: between the City and Westminster was built the modern West End of residential terraces and squares. It was the obvious location. As Sir William Petty explained 'because the winds blowing near three fourths of the year from the west, the dwellings of the west end are so much more free from the fumes, steams and stinks of the whole easterly pile; which when the sea coal is burnt is a great matter.'[41] Much of the land was originally occupied by gardens and by the aristocratic palaces which lined the Strand. These were torn down – only twenty-two remained by 1682 – and in their place rose tenement buildings and commercial premises such as shops, warehouse and breweries. The New Exchange with its arcade and galleries of shops was built on the south side of the Strand, so too was the Dorset Garden theatre. In 1670 the Earl of Leicester was licensed to build what became Leicester Square, Lisle Street and King (later Soho) Square. Charles Lord Gerrard developed Gerrard Street. Old Compton Street dates from the same decade; the Earl of St Albans' St James's Square and the Earl of Southampton's Bloomsbury Square were slightly earlier. In 1674 Sir Edward Dering, Kentish landowner and minor official, built a house in Great Russell Street, Bloomsbury, and let it to the Countess of Middleton for twenty-one years at £70 a year; the following summer he built another for himself in the same street; but by 1679 he had built a house in Gerrard Street and moved there.[42] In these new, fashionable, residential squares the nobility and the gentry often rented town houses rather than maintain their own establishments. They were followed by retailers like mercers, lace and silk men who opened up shop in Covent Garden, and Bedford, Henrietta and King Streets, and their 'shops were so resorted unto by the nobility and gentry, in their coaches, that oft times the streets were so stopped up' that pedestrians could not pass.[43] Leisure facilities were concentrated in this new district. Not only shops, but parks like Pall Mall, Hyde Park, St James's Park, the two theatres, and the coffee-houses and taverns, made the West End the epicentre of elegant and fashionable life. Very few, however, of the merchant elite of the City of London could be persuaded to move here; some of those with a gentry background or aspirations set up home in Hatton Gardens, a suburban development which was strategically placed between the City and the West End: but in general the segregation of the denizens of the City and of the West End was just one more inescapable contradiction of the metropolis.

Contemporaries liked to talk of the 'Town' and the 'City', but these were places of the imagination. The distinction between the City and what had long been known as the 'Town' was deep and complex. If one listened to the dramatists, the City was to be identified with the hard-headed, even grasping, merchants, who were usually dull, covetous, and hypocritical, with insubordinate apprentices and employees and frivolous and frumpy wives. The 'Town' meanwhile was equated with wit and gentility, but also with slavish fashion, empty-headed rowdies, conmen and whores. The pamphleteers and poets wrote confidently of the characters of the Town wit, hero, gallant, hector or miss, and derided the 'cit'. These are caricatures and comic 'types', easy targets and stereotypes – 'he's as jealous of her as a Cheapside husband of a Covent Garden wife'.[44] The 'City' was the place of work and business and therefore perhaps more easily located within the City of London. The 'Town', on the other hand, was the arena of display and consumption. Physically centred on the West End, in Covent Garden, the coffee-houses, the theatres, the parks and pleasure gardens, but also encompassing the stews and alehouses of the City, the 'Town' was imaginatively located in a space also known as 'Covent Garden' or the 'Mulberry Garden' where men of leisure and women of spirit pursued their amours. This was a world apparently detached from commerce or farming, religion, politics, court or parliament, or all the other humdrum concerns of the majority of the population. Consumption was the business of 'Town' life, largely because it spoke of wealth and gentility. So off trooped the ladies and gentlemen of fashion to their tailors and milliners, to the theatres, to the pleasure gardens, to the fancy French meals of 'ragoos' and 'kickshaws' at Locketts in Charing Cross or to buy the sixpenny China oranges (which were in fact from Portugal). They organized their own entertainments, balls and visits, gambling and affairs. The gentlemen had mistresses but also availed themselves of the whores of Covent Garden or Whetbury Park. The bathhouse offered another sensual pleasure. City merchants who had experienced baths in Turkey built the Royal Bagnio in Newgate Street for 'sweating, rubbing, shaving, hot-bathing, and cupping, after the Turkish model' while the Duke's Bagnio was to be found in Long Acre.[45]

Whether it was at the theatre, tavern, coffee-house, bathhouse or brothel, the inhabitants of and visitors to Restoration London seem to have enjoyed easy-going relations with each other irrespective of social standing. London, for all its size, was still a face-to-face society. The *Gazette* for 2 March 1674 carried an advertisement encouraging those interested in the new method of sheathing ships' hulls with lead to 'repair to the person employed by the undertakers in the management of this work, viz. Mr Thomas Rastel at the Jerkers office in the Customs House, or to the said Mr Thomas Rastel, or Mr Francis Dracot, every Tuesday and Thursday, from twelve to one o'clock at Mr Garraway's Coffee House and afterward the same days in the West Indies Walk upon the Exchange'. When Mrs Makin set up a school for gentlewomen at Tottenham High Cross, she advertised that her representative would offer a 'further account' between 3.00 p.m. and 6.00 p.m. every Tuesday at Mason's coffee-house in Cornhill and every Thursday at the 'Bolt and Tun' in Fleet Street.[46] His subjects could even observe their King playing tennis, or walking in the parks, or in the playhouse: when Italian players put on daily performances of *Scaramuccio* in the hall at Whitehall, there were 'all sorts of people flocking thither, and paying their money as at a common playhouse; nay even a twelve-penny gallery is builded for the convenience of his majesty's poorer subjects' – much to John Evelyn's disgust.[47] This is not to say that marks of distinction and rank went unnoticed, nor that it was not easier for a gentleman to participate in the pastimes of the lower orders than for a plebeian to pass themselves off as a lady or gentleman, but it is simply to suggest that the metropolis, and especially its leisure facilities, offered a more socially diverse and fluid environment than did other parts of the country.

Leaving London, wrote Henry Bulkeley, 'is a sort of dying'. The chasm between 'the city' and 'the country' was a literary convention. The comedies played upon the stultifying effects of rural life – 'I see a little time in the country makes a man turn wild and unsociable and only fit to converse with his horses, dogs and his herds,' sneered Horner – and on the revivifying effects of metropolitan existence – 'people really do live no where else, they breath, and move, and have a kind of insipid, dull being, but there is no life but in London'.[48] Life in Hampshire or

Somerset was synonymous with going to seed among one's hounds and tenants, with hunting, shooting and fishing rather than wit and sophistication. This, of course, is an argument about what constitutes a gentleman's lifestyle, and it was just as easy to fail the test of gentility in London, by, for instance, succumbing to foppishness, as it was in the shires. Yet for the well-off, life was different in the countryside, and it was a difference to be savoured for its own sake and for the contrast: 'to make the town new to me I have been airing myself for near three weeks in the country.'[49]

Life in the English counties certainly did move at a slower pace than the hectic metropolis, but it was not without incident. A random example might be the report filed from just outside Spalding, Lincolnshire by a local correspondent of Harris's *Domestick Intelligence*: a gentleman and his lady had been robbed by six highwaymen, the thieves had been pursued 'and 'tis said that two of them were taken . . . about ten miles from this place'; 'we have a strong report here, that a strange and monstrous fish has been seen to play in the ocean,' it is thirty feet long 'with a head like a lion'; 'the snow having fallen incessantly in these parts, so that 'tis confirmed from all hands, several small cattle were covered in one night, and are not as yet found, and several great cattle perished in the fens.'[50] What was valued in the countryside was independence, innocence and integrity. Shadwell's *Epsom Wells* features Clodpate, 'a clownish country fool' who abhors London and treats his guests to 'dull encomiums upon a country life, and discourse of his serving the nation with his magistracy, popularity and housekeeping'.[51] Yet there is a kernel of something admirable even in this caricature. Even while 'the country' was guyed on stage, political pamphleteers were eager to associate their message with the sturdy political independence of the country gentry. All those *Letters* to 'friends in the country' or *Appeals* to and from 'the country' were attempts to mobilize a certain self-image, a set of convictions and attitudes, which were, for all their paternalism and tradition, a salutary political stance in the face of parliamentary 'corruption' under Danby.

Behind the slogans and slanders the reality was that life for the gentry and aristocracy revolved around both city and country. They divided their year between London and their estates; many of them sent younger sons into the professions or even commerce; and many squires were entrepreneurial, 'improving', landlords rather than sack-soaked foxhunters. In the shires there were many of the appurtenances of civility such as coffee-houses, bowling greens, parks and walks. When Thomas Baskerville visited Norwich he not only admired the cathedral, city walls, castle, town hall and enormous market place, but also 'a fair walk before the prime inns and houses of the market place, called the gentlemen's walk or walking place, which is kept free for that purpose from the

encumbrance of stalls, tradesmen, and their goods'. Baskerville praised
Norwich's civic pageantry and 'the fine shows in the streets, in some
measure like that of the Lord Mayor's Day of London'.[52] On his
journeys Baskerville constantly drew these sort of comparisons with
London and, as Peter Borsay has pointed out, Celia Fiennes and
Daniel Defoe measured the provinces against the metropolis and
inevitably found both the provinces wanting and the capital's superior-
ity confirmed.[53] The experience of the metropolis spoiled one for the
provincial town, joked Henry Savile; 'the fall being much more tolera-
ble from London to a hermitage, than from London to Leicester or
Northampton.'[54]

London was not only the yardstick, it was the source of much of
England's taste and style. The 'country women [were] slavish for town
fashions'; the farmers eager for information – in 1669 John Witter sent
four pecks of sainfoin, a new grass seed, home to his parents in Cheshire
with instructions on how and where to sow it.[55] The architecture of the
capital was carried to the shires: Edward Taylor, carpenter of Newent,
worked in London for Wren before returning to his home town to build
a classical nave for the church in the mid-1670s; Christopher Kempster,
one of Wren's principal masons, was developer and possibly designer of
Abingdon's splendid classical town hall begun in 1678. Even the
manners and vices of the city could spread. One critic of 'raillery' coun-
selled his country readers to be as wary of receiving London letters
which might spread this infection as they had been of letters during the
Great Plague.[56] In a flight of fancy, Marvell described the dissemination
of a pamphlet across London and then out into the counties. The metropolitan author 'ubiquits himself, peeping at the key-holes, or picking
the locks of the bed-chambers of all the great ministers, and though they
be reading papers of state, or at the stool, more seasonably obtrudes his
pamphlet. Next he sends it by an express to his friends at the universities, but especially to his own college'.

> The country cathedrals learn it latest, and arrive by slower degrees to their
> understanding, by the carrier. . . . Those of 'em that can confide in one
> another, discourse it over in private, and then 'tis odds, but, before the
> laity get notice of it, they first hear it preached over by him whose turn it
> is next Sunday in the minster . . . if the dean foresee that 'tis a very
> vendible book, he, you may imagine forestalls the market, and sends up
> a whole dicker of 'em to retail at his best advantage. All this while the little
> emissaries here in town are not idle, but hawk about them from London
> to Westminster with their britches stiff with the copies, and will sell them
> to any one for commendation.[57]

Although in general, money and manners, fashions and books, are
perhaps too easily assumed to flow out from London and spread across
a supine country, this was the pattern in Restoration England. By the

early eighteenth century, provincial English towns would be generating many of their own cultural practices and displaying a significant independence of the metropolis. But in Charles II's reign this urban renaissance had not yet taken place, provincial society was still tied to London's apron strings, not least because the ruling elite divided their time between county and metropolis.

3   The Talk of the Town

this diffusive age, greedy of intelligence and public affairs
John Evelyn to Samuel Pepys, 28 April 1682

All we have told us is but a pennyworth of news in the *Gazette* every week. Sometimes we know things they do not tell us.
William Garway MP, May 1675

Sir for news or town discourse I must not pretend to know much, being I visit not taverns nor coffee houses, nor do I converse much with any persons that do . . .
James Hicks to Sir Joseph Williamson, 21 July 1673

Nothing seems to have circulated so fast in Restoration England as news, gossip, rumour, scandals, scares and the spoken word. The talk of the town was the most effective publicity available. As we have seen, people expected to deal with each other in person. The diaries of Pepys, Evelyn, Reresby or Hooke reveal the constant visits, the bumping into people at court and on the Exchange, in the park or at a theatre, the shared meals and coach journeys, the meeting and the mingling, and the endless talk. Susan Whyman has reconstructed the daily route of the merchant John Verney: he 'would meet others at the Exchange at eight o'clock precisely, and thence . . . to two or three merchants' houses, and before 10 I must be at [the] customs house'. He often attended at the Levant Company in Ironmongers' Hall on Fenchurch Street and the Royal Africa Company in Leadenhall Street, and visited the goldsmiths in Lombard Street. He might then pop into Jonathan's or Garraway's coffee-houses in Exchange Alley, before appearing in 'the Turkey walks' of the Royal Exchange. Thence he strolled along Cornhill to Cheapside and the book stalls of St Paul's churchyard and loitered in the aisles or 'walks' inside St Paul's where so much news and gossip was exchanged.[58] To promenade the town in this way, mixing business and pleasure, had been the practice of merchants and gentlemen for decades. But two recent developments had dramatically changed the talk of the town in Restoration England.

The first was that civil war and revolution had emboldened the lower orders who now expected to debate public affairs and private vices as freely as their superiors. The genie was out of the bottle and even those who abhorred it had to make the best of a bad job. Roger L'Estrange claimed in the first issue of his short-lived newspaper, the *Intelligencer* (1663), that he would rather not have been producing such a journal because news 'makes the multitude too familiar with the actions and counsels of their superiors, too pragmatical and censorious, and gives them not only an itch but a kind of colourable right and licence to be meddling with the government'.[59] The second was the advent of a new and egalitarian venue for conversation, the coffee-house. The coffee-houses served as the forum for political conversation or public opinion. What was variously known as the 'talk', 'humour', 'noise' or 'reports of the town' was largely the views expressed in the coffee-houses. 'The common people talk anything, for every carman and porter is now a statesman, and indeed the coffee houses are good for nothing else,' complained Sir Thomas Player in 1673. He pinned the blame on sobriety: 'it was not thus when we drank nothing but sack and claret, or English beer and ale. These sober clubs produce nothing but scandalous and censorious discourses, and at these nobody is spared.' Or as Clarendon had opined, they were 'places where the boldest calumnies and scandals were raised, and discoursed amongst a people who knew not each other, and came together only for that communication, and from thence were propagated over the kingdom.' 'It is become a custom after chapel,' wrote Roger North of Cambridge, 'to repair to one or other of the coffee-houses (for there are divers), where hours are spent in talking, and less profitable reading of newspapers, of which swarms are continually supplied from London. And the scholars so generally entête after news (which is none of their business) that they neglect all for it.' In Oxford, too, 'most scholars retire' to the coffee-house 'and spend much of the day in hearing and speaking of news'.[60] It is this association of news and talk in the coffee-house and elsewhere which is so characteristic of the age.

What was 'news' in Restoration England? Then, as now, 'news' was an elastic category which stretched from the most formal activities of monarch and government to the most salacious gossip. Those with an interest in matters of state assumed that real news emanated from the court and parliament: it was the standard line of newsletters in the summer to explain that 'the absence of his majesty and the court is the cause of the scarcity of domestic news'; or as the Danish envoy reported, 'because of the absence of the king and the entire court, very little is happening here worth writing about'.[61] The newspapers which came onto the scene in 1679 were occasionally able to tell their readers what the king and courtiers were up to at Windsor or Newmarket in the long summer months. But the news worth talking about was not simply the broadsheet material of politics and policy, foreign affairs and taxation, it also included the mundane details of trade and agriculture, the excitements of new scientific discoveries or bizarre events, and the sensation of crime, rumour and scandal.

Wagers were laid in the coffee-houses about when and whether parliament would meet, anxieties were expressed about the safety of English ships and a European land war 'furnishes the town here with millions of stories and conjectures'. We have already eavesdropped on Robert Hooke's and Andrew Yarranton's happy evenings discussing the secrets of tin-plating – on other occasions Hooke might discourse 'about watches for pocket and for longitude' with Wren, or 'about the particles of body, figures of ice, frost and snow' – and much of the talk of the town may well have been about such practical matters.[62] A good murder or the latest affair was lapped up; when trying to raise a laugh from Rochester, the quarrelsome courtier Henry Bulkeley described how the fops assemble 'daily to talk of nothing but fighting and fucking at Locketts', the fashionable Charing Cross tavern.[63] Or the coffeedrinkers may have whiled away their time tutting over the failings of the clergy or the self-seeking and bigotry of the bishops. In all the hubbub which constituted the news of the day, the talk of the moment, there was a predictable mixture of 'intelligence' of current affairs and opinions and speculations and idle chat.

We know that similar exchanges occurred, too, over the gentry's dinner tables, at provincial bowling greens or in private letters. News and opinion was, after all, a national phenomenon, not a metropolitan one. It may be that the events in the provinces were less earth-shaking than those in Westminster and Whitehall, but they were all related. The government needed to know what was going on in the shires, it needed to know how declarations of indulgence or of war, dissolutions of parliament or campaigns of persecution, were received in the counties. Sir Joseph Williamson envisaged his own system as one of gathering as well as disseminating news. He urged his aides to 'above all be busy at the desk, working at the correspondents' business, acknowledging, encouraging and pressing our correspondents everywhere to be diligent'.[64] The direct relationship of national news and local feelings was brought home to Nathaniel Thompson after he published a Shrewsbury correspondent's hostile report on the Whig MP and Shropshire gentleman Francis Charlton in the *Loyal Protestant*. A few weeks later, while walking near Temple Bar in London, Thompson was assailed by a young man wielding a cane and shouting, 'God damn you, my name is Charlton; and I am resolved to be revenged upon you, you dog, you have abused my father.'[65]

Slowly but surely the appetite for news in Restoration England meant that it was becoming a commodity: during the popish plot crisis 'everybody was so to desirous to hear news, that they would buy it, if they left

no other penny in their pockets.'[66] The commodification of news and
the advent of the coffee-house as a commercial public space had profound consequences. Three are particularly pertinent here: an insatiable
hunger for news which fuelled political tensions and was certainly one
ingredient in the popish plot furore; increasing specialization or the tailoring of 'news' to a certain audience; and the tendency of commerce
to compromise or thwart censorship. News was available for purchase
in several forms. The only officially permitted, *printed* newspaper in the
1670s was the *Gazette*, a folio half-sheet in double columns on both sides,
published on Mondays and Thursdays, and priced at one penny. The
Gazette, which was edited by Williamson, was given over to official notices
and proclamations, the movements of the King and court, foreign news
and shipping and to some advertisements. It was obvious that the metropolitan demand for news of all sorts and for the commercial services
which accompany newspapers, above all advertising, was not going to be
satisfied by the *Gazette*. There were attempts to produce rival newspapers
in London in the early 1660s and a trade-centred paper, *The City and
Country Mercury*, in 1667, but government restrictions on the press
thwarted such commercial initiatives. The *City Mercury* which appeared
from November 1675 was a weekly advertising paper and at first
seems to have been distributed for free; the short-lived *Poor Robins
Intelligence* of 1676–7 was given over to banter and chat.[67] The government's prime concern was not facilitating trade but protecting the peace
of the kingdom from 'idle and malicious reports', the 'lies and vain
reports' collected or invented to 'disturb' the people, 'to scandalise the
government or for other indirect means'.[68] The *Gazette* was distributed
around the country, but those who hungered for hard news, turned to
the various hand-written newsletter services. In 1678 Edward Seymour
asked Secretary Williamson 'to send me some intelligence, that I may
barter with my neighbours, who are well furnished from the coffee
houses'.[69]

   The two licensed newsletters were produced by Williamson's office
and by Henry Muddiman from his office at the Peacock tavern near
the New Exchange. These were substantial news services. From about £5
a year, subscribers received weekly, twice weekly or by every post, a
digest of news which had been sent into the office and supplied by
various officials and correspondents. Williamson's newsletter relied
heavily on a network of postmasters, customs officers, naval storekeep-
ers, garrison officials and others, who sent in weekly reports and received
the newsletter in return. It is likely that these officials were then able to
make a profit by retailing the news to their informants and friends and
in the tavern or coffee-house of their town. Birmingham's postmaster
probably profited from this kind of arrangement until 1673 when an
interloper, Simon Heath, wrested control of the town's wine licenses
from him, set up a coffee-shop, and asked a Newgate ironmonger to

procure either the Williamson or the Muddiman newsletter for his new establishment.[70] Surviving lists of those who received these two newsletters also show a mix of professional men – clergy, doctors, lawyers, soldiers – merchants and civic officers, gentlemen and aristocrats. 'Being very inquisitive after news' while at Newbury in 1678, the Marquess of Worcester 'enquired if there was no Muddiman's letter in the house' and eventually tracked down a copy thanks to 'a man in the house that had the liberty to peruse a parson's letters that lives at Hamsted, who uses to have the news.'[71] Williamson and Muddiman ran efficient, government-approved, long-standing news organizations, but they had rivals. In the mid-1670s John Starkey and Thomas Collins, two booksellers with shops near Temple Bar 'poison both City and country with false news'. Here, according to Danby, young lawyers, 'ill-affected' gentry and citizens, and the 'agents of the several parties and factions about town' resorted every afternoon for political news 'so penned as to make for the disadvantage of the king and his affairs'. The disaffected 'take care to communicate' resolutions, speeches, petitions and propaganda 'by letter all over the kingdom and by conversation throughout the City and suburbs'; while Starkey and Collins 'together with their servants are every afternoon and night busied in transcribing copies, with which they drive a trade all over the kingdom'.[72] There were other, shorter-lived, more informal newsletter services which, like the Starkey and Collins operations, catered for a specific clientele; and of course the news was constantly being repeated and spread further. Sometimes it is difficult to distinguish partisan news dissemination from mere curiosity. In 1677 Giles Hancock explained to Williamson that since the landlady of his coffee-house received a weekly 'paper of written news', which she said she had by authority, 'I thought it no harm to take an exact copy thereof, and give some copies of it to get a little money'.[73] The disingenuous Hancock was, however, a political activist who would later become a whig.

In addition to the newsletters and the newspapers, Restoration England derived its news and views from a variety of other topical material, ranging from substantial printed books and pamphlets to manuscript squibs. Marvell described how Bishop Herbert Croft's anonymous work, *The Naked Truth* (1675), circulated:

> The author caused four hundred of them and no more to be printed against the last session but one in parliament. For nothing is more usual than to print and present to them proposals of revenue, matters of trade, or any thing of public convenience, and sometimes cases and petitions ... but ... the parliament rising just as the book was delivering out and before it could be presented, the author gave speedy order to suppress it till another session. Some covetous printer in the meantime getting a copy, surreptitiously reprinted it, and so it flew abroad without the author's knowledge, and against his direction.[74]

The controversy aroused by Croft's book was largely a result of his arguments against the claims made for episcopacy and of the vitriolic replies and defences his work provoked. Other tracts were more overtly seditious, partisan and slanderous. Laurence Womock complained of a pamphlet that 'comes forth slily as if it were intended to do mischief' and is 'privately conveyed into the hands' of sympathetic MPs.[75] In February 1668, 'a fellow brought a bag of about 400 letters for the parliament to the door, and slunk away; they were printed books of verses, a downright libel.'[76]

Not all news or propaganda was printed. In November 1670 Marvell told Mayor Acklam of Hull that the speeches at the opening of parliament 'were by order from the Lord Arlington prohibited printing, but you will nevertheless receive a written copy'.[77] Marchamont Nedham remarked that Shaftesbury's 1674 letter to the Earl of Carlisle 'was intended for a fireball among the citizens here; as appeared by the industrious spreading copies of it in all the coffee-houses . . . and which lately inspired Mr Jenks with the wisdom of a statesman, to instruct his majesty, and move the matter at Guildhall in common council.'[78] Handwritten papers were often used to make a political or a personal point or sometimes both, as in the 1675 quarrel of Thomas Howard and Lord Cavendish, or in the 'Alarum', a denunciation of Arlington and his supporters 'scattered in Westminster Hall, 20 October 1669, at the meeting of parliament'.[79] Such manuscript 'libels', satires, lampoons or other personal attacks, were often simply 'found' (or so it was claimed) at the doors of parliament, the royal bed-chamber, the Inns of Court, in the street or on the benches of St James's Park. In the summer of 1680 an answer to the King's declaration on the succession 'in about three sheets of paper' was thrown into coaches and one copy 'dropped at the King's feet at Windsor as he was walking in the court, supposed to be flung by somebody out of Prince Rupert's Tower'.[80] At moments of crisis there were 'many papers dropped about town' and they were avidly passed from reader to reader: 'it is notorious that not one in forty libels ever come to the press, though by the help of manuscripts they are well nigh as public'.[81] In samizdat style, clandestine distribution virtually ensured popularity: 'you shall sometime find a seditious libel to have passed through so many hands that it is at last scarce legible for dust and sweat,' observed Edmund Bohun; 'whilst the loyal answer stands in a gentleman's study as clean and neat as it came from the press'.[82] Many libels were simply scurrilous, personal attacks, emanating from the self-regarding and vicious world of the court. But even these could command a market. 'Captain' Robert Julian, a one-time naval clerk and debtor, who, after apparently serving as a scribe for Rochester and some of the court poets, set up as an entrepreneurial distributor of lampoons, dealt on cash terms only: 'you want new papers, damn me where's my fees / Of guineas tossed with Julian [,] you're a rogue / we are straight presented with what's new in vogue'.[83]

It was possible therefore to visit a coffee-house, either in London or in a provincial town, and for the price of a penny dish of coffee to see the official *Gazette*, a newsletter, and even a new satire or libel, and no doubt to join in discussion of such news. All of this contributed to what was – in some eyes at least – the unruly and discordant talk of the town. Authoritarian by nature, all seventeenth-century governments were nervous of public debate, but the Restoration monarchy, preoccupied with the problems of dissent, unruly parliaments and foreign relations, was deeply suspicious of the unfettered circulation of news and opinion. 'What can be done for the suppressing of seditious prints and papers [?]' wondered Danby in one of his memoranda. He went on to raise the possibility of 'directing some body to write both about the present state of things to give the world a better impression of them than they are now possessed with and to give constant weekly accounts of what is done at any time which may be for the satisfaction of men's minds'. Or as Lord Chief Justice North later put it, the best way to deal with seditious publications was 'to set up counter writers, that, as every libel came out should take it to task, and answer it'.[84] The government enjoyed numerous advantages. It could employ 'counter-writers' of talent and experience such as Nedham, L'Estrange, Nalson and Dryden to direct and channel opinion. Also working in its favour was the tremendous weight of tradition, prejudice and unconscious propaganda which insisted upon the legitimacy and necessity of authority. Everything from the Sunday sermon to the judicial system reinforced the message of subservience. But this was not enough. The authorities felt compelled to manage, curb and control information and speculation. Yet what could be done to ensure a compliant press, to control the spread of manuscript news or libels, or to influence the talk of the taverns and coffee-houses?

On paper the government was well equipped to control the press.[85] The 1662 Licensing Act established a system of pre-publication censorship by such authorities as the church, universities, Lord Chancellor and the secretaries of state; it also gave the last of these the power to issue warrants for the investigation of unlicensed publications. A further ally was the Stationers' Company, which held the monopoly of printing and which was expected to enforce government policy and its own interests through its powers of search, seizure and arrest of unlicensed publications and their printers. In addition to these statutory and trade controls, in 1663 Roger L'Estrange was appointed Surveyor of the Imprimery, responsible to the secretaries of state, and aided by Messengers of the Press, 'instruments for discovery and intelligence'. Naturally the crown also retained the right to issue orders, warrants and patents concerning the press in all its manifestations: L'Estrange, for example, briefly enjoyed a royal patent giving him the sole right to publish news before this was effectively transferred to Williamson and the *Gazette* in 1666. Yet the effect of this legal apparatus on authors and publishers is difficult to judge. No doubt the example made of the bookseller John Twyn, executed for treason in 1664, after L'Estrange discovered that he had printed a call for Charles II's overthrow, was salutary. But the extent of self-censorship is imponderable; and we know of only a few cases where authors, such as Baxter, Hobbes and Rushworth, laid their work before the licensers and accepted their judgement.[86] The simple reality was that most subversive or scandalous publications appeared covertly, without licenses or authors' names or genuine imprints, and had entered the public domain long before the authorities had got wind of them.

The authorities were reducing to bolting the stable door after the horse had fled. Richard Chiswell had distributed two hundred copies of Denzil Holles's *The Grand Question* (1669) before the House of Commons seized the remaining copies; the subversive appendix to Lord Lucas's speech of 1671 had spread far and wide before it was burned; and John Starkey may have dispersed more than two hundred and fifty copies of 'an unlicensed and dangerous book' on contractual monarchy before his stocks were seized at the Temple in 1677.[87] There is something slightly pathetic about the warrant issued to L'Estrange on 29 March 1676 to search out the publishers of *A Letter from a Person of Quality, Two Seasonable Discourses, The Naked Truth,* and the *Speeches* of Buckingham and Shaftesbury calling for a dissolution of parliament. This roll-call of critical pamphleteering hardly suggests an effective gag on the press.[88] Unable to prevent publication, the authorities harassed authors, printers and publishers. When the votes of parliament were printed without authorization in 1673, John Starkey, Francis Smith and John Ayloffe were all interrogated and imprisoned; Henry Brydges, who printed Jenks's Guildhall speech in 1675, had his press broken up, his type defaced, and the privy council demanded his prosecution to the 'utmost severity of the law'; John Darby was convicted and pilloried for printing *Some Seasonable Queries* against the Conventicle Act, while its reputed author, the Independent Nicholas Lockyer, fled abroad. In 1677 the Lords fined Dr Nicholas Cary £1000 and imprisoned him until it was paid for the contempt of arranging the printing of Holles's *Some Considerations*; that summer a city attorney Browne was convicted at the Guildhall of publishing *The Long Parliament Dissolved* and sentenced to a 1000 mark fine, imprisonment until its payment, and barred from legal practise.[89] A small, obstinate group of ideologically committed printers and publishers refused to be intimidated: the 'forty-one imprisonments' suffered by the baptist Francis Smith were a badge of honour; whereas

John Starkey displayed considerable ingenuity in dividing the printing of an unlicensed work between several different printers. Little it seemed would stop them.

L'Estrange believed that his efforts to track down unlicensed publications were hampered by the Stationers' Company's reluctance to help and by its preoccupation with the privileges and profits of its members. The canny stationers knew all too well that licensed books were regarded as staid by the book buyers, whereas the unlicensed works were sure of a ready sale: Hobbes's subversive *Leviathan* (1651) was selling for three or four times its original price in the 1660s and few were surprised by attempts to reprint it in 1670 without a license and with a false date of '1651'.[90] Some of the Company's most eminent members paid lip-service to the rules on licensing while surreptitiously having a hand in profitable illicit publishing.[91] L'Estrange, who suggested a series of reforms and bylaws to make the Company a more effective regulator, seems finally to have adopted his opponents' tactics. In February 1677 it was reported that *A Pacquet of Advice*, a reply to Shaftesbury's *Letter from a Person of Quality*, 'has lately been underhand published and dispersed'. Shaftesbury protested to the Company about its failure to seize this unlicensed tract, and a few copies were called in, but then the Warden of the Company, Samuel Mearne, entered into the Company's minutes a letter from L'Estrange asking him to allow *A Pacquet* to appear with the same 'stealth' as Shaftesbury's pamphlet in the hope that it would be just as effective.[92] Resorting to underhand methods did not mean that L'Estrange had abandoned his raids on printing houses, but it does foreshadow what was to be a far more effective role for the surveyor in the 1680s when his periodical *The Observator* turned the table on whig propagandists.

Scribal publication was still less amenable to government control. Unlicensed newsletters were a constant thorn in the side of the government, while the various manuscript pamphlets, poems, satires and other 'libels' in circulation were even harder to hunt down. L'Estrange, who had suggested that the Stationers' Company should extract an oath from its members to have no part in the production of printed libels, was equally annoyed by manuscript libels. Copies passed 'indifferently' through several hands, 'yet some stationers are supposed to be the chief, and professed dealers in them, as having some affinity with their trade'. But when they are questioned, 'the common pretence is, *they were left in my shop*, or *sent in a letter, I know not by whom*: which may be true in some cases, though but a shift, for the greater part.' His solution was that anyone who received such a libel should be obliged to report it to a JP and name the sender or be held responsible as the author of the libel.[93] Just how unfeasible such a scheme was becomes apparent when one leafs through the collections of satires, libels and other material that country gentlemen built up, especially when, like John Pye, they have recorded the provenance of these writings: one had been taken up by a Leeds gentleman and passed to Pye by the minister of Tothill Street chapel in Westminster; another, 'Rochester's Farewell', came from Mr Ellasby of Chiswick and the original was returned to him four days later 'by the boy sealed up'.[94] The difficulty of pinning down the source of a libel and the impotent rage this caused is seen in the notice that Francis Coventry pasted on Bedington Wall when his new wife was lampooned in verse:

> Whereas a libel (vainly) intended against the honour of some persons of my relation, is lately crept abroad, whilst the author thereof stays at home. This is to declare to all the world, that whosoever has made the said libel, and shall not own it, is a malicious coward, and poltroon, and if he shall own it, is a villain and a rascal. Subscribed Francis Coventry

Perhaps fortunately, Coventry was unaware that copies of his own notice were being distributed to other gentlemen by Sir Nicholas Carew, who was 'thought to be' the author of the offensive verses.[95]

The government found itself just as impotent when it accused the young lawyer and republican John Freke of distributing a manuscript verse satire, *The Chronicle* or *The History of Insipids*, in 1676. Freke was accused first of dispersing a seditious libel and then of treason, but the prosecution was a shambles: lack of evidence allowed Freke to gain bail and when he was eventually tried for the 'misdemeanour in publishing a scandalous libel . . . the witness was one simple bookseller's boy that had an ill memory. Only that coming in he found a libel called the Chronicle and writ it out, upon the table. Freke's counsel spared all defence and the jury without going from the bar forthwith acquitted him.'[96] Even more galling, the verses seem to have continued to circulate even while the authorities were hunting them down: the 'very abusive paper' arrived in Great Yarmouth in January 1676 and was also soon circulating at the other side of the country in Gloucester; there the authorities were determined to prosecute the local distributors of this 'hell-bred paper' and indeed bound over some individuals to appear at the Michaelmas sessions, but on the acquittal of Freke, they were advised that the King was content for the prosecution to lapse if the people should take warning from the episode.[97]

What, finally, were the chances of controlling or suppressing the spoken word, of policing the talk of the town? Treason, both in speech and writing, was covered by legislation. Inflammatory talk could get you hauled up in front of the privy council, parliament or a local magistrate. Objectionable political comment was broadly construed: a Portsmouth man appeared before the local sessions in 1676 accused of saying that the Duke of York had declared himself a papist and that he would fight the Duke according to the oaths of allegiance and supremacy; while John Harrington, a 'cousin' of Shaftesbury, was tried and convicted at the London Guildhall 'for words to this purpose, viz. that in a government consisting of three estates, treason must be against all three, not against one of them only.'[98] Meanwhile many, if not the majority, of those indicted at assizes for scandalous and seditious words or false news were nonconformists and Quakers giving voice to their religious principles. But such proceedings were perhaps rather draconian for the murmurings and gossip of the taverns and coffee-houses. Much more effective was to exert some control over the venues for talk.

After 1663 coffee-houses operated under license and while this gave the government some leverage – allowing, for example, the prosecution of fifteen owners of unlicensed Westminster coffee-houses in 1672[99] – it did not prevent a steady stream of complaints from the government and its agents that they were nurseries of sedition, echoing to 'bold and licentious discourse'. They were certainly exploited by agents, especially those of foreign powers. In 1677 Charles summoned the keeper of the Amsterdam coffee-house near the Exchange because a 'part of the Spanish memorial in a paper [had been] passing from table to table'.[100] To some observers, it was plain that particular coffee-houses attracted a dissident clientele. A hostile commentator on dissenters denounced them all as proud and censorious, frequenters of coffee-houses and 'great improvers of any little matter that is but whispered against the court and government', along with 'hypocritical loyalists' they spread such news and 'scandalous verses . . . of which many have been abroad of late'.[101] A few coffee-houses were run by radicals such as Edmund Chillenden or John Wildman and attracted like-minded clients: according to one gentleman, Richard's at Temple Bar was a 'damned republican fanatic coffee-house'; the Earl of Shaftesbury liked to 'vent out all his thoughts and design' in John's coffee-house and later at the Nag's Head tavern in Cheapside.[102]

It would be naive, however, to assume that coffee-houses were in themselves bastions of 'opposition' in the 1670s. The coffee-house had, after all, been part of the way of life for many thousands of English men (and some women) for more than a decade. The authorities used the coffee-houses to distribute the *Gazette* and Williamson's newsletter and to collect information. It is perhaps in the nature of our evidence that we hear less of the daily drone of banalities than of the occasional outspoken criticism. In August 1673 the nervous Henry Ball reported that everyone dreaded the meeting of parliament, 'all people will have it that we must break off our league with them [the French], or suffer ourselves to be ruined, but I dare not write half what is spoken in public in every coffee-house.' Others, however, did not set such store by the coffee-house gossip; the urbane Sir Nicholas Armourer reported no 'considerable' news a few weeks later but 'a 1000 coffee-house reports and libels sans number' about who's in and who's out at court.[103] Sir Leoline Jenkins declined to 'measure the temper of the nation by the humour of our coffee-houses, and by the venomous bitterness of a few writers of libels'.[104] Most of what was said over the coffee cups was frankly laughable. The knockabout pamphleteering of the 1670s offered portraits of the coffee-houses as academies of civility and dens of dissent, but then subverted both caricatures. The whole point of the witty *Characters*, *Petitions* and *Complaints* about the coffee-houses was to expose the coffee-house bores who took themselves too seriously and to ridicule those who took them at their own valuation. In all likelihood, then, it was less what was said at the coffee-house, than their function as distribution centres for news and pamphlets which alarmed the authorities.

Information needed to be managed. In December 1675 the government's tame coffee-seller in Yarmouth pleaded with Williamson for 'reliable' news to be sent for display in his coffee-house: 'we are well stored with speeches and votes, as the Earl of Shaftesbury's, the Duke of Buckingham's, Sir John Holland's, and the Test, so that no endeavours are wanting to make the court odious to the people, and all men being dissatisfied are too credulous, so that now but to accuse is sufficient to condemn. The want of your *Letters of Intelligence* and *Gazettes* to pleasure others makes me more barren to serve you.'[105] In 1677 Secretary Henry Coventry appeared on the Exchange to deny rumours that the Spanish government were planning to seize English ships. 'There is not a place in the world so fruitful in lying stories as London, and, though the falseness of these stories is usually within two or three days laid open to the world, yet the people are ready to receive new ones, and to believe them 'till they also are detected.'[106] When it suited the government they too would spread lies. Pepys was asked to spread stories of Dutch maltreatment of English seamen in the coffee-houses where it would 'spread like the leprosy'.[107]

It was critics of the government who were more effective in spreading their propaganda through coffee-houses. The report from Yarmouth in 1675 must have touched a nerve in Whitehall at the end of a bruising year. Not only were Shaftesbury's *Letter from a Person of Quality* and other pamphlets to be found in the capital's coffee-houses, so were manuscript libels like Freke's *History of Insipids*; meanwhile a parallel pamphlet campaign sought to identify 'the coffee-houses' with the values of the campaigners for a parliamentary dissolution. Danby felt impelled to move against the coffee-houses and against libels. A proclamation of New Year's day 1676 ordered the closure of all coffee-houses. Some claimed that it threw the town into 'a mutinous condition' and concluded that 'if the government show itself to fear the people . . . the people will hardly fear the government'. Others, like Robert Hooke, barely noticed the proclamation. Within ten days, the order had been withdrawn and the coffee-houses were given six months' grace. The coffee-house keepers took the oaths of allegiance and supremacy and gave bonds not to permit scandalous papers to be brought into their establishments nor to allow false and scandalous reports against the government to be uttered there. On 7 January 1676, a few days after the first proclamation against the coffee-houses, another was issued which offered a reward of £20 to any informant who identified the source of either printed or manuscript libels.[108] Although there is no hard evidence as to Danby's thinking, it seems perverse to interpret this episode as a genuine attempt to abolish coffee-houses. It is more in keeping with an attempt to intimidate the coffee-sellers and with a series of petty but deliberate attempts to break the links being forged by Shaftesbury and Buckingham in the City of London. The proclamation may have been an outburst of exasperation, it was certainly ill-planned, clumsy and open to legal challenge, but its speedy withdrawal suggests that it had fulfilled whatever immediate purpose had been intended.

In the longer term, this shot across the bows of the coffee-houses misfired. It confirmed the coffee-houses' reputation, which was being carefully nurtured by pamphleteers, as centres of radical thinking. It did nothing to smother libels: to quote but one 'libel' on the order to close the coffee-houses;

> By which I'll be bold,
> That his Lo[rdshi]pp doth hold,
> And so must all men in high station,
> That subjects may drink,
> But not soberly think
> On the real state of the nation.[109]

Danby's warning did not deter the coffee-houses, nor 'that damnable trade' of furnishing them with newsletters. In the autumn of 1677 the government issued warrants for the arrest of several coffee-house keepers, but this time it was concerned with named individuals like Edmund Chillenden who 'publishes and disperses false news'. It was reported meanwhile that Charles was incensed by the coffee-sellers who 'to gain a little money had the impudence and folly to prostitute affairs of state indifferently to the views of those who frequent such houses, some of them of lewd principles, and some of mean birth and education.'[110] The King, then, recognized that 'a little money' was the main incentive here, that the prospect of profit emboldened coffee-house keepers, printers and many others to maintain the venues and information services which allowed the town to talk and which in turn was open to exploitation by that dangerous minority with 'lewd principles'.

Communication has been a theme of this chapter. The trafficking of information and opinion demonstrates once more the power of commerce and the limits of regulation in the late seventeenth century. Restoration London, with its 'Town' and 'City', exemplifies the division between the impulse towards consumption and the drive for profit. The work of the surveyors and cartographers reveals rival procedures and different ways of imagining geographical space. Such contradictions and tensions proved fruitful. They do much to explain the energy and dynamism of England in the 1670s.

7

Tyrannic Love: Sex, Marriage and Politics

> Restless he rolls about from whore to whore,
> A merry monarch, scandalous and poor.
>
> Rochester, *On King Charles* (1673)

> The majesty of historical matters will not allow a judicious author to dilate
> upon accidents of love, he speaks of them but *in transitu*, and it must be
> no less an eminent battle, or the subversion of a state, can tempt him to
> a digression.
>
> *The Annals of Love* (1672)

In Dryden's tragedy *Tyrannick Love, or the Royal Martyr*, first performed
in June 1669, St Catherine, 'a pattern of piety', and her mother Felicia
suffer martyrdom at the hands of the lustful Emperor Maximin. The evil
Maximin, who at one point believes that he loves Catherine, dwells sadis-
tically on the gruesome death which awaits her and orders, among many
other barbarities, the execution of his own wife. In the final act the
tyrant's virtuous daughter Valeria, played by Nell Gwynn, overcome by
her father's cruelty and thwarted in love, stabs herself and expires.
However in the famous epilogue to the play, Nell comes back to life and
out of character to address the audience as 'the ghost of poor departed
Nelly', who must walk the earth as a spirit because the great comedienne
had played 'out of my calling in a tragedy':

> O poet, damned dull poet, who could prove
> So senseless to make Nelly die for love!

Nell has the last word, trusting no poet, but writing her own epitaph:

> Here Nelly lies, who though she lives a slattern,
> Yet died a princess, acting in St Cathar'n.[1]

The joke was as complex as it was instant. Gwynn was not only playing
against type in this tragedy, she was being used by Dryden to voice a
cynical, even subversive, coda to the action. The play had contrasted the

perverted 'love' felt by Maximin with the noble true loves experienced by his victims. The epilogue's frank distinction between Nell Gwynn's free-wheeling sexuality and romantic love cast doubt on the play's stance. Even more daringly, it trespassed on personal ground. This was not the first time that Nell Gwynn had publicly alluded to her own love life, but to call herself a slattern was bold indeed at this moment. Nell had been the mistress of the actor Charles Hart, who played her unrequited love interest Porphyrius in this piece, and had then moved on to Lord Buckhurst, and by the time that Charles II himself probably attended a performance on 24 June, she was in all likelihood the King's mistress too. Nell was certainly pregnant by Charles II later in the same year.

So this was a daring epilogue, just as tyranny, lust and love were brave subjects for the poet laureate to explore on stage. There is no evidence that either play or epilogue was intended or perceived as critical of Charles II and his court. Yet in the political climate of the day, such a reception could not have been ruled out. Only the previous year the apprentices of London had destroyed the capital's 'bawdy houses' or brothels while mocking the whores and whoremasters at Whitehall.[2] And Pepys had watched Sir Robert Howard's *The Duke of Lerma*, 'a very good and most serious play', in acute anxiety since he quite wrongly believed that it was 'designed to reproach our King with his mistress'.[3] Suspicions about the sexual mores of Charles II and his court deepened and took on a darker tone as the 1670s progressed, in part because of the court's growing association with tyranny and popery, but also because royal sexuality was seen, rightly or wrongly, as some kind of challenge to patriarchal society.

Restoration England was (and still is) often proclaimed 'merry England'. But this merry England, epitomized by 'a bold, merry slut' like Nell, was little more than a mirage.[4] It was largely the projection of the dissolute court and of a coterie of poets and playwrights. Nelly's earthy assertion of her uncomplicated persona – the orange girl who slept her way to the top – might be complemented by a few lyrics advocating equal sexual pleasure between men and women or the frankness of the sex comedies in which the ladies were as randy as their gallants. But there was no sexual revolution in seventeenth-century England. There were some signs of female emancipation or assertiveness: the arrival of professional actresses on the stage; the appearance of at least one successful professional female dramatist, Aphra Behn; the advocacy and practice of upper-class female education by Bathsua Makin; and, of course, the prominent role of women in nonconformity and the sects. Gender roles were not, however, under threat in Restoration England. The patriarchalism of the era was almost complacent. The translator of the French writer Poulain de la Barre's *The Woman as Good as the Man, or the Equality of Both Sexes* (1677) claimed condescendingly that of all nations the English most respected women 'and what in this matter the virtuosi, and enquirers of that nation [France], squeeze from subtle speculation and logic, is no more than what every English man practises by common sense and natural inclination.'[5] Even if they could be measured, the scale of sexual promiscuity or of equality between the sexes in Restoration England are besides the point here. This chapter is concerned with the power of sex as a symbol, and especially as a symbol of what was wrong with England and its government in the 1670s.

1 Sex and Marriage

a wild unthinking dissolute age; an age whose business is senseless riot, Neronian gambols and ridiculous debauchery.

> Nathaniel Lee, *The Rival Queens* (1677), dedication to Mulgrave

like Sardanapalus, we spin amongst the women, who by their artifices have so wholly gain'd us, that we speak or think of nothing else.

> *Angliae Speculum Morale* (1670)

Sex was much on Restoration minds. We know this both from those who resisted its temptations, like the Earl of Anglesey who thanked God for never suffering 'me to be polluted with strange women, the sin of the times', and from those who succumbed.[6] Samuel Pepys's sex life is known in intimate detail. His harassment of women in church, taverns and shops, his relations with the wives of his own employees and with his own maids, and his interest in pornography, raise the question whether this behaviour was typical of men in his position? Robert Hooke, a rather different kind of diarist, left a meticulous and chilling record of his sexual liaisons with his female servants, in which he seems to equate orgasms with other kinds of purges and vomits as part of his health regimen. His relationship with Nell Young, a married seamstress who appears to have been his housekeeper, benefited the Youngs materially; it is not clear what other servants, such as Betty Orchard or Doll Lord, gained from sex with the great scientist, nor what kind of sexual relationship he had with his teenage niece.[7] Sir George Downing, the financial wizard and diplomat, was renowned for his sexual voracity. Gossip had it that he enjoyed the favour of six mistresses concurrently; and when all of Whitehall lusted after a visiting fifteen-year-old French actress, the King 'sighs and despairs, and says nobody but Sir George Downing or my lord Ranelagh' could win or buy her.[8] Similarly metropolitan mores were evoked in the naturalistic opening lines of Rochester's *A Ramble in St James's Park*;

> Much wine had passed with grave discourse
> Of who fucks who and who does worse,
> Such as you usually do hear
> From them that diet at the Bear,
> When I who still take care to see
> Drunkenness relieved by lechery,
> Went out into St James's Park
> To cool my head and fire my heart.

Rochester's speaker then offers a dyspeptic vision of a society gone mad with lust, in which all the world, high and low, 'do here arrive, / And here promiscuously they swive.'[9]

Promiscuity was the norm in some circles of the court, the nobility and the theatre. John Evelyn claimed that appearance of 'foul and undecent women' on the stage, 'who inflaming several young noblemen and their gallants, became their misses, and to some, their wives', led 'to the reproach of their noble families and the ruin of body and soul'. Critics of the nobility complained that 'fornication is no sin with them, and adultery is the least; they not considering in every such act, that they invade their neighbour's freehold.'[10] But upper-class promiscuity was nothing new: the prevailing double standard which allowed men extra-marital affairs but denied them to women was deep rooted, and it was particularly applicable to those with the wealth, power and leisure to indulge it. While the kept women of the town were known as 'misses', their male lovers were called 'keepers'.

'Our crying sin of keeping' was much lamented. The 'kind keepers' satirized in plays were sexual fumblers and naive gulls, easily cheated and betrayed by their mistresses. Up they came to London with their wives and families, then they slipped away to visit a supposed 'lady of quality' who has borrowed her clothes and her lodgings 'in some modish place, as the Piazza, Southampton Buildings or Suffolk Street'.[11] Mistress was a suitable role or career for actresses or up-market prostitutes. Lord Culpepper's mistress, Sue Willis, who had two daughters by him, was also one of London's leading madams or 'bawds'. In 1677 Culpepper took her to Paris 'to buy whatsoever pleased her there and this nation could not afford'. George Porter, a groom of the bedchamber, took Jane Long, actress and one-time mistress of the Duke of Richmond, from the stage to be his mistress. Porter set her up in London, deserted his wife Diana, and retired to Berkshire, whence he made visits to London to gorge on its delights: 'the rogue is grown so ravenous,' wrote Henry Savile, 'that now he surfeits of everything he sees but Mrs Long and his son Nobbs which he can never have enough on.'[12] Such arrangements were clearly suited to the ageing aristocrat or gentleman. What of the predatory young male, the rakish gallant or hector?

Young men of fashion with an entrée to the court might prey upon the maids of honour to Queen Catherine or the Duchess of York; but even these would descend on the theatres, taverns and streets of London, accosting respectable women, hunting for whores or bawdy houses. After an evening of drinking and 'mad bawdy talk', courtiers like Henry Killigrew, 'were ready to take hold of every woman that came by them'. In February 1670 Richard Legh wrote to his wife about one tragic encounter which seems to have arisen from drunkenness and an assumption that a passing woman was a whore:

> one Cooke, was drunk in Covent Garden, and coming home, met the Duke of Monmouth's valet de chambre who had his own wife by the hand leading her homeward. This Cooke would needs take her from him, and being rude with her, the woman gave him a box of the ear. Cooke drew and pricked her in the buttock; then the French valet drew at the first pass run Cooke into the right pap, and he fell and has never spoken since. He cannot outlive two days. The Frenchmen is fled though he needs not.[13]

The anecdotal evidence of aristocrats and their hangers-on chasing women, abusing and violating them, is substantial, but it does not lend itself to measurement or comparisons. Nor is it clear how one might ever assess whether the middling and lower orders found themselves more preoccupied with sex than in other ages. There are no obvious measures, no diaries, no usable records of sexual desire or practice, no index even of prostitution or sexual crime. And in the absence of a seventeenth-century Kinsey Report, what might substantiate or explain the perception of this as a sex-obsessed age, 'a wild unthinking dissolute age'?

A possible clue might lie in the commercialization of sex. Sexual services were a commodity like any other, and in Restoration London these services were flourishing. Prostitution catered for all ranks of society, but it is a safe bet that market forces applied and the finest whores of Covent Garden were able to choose their clientele. Magalotti, an Italian visitor, reported that 'the public brothels are numerous and all very safe', at least from theft and violence, if not from the pox. A brothel was usually the house of the madam who brought 'in as many girls as you like, to show you, who go to search in the neighbourhood until one or more please you. With this they leave you alone with her until they are called to send her away.' Afterwards clients were expected to share sweetmeats, tarts and drink with their girl, 'so that between the pay for the girl, which regularly comes to a crown, that for the procuress, and the cost of the collation, the amusement gets away with a pound'.[14] There were many prominent 'bawds' and whores: Damaris Page, Mother Moseley, Mistress Cresswell, 'Roberts, Thomas, Mistress Dutton'; Mrs Cuffley, 'that whore paramount'; and at least two specialists in flagellation, Betty Bewley and Jenny Cromwell. Between 1675 and 1683 Sue Willis, Culpepper's mistress, kept a brothel at a house in Lincoln's Inn Fields with two white balls on the gateposts; Betty Morris, 'bonny black Bess', was based in Brick Court, Westminster, and according to Lord Buckhurst,

> to those that have had my dear Bess in their arms,
> She's gentle, and knows how to soften her charms;
> And to every beauty can add a new grace,
> Having learned how to lisp, and to trip in her pace;
> And with head on one side, and a languishing eye,
> To kill us by looking as if she would die.

'In Milford Lane near to St Clement's steeple / There lived a nymph kind to all Christian people': this was Lady Bennet, whose house between the Thames and the Strand offered the young blades many delights including a nude revue. So notorious was Lady Bennet that Wycherley dedicated *The Plain Dealer* to her in a witty, but genuine, acknowledgement of her profession's lack of hypocrisy.[15] Not all whores were based in brothels, and those who plied their trade in the streets may have recognized the scene in Dryden's *The Kind Keeper*, where Aldo, in his guise as pimp and adjudicator, demarcates territories: 'you shall have the City from Whitechapel to Temple Bar, and she shall have to Covent Garden downwards: at the playhouses, she shall ply the boxes, because she has the better face; and you shall have the pit, because you can prattle best out of a vizor-mask.'[16]

Once commodified, sex easily becomes a playground, an invitation to experiment with all manner of forbidden and foreign delights. Commercial pornography arrived in England in the later seventeenth century. The Italian painter, James Barnardi, set up shop at the sign of the Cross in St James's Street, Westminster, and dealt in all kinds of erotica including playing cards showing 'divers obscene postures and figures not fit to be expressed among Christians'.[17] The thirty-six 'postures' or erotic prints attributed to the sixteenth-century Italian pornographer Aretino seem to have been available. The satirists suggested that the town gallant's 'mind is a room hung round with Aretine's pictures'; and Pepys probably found them bound with the pornographic *La Puttana Errante*, 'the wandering whore', which was later surpassed in obscenity by the French *L'Escole des Filles*. When questioned about these items, a bookseller who had imported them from Amsterdam said that he 'did not conceive [them to be] any way prohibited in England'.[18] Along with erotica from abroad, came sex toys. A bizarre attempt by Rochester and his cronies to import a consignment of dildoes in 1670 led to disaster for these leather 'martyrs' when they were seized and 'burned without mercy' by customs officials allegedly at the instigation of their wives. The whole episode, which was probably some kind of practical joke, fuelled a minor literary industry as the court wits assailed each other with jokey letters, burlesques like *Dildoides*, and rollicking satirical songs such as *Signior Dildo*.[19]

Even sodomy has been portrayed as an alien import. The famous episode when a drunken and naked Sedley abused scripture and acted 'all the postures of lust and buggery that could be imagined' from the balcony of a Fleet Street tavern in 1663 led to the reflection that 'buggery is now almost grown as common among our gallants as in Italy, and that the very pages of the town begin to complain of their masters for it.'[20] Understandably the evidence in support of this assertion is flimsy. Rochester and Savile seem to have shared a liking for young French valets and musicians, and there are famous references to 'the well-looked linkboy' and to a 'sweet soft page' in Rochester's poetry.[21] Rumours also surrounded Buckingham and his friend the actor Edward Kynaston, who had specialized in female roles. But in so far as this subject has been explored, the consensus is that these aristocratic libertines, for all their talk of smooth-faced boys and Ganymedes, were simply indulging their taste for excess and their delight in breaking taboos. In such sexual relations they remained the dominant, 'male', partner. There is little here which can be regarded as homosexuality or even bi-sexuality. Whether Restoration England had a community of homosexuals (in the sense of adult men seeking sex exclusively with other adult men) remains to be established. It has been argued that a distinctly homosexual identity only emerged in the early eighteenth century, but of course since buggery was illegal there was good reason to maintain secrecy – and there are strong hints, as in the case of Titus Oates, of men who moved in a clandestine homosexual world.[22]

The strongest case for regarding this as an especially dissolute age must, however, rest on taste in the theatre. By far the most obvious way in which sex was packaged and sold in Restoration England was through the stage and printed plays; this was not mass entertainment, of course, but it probably had an influence far beyond the audience of the two London theatres. The taste for sex was served in different ways. Tragedies presented sex as spectacle, women bound, dishevelled and semi-naked, frequently the victims of rape or sadistic martyrdom: 'the Restoration tragedy staged male lust being directly aroused by a real female body.'[23] In *Tyrannic Love*, Maximin almost salivates over the 'wheel' on which he intends St Catherine to be martyred; 'by degrees her tender breasts may feel, / First the rough razings of the pointed steel: / Her paps then let the bearded tenters stake, / And on each hook a gory gobbet take'.[24] Comedies were more suggestive. Plays with 'a room, and couch within' will 'oblige the town, the city and the court' claimed Dryden.[25] 'Nothing but bawdy, downright rank bawdy, will do now,' says one character in Durfey's *The Fool Turn'd Critic* (1678), ''tis a lewd age.'[26] Wycherley, responding to the outrage caused by his comedy *The Country Wife*, prefaced his next play with the observation that 'from some many ladies will take a broad jest as cheerfully as from the watermen and sit at some down-right filthy plays (as they call 'em) as well satisfied and as still as a poet could wish 'em'. He had to conclude that the fault must lie with 'the doubtful obscenity of my plays' or, in other words, that they were not 'filthy' enough.[27] Joseph Arrowsmith certainly advised that comedies be written 'with double sense and brisk meaning songs . . . the ladies laugh at a little bawdy jest as if they would bepiss themselves'.[28] Comedies were risque, making much use of innuendo and double-entendre – as in the notorious 'China scene' of *The Country Wife* – and often farcical, with a succession of bed-hopping confusions in which enforced marriages are prevented, characters in disguise or in the dark sleep with the wrong partners, and fools unwittingly assist in their own cuckolding. The craze for sex comedies which literary historians regard as such a feature of the 1670s probably began with Thomas Betterton's *The Amorous Widow* (*c.*1670). Its zenith was represented by *The Country Wife*, *The Man of Mode*, and *The Virtuoso*, all staged in 1675–6.[29] Sexual intrigue, adultery, the casting off of one mistress and the seduction of another, are what motivate these plays, and what shocks and titillates the audience is innuendo, the repudiation of conventional morality, the admission of sexual appetites, especially if depraved or illicit, and the suggestion of off-stage sex. Audiences enjoyed the exposure of hypocrisy, as in the scene in *The Virtuoso* where Snarl, the sanctimonious puritan, is revealed as a masochist, urging his mistress, 'Do not spare thy pains. I love castigation mightily.' In the end Snarl marries his whore, 'for better marry my own than another man's', and most of the characters are paired off as convention required.[30]

For it is in the nature of seventeenth-century comedies that they end in marriage, that the disorderly sex of the play's action is brought under control and harmony is restored. It is a matter of debate whether all the comedies do offer convincing resolutions in which the rake is reclaimed by marriage and the moral order reasserted. But the run-of-the-mill comedies and farces aspired to this neat ending. A crude weak farce, *The Milkmaid of Islington*, supposedly performed for courtiers at Newmarket in 1679, features Lovechange, the alleged 'stallion' of Lady Jilt, telling her husband that 'you cannot choose but to know the frailty of the times, the surfeits of the womb, and how great ladies use to relieve their appetites' and better Lady Jilt select him than 'sin with feeble ushers and withered dwarfs'. It eventually transpires that there has been no cuckolding and true love wins out. One of the lessons for the gallants is 'henceforth account not every lively wife / Wanton, because she lives a merry life'.[31] It should not surprise us that audiences wanted lash-

ings of sex in their comedies but still wanted everything to come right
eventually. As Wycherley complained, the audiences want to be shocked,
but not too much; they wanted to be wicked, but not too wicked. In 1676
the epilogue to John Crowne's play *The Destruction of Jerusalem* 'is much
praised that tells 'tis not like to please this age to bring them a story of
Jerusalem who would more delight in one of Sodom'.[32] Was it a perverse
bravado that so many took delight in the idea that theirs was a particularly debauched generation? Was it a response to the stuffy piety and
moralism of earlier generations? Was it even true? Dryden believed that
The Kind Keeper had been panned because its satire was too near the
bone: 'name but a cuckold, all the city swarms,' he claimed, as if the
population were living in fear that their own vices would be exposed by
the playwright.[33]

I

If we are to judge by the number of poems and plays, pamphlets and
private letters, devoted to romantic love between men and women,
Restoration England was as familiar with this noble passion as it was with
sexual appetites. Something of the English attitude to love may be
revealed in Sir William Temple's unflattering description of Dutch
mores. He describes the Dutch as being less passionate than other
peoples. Their temper was not conducive to quarrelling, joy, jokes, 'nor
warm enough for love. This is talked of sometimes among the younger
men, but as a thing they have heard of, rather than felt.' Temple, who
knew that of which he wrote, believed love would brook no rival nor
allow 'any bent of thought another way'. And yet the Dutch stolidly
pursued their business: 'I have known some among them that personated lovers well enough but none that I ever thought were at heart in
love; nor any of the women that seemed at all to care whether they were
so or not.' On the other hand, this same lack of passion might explain
the high reputation of married Dutch women; 'a certain sort of chastity
being hereditary and habitual among them.'[34]

Were the English then a passionate people? Their poets and playwrights certainly presented them with an inspiring image of human love.
'Love's a heroic passion which can find / No room in any base degenerate mind,' proclaims Queen Isabella in *The Conquest of Granada*; 'It
kindles all the soul with honours fire, / To make the lover worthy his
desire.'[35] Even the intellectualized abstractions of *All for Love*, Dryden's
version of the Antony and Cleopatra story, cannot contain love: 'I could
not counterfeit; / In spite of all the dams, my love broke o'er / And
drowned my heart again,' weeps Cleopatra. She loves with 'transcendent
passion', while Antony brings 'half the globe . . . in dowry with my heart';
and the play's final verdict is that 'no lovers lived so great, or died so

well.'[36] Thrilling, tragic, noble love of this kind could be set against more mundane heartbreaks. Aphra Behn poignantly chronicled the devastation wrought by love on our pretensions and self-control:

> Some dear, some secret, youth that gives the wound
> Informs you, all your virtue's but a cheat
> And honour but a false disguise,
> Your modesty a necessary bait
> To gain the dull repute of being wise.[37]

Restoration love poetry, which owed much to Ovid among others, was both lyrical and worldly. The comedies often just seem worldly. Although acknowledged, the power of love is kept at arm's length by banter and by its assimilation to a kind of warfare. Dorimant is on record as intending to marry 'a good estate', but Harriet creeps beneath his defences, 'I have took the infection from her, and feel the disease now spreading in me.' Love is a contest: 'I love her and dare not let her know it, I fear sh'as an ascendant over me and may revenge the wrongs I have done her sex.'[38]

Perhaps property was a better guide than poetry to successful relationships in the seventeenth century. 'The passion of love is very much out of fashion in this country,' Charles II had written to Minette in 1664, 'a handsome face without money has but few gallants, upon the score of marriage'.[39] A gentleman like Sir Edward Dering had a duty to his family to arrange the best marriages possible for his children. Dering happily married his daughter Mary to Thomas Knatchbull in 1673. 'The estate was not much but being a very civil man, well beloved by all that knew him, one that seemed to love my daughter very well, and the hopes of future kindness from Sir Norton [Thomas's father] to him, and my own friendship with the family, induced me into it.' The same summer Dering negotiated for a match between his eldest son and the daughter of Lady Culpeper: 'this was a very considerable family in our own country [ie. Kent], and the young lady of competent beauty and of great repute of prudence, sweetness and obedience to her mother, so that I resolved to take £5000.' Lady Culpeper was 'very high and resolute' and offered him less, 'either not being able to give £5000 or believing my son had an affection for her daughter'. Whatever the young man's affections, Dering 'had as much care of him as of myself in his marriage' and broke off negotiations.[40] John Verney, an overseas merchant of gentry family, returned to London seeking a wife and lighted upon the daughter of Mr Edwards, a cloth merchant ('which possibly may be of good advantage to me in his advice'), whose daughter was reputed a 'good housewife never bred to plays or parks but a sober, discreet and godly young woman'. Nevertheless John would not visit her until he had arranged a substantial dowry with her father.[41] Intermediaries were vital to these delicate negotiations. Clients like Sir John Bramston and Dymock Walpole, a Lincolnshire gentleman, used the banker Sir Robert Clayton to look out for suitably wealthy brides for their sons: 'you have all the money and women at London.'[42] In rural Essex, the clergyman Ralph Josselin, like many of his brethren, often acted as a go-between in marriage discussions. Marrying off his own daughters was a protracted affair. The Josselin family seemed to like a young Mr Smith from London who 'proferred his love' to Mary Josselin in September 1676, but 'she refused him, as she had formerly done another of good estate' and he went away 'very sorrowful'. In December the family set aside a day for prayer on the subjects of their profligate son and a young Londoner's offer to another daughter Elizabeth to which she seemed 'very averse'. The young man, Gilbert Smith, presumably the same man who courted Mary, spent Christmas with the Josselins and departed for London, according to Ralph, 'with hopes of my Elizabeth's love; God seen in inclining her heart, which was very awkward at first: my affections drawn from the hopes his sobriety and good nature gave, that grace and industry might meet to make him a good husband, for his estate was small.' Gilbert married Elizabeth the following June.[43]

Affection was not irrelevant even to the grandest of matches. Suitors were expected to talk of romance. When Sir Edward Bayntun was hoping for a match between his son and Danby's daughter in 1674, he took care to mention to the Countess of Danby that 'Harry seemed transported the other night when amongst twenty it was his good fortune to draw your pretty daughter, my lady Sophia, for his valentine.'[44] But the harsh reality was that marriages at this social level were property transactions – as the Danby family were all too aware. One of the great scandals of the 1670s involved an heiress named Bridget Hyde who was secretly married off at the age of twelve to a John Emerton by her aunts to protect their own property interests. Despite this admittedly dubious marriage, the Earl of Danby ruthlessly pursued her for his son Peregrine, Viscount Dunblane, while her step-father, Sir Robert Vyner, played off all parties against each other in the hope of securing his own best interests – it was, as Marvell said, a 'detestable and most ignominious story'.[45] It casts a lurid light on the complacent portrait of Sir Robert Vyner and his family painted by Wright at this time (see plate 13). There was a real fear that heiresses like Bridget Hyde were in danger of abduction, either from ill-advised gallants attempting elopements or from grasping relatives: to the King's fury, Bridget herself was temporarily snatched at gunpoint by a Cornet Wroth; Rochester's abduction of his future wife Elizabeth Malet was notorious; and the Earl of Sandwich was so concerned that Mrs Wortley, an heiress in his care, was in danger of 'having violence used to get her into possession of others whilst the court and myself were out of town' that he took steps to prevent 'the stealing of her'.[46]

Plate 13   Sir Robert Vyner and his family (1673), by John Michael Wright. Vyner, a gold-smith banker who became Lord Mayor of London, was deeply involved with Danby. They were both tainted by scandal when Vyner attempted to marry off his stepdaughter, Bridget Hyde, to Danby's son, despite the fact that she was already married.

The marriages of the later seventeenth century were just as various as they are today. Married couples were not strangers to love and passion. 'My dear heart,' wrote Sir Robert Paston MP to his wife on his way home from parliament, 'let my coach meet me at Norwich and for any women to entertain me there fear for none but yourself and [I] desire to meet you alone at home'.[47] Josselin was 'sensible of the comfort of my wife, my love; seeing everything more pleasant because I have her'. The pious Sir Edward Harley enjoyed a close relationship with his wife Abigail, whom he addressed as 'my dear heart'. On their wedding anniversary he wrote to her:

> After I have upon my knees rendered thanks to the God and father of mercies for twelve years happiness in your embraces, I most gladly tell you that our love is of more excellent nature that what is called the gallantry of the age, and it is no less in degree. Our relation and our love are the gift of God, and the end is to endear our love to God.[48]

Many gentlemen stuck in London pined for their wives: 'this town affords no satisfaction to me in compare of thee and my dear bantlings, thy entirely affectionate husband, R. Legh'.[49] There is evidence of wifely affection, too, in the replies sent from the country, full of family and estate news, details of preventatives and cures, enclosing favourite clothes or hampers of home-made delicacies. Occasionally women made outright statements of love. 'Dear,' wrote the dying Margaret Godolphin to her husband in 1678, 'believe me that of all earthly things you were, and are the most dear to me; and I am convinced that nobody ever had a better, or half so good a husband.'[50]

Just as predictably, there were also wretched unions. Unhappy husbands took consolation elsewhere, but what could miserable wives do? How many were there like Pepys's unhappy young wife, Elizabeth, who chafed at the lack of money and liberty, or Rochester's wife, closeted in the country, while he pursued his amours in town and court? When the Earl of Anglesey's daughter, Philippa, asked his permission to marry, 'I told her it would be purely her act then which she agreed to'. She married Charles, Lord Mohun early in 1674. By June she was complaining of his ill-treatment, and possibly of his violence, and by September they were 'desperately out again'. Anglesey blamed both parties, but Philippa most since she was an 'ungracious daughter', rejecting his advice 'and carrying herself irreligiously, among other expressions she said she would be a common whore before she would submit to her husband's will in what I thought fit, if she had not been married I had beat her; I did call her impudent baggage and said that she carried herself like a whore and left her with a resolution to see her no more.'[51] Yet Anglesey spent most of 1 December reconciling the couple and after dinner left them tucked up in bed. This was not, however, destined to be a long marriage, since the quarrelsome Lord Mohun died in 1677 from wounds received while fighting a duel.

One key to the happier marriages may have been the wife's acceptance of the subordinate role. Marriage was not meant to be egalitarian. Richard Leigh, poetically extolling the delights of friendship, drew unfavourable comparisons with 'arbitrary families, / Which seem domestic tyrannies' where the wife is 'the husband's prime she-slave' and 'parents with Turkish rigour sway'.[52] The doting Lady Abigail Harley began her replies to her husband, 'my dear master'. Lady Mohun might have been happier – or so her father thought – if she had been both a more deferential daughter and more submissive wife. Well-to-do husbands left their wives in the country where they were needed to run the household and supervise the estate – but where they were also out of danger. The plot of *The Country Wife* turned on Pinchwife's attempts to keep his country-born wife Margery away from the moral and sexual dangers of the city – and this no doubt touched a nerve among the gentle audience. Rochester and Henry Killigrew came to blows in the royal presence after the tipsy Killigrew spoke 'bold raillery (according to his custom) upon my Lord the Earl of Rochester concerning his keeping his wife in the country and not letting her see London'.[53] In marriage, as in love affairs, the balance of power was delicate and male authority precarious. In a comic dialogue on marriage Buckingham had 'Bellair' pronounce 'let a husband be never so much the superior, and flatter himself with an imaginary preeminence, yet if he affects a despotic sway, takes more upon him than the laws allow him, and violates the original contract, 'tis as natural for wives as for subjects to rebel.'[54] Buckingham, of course, was notorious for bringing his mistress, the Countess of Shrewsbury, to live with him and effectively ordering his wife out of the house.[55]

Love and marriage among the upper classes may reflect little of humbler people's passions. At this level love might not be constrained by property but it was certainly confused by lust. The nonconformist minister Philip Henry jotted in his diary that 'most people look upon marriage only as a license to lie together, which they might not before, and not as an ordinance of God.' But other comments suggest that cohabitation was not unusual: "'tis the shame of this generation that so many men and women live in common.'[56] In most families, of course, the subordination of wives and women took the prosaic form of drudgery and child-bearing with little hope of escape. Inevitably, some marriages took a tragic turn: John Smithson, vicar of Berwick, and a wife-beater, had often been heard to say that he would be his wife's death or she would be his, before he stabbed her to death in June 1672. Elizabeth Lillyman who had murdered her husband 'was burnt to ashes' on 18 July 1675.[57] Thus was the sanctity of marriage upheld.

None of this would merit discussion in an account of the age of Charles II, if it was not for the contemporary debate on the point and purpose of marriage. Associated with the *querelle des femmes*, this was a highly artificial literary and journalistic exercise, designed to sell witty pamphlets, poems, ballads and broadsheets, to supply material for the badinage of the comedies and to enhance reputations. The attack on marriage was managed by 'some shallow-brained fellows (pretenders to poetry) who have thrown about lampoons and satires, to their follow-ers, who at coffee-houses and taverns vent the ware; this is done in the country too according to their little wit'.[58] As so often in Restoration England, much of the debate is conducted through a literary ventrilo-quism, with pamphleteers advancing their case by castigating the sup-posed behaviour or opinions of a stereotyped character or by replying to an opponent in an assumed persona. According to such witty writers the stock of both marriage and wives was falling fast.

The 'town gallant' was 'so bitter an enemy to marriage' that 'con-tempt of wedlock grows very strong'; marriage was 'a peevish subject' said the 'town miss' or kept-woman. Marriage was 'the enemy to mirth, wit, valour, all / That we can virtuous, good or pleasant call'; it was sexual drudgery and financial ruin; the end of freedom and the beginning of hypocrisy, anxiety and even hatred:

> W is double woe
> I Nought else but jealousy
> F is fained, flattering, fraud
> E is naught but enmity.

Or in the words of an unpleasant squib of the mid-1670s 'on marriage':

> The clog of all pleasure, the luggage of life,
> Is the best can be said of a very good wife
> But if she prove whorish and peevish beside
> Her fortune but narrow and her c–t very wide
> Marriage then seems by the devil invented
> In the height of his malice when over tormented
> And the portion he gave with madam his daughter
> Is a hell upon earth worse than any hereafter.

Some denounced marriage as a 'holy cheat', 'a licensed way to sin; / A noose to catch religious woodcocks in'; others more temperately argued 'marriage is an honourable state, yet crowned with thorns'.[59] Wives were 'scolds' and husbands often drunken and violent – according to *Poor Robins True Character of a Scold* (1678) and the reply *A Scourge for Poor Robin; or, the Exact Picture of a Bad Husband* (1678). The satirists advised sleeping with other men's wives, or with prostitutes. With whores all that is to be feared is disease, 'and disease, you know, may hope to be cur'd, / But the torment of marriage can ne'er be endur'd.'[60]

On the other side of the debate were high-minded and practical arguments. Marriage is 'the noble centre of the mind'. 'Marriage puts the world into discipline and a happy government.'[61] The proverbial truth that an old hedge offers the best shelter is quoted by an author who justifies his supposed intention to marry a woman twenty years his senior by saying she will 'be the delight of my soul rather than my eye', that his affection is based on reason rather than physical attractions, and that 'in marrying her I marry happiness; not the stoical happiness of content with a little, but with much, even whatsoever I can wish for, within the power of wisdom and policy.'[62] Even real domestic tragedies became vehicles for the moralizers. One day in May 1677 a tubman intervened to prevent a Thames lighterman from murdering his wife with a half-pike in Nightingale Lane – or, as the author of *A Caution to Married Couples* (1677) 'wittily' put it, 'observing the unnatural combat between the two that were (or at least should be) both one flesh, and that the head was going to spit the rib', the tubman stepped in and received a fatal blow. Such tragedies were only to be expected in light of the 'discontents, hatred and cruelties' witnessed every day because people married for lust, money or 'some other sinister bias' and neglected 'virtue and equality or agreement, as well in fortune and quality, as humour (the great or rather only cement that can firmly knit the matrimonial bond)'. Marriage was not only the path to true happiness, according to these writers, but a safeguard for morality and property. During the Lords' debate on the Roos divorce, the Earl of Bristol protested that divorce would destroy 'domestic peace' in families and observed that, while ladies of quality had in the past admitted adultery so as to be free 'to enjoy her love', allowing a way 'to be unmarried again' would unleash disaster.[63] We have already heard passing references to adultery as the invasion of another's freehold, and have noted the property transactions at the heart of many marriages, so it comes as no surprise to learn that marriage was the first manifestation of property rights, and that 'by marriage, and the issue of the bed, men had within themselves a lordship and dominion'.[64]

Patriarchalist arguments of this kind were aimed particularly at the libertine outlook and 'the fanatical definitions of the self-conceited Malmesbury philosopher', Thomas Hobbes. Libertines, it was alleged, 'think that the satisfying of an ungoverned appetite is more important than the being kind and obliging to common nature'.[65] Narcissistic, egocentric, extravagant, they value their own passions above their duty to others, whether spouses, family, community, or posterity: but love, 'an impetuous and lawless appetite', needs to be tamed by marriage or it will consume 'the manly temper and vigour' of England's youth.[66] If asked where these libertines were, their critics would talk darkly of the influence of Hobbes, the stage and the poets, and refer to the rowdy gallants of London who practised what they taught. Libertinism of many kinds was seen on the stage. Comedies and romances were full of characters avoiding marriage as a condition hardly to be endured; and villains routinely denounced 'marriage, thou curse of love; and snare of life, / That first debas'd a mistress to a wife'.[67] The libertine figure, Philander, in Behn's novel *Love Letters*, scorns the bond of his marriage to Mertilla, telling his love Silvia,

> my soul was married to yours in its first creation; and only Silvia is the wife of my sacred, my everlasting vows; of my solemn considered thought, of my ripened judgement, my mature considerations. The rest are all repented and forgot, like the hasty follies of unsteady youth, like vows breathed in anger, and die perjured as soon as vented, and unregarded either of heaven and man.[68]

Philander is eventually exposed as a broken reed, as are most literary libertines.

Maximilian Novak has written of a libertine campaign against marriage, but that oversimplifies and overstates the literature.[69] These pam-

phlets also discussed wit and heroism, town and country, they were part
of the wars surrounding Dryden and Hobbes and their pretensions, and
yet at the same time these were pure exercises of the pen, displays of virtuosity in which the same author might write in favour of marriage one
day and against it the next, and, perhaps above all, they were commercial enterprises; the author and bookseller wanted to sell copies. There
was no serious attempt to undermine the institution of marriage or to
subvert patriarchy – as we have seen these trundled along in the time-
honoured fashion. Yet the popularity of the subject both for authors and
readers may be a symptom of an unease about sex, love and marriage
in Charles II's England. Why should marriage present itself as a ready
subject for poets and playwrights? Perhaps the commodification of sex
which we have already noted, and the possibility, at least in sophisticated
metropolitan minds, of separating sex and love, had their parts to play.
It is also possible that the rampant sexuality of the merry monarch and
his court prompted some of his subjects to wonder whether sex and marriage were important, even politically important, subjects. It is that possibility which the rest of this chapter explores.

2   Sex, the Court and Opposition

> With a court, & a stage, with a lie
> I corrupted the age with a hoe
> I have made the city drunk, & the senate's my punk,
> With a hey tre, nonny, nonny noe
>
> 'A base song' on Charles II,
> from Sir William Haward's manuscript miscellany

> Now all I have to say for myself is that you know, as to love, one is not
> mistress of one's self . . .
>
> Duchess of Cleveland to Charles II, 28 June 1678

The sex lives of the monarch and his courtiers were common knowledge. Charles's sexual history was long and involved. After a series of
youthful liaisons, in 1660 he fell for Barbara Palmer, who in due course
became the Duchess of Cleveland, and the pre-eminent royal mistress.
But there were others, actresses and singers like Moll Davies, Elizabeth
Farley, Mary Knight and Nell Gwynn, maids of honour and, it was
alleged, common whores brought to the King up the private backstairs
controlled by William Chiffinch, page of the King's bedchamber. By the
late 1660s, Charles and Cleveland had drifted apart, and in 1671 Louise
de Quérouaille established herself in the King's affections and became
the second great royal mistress of the reign. Although their sexual relationship may have finished by 1676, the grip of Louise, now Duchess of
Portsmouth, over her former lover remained firm. Charles continued to

have other relationships: when Hortense Mancini, Duchesse de Mazarin, arrived in London in 1675, he set her up in apartments at St James's Palace and granted her an annual pension of £3000. Some women got away – Frances Stuart, Duchess of Richmond, never succumbed to the King – and others were turned down – Charles apparently declined the pleasures of the Countess of Clanbrassil.

Nicknamed 'Old Rowley', after a stallion in his stud or a pet goat, Charles was clearly a virile and sensual man with a large sexual appetite, and the opportunities to satisfy it. Incidental glimpses of his sexual foibles probably mean little. Pepys had it on good authority that at the height of the second Dutch war, 'the King's greatest pleasure hath been with his fingers, being able to do no more'.[70] Rochester advised Nell Gwynn both in letters and verse to 'cherish' the King's 'love wherever it inclines, and be assured you can commit no greater folly than pretending to be jealous; but on the contrary, with hand, body, head, heart and all the faculties you have contribute to his pleasure all you can, and comply with his desires throughout.'[71] There was always much 'toying' with mistresses in private, and Charles found it impossible to restrain himself from stroking and petting Louise in public. Of all the commentators, it is Halifax who offers the most convincing portrait of Charles's love life. The King's 'inclinations to love were the effects of health, and a good constitution, with as little mixture of the seraphic part as ever man had.' There was 'an implied bargain' with his easy-going mistresses that precluded jealousy, while 'his patience for their frailties showed him no exact lover.' Charles and his mistresses were not 'heroic refined lovers' who sought their pleasure in difficult courtships and passionate commitments.[72]

Charles's liaisons were fruitful. A satirist was tempted to compare him to Henry VIII, but Charles was resolved to have only one wife, 'and other men's he never swives. / Yet hath he sons and daughters more / Than e'er had Harry by threescore'; another writes of 'seventy-five royal bastards boys and girls'.[73] In fact fourteen 'natural' children were acknowledged by the King. The eldest was James, Duke of Monmouth, born to Lucy Walter in 1649 and the youngest was Mary Tudor born to the actress Moll Davies in 1673. Charles also had children by Portsmouth and Elizabeth Killigrew (one each), by Gwynn and Catherine Pegge (two each), and by Cleveland, who produced six.[74] In addition, there were the reputed children, such as Lucy Walter's daughter Mary Taafe, who was nicknamed 'the princess' and boasted of her brother Monmouth, and who was granted an annual pension of £600 in the 1670s. Charles created an extensive alternative royal family of mistresses, ex-mistresses and their children, many of whom enjoyed the title of duke or duchess and all of whom received pensions or other perks at the hands of their generous King and father.

Where Charles II led, his court was sure to follow. Whereas a royal court was, by convention, an arena for gallantries and amours, and the natural meeting place for unwed sons and daughters of the elite, some Restoration courtiers went far beyond the bounds of courtly love. The Duke of York was notoriously promiscuous. He was alleged to have 'come out of his wife's bed and gone to another laid out for him'; and Pepys was worried when James 'did eye my wife mightily' in the park.[75] The King's one-time best friend, the Duke of Buckingham, flaunted his affair with Anna-Maria Brudenell, Countess of Shrewsbury; the Duke of Monmouth was a chip off the old block, pursuing numerous and concurrent intrigues. Of course there was always an inclination to romanticize these liaisons. In 1675 one of the Duchess of York's maids of honour, Mrs Needham, 'having managed an intrigue of love with his grace the Duke of Monmouth a little too grossly, has forsaken her service and is retired, nobody knows whither nor how, but there are romantic stories told of her, which exceed all the adventures of errant ladies that were ever heard'.[76] Courtiers such as Rochester, Montagu, Jermyn, Sedley, Buckhurst, Fanshaw, Porter and Killigrew, were seducers and adulterers. In the small world of the court, affairs and marriages took on an almost incestuous character, with rakes seducing both a mother and daughter or sharing mistresses, and mothers losing track of the paternity of their off-spring. Monmouth had an affair with Lord Grey's wife, Mary, with Grey's apparent approval; meanwhile Grey embarked upon an affair with his wife's younger sister, Lady Henrietta Berkeley, which led in 1682 to his trial for abducting his lover and later their flight abroad – this was the germ of Behn's novel *Love Letters between a Nobleman and his Sister.*[77] Other husbands were less compliant. The inveterate duellist Henry Bulkeley was sent to the Tower in 1675 for challenging Ossory who had been too free with Sophia, Bulkeley's wife; two years later the two men fought a bloodless duel and 'the old quarrel about Mr B[ulkeley's] wife is the town talk.'[78]

The court was a strangely eroticized institution. It was a hothouse of intrigue, both political and sexual, all fuelled by the gossip, the nocturnal visitors on the private stairs, the assignations in private rooms, country houses, masquerades, boxes at the theatre and dark corners of the rambling palaces. Even the court's most enthusiastic habitues could find it wearing: Rochester complained that one could not think at court 'or at least as if you were shut up in a drum, you can think of nothing but the noise [which] is made about you'.[79] That noise was, in part, a thrum of sexual energy which emanated from the febrile, drunken young courtiers, from their more jaded seniors, and above all from the insistent interest of Charles. Frances Stuart had to flee court to escape prostituting herself to the King; Pepys heard of a Suffolk parson's daughter leaping to her death rather than submitting to royal advances; and

– as we have noted – courtiers' wives were sent to the country for their own 'safety'. The oppressive sexuality of the court can be sensed in the ghost-written memoirs of the Comte de Gramont or in the uneasy observations of the prim diarist John Evelyn. It is discernible in the portraits of several of the court's ladies, some of which were titillating 'closet pieces', nude studies of Nell or Barbara as Venus meant for private viewing only. The so-called Windsor beauties, the series of portraits of court ladies painted by Sir Peter Lely for the Duke of York, or Lely's portraits of Louise and the other mistresses, offer a glimpse of a contemporary sensuality. One example is the portrait of Margaret Hughes, Prince Rupert's mistress, which is reproduced on the cover of this book. All of Lely's pictures famously 'had an air one of another, all the eyes were sleepy alike', but the languor of his women was intended to appeal to his patrons and their tastes.[80] However, it was probably the verse produced by the courtier poets which contributed most to the court's atmosphere of heady sensuality and which now offers us the most intimate view of the behaviour and values of the court.

This was coterie verse, designed to be tossed off as a lyric or a satire and to be enjoyed by the small and self-regarding circle of courtiers and hangers-on, and yet it was meant, too, to capture and express a certain insouciance or disdain towards convention and morality; it was, in short, libertine, aristocratic and care-free. So the poets complained of the pangs of love and then, in their next breath, appealed to 'tell me no more of constancy'; these were light-hearted songs or worldly acknowledgements of the paradoxes of love and sex. Let the 'meaner spirits of your sex' confine themselves to just one man, says the speaker in Rochester's *Upon His Leaving His Mistress*, 'and shall my Celia be confined? / No! Live up to thy mighty mind, / And be the mistress of mankind.' The apparent advocacy of free love was matched by a willingness to contemplate mutual pleasure: ''Twixt strifes of love and war the difference lies in this: / When neither overcomes, love's triumph greater is.'[81] This seductive vision of sexual freedom, albeit tinged with the jealousies and regrets inherent in the human condition, was only one side of the courtly versification practised by Rochester, Buckhurst and friends. The other was the satire, lampoon or libel, frequently impromptu, usually scurrilous and often brilliant, but always designed to appeal to those, primarily courtiers themselves, who were fascinated by the doings of the court. One lampoon begins 'this way of writing I observe by some / Is introduced by an exordium / But I will leave to make all that ado / And in plain English tell you who fucks who.' Another set of verses begins, 'Cary's face is not the best . . .', and then catalogues the attractions and defects of eighteen of the court ladies.[82] The famous *Signior Dildo* slanders a long list of court ladies and whores, or as one contemporary put it, 'it reaches and touches most of the ladies from Westminster to Wapping.' Attributed to Rochester, and composed as a comment on the Modena marriage, *Signior Dildo* is a song to the tune of 'Peg's gone to sea with a soldier' and it was probably intended that further verses should be added at will. Although the ludicrous conceit that 'a rabble of pricks' ambush the signior and run him out of town balances the poem's misogyny with a suitably sour note about masculinity, yet it cannot disguise the fact that satire was a man's world in which women were the object of ridicule or worse.[83] The scabrous attacks on Cleveland, such as *Mistress Knights Advice to the Duchess of Cleveland in Distress for a Prick*, were violent and obscene. As Lady Frances Brudenell wrote to Lady Hatton in 1680, 'the lampoons that are made of most of the town ladies are so nasty that no woman will read them or I would have got them for you.' And it was not only in verse that women came off badly.[84]

For all the talk of mutual joy and freedom in love, the women who became caught up with the fast-living court seem to have been ill used, in Rochester's words 'to suffer the general fate of errant woman / Be very proud awhile, then very common'.[85] Insulted, abused, betrayed and abandoned, many of these young women have sunk back into the obscurity from which they came. Rochester began his affair with Elizabeth Barry when she was seventeen, she had borne him a child, and their affair had ended, in acrimony, before she was twenty. Mrs Barry, at least, had the talent, and in part thanks to Rochester the training, to make a career on the stage. Others were less fortunate. In 1678 Henry Savile met Jane Roberts, who had been mistress of both Rochester and the King, in a 'sweatshop' in Leather Lane where both were undergoing treatment for venereal disease. Savile was no stranger to the ravages of the disease nor to the horrors of its treatment with mercury, but even he was taken aback by her suffering, 'what she has endured would make a damned soul fall a-laughing at his lesser pains it is so far beyond description or belief.'[86] Jane Roberts died the following year.

Court ladies might hope to rise above some of the consequences of promiscuity. Lady Elizabeth Howard whose lovers included Monmouth, William Cavendish and Frank Newport, eventually 'stole a wedding' or eloped with Thomas Felton of Playford, a groom of the King's bedchamber, whom the King soon forgave 'though it is believed several others never will'.[87] At sixteen Cary Fraser, daughter of Sir Alexander Fraser, the King's principal physician, and reputed procurer of abortifacients for the court ladies, became a maid of honour to Queen Catherine. Courted by Sir Carr Scroope, mistress of Mulgrave and then Mordaunt, who secretly married her when she became pregnant, Cary was sufficiently ambitious to set her cap at the King in 1677: 'She vowed the King . . . must take 'er / Rowley replied he was retrenching / And would no more of costly wenching.'[88] Mary or Mall Kirke was a maid of honour to the Duchess of York from 1673 to 1675 when she lost her position after unexpectedly giving birth at St James's Palace. The newsletters cruelly mocked her. It was said that as soon as she had realized that she was pregnant, Mall became a Catholic and announced her intention to retire to a nunnery, but she was persuaded to remain at court a while to disprove the 'scurvy suspicion' that she was with child. She almost got away with it but unfortunately dallied too long, 'being unskilful in such affairs, mistook her reckoning and was surprised' by the onset of labour.[89] The scathing tone of this account may reflect moral outrage at so indecent a scandal at court, or it may arise from the associations with Catholicism. Mall had apparently been mistress of the Duke of York, the Duke of Monmouth and the Earl of Mulgrave simultaneously. Mulgrave, who wrote an erotic verse account of a sexual relationship that might well have its origins in their affair, was suspected by some of fathering Mall's baby. When Mall's brother, Captain Percy Kirke challenged Mulgrave for debauching his sister and then wounded him in the duel, the scandal-mongers had a field day: 'we know that this or something else has caused a thousand stories to be raised about the father of the child.'[90] After a decent interval in France she returned to become first the mistress and then the second wife of a Shropshire gentleman.

A very few women were able to turn the tables on men. The Duchess of Cleveland and the Countess of Shrewsbury took lovers in what was almost the current masculine fashion – Cleveland's lovers included soldiers, acrobats, actors, and playwrights, young men on the make like John Churchill and William Wycherley. Naturally these ladies and their appetites became the satirists' targets. Cleveland was accused of 'disabling stoutest stallions ev'ry hour'. This was a vision of the female harpy; 'husbands and lovers, all she makes her prey'. Such women will 'play, they'll drink, talk filth'ly and profane, / With more extravagance than any man'.[91] Reckless by nature, these exceptional women ultimately relied on the protection of powerful men, and were not above using their protectors to defend their honour. Henry Killigrew was banished from court for insulting remarks about Cleveland's juvenile lechery. He did not learn his lesson, however, and later defamed the Countess of Shrewsbury; 'they say that of late he had showed about publicly a paper signed by her (as he affirmed) when they were kind one to another, attesting the ability of his performance (viz. thirty-four or thirty-five times in three nights).' The Countess's servants waylaid Killigrew's coach on the road to Hammersmith and beat him. Just as shocking as the attack and its motive was the fact that since the Countess was now Buckingham's mistress, and as Buckingham basked in royal favour, no action was taken: 'this makes it worthy observation. Being a riot of so heinous a nature to all government.'[92]

I

'The court,' wrote one English author, 'is the epitome of a kingdom, or rather a mirror . . . [and] the royal presence is the only soul that animates a court.'[93] Unfortunately he was writing in praise of Louis XIV, the diligent, self-restrained, master of France. The English court was far from laudable. And everyone knew it. Evelyn famously thought that it more resembled 'a luxurious and abandoned rout than a Christian court'. William Lawrence, a Gloucestershire squire, would have given a correspondent an account of the intrigues of Charles's court, for 'here is room enough for all the whips of a satirist, but it is neither decent nor safe to peep into the cabinets or pry too nicely into the amours of princes'. That said, Lawrence continues, 'the royal example spreads too fast, and now the only stratagem of a great man is how to betray a beauty and undermine the chaste.' 'Vice now throws off the mask,' he remarks as he launches into the story of Buckingham's child by the Countess of Shrewsbury.[94] The court and courtiers fascinated many onlookers. Doubtless Pepys was not the only man to dream 'that I had my lady Castlemaine in my arms and was admitted to use all dalliance I desired with her'.[95] The English were transfixed by these gilded figures and horrified by their debauchery; if the court was a mirror of society what did it say about them? And if the King was its soul what did it say about him?

That 'the royal example spreads too fast' had long been acknowledged. From the Restoration, Charles's sexual behaviour was the subject of criticism among his subjects. In 1674 John Weedon was prosecuted for saying that the King keeps 'nothing but whores' and was 'a scourge to the nation'; in 1677 a Yorkshire yeoman stated that 'the King minds nothing but women'; rumours circulated that he had been taken at a 'common house' or arrested at a brothel. The popular charge that Charles was a 'whoremaster', that he was 'sick of the pox with using so many whores', merged with the other scurrilous accusations that he was a knave, rascal, liar, thief, bastard and papist.[96] This unfocused popular abuse was worrying, but not so alarming perhaps as the better informed criticism heard in some of London's coffee-houses, never mind the explicit criticism of the King's behaviour by those such as clergymen who could speak with moral authority. Pepys was alarmed by Dr Robert Creighton's 'strange bold sermon . . . against the sins of the court, and particularly against adultery, over and over instancing how for that single sin in David, the whole nation was undone'. In a 1675 sermon before the King and court Edward Stillingfleet read them a long lecture on sexual laxity. In January 1681 Gilbert Burnet wrote to Charles setting 'before him his past ill life, and the effects it had on the nation, with the judgements of God that lay on him'.[97]

Why did Charles's bad example matter so much? It was axiomatic that as father of the nation Charles was its moral exemplar; the patriarch had to exemplify virtue and to maintain discipline in his immediate household and in the national family. Vices were believed to spread down the social hierarchy until they infected the masses. The malign influence of the court was a hackneyed theme of many different kinds of work, from those analysing the economic woes of the nation to those criticizing foreign policy: they lament 'the luxury of our court, whereby thousands, specially of the youth, are debauched, from all virtue, and those sums, which might be a great accession to the trading stock of the nation, turned out of that channel, to the maintenance of prodigality, and that beggarly villainous train, wherewith they are attended'.[98] The supreme governor of the Church of England should be a godly prince upholding protestantism and Christian virtue. A debauched and vicious ruler was a provocation to God, and although few preachers, Anglican or dissenting, pointed a finger directly at Charles, the burden of many of their sermons was that the nation would be punished if it continued on its immoral path. Protestant providentialism taught that bad rulers were a divine chastisement visited on a godless people, that prince and people could mirror each other.

An obvious case of the sort of bad example that was held to be both offensive to God and subversive of a central institution of seventeenth-century society is the court's attitude to holy matrimony. Courtiers mocked marriage by their sham marriages. Some of these were mere deceits to inveigle their mistresses into bed: the Earl of Oxford went to elaborate lengths to persuade Hester Davenport that they had been properly wed. Sir Charles Sedley, whose mad Catholic wife was in a Belgian nunnery, went through some form of marriage with Anne Ayscough in April 1672: as he wrote *To Cloris*, 'What a priest says moves not the mind, / Souls are by love, not words, combin'd.' In exile Monmouth treated Henrietta Wentworth as his wife and on the eve of his execution maintained that she was his lawful wife before God. The Duke of Norfolk told Evelyn that although he kept 'that idle creature and common whore', Mrs Jane Bickerton, and had children with her, he would not marry her; but in 1678 they did indeed marry. And most notoriously of all, Buckingham treated the Countess of Shrewsbury as his wife, and added injury to the insult by wounding the Earl of Shrewsbury in a duel. When the Countess bore Buckingham a son, the infant was baptized with the King standing as godfather; and when the child died, he was buried as a legitimate child of the Villiers' line. This disdain for marriage was even echoed in the King's dealings with his mistresses: in October 1671 Charles stayed at Arlington's country house, and according to Evelyn, who was also a house guest, 'it was universally reported that the fair lady [Louise] was bedded one of these nights, and the stocking flung, after the manner of a married bride.' Evelyn categorically denied that he was present at such a 'ceremony', but it was widely believed that 'she was first made a *miss*, as they call these unhappy creatures, with solemnity at this time.'[99]

Marriage seemed to be a matter of mere convenience – 'a ceremony imposed on man by custom . . . a trick devised by the wary old, only to make provision for posterity' (in the words of Behn's libertine Philander).[100] But these were not negligible matters to the propertied classes of seventeenth-century England. Paternity, legitimacy, succession, ownership went to the heart of the concerns of those with broad acres, noble names or other riches to pass on to the next generation. Recall the scandal that surrounded Lord Roos's divorce bill in 1670. The dissolute Roos had already separated from his unfaithful wife, he had already had both of her sons declared illegitimate, but what he needed now was the freedom to remarry and father legitimate children to inherit his title and his estates. *Mutatis mutandis* these issues were relevant to Charles's own situation. 'The King disavows' divorce, reported Marvell, 'yet he has said in public, he knew not why a woman might not be divorced for barrenness, as a man for impotency.'[101] And not only did the security of the monarch's claim to his inheritance act as a kind of guarantee for all the subordinate property holders, it was a fundamental prerequisite of political stability. The importance of the succession in a monarchy meant that the monarch's sexuality and virility were vital political issues.

The Stuarts clearly had a virile dynast in Charles II; it was scarcely his fault that his wife was barren, that he was harnessed, in Dryden's words, 'to a soil ungrateful to the tiller's care'.[102] If he could not bring himself to follow Roos's example and divorce the Queen, then why not legitimate a royal bastard? Despite his casual liaisons, Charles was careful about which of his putative children he acknowledged. He was implacable in refusing to acknowledge as his own Cleveland's child by Henry Jermyn in the face of her threats and tantrums. In the crisis years after 1678 some thought Monmouth a natural choice as heir. Rumours flew around that he would be legitimized; York was furious when the usual phrase 'our natural son' was omitted from Monmouth's patent as Captain General in 1678. Monmouth's supporters persisted, despite Charles's repeated and formal denials, in their claims that Charles had secretly married Monmouth's mother. Others claimed that Monmouth had a right by the 'law of nature' and that the laws of marriage and legitimacy were a clerical con trick.[103] This kind of argument, with its distant echo of libertinism, was exactly what the conservative squirearchy feared. And it was, they believed, the direct result of the King's own sexual laxity. John Lacy accurately captured their thinking in his 1677 satire on Charles.

Thy base example ruins the whole town,
For all keep whores, from gentleman to clown;
The issue of a wife's unlawful seed,
And none's legitimate but bastard breed.
Thou and thy brachs have quite cross'd the strain;
We ne'er shall see a true-bred whelp again.
An honest, lawful wife's turn'd out of doors,
And he most honour has that keeps most whores.[104]

The debauched court was not only a bad moral example, it was a burden on the nation. The expense of Charles's sexual self-indulgence was staggering. Charles's two chief mistresses, Cleveland and Portsmouth, reaped huge rewards for their favours. During the 1670s the two duchesses and their children were in receipt of permanent grants worth more than £45,000 a year. Nell Gwynn received £8000 in gifts between 1670 and 1677, but Portsmouth enjoyed an annual pension of £12,000. These women flaunted their wealth. In Hyde Park Cleveland's coach was pulled by eight horses, when even the King's only had six. Gwynn bought the lease of her Pall Mall house 'in ready money' and planned 'to have it richly furnished'. Portsmouth's apartments had 'ten times the richness and glory beyond the Queen's, such massy pieces of plate, whole tables, stands etc, of incredible value', observed Evelyn in 1675.[105] In 1679, Danby was anxious lest secret service payments of more than £55,000 to Portsmouth should become public knowledge.

While bemoaning Cleveland's wealth in 1671, Marvell also lamented that 'all promotions, spiritual and temporal, pass under her cognisance'.[106] The mistresses used their influence incessantly. Petitioners naturally sought the aid of 'Madame Gwynn or some other powerful person'. Portsmouth was systematic and effective: she made the careers of some politicians, such as Sunderland, and saved those of others: at Newmarket in the spring of 1676, 'there was a great falling out between the Duke and the Treasurer, whose friend, Portsmouth (tho she had but newly miscarried) went down immediately to keep the staff where 'twas.'[107] Portsmouth was not just a tool of domestic factions, her most important role was as a go-between for Louis and Charles. In 1678, for instance, Reresby did not believe talk of war, because he had seen 'the King, Duke and French ambassador so often very merry and intimate at the Duchess of Portsmouth's lodgings, laughing at those that believed it in earnest'.[108] Unpopular with the masses, these mistresses were the object of parliamentary animosity. In 1679 MPs openly compared Louise to Delilah and she was alleged to be on her knees begging the King for a prorogation of parliament to prevent further attacks upon herself.

The unpopularity of Charles's mistresses was an amalgamation of many preoccupations. The romantic arrival in London of Hortense

Mancini, Duchesse de Mazarin, in mud-spattered long coat and boots, 'furnishes the women with some tattle' reported one MP. But in the coffee-houses in the winter of 1675–7, Mazarin's arrival 'does afford matter for politic reflection'. Perhaps she had been sent over by Louis to reinforce the efforts made by Portsmouth on behalf of the French interest? Or perhaps Montagu had sent her to aid Arlington's struggle against Danby and his supporter Portsmouth? Or perhaps the Duke of York was drawn to her bed 'though devotion has given his highness a new turn, the bowls, you know, will still to their bias'. Whatever the explanation, it was likely that 'the nation, already too sensible of the amorous excesses of their prince, may be more inflamed by such an accession of great expense that way.'[109]

In a court-centred political system the implications of personal preferences were legion. Halifax put it succinctly when he observed of Charles that 'mistresses were recommended to him; which is no small matter in a court, and not unworthy the thoughts even of a party.' When Lady Clanbrassil offered herself to the King in 1671, she thought 'to trip up Nell Gwynn's heels, and you cannot imagine how highly my Lord Arran and many others do value themselves upon the account of managing Lady Clanbrassil in this affair'.[110] In 1678 Henry Savile reported on a byzantine conspiracy launched by Ralph Montagu and his sister Lady Hervey to undermine Nell (and simultaneously discredit Portsmouth) by dangling the sixteen year old Jenny Middleton before Charles:

> my lady Hervey who always loves one civil plot more, is working body and soul to bring Mrs Jenny Middleton into play, how dangerous a new one is to all old ones I need not tell you, but her Ladyship having little opportunity of seeing Charlemagne upon her own account wheadles poor Mrs Nelly onto supping twice or thrice a week at W[illiam] C[hiffinch's] and carrying her with her; so that in good earnest this poor creature is betrayed by her Ladyship to pimp against herself . . .[111]

The devastating effect of this combination of the sexual and the political is best demonstrated not by any of Charles's relationships but by the debacle unleashed when Cleveland fell out with her lover Ralph Montagu in 1678. The direct consequence was the revelations to parliament which culminated in Danby's fall. In the summer of 1678 Henry Savile wrote of 'terrible doings at Paris betwixt my Lady Cleveland and her daughter Sussex'. Cleveland and Montagu had enjoyed a long standing, if not exclusive affair; while Cleveland was visiting England in the spring of 1678, Montagu had begun a very public affair with her seventeen-year-old daughter, Anne, Countess of Sussex, who was almost certainly the daughter of the King. Cleveland appealed to Charles and accused Montagu of disloyalty to his monarch; the ambassador returned to London, but Charles refused to see him. 'The King being very angry with the ambassador and his friends and enemies now struggling at court to support or ruin him,' wrote the cynical Savile, 'the latter is I think the likeliest in every court it being the easiest and the worst natured.'[112]

II

It has rightly been remarked that 'stories about royal or court sexuality' were a legitimate part of political discourse in Restoration England just as they were in *ancien régime* France.[113] Discussion of royal sexuality and its dangers was most explicit in manuscript satires, libels, and ballads distributed through 'scribal publication' and in some surreptitiously printed material. What has been called the 'Marvellian tradition' of political satire, exemplified by the *Advice to a Painter* poems, launched attacks on the government across a wide front, with sexual accusations mixed in among all the rest. Thus the manuscript mock bill of sale advertising forty-four lots to be sold on 29 May 1673 at the royal coffee-house included such items as national honour, the Protestant religion, parliamentary independence, offices, plans for a royal divorce and for legitimizing Monmouth, while lot one was 'one whole piece of the Duchess of Cleveland's honesty', lot two was 'two ells of Nell Gwynn's virginity in three pieces', and lot thirty-five was two dozen French wenches, one half 'paid by his Majesty to keep him to the right in the Protestant religion, the other half to incline him to the Catholic, managed by the two factions in the Cabal'.[114] Other verses and ballads prophesied the end of English liberty, the destruction of law and property, the abolition of Magna Carta – 'then the English shall a greater tyrant know, / Then either Greek or Gallic stories show; / Their wives to's lust expos'd, their wealth to's spoil, / To fill his empty treasury, they must toil.' Or 'now the world's ruled by cheating and swiving' according to a ballad of the early 1670s:

> Of a vast new supremacy the plot,
> First laid in Scotland by Lauderdale the Scot.
> His, and Jack Barclay's army shall make good
> A Scottish union, laid in English blood.
> Lust chang'd our religion first:
> Lust makes a new supremacy. Which is worst?
> Lust banisht the chaste Spanish Katherine.
> Remarry Roos, and do the same again.[115]

This kind of outright attack portrays royal sexuality as part and parcel of misgovernment. In other satires, tyranny itself was represented in sexual terms. In John Ayloffe's *Britannia and Raleigh* (1674–5), for

example, a female form speaks for absolute government and urges
Charles to

> taste the delicious sweets of sovereign power
> 'Tis royal game whole kingdoms to deflower
> Three spotless virgins to your bed I bring,
> A sacrifice to you their god and king.[116]

But there is perhaps more going on here than the use of rape as a
metaphor for arbitrary rule. It was not only the exercise of tyranny, but
also its psychology, which was explicable in terms of lust.

The great tyrants of history were men of unrestrained lust – Nero,
the Tarquins, Tiberius, Heliogabalus and the Assyrian Sardanapalus.
These were all voluptuaries: they knew no restraint, no limits but their
own appetites, and they followed their lusts into luxury and even self-
destruction. *The History of Insipids* (1674), a corruscating republican satire
suspected to be the work of John Freke, declared that Louis and Charles,
the French wolf and the British goat, 'know no law but their own lust'.[117]
And the courtier, Rochester, in more humorous vein, wrote of Charles's
as 'the proudest and peremptoriest prick alive / What e'er religion and
his laws say on it / He'll break through those to come to any cunt.'[118] In
Sodom, a pornographic satire of the mid-1670s often attributed to
Rochester, the tyrant Bolloxinian enters with the line, 'thus in the zenith
of my lust I reign / I drink to swive, and swive to drink again' – he later
boasts that 'with my prick I'll govern all the land.'[119]

No-one seems to have doubted that Charles II was a monarch who
could be led by the prick. He hates all business and thinks of nothing
but pleasure, Pepys was told: Castlemaine 'rules him' because she has
'all the tricks of Aretino that are to be practised to give pleasure – in
which he is too able, having a large ****'.[120] Or as Rochester has it, 'his
pintle and his sceptre are of a length / And she may sway the one who
plays with the other.'[121] The King might vow that 'whatever it cost I will
have a fine whore / As bold as Al'ce Pierce and as fair as Jane Shore,
/ And when I am weary of them I'll have more,' but like his medieval
predecessors whose mistresses Alice and Jane had been, he would be
the prisoner not the master of his whores.[122] Charles was a victim, or so
the satirists lamented: 'women have grossly snar'd the wisest prince';
'was ever prince's soul so meanly poor, / To be enslav'd to ev'ry little
whore.'[123] Talk about the visits of Nell Gwynn and Portsmouth became
very personal – 'now they let not his sacred body alone' – when it was
rumoured that Charles suffered a fit in Portsmouth's presence in 1673:
the insinuation being, presumably, that the royal strength and health
were being drained away by his amorous activities.[124]

Royal potency was constantly called into question. The attack on
Coventry for his gibe about the King's pleasure among the actresses was

commemorated in 'a woeful ditty', *A Ballad called the Haymarket Hectors*
(1671), which portrayed 'our amorous Jove' compensating for his impotence with Nell by sending his life guards to avenge her honour, heedless of the nation's needs and parliament's honour. If Charles would
venture his parliamentary subsidies to placate Nell, asks the ballad, what
would he unleash to defend Cleveland, 'the prerogative whore'?[125] The
effect of Portsmouth was even more damaging, said the satirists:

> his fair soul, transformed by that French dame,
> Had lost all sense of honour, justice, fame.
> Like a tame spinster in's seragl' he sits,
> Besieged by whores, buffoons, and bastard chits;
> Lulled in security, rolling in lust,
> Resigns his crown to angel Carwell's trust.[126]

This was the very image of the effeminate king, enslaved to private pleasures and those who provide them: 'nothing but wickedness and wicked
men and women command the King,' observed Evelyn, 'it is not in his
nature to gainsay anything that relates to his pleasures.'[127] Charles was
beyond repentance, said John Lacy;

> Go practice Heliogabalus's sin:
> Forget to be a man and learn to spin,
> Go dally with the women and their wheels
> Till Nero-like they drag thee out by the heels.[128]

It was an effeminate King who 'seems like bold Mars only in the works
of Venus, but like Venus in the arms of Mars', who shuns war for the
battles of the bedroom.[129] The Gloucestershire squire, Lawrence regret-
ted that Charles 'too much softened by his long converse with the softer
sex, seems so little inclined to the rough salutes of war'. Lawrence compared the life of Charles's subjects to that of a dog who fears and loves
and that of the King to a duck 'who swives and tipples'. But kings should
concern themselves with 'sublimer things'. 'It is much more heroic . . .
to conquer other nations, than enslave their own.'[130] Unflattering comparisons were often drawn between amorous Charles and his bellicose
French cousin, 'the cully of Britain' and 'the hector of France':

> More tolerable are the lion king's slaughters
> Than the goat's making whores of our wives and our daughters.
> The debauched and the cruel, sith they equally gall us,
> I had rather bear Nero than Sardanapalus.[131]

Evelyn told Pepys that Louis had mistresses, 'but laughs at the foolery
of our King, that makes his bastards princes, and loses his revenue upon
them – and makes his mistresses his masters'.[132] John Oldham brought
out the same contrast between the hero and the lover in an ironic
refutation of those 'saucy pedants and historians', who object to

Sardanapalus's devotion to sex, with the argument that his fame will last, 'and where in fame does the vast difference lie / T'have fought, or fucked for universal monarchy?'[133]

This was the illusion at the heart of tyranny. Potency, sexual energy, was not sufficient to rule the world:

> As Nero once, with harp in hand, survey'd
> His flaming Rome and, as that burn'd, he play'd
> So our great prince, when the Dutch fleet arriv'd,
> Saw his ships burn and, as they burn'd, he swiv'd.
> So kind was he in our extremest need,
> He would those flames extinguish with his seed.
> But against fate all human aid is vain:
> His prick then prov'd as useless as his chain.[134]

As the King aged, his potency waned. An attack on Portsmouth described her as the power behind the throne, her 'slaves' steering the English 'man of war',

> Yet without doubt they might conduct
> Him better, were you better f-ck't
> Many begin to think of late
> His crown and cods have both one date
> For as these fall, so falls the state
> And as the reins prove loose, and weak
> The reins of government must break.[135]

The poets constantly reminded their readers that the sexual drive was doomed to disappointment, it was an imperfect enjoyment, 'our joys . . . lessen still as they draw near', and for men especially the moment of sexual satisfaction brought 'a loss of power and substance'. This, argues Rachel Weil, was what, for seventeenth-century minds, made lust so insatiable, power so 'elusive and unstable', and tyranny a condition in which the location of power was unknown.[136]

These satires, all of which converge in their portrayal of Charles II as an impotent, effeminate, slave to lust, deserve and are receiving recognition in their own right. The political pornography, the 'pornopolitics' as it has been called, of England in the 1670s is an interesting phenomenon; but did it have a significant effect?[137] Some still doubt it. Even while remarking upon Rochester's extraordinarily sexualized attacks on Charles, their significance is dismissed by a recent account of rakes and libertines (although to be fair, one written with an eye to the emergence of civility).[138] Yet, as we have seen, Rochester was not alone. The voluminous political pornography was an irritant to the government: the abortive prosecution of John Freke or the efforts of L'Estrange to control manuscript dissemination prove that. Rochester fled the court after mistakenly handing Charles his acerbic satire, 'In the isle of Great

Britain . . .'; and in 1677 Buckingham appealed to Rochester to come to court to rebut their enemies' attempts to father 'a new treasonable lampoon' (probably Lacy's satire against Charles) on Rochester.[139] Satires hit home at court.

One might reflect on how this satire went down with other readers, in coffee-houses, taverns or country mansions. Obscene satire is a tricky language to use. John Oldham's modern editor, for example, believes that while there are implied parallels with the King, 'sexual conquest . . . not Charles is the focal subject' of *Sardanapalus*.[140] More prosaically, the medium can obscure the message, readers might find their attention wandering from the political satire to the pornographic effect. Further confusion is caused by the layers of irony so characteristic of wit literature. Is it a paradox that a libertine poem attacks the libertinism of the court? Or does the explanation lie, as Weil suggests, in the poet's need to adopt a libertine voice to escape accusations of killjoy, prude and puritan?[141] It might also be objected that since pornographic satire is primarily a language of mockery, it has at best a limited role to play in mounting a constructive critique of the political status quo. Yet, as Weil has observed, one of its most important functions was to connect 'popery' and 'tyranny', to help construct a common element of 'debauchery' between these two evils which opposition ideologues could then deploy.[142] This is undoubtedly true, even if it downplays the generations of theological and political argument which had established a connection in one direction, that is, that popery was tyrannical. Finally, there is, of course, a danger that these satires would be preaching to the converted. Surely only those already deeply suspicious of Charles II and all his works would relish these ferocious and obscene attacks? This does not, however, seem to have been the case.

Pornographic political satire was read and presumably appreciated by many people who were far from committed opponents of Charles II. This is obvious from the scale of manuscript dissemination. It was not only courtiers and diplomats who made copies of these verses, but provincial gentlemen in Leeds, nonconformist ministers in London and Lincolnshire landowners. What they copied into their commonplace books was also circulating around the coffee-houses. Is the impact of this material calculable? It would be naive to think that such gentlemen were immune to the pleasures of pornography, or that they were incapable of compartmentalizing parts of their life – it is still striking to encounter strange juxtapositions in their manuscript compilations, to find *Signior Dildo* side by side with a pindaric ode on the Bible. But the cumulative effect of all these 'base songs' and libels about the court and the monarch might well have been to create a sense of unease among individuals who thought of themselves as loyal subjects. It is also worth recalling that while some of the satires were by republican or Dutch opponents of Charles, most were the work of good royalists and many were by men who served the King. Obscene satires from within the court itself may have brought fears into focus for some or sown the seeds of doubt in others. And, although a direct effect cannot be demonstrated, we can imagine how the satires might have tainted the political atmosphere if we consider some of the more innocuous and politically orthodox publications of the decade in the light of these pornographic satires and the general concern about Charles's sleazy court.

In 1672 a pocket-sized book was published in London called *The Annals of Love, Containing Select Histories of the Amours of Divers Princes Courts, Pleasantly Related*. The anonymous author was at pains to stress that his book's twenty-one stories of love and romance were grounded in fact and authority.

> These annals of love are really history, whose fountains and originals I have on purpose inserted in the ensuing table. They are no witty and facetious inventions . . . but faithful touches taken out of history in general . . . Let no man expect a scheme of our present hypocrisy in this book; he that does will be mistaken, and find nothing but a faithful relation of the iniquity of old times. I confess I have added some ornament . . . If in the conferences and passages I have invented there happens any resemblance with the intrigues of our age . . . I protest I thought nothing of the present, when I spoke of what was past.[143]

What are we to make of this? Surely this author protests too much? The repeated denial of any relevance to the amours of Charles II's court only alerts us to the possibility of resemblances – a possibility strengthened when we notice that the *Annals* was published by the bookseller John Starkey who had repeatedly clashed with the government. The work contains passing remarks about the evils of debauchery and dissolute examples, yet the parallels with Restoration England are not strained. A long account of a medieval Aragonese king who divorced his wife and contracted a secret marriage in order to father an heir is wrapped up with an offhand comment, 'but we do ill to employ so much leisure on so barren a story'. No explicit criticism is made of Charles II, no coded references are employed, this is simply a collection of stories, but it suggests how confused questions of love, marriage, divorce and sex had become with domestic politics. Like Pepys racked with anxiety when he thought that the drama *The Duke of Lerma* was attacking Charles for his mistress, the attentive reader of the *Annals* would hear distant alarm bells.

The political echoes of sexuality may be audible in Dryden's double-plotted romance *Marriage à la Mode* which concerns mistaken identities, crossed lovers and the legitimate ruler of a pastoral 'Sicily'. The comic plot deals with the incompatibility of sexual passion and marital fidelity:

'our marriage is dead, when the pleasure is fled,' sings Doralice. The resulting comedy of manners is finally resolved by a pact based on mutual self-interest and the preservation of marriage. In the romance plot the rightful ruler only regains his crown thanks to the sacrifice of a noble woman and so one modern critic concludes that the conservative political control re-established at the play's end is illusory, 'the result of feminine self-exclusion rather than patriarchal mastery'. Although we cannot know whether such a reading would have suggested itself to seventeenth-century audiences, it certainly seems feasible that at some level Dryden was wrestling with the difficulty of containing sexuality within the neat confines of dramatic plots. Harold Weber has made a parallel point about the often explicit recommendation of the obscene satires that Charles should restore his authority, his relationship with men, by putting women to one side.[144]

The subversion of government by a ruler's sexuality was a constant theme of the stage. In view of the satires on Charles, consider the judgement of Vendentius, spokesman for Roman honour, on the fate of Antony at the hands of Cleopatra:

> She has left him
> The blank of what he was.
> I tell thee, eunuch, she has quite unmanned him.
> Can any Roman see and know him now,
> Thus altered from the lord of half mankind,
> Unbent, unsinewed, made a woman's toy . . .[145]

Even Maximin, the debased ruler of *Tyrannic Love*, exemplifies these issues. 'Free will's a cheat in any one but me: / In all but kings 'tis willing slavery,' he huffs. And yet a few minutes later, he is excusing himself:

> My loves are like my old Praetorian bands,
> Whose arbitrary power their prince commands:
> I can no more make passion come or go,
> Than you can bid your Nilus ebb and flow.
> 'Tis lawless, and will love, and where it list:
> And that's no sin which no man can resist . . .

The response to this pitiful plea was swift and unanimous: St Catherine praises 'kings who rule their own desires'; and some no doubt thought of Louis XIV who 'is a perfect master over himself, not tainted with any passion that might eclipse his other excellent qualities'.[146] So although it would be rash to make sweeping claims about the unsettling effects of obscene and clandestine satires on Charles's loyal subjects, just a moment's reflection begins to suggest what they might have implied for readers of perfectly respectable romances or for the audience of heroic tragedies.

This chapter has concentrated on a darker side of 'merry England', on a widespread sense that sexuality, especially the casual promiscuity of a section of elite society, symbolized much of what was amiss with the nation. These were difficult issues to articulate for many of Charles II's subjects, especially within the bounds of political loyalty and conventional decency, but gossip about the goings-on at court and dog-eared manuscripts of libellous and obscene verses may have put a name and face to all manner of nameless fears. Nor is it difficult to see why the banal and artificial debate on marriage, or the Roos divorce, touched a nerve. The fascination of theatre audiences with sex and libertinism more than hints at an anxiety about the power that women wield through their sexuality. Many subjects were critical of their monarch's self-indulgence, they were hostile to gold-digging harlots or sinister French paid Catholic mistresses, and they perhaps registered the more subversive message of the pornographic satire that a monarch's lusts are a direct route to tyranny.

8

Politics, Piety and Toleration

The satirical, obscene, negative language used to decry the court and monarch may, as the previous chapter argued, disclose the deeper fears of Charles II's subjects, but it was not mainstream political discourse. Among the more conventional idioms for the discussion of politics were an historical and legal idealization of the constitution, a descriptive language which concentrated on such issues as electoral 'interests' and 'service' to the monarch, and the abstract terminology of political philosophy. These political 'languages' are the starting point for this chapter. As we have seen in a different context, such languages can infect each other; muted echoes of one may be heard in another. We may even discern in these idioms the values and ideals which were supposedly under threat from 'popery and tyranny'. This chapter also explores the disparity between the ideals and the political practice of the 1670s. No greater disparity existed – and no domestic political problem was more troublesome – than that between the 'ideal' of religious uniformity and the reality of religious pluralism. The ideal enshrined in the religious settlement of 1662 was out of date by the 1670s. For many sober protestants, the threat now came not from the heterogeneous 'dissenting interest' created by 1662, but from the old enemy of popery and the new opponents of profanity, rationalism and atheism. Yet even as the religious landscape was changing around them, and even though they were sensitive to the new pastoral agenda, ministers of all denominations remained of necessity stout defenders of their confessional and institutional identities. Many walked a delicate line between their pastoral mission and their church's claims. Nowhere was this more acute than among the Anglican clergy. It was the debate about the Church of England's pretensions and the persecution of its opponents that raised some of the period's most fundamental questions about the role of the civil magistrate in religion.

1 Religion, Liberty and Property

> Who cannot but remember that religion, liberty and property were all lost and gone when the monarchy was shaken off; and could never be revived till that was restored.
>
> Charles II's Declaration of 8 April 1681

The trinity of religion, liberty and property was invoked in almost every speech at the opening of parliament in the 1670s and in countless seventeenth-century assize sermons and charges to the grand jury. 'The commons of England for hereditary fundamental liberties and properties are blessed above and beyond the subjects of any monarch or state in the world,' asserted Edward Chamberlayne; and in 1673 Charles assured critics of the Declaration of Indulgence that he did not 'pretend to the right of suspending any laws wherein the properties, rights, or liberties of his subjects are concerned'.[1] These are slippery terms. 'It's our reproach, that when foreigners ask us, what we mean by these liberties, rights, privileges, and properties of the subjects, they cannot find one in a thousand able to solve the question.'[2] But then there were advantages in ambiguity.

Religion, for example, meant that protestantism of which the English were so proud and protective; but by the 1670s there were several denominations of English protestants, some of whom vied with 'the church established by law' for the right to be thought definitively protestant while others, notably the Quakers, had begun to question the whole inheritance of the Reformation. And liberty, in the opinion of one modern scholar, 'came to mean those rights which had been granted by God to his people and which had never been surrendered by them to their kings'.[3] These rights were part of the status of English people as 'freeborn subjects' and that was a status much prized and often asserted in a bewildering range of circumstances from land disputes to protests against martial law. In July 1670 L'Estrange's men raided John Streater's printing-house with warrants to search and arrest suspects, but twenty people 'fell into an uproar, and begin crying out that they were freeborn subjects, and not to be meddled with by such a warrant'.[4] When the speculative builder Barbon stood upon the liberty of the subject in 1675 to redevelop the site of Essex House in the City against royal and civic opposition, he caused Attorney General Jones acute embarrassment. 'Knowing well the danger of splitting upon Magna Carta,' Jones demurred at proceedings, but was caught between those asking who if not the Attorney General would maintain the royal prerogative and those who wondered that Jones of all people should be 'against the liberty of the subject'.[5]

Property was often taken to be fundamental: property 'that is, right and title to your own lives, liberties and estates,' in William Penn's words;

and Sir Robert Howard agreed that 'life, liberty and estate is property.'[6] What this right consisted of, beyond some vague moral claim, was legal title, a right which could be upheld in law against all opponents. Subjects have the same right in their property as the King has in his 'regality', explained Marvell, 'and in all cases where the King is concerned, we have our just remedy as against any private person of the neighbourhood, in the Courts of Westminster Hall or in the High Court of Parliament'.[7] As Professor Nenner points out, the argument about property rights applied just as forcibly to the Duke of York's right to succeed to his patrimony, the crown of England.[8] Liberty could be asserted through the courts, but perhaps not as easily. In 1677 Shaftesbury was imprisoned by order of the House of Lords and sought his release through a habeas corpus action in King's Bench, where he unsuccessfully argued that although the House of Lords was a superior court, King's Bench could still judge any of its orders designed 'to deprive any subject of his liberty' and find it 'void if it be against Magna Carta'.[9] The intense interest taken in the freedom of the jury from judicial interference during this decade, or indeed the largely unfounded complaints about royal encroachment on judicial independence, are simply further examples of this assumption that 'liberty' was protected by the law.[10]

If the law was one putative safeguard of liberty, property and religion, another was the nature of the English monarchy. It was, wrote Sir Philip Warwick in 1678, a mixed monarchy. Charles's government 'does manifest that he himself affects only a temperate monarchy to govern by law' claimed Nedham.[11] The nature of monarchy had to be carefully spelt out. 'Unless a man will wilfully shut his eyes,' argued Sir Peter Leicester, it is plain that the English monarchy is 'an imperial crown monarchical having the supreme power of rule in itself only'. Leicester wanted to debunk the false notions of the 1640s and 1650s that 'the people' might have 'a co-ordinate power' with the crown or that they might even be the supreme power; and having done so, he proceeded to rule out any right of resistance.[12] In Sir Matthew Hale's learned opinion the English monarchy was 'not absolute and unlimited, but bounded by rule and law', although 'in some points the government is absolutely monarchical . . . wherein the King has absolutely and alone power to do as he pleases.'[13] Similar views were expressed in parliament. In 1675 Sir Edward Dering opposed an address for recalling the King's subjects from the French army because this was one of the issues wholly in the King's power, not contrary to any fundamental law, nor injuring any individual. But 'in matters of a higher nature, such as we think shake the foundations of our laws and liberties, and that was the case of the late Declaration [of Indulgence], in matters of religion, we then were as with good reason we might be, something more earnest and pressing till the danger was removed.'[14] Warwick's bluff view, and one repeated by many others, was that the King was absolute because all power is his, but limited by the law and therefore not an 'arbitrary' ruler; the monarchy was truly absolute in parliament. Or in Nedham's words, although the English king is supreme, 'he does not govern by an arbitrary will, but by laws first composed by parliaments, and afterwards enacted by royal assent.'[15] Everyone accepted that Charles II's sovereignty rested on the trusty notion of 'king-in-parliament'. No less a commentator than the Earl of Shaftesbury asserted that 'the King is king by law, and by the same law that the poor man enjoys his cottage.' As he told the Lords in 1675, 'the King governing and administering justice by his House of Lords, and advising with both his Houses of Parliament in all important matters, is the government I own, I was born under, and am obliged to.'[16]

Parliament was Charles II's glory. He relied upon 'the hearts and affections of his people', as MPs were repeatedly told, and he had an unshakeable interest in the maintenance of religion and liberty; 'for, as religion, the protestant religion, commands your indispensable obedience, so it is a just and lawful liberty which sweetens that command, and endears it to you. Let other princes therefore glory in the most resigned obedience of their vassals.' Parliament, patriotic, wise, loyal and generous, was the natural expression of his people's love. MPs needed no convincing: Sir Charles Harbord claimed that we 'support the prerogative by the affections of the people; they are twins'.[17] MPs saw themselves as balancing different responsibilities: Sir John Reresby MP wrote to Danby in 1679 that he was 'a true servant to the government (so long as I find it doth not entrench upon the liberty of the people)' – although he later thought better of the parenthesis and struck it out; Sir John Holland sought a moderate ticket for the 1681 Norfolk election on a basis 'of loyalty to our king, of faithfulness to our religion, the government and ancient constitutions of our kingdom'.[18] Andrew Marvell, MP for Hull, assured his constituents that he would further their private and particular interests, and that 'in the more general concerns of the nation [I] shall God willing maintain the same incorrupt mind and clear conscience, free from faction or any self-ends, which I have by his grace hitherto preserved.'[19] Members of parliament and others idealized balance:

> I would neither disobey any lawful command of his majesty, nor diminish the just English regal power. I would not crop a leaf of any flower of the crown, yet I make as much conscience not to betray my country, or easily yield up the ancient laws and government of England, by parliament, to the king's will, to make English freemen tenants at will to the king, of their laws, their parliaments, their liberties and lives.[20]

It was almost impossible to enunciate this fine sentiment without an implied threat: subjects would maintain the balance if the monarch did. Shaftesbury owned the balanced government he was born under, but in the next breath he warned that 'if ever there should happen in future (which God forbid!) a king governing by an army without his parliament, it is a government I own not, am not obliged to, nor was born under'.[21] Like any ideal, the notion of a monarchy bound by law and working in partnership with parliament was a rallying call. It was a standard around which the forces of consensus and co-operation could gather. And like any ideal, it was constantly in question.

2   The Practice of Politics

Politics in the 1670s was an intensely personal business at every level. At the top of the political tree, the key to success was gaining the King's ear and attention, finding a moment to sway him and then having the resources to keep him to his chosen course. Allies and information were indispensable, as were finely tuned political antennae. But it was never easy to see beyond Charles II's mask and predict the vagaries of royal favour. When Arlington returned empty-handed from his mission to the Netherlands in the New Year of 1675, his influence was undoubtedly on the wane. Yet at precisely this moment Southwell was gushing that Arlington 'is as close in his majesty's favour as at any time before, and having skill in suiting the King's genius, 'tis not believed that many contrary winds will be able to shake him'.[22] Government rested on a delicate web of personal relationships. In the summer of 1671 Anglesey was led on by Buckingham at a dinner party with talk of appointment as Lord Chancellor or Lord Keeper. Buckingham flattered him and said 'he thought they might live easily with me as a friend', but then enjoined secrecy 'for the Lord Arlington if it were known would tell it as news to the King to disappoint it.' Anglesey did become Lord Privy Seal and never was trusted by Arlington, although in 1673 Clifford was eager that they should be reconciled, 'it being for the King's service that we should agree well.'[23]

Charles was himself temperamentally suited to exercising the personal touch. Ministers, ambassadors, MPs and others were brought to his privy chamber or to his mistresses' apartments so that he could cajole and woo them. Reresby's pious claim that he understood the duty of an MP 'to be moderate and healing between the two extremes, and to have a due regard to the King's prerogative as well as the liberty of the subject' was supposedly made in a private interview with Danby in February 1677. It led directly to his presentation to Charles II in the lobby of the House of Lords, 'there being nobody present but the King, his lordship and myself', and so flattered was Reresby by the attention shown to 'so mean a person' as himself that he was convinced of the sincerity of Charles's assurance that 'there is no person that lives under me whose safety and well doing I desire less than my own, and should be as sorry to invade his property and liberty as that another should invade my own.'[24] The blandishments offered to Reresby show the government's need for friendly faces in parliament: the same year Henry Savile concluded that 'measures now at court are so taken that it is essential to a man's succeeding there to be of parliament.'[25]

Courtiers come in many guises. Some were the 'men of pleasure', the merry companions, who were, opined the Earl of Essex, 'the very pest and ruin of all such courts'; while others were, like Essex himself, models of service and probity. Sir William Temple, one-time diplomat and courtier, advised Essex

> to make court as much and as personally as one can to the King, to live fairly with all the ministers in the charges of a court, but to stand upon one's own legs and the merits of serving well, and where all these will not carry one the best I think is to be content to alight and be quiet at home. The men of court and ambition can talk of other ways. But none into which I believe your lordship's temper and thoughts can run, the servitude in them is not to be endured by a man that has bread enough at home . . .[26]

It was quite possible to pay court and yet not have influence. In 1678 Buckingham was said 'to advance in favour', but Southwell did 'not hear that it ends in any other advance than that of conversation and merriment.' The 'other ways' of succeeding at court presumably included the kinds of personal services performed for the King by his mistresses, and by courtiers like Bab May, rewarded for his pimping for Charles, and Lord Buckhurst, supposedly pensioned for giving up his mistress, Nell Gwynn, to the King. Even the Commons was alleged to be full of members who had earned rewards for marrying cast-off mistresses or 'making provocatives for lechery' for Charles.[27]

The self-interest of those at court or in government should not be overlooked or condemned. Every place carried income and costs. The offices of household and state almost never changed hands without elaborate financial provision; it took Arlington months to buy the office of Lord Chamberlain, and it was a mark of peculiar obloquy that Sunderland was sacked as secretary of state without financial compensation. Sir Edward Dering, who originally took office for the honour, for his family and to serve the King rather than for profit, was subsequently passed over for preferment because of his refusal 'either to pray or pay for court favours (the two most prevailing topics in our time)'. When Sidney Godolphin nominated him as a treasury commissioner in 1679,

it was to me a wonderful thing and of which I believe there are few
instances in our court (or indeed in any) that one gentleman should
prefer another to so considerable a place as this without any consideration of friendship, alliance or interest, without importunity, without application, indeed without the knowledge of the person himself or of any
friend or relation of his.[28]

Government was a perpetually shifting balance of factions and
networks, stretching across the court, administration and parliament,
and reaching into the localities and the worlds of finance and commerce. Every move might jeopardize a carefully created political
position and virtually no-one was above the game. When Danby found
that Buckingham was once again in favour at court in 1678, and that
Nell Gwynn had been an intermediary, he wrote to his own wife asking
her to let 'Nelly' know that she was surprised that Nelly should oppose
Danby 'that has always been so kind to her, but you wonder much more
to find her supporting only those who are known to be the King's
enemies, for in that you are sure she does very ill.'[29] Intimidation and
insinuations, opportunism and cynicism, were part and parcel of the
political process.

I

MPs, as we have heard, paid fulsome lip-service to the ideal of serving
King, constituents and conscience. Nowhere then should the political
virtues of balance, restraint and consensus have been more evident
than in the process of choosing MPs . 'Times have much changed now,'
observed Waller in January 1674. 'Formerly the neighbourhood desired
him to serve; there was a dinner, and so to an end; but now it is a kind
of an empire. Some hundred years ago some boroughs sent not; they
could get none to serve; but, now it is in fashion and a fine thing.'[30]
Whether or not there was a trend in this direction – and several scholars suspect that there was – it found little opportunity for expression
during the eighteen-year life of the Cavalier Parliament. The small
number of by-elections in the 1670s, and the even smaller number of
those by-elections which led to an open contest, warn us not to place
too much emphasis on the electioneering of the decade. Counties or
boroughs (where the franchise was often restricted to a mere handful
of inhabitants) might well prefer to select their candidate before the
election day and thus avoid the expense and discord of a contest. The
wishes of a powerful figure were often decisive. When Sir Edward Dering
was elected unopposed at Retford in 1670, Henry Savile rebuked his
brother, Lord Halifax, for not naming him as a candidate: Savile 'was
pretty sure the court commendation for Sir Edward Dering would not
stand in competition with such an interest as I am certain is in your

power to procure for me'.[31] If the King or his agents did not take an interest, it was often the local power brokers, magnates like Halifax, gentry clans and alliances, who determined the outcome. They might either impose or agree upon a nominee or if irretrievably divided among themselves they might opt for a full-blown contest with a 'view' of the supporters of each candidate or even a poll of the voters. Not that a contest implied any sophisticated political debate. When Lord Lindsey challenged the Cecil interest at Stamford in 1676 his candidate 'furiously treated' the townspeople at a cost of over £1000 to ensure their votes. 'Treating', the provision of abundant free booze and food, was commonplace: the 1677 contest at Shrewsbury was said to be between the 'drinking party' and the 'rabble party'; and in 1675 Danby spent more than £7000 treating the voters of King's Lynn on behalf of his son-in-law. Other forms of bribery and persuasion were used. In 1673 William Broxholme, 'a true son of the Church of England . . . and a loyal subject to the King', won the seat of Grimsby, where the electorate numbered fifty freemen, by spending 'more to obtain their votes than three parts of four of the men were worth'.[32] Candidates were often concerned to challenge the existing franchise in a borough if they thought that either its extension or restriction would be of electoral advantage.

Contested elections were fought on personal grounds. The candidates were described by such epithets as 'honest', 'loyal', 'worthy' or 'patriotic' and were seen as the candidates of particular individuals, families or networks. Vanity, prestige, and avarice all played a part and some elections became many-sided factional contests. Aristocratic struggles at court were inevitably played out in local elections: the Lindsey campaign against the Cecil interest had roots at Whitehall; the contest at Liverpool in 1670 between Sir William Bucknall and Sir George Lane was also a contest between their respective patrons Ormonde and Arlington.[33] There was nothing, however, to prevent MPs from modifying their stance after election. Reresby was elected for Aldborough in 1673 as the protégé of the local supporters of the Savile family and in opposition to the local interest of Sir Thomas Osborne; but once Reresby arrived at Westminster, where he had a long struggle to win the right to take his seat, his Yorkshire allegiances paled by comparison with the duty he owed to Sir Thomas Osborne, who was, of course, also Lord Treasurer Danby. In all the by-elections of this decade the only real sign of the role of political ideology or principle is in appeals to religious interest groups. The backing of nonconformists or the support of 'the church interest' was a significant factor in the elections in Derbyshire in 1670, Dover, Chester and Suffolk in 1673, Norfolk in 1675 and Great Yarmouth in 1678 where one candidate was 'ever loyal to the King and true to the Church' and the other a dissenter.[34]

II

The practice of parliamentary politics is too diverse a subject for more than a cursory discussion here. But there are obvious points about parliament which are often overlooked. One is that many MPs failed to turn up. In 1675 Dering calculated that of the 508 MPs, only about 300 were in London and of these only 180 bothered to attend regularly. This poor attendance allowed a small number of vociferous members to dominate debates and proceedings. It was the assiduous professional politician, of whom Sir Thomas Meres, MP for Lincoln, is the decade's outstanding example, who wielded real influence in the Commons. If such individuals were not firmly under ministerial control, as Meres was not, then the Commons could become a serious thorn in the flesh of ministers. Attempts to organize business in the house, whether by the government, as in Danby's daily sessions in 1675, or on behalf of aristocratic patrons, as the group sitting in the south-east corner attempted during the 1674 baiting of the bears, had limited success. The lesson drawn by Danby was that greater discipline was needed among the government vote, but he was unable to achieve this. As demonstrated earlier, MPs found it perfectly natural to hold other offices, and some of them had been, were, or hoped to be paid government officials at the same time as being members.[35] This strong vein of self-interest is another significant characteristic of parliamentary politics. Unfortunately it can only be properly demonstrated by a detailed exposition of the vested interests of MPs and their many obligations to patrons, electorates, and educational, religious, professional, commercial and family connections. Complex, often unquantifiable, loyalties tied MPs to members of the court and the House of Lords.

Parliamentary oratory can be revealing of political values. During the 1670s parliamentarians frequently insisted on their fear of France and its territorial, commercial and religious ambitions, and on something even more ominous, the danger of emulation: 'our jealousies of popery, or an arbitrary government, are not from a few inconsiderable papists here, but from the ill example we have from France.'[36] Some orations achieved notoriety. On 22 February 1671 John Lord Lucas, an old cavalier warhorse, made a 'smart speech' on the subsidy bill in the Lords. He complained that the Commons neither knew what their bill gave the King nor what it was for; and he followed up this insult with the offensive claim that the Lords could and should amend or deny taxes voted by the Commons. On 12 March the Foreign Affairs Committee discussed how to vindicate his majesty's honour and gain satisfaction from Lord Lucas for the speech he had made in the King's presence 'in which many things [were] said very seditiously and undutifully towards his majesty and his government, and copies of it being now since spread abroad, and become very common'.[37] Within a week Lucas had been confronted with a pirated version of his speech, but he disputed that as a false copy and offered to produce a true copy; the Lords, in a move which could be seen as protecting Lucas, as well as demonstrating their abhorrence of the versions circulating, ordered that the 'speech' be burned and the hangman ceremoniously lit one with a link in Old Palace Yard. In Essex, Josselin heard that Lucas might be sent to the Tower 'for speaking freely against the taxes which are heavy beyond measure'.[38]

No authentic copy of Lucas's speech survives, and there may never have been one, but it is possible to collate manuscript versions, news-letter reports, and the text as printed in 1673, to establish a clear idea of what Lucas said and why it offended.[39] Lucas made a blatant appeal to the landed interest, playing on cavalier sentiment, biblical piety and even Augustan imagery. At the Restoration, he asserted, hopes were high that our burdens would be lifted, that every man would dwell under his own vine, and Astrea would return to England. But we have fallen very short of our expectations. Under the usurper we were taxed heavily, but at least had the means to pay. Now our taxes weigh more heavily, and our lands are thrown up, corn and cattle bring in nothing, and money is scarce. What we have given is swallowed up by parvenus.

> Is this, my lords, the reward of our services? Have we for this borne the heat of the day, been imprisoned, sequestered, and ventured our lives and our families, our estates and our fortunes? And must we, after all this, sac-rifice so much of our poor remainder to the will of a few particular men, and the maintenance of their vanities?

Lucas then questioned the King's need for supply and wondered whether Louis was inducing 'us to consume our treasure in vain preparations against him'? Once we had exhausted our treasure on fleets and armies, we would be an easy prey. What is this, Lucas asked, presumably with Charles looking on, but 'for fear of being conquered by a foreigner, [to] put ourselves in a condition almost as bad; pardon me, my lords, if I say in some respects a great deal worse,' for under a victor we know we can fall no further, but there may be no end to demands for taxes. By reducing the proposed tax, the peers would do the King the greatest possible service, 'for though you shall thereby take from his majesty a part of the sum, you will give him a great deal more in the love and hearts of his subjects.'[40] Lucas was troubled that our money was 'too much consumed in pleasure; that his majesty was a good, a gracious, and a strong prince, and so was Samson yet he suffered his locks to be clipped by his Delilah.' This account adds that Lucas's speech was seconded by Bolingbroke, Halifax and Clare, 'which last spake against the King's sitting in the house, upon which they had not freedom of debate'.[41]

Forthright but loyal, anti-tax and anti-war, suspicious of the executive, this is classic back-bench, 'country party', oratory, but it had other overtones, as in the reference to Samson and Delilah, and it was open to appropriation. *The English Ballance* (1672) opposed the Dutch war and sympathized with dissent, but it also heaped praise upon Lucas:

> the consumption of the nation is visible in its countenance, its soul and substance is consumed; (as was excellently laid open in that first and second discourse of my lord Lucas, before the House of Lords, in whom alone the ancient gallant spirit of the English nation did show itself and shine forth, and who, by that heroic act, has erected to himself a monument in the heart of all true Englishmen, and proposed himself as a worthy pattern of imitation, to all who affect the glory of being true patriots) . . .[42]

Late in 1673 Lucas's speech appeared in print, adorned with an epigraph from Juvenal's Satire 1, a preface extolling Lucas's loyalty and prescience, and an appendix of twenty-six ominous developments since 1671, including the war, the Stop, the Indulgence, the Test, the Modena marriage, and also the creation of Louise, 'French Carwell', as an English duchess and, item fifteen, 'debauching the nation by masquerades'. The hand of Dutch agents is rightly to be suspected in this work, and according to an anonymous denunciation it was the baptist bookseller Francis Smith who 'printed Lucas's speech with those damned reflections at the end of it squinting at the government'.[43]

The Lucas speech and its fate can be compared with a paper of early 1673 on how 'this monarchy has much declined and lessened itself'. Written for another peer, Basil Feilding, Earl of Denbigh, this analysis highlights the favour shown to papists, the offence to the Commons by assuming 'a power to suspend their laws at pleasure', the misuse and waste of money, and military disgrace as the four causes of decline. Seven remedies are offered to 're-estate his majesty in the former love, confidence and devotion of his loyal subjects'. The first is to secure the kingdom against popery, others include guaranteeing 'laws and liberties', abandoning any 'appearance of a standing army', cut-backs on expenditure and taxation, tailoring foreign policy to public opinion, and, finally, a declaration from the Duke of York in the Lords that whatever his private 'scruples' he will always maintain the established protestant religion.[44]

The tax burden and governmental mismanagement were also themes of Sir John Holland's speech on 18 October 1675. This loyal and moderate Norfolk gentleman worked into his oration the trade imbalance with France, the 'prodigal' consumption of the nation, the decay of rents and trade, the depopulation of the countryside and the flight to London, the changed 'humour of the yeomanry' and 'breeding of the youth', all to support his central contention that 'the charge of the government is greater than the nation can bear.' If the people could not bear the charge, he added darkly, 'the government cannot stand, though it be supported by arms. But, should it be endeavoured, it cannot be long endured by the temper of the English nation.'[45]

What is most striking about these speeches and tracts is that, even while they are essentially conservative and loyal, preoccupied with the interests of the landed class and the rural economy, they raise the spectres of popery, military rule, royal luxury, national moral decay and all the other bugbears of the government's more radical critics. Surprisingly their arguments stand on the same continuum as those of Andrew Marvell's famous indictment of Danby's government, *An Account of the Growth of Popery and Arbitrary Government* (1677). But then Marvell's tract was no republican rant or witty diatribe; it is a rather dull and prosaic history. No doubt Marvell was deliberately appealing to the loyal and moderate when he claimed to be writing 'out of mere fidelity and service to his majesty', when he took care to absolve York from all blame, when he seems to identify himself with a cavalier position, or when he skirts around the issue of nonconformity.[46] This middle-of-the-road authorial stance helps give credibility to the long chain which Marvell forges out of unrelated events and policies. The common thread – to change metaphors – between, say, the Declaration of Indulgence and Danby's Test Oath is the unnamed conspirators who owe 'their fidelity to the French King' and possibly to Rome. Peculiarly impersonal – Danby is never mentioned and Charles, the only real common denominator in all these events, is praised – Marvell's account is a foreshortened history of the 1670s. What this demonstrates is not that there was some infinitely flexible 'country' ideology which could be embraced by a figure like Lucas and by Marvell, but rather that there was a register of political criticism which was available to many commentators and open to diverse inflections.

III

The practice of politics in the 1670s was not a pursuit of political principles through parliamentary parties, it was the advancement of men and measures, the chase after profit and honour, and the naked rivalry of ambitious men and their connections. Yet oleaginous professions of 'service' to the King, to the county or corporation, to the Church of England and to one's patron, should not be dismissed too lightly. Deference and hierarchy made 'service' a legitimate political ideal.[47] It was easily reconciled with multiple loyalties of the kind experienced by office-holding MPs and some felt that it could even be accommodated to competing 'interests'. Politics, after all, was about meeting and even reconciling the various 'interests' of the nation. 'Interest', that buzzword of the decade, had several political overtones. It was used to denote the local electoral support of an individual or group, which often relied on something close to self-interest. Horrified when a local rival blocked one of his nominations for office, the Earl of Lindsey complained to Danby that the county noticed 'that those who stick to me are preferred' which was 'a very powerful and engaging argument for persons to adhere to our party, for the world will be governed by interest.'[48] Parliamentary critics of the court were fond of announcing that 'the nation's interest is laid aside for private interest,' that the nation was in thrall to the 'French interest' or that 'the protestant interest' was in danger.[49] Closer to home MPs professed to abhor vested interests, but most, if not all, had them. Sir William Coventry loftily remarked when declaring that he had no interest in a matter under debate that he found such a declaration 'sometimes very necessary in this house'.[50]

Partisanship was similarly deplored – and practised. In the light of the infighting in the Commons, sentiments such as Henry Powle's that he 'always had, and still had, an unwillingness to accuse great men, it looking like faction, they being more exposed in their actions than other men' – uttered during the 1675 impeachment of Danby – ring hollow.[51] There was a 'court party' within parliament, but the pretence was that no partisanship ever disturbed the pure consciences of those debating the nation's business. A charade was played out in 1673 when Henry Coventry attacked Sir Thomas Meres for distinguishing 'between the country gentlemen and the courtiers, whereas there was none, nor ought to be none'.[52] Meres may not have used the precise terms 'court' and 'country', but many of his contemporaries did so without turning a hair.[53] And Coventry may have been correct that it was not 'parliamentary' to refer to opposing 'sides' of the house, but they existed. Diarists and newsletter writers had to coin terms like 'Yorkist' and 'anti-Yorkist', 'Treasurist' and 'anti-Treasurist', or those in 'the south-east corner' of the chamber, to describe them.[54] These were not, of course, modern political parties and contemporary parliamentarians tended to shy away from anything which smacked too much of the late civil wars. Not that this prevented political pamphleteers from 'reviving the old names of distinction'. 'What is this but to set the old quarrel on foot again?' they asked as they gleefully accused each other of the principles of rebels or of tyrants.[55]

The past not only taught a grim lesson about partisan politics, it also encouraged the hunt for conspiracies. For more than a century the English had been steeped in the mythology of popish plots and in recent years they had been taught, especially by Dutch propagandists, to be suspicious of government by cabal or Foreign Affairs Committee. In this context 'popery' was a wonderfully flexible rhetorical tool. 'Popery' was always implicit in any authoritarian government, just as any Catholic regime was always disposed towards tyranny. For the Church of England, 'popery' embraced the sects and regicides; and for nonconformity, much of the established church's worship and teaching was tainted with popish superstition or arrogance. As it was deployed by Shaftesbury in 1675, 'popery' meant any aspiration to diminish the civil magistrate's ecclesiastical power and to emancipate the church as an autonomous institution. Thus 'popery' might emanate from Rome or from Anglican bishops who sought to seduce gullible princes into absolutism. Politics and religion merged almost seamlessly.

3 Piety, Profanity and Persecution

Begun the bible again. This morning considering the great decay of piety and increase of profaneness and atheism and particularly my own standing of a stay if not declining in grace I fixed a resolution to renew the course I had in former times held of watching over my ways and recording the actions and passages of my life both to quicken me in good ways and to leave a memorial thereof to my posterity for imitation, and to give God the glory of his guidance and mercy towards me and mine: proposing also to review the time past of my life and for the same ends to reduce all the passages thereof to writing that I could find memorials of or recollect. So to redeem the time because the days are evil.

The Earl of Anglesey's diary for 26 May 1671

In the 1670s denominational boundaries were easily blurred. Aristocrats like Anglesey mixed with bishops and leading nonconformists like John Owen, while gentlemen such as Sir Edward Harley entertained nonconformist clergy and yet outwardly conformed to the Church of England.[56] More importantly, as the Compton Census revealed, large numbers of humble parishioners attended both the Church of England and nonconformist meetings. There was an overlap between the church and moderate nonconformity. 'All acknowledge there is at this day a number of sober peaceable men both ministers and others among the dissenters,' wrote Philip Henry in 1671, and he wondered why steps were not taken to reunite them with the church.[57] By the same measure, moderate dissenters recognized that the preaching and ministry of many Anglican ministers was godly and fruitful. The Church of England's routine preaching concentrated upon the protestant fundamentals and urged the amendment of life. In 1675 the bishops had demonstrated their eagerness to embark upon a moral crusade. The church had warily lent its support to nonconformist initiatives for a new missionary effort in Wales.[58] The present parliament clearly no longer had the political will to promote persecution of fellow protestants and, as Danby admitted in 1673, any new parliament would lean towards the comprehension or even toleration of protestants. The rifts among English protestants appeared to be slowly healing.

One of the most obvious reasons for such irenic attitudes was quite simply that pious protestants spoke a very similar language. The idiom in which John Bunyan described his religious experiences in his autobiography *Grace Abounding to the Chief of Sinners* (1666) or in *Pilgrims Progress* (1678) is very like that of the diaries of Philip Henry, a presbyterian minister, or Ralph Josselin, a nominally conformist Anglican clergymen. Their souls are refreshed with the sweet word of God; God is good to them in his ordinances; and they hope to 'sanctify' every dispensation of divine providence. Pious members of the upper classes were just as familiar with this outlook, as Anglesey's diary shows. The Bedfordshire gentleman John Crew prayed that God would 'sanctify' the death of his son so 'that one great affliction may not make me forget many mercies.' Sir Edward Harley spoke the same dialect: 'an interest in Christ, in whom we are complete, is a remedy for all sorts of crosses and disappointments,' he reminded his wife. Meditation and introspection are fundamental duties. 'Be you very watchful over yourself that not anything divert you from your morning and evening worship of God in secret and constant reading the scripture and some other good book,' he instructed his daughter. 'Warn your sisters from me to do the like.'[59] Peers, gentlemen, ministers and yeomen, and their wives and daughters, shared in this bible-based piety, with its emphasis on personal experience of God, its providentialism and deep sense of personal and national sinfulness, and its determination to manifest the individual's calling in a godly life.

Pious protestants spoke with virtually one voice when they warned that 'the days are evil'. No age had been as guilty as 'the present time is, of a spreading and bold profaneness', claimed Robert Boyle. It was a 'drolling degenerate age', said Lucy Hutchinson; 'an age of so much profaneness and atheism,' lamented Thomas Barlow to Sir Edward Harley. Or, as Bishop Fell complained, 'this age of ours has somewhat of mockery for its particular genius.'[60] Our encounter with wit has already revealed that the profane liked nothing better than to laugh at religion. In Oxford Anthony Wood, who detested the common 'bantering', 'prating of news' and the refusal 'to be earnest and zealous', claimed that 'people [are] taken with fooleries, plays, poems, buffooning and drolling books' among them Marvell's *Rehearsal Transpros'd* (1672) and John Eachard's *The Grounds and Occasions of the Contempt of the Clergy* (1670).[61] Complaints of 'scoffing', of worldliness and levity, might be regarded as no more than the stock-in-trade of preachers and moralists, if it was not for the extraordinary confluence of these traits in a wave of hostility towards the clergy. This anti-clericalism (for that is what it was) took all clergy and their pretensions as its target. In one 'letter to a witty gentleman' a minister protested that the wits want the people to 'confess we have been fools all this while, and miserably bewitched into vain hopes, by the charming voices of a company of crafty priests'.[62] 'Priestcraft', the self-interested elevation of religion into a mystery by the clerical profession, was a powerful accusation to level against the clergy. Many were content to jeer at the failings of the clergy. John Eachard's book, for instance, sparked a furious row. Far from being a helpfully dispassionate analysis of the clergy's problems, it was taken up as ammunition by their enemies: 'as some things in your book were matter of chat in coffee-houses in C[ambridge] before it was printed; so now since it was printed, they be matters of pastime in taverns in L[ondon] where wit, and wine, and profaneness, *sport themselves in their own deceivings*: and make the faults of God's ministers (for which all that fear God do grieve) the matter of unhallowed mirth.'[63] Marvell was to do even more damage with *The Rehearsal Transpros'd*, his attack on the extreme Anglican Samuel Parker, and *Mr Smirke: or the Divine in Mode* (1675), a defence of the moderate Bishop Croft.

Scoffing and anticlericalism were among the symptoms of profanity. And profanity had a myriad of causes. For some it was a product of sin, but it was also recognized as a reaction against the misguided zeal and the 'enthusiasm' of mid-century and the hypocrisy of contemporary pretenders to godliness. Charles II amused himself by 'showing the cheat of such as pretended to be more holy and devout than others, and said they were generally the greatest knaves', and then proceeded to name 'some eminent men of the present age' including bishops.[64] Many of the pious found a handy culprit in Thomas Hobbes. In the 1650s Hobbes had advanced an account of human nature, the physical world and political society in which egoism, the individual's drive to satisfy his own interests and desires, was a prime force. Hobbes's doctrines were beyond the pale for the orthodox protestants of Restoration England, but he shaped the debate, not least because his views were part of a much broader re-evaluation of human motivation. Human nature was at the centre of attention thanks to the writings of Descartes and Gassendi, the revival of interest in Epicurus and in the Stoics, theological debates about free will, and scientific work in human physiology.[65] One suggestion which emerged was that the springs of human behaviour are natural, that our actions are rooted in the material world, in our physical drives such as lust and fear. Several thinkers were drawn to a rather mechanistic view of human nature; John Locke began to make notes about pain and pleasure as the motivation of our actions, and he translated a work on morality by Pierre Nicole, a French Jansenist.[66] Some propagandized for a Stoic ideal of virtue in the shape of the 'man without passion', but others wondered whether the passions, rather than being the source of all human ills, might be a potential force for good.[67] An intriguing translation of Pierre Nicole's *The Grounds of Sovereignty* appeared in October 1675 with the explicit intention of influencing the new session of parliament. This, says the translator, is a 'loyal' work, designed to show that subjection among men is not only natural but useful. A straightforward advocate of absolute sovereignty and complete obedience, with not a hint of the English tradition of law and parliament, Nicole also argues that self-interest or 'cupidity', if harnessed and controlled, will promote the common good. The English were slowly becoming acquainted with the idea that self-interest, still widely regarded as a reprehensible passion, might also be a key to social improvement.

These debates about human nature went hand-in-hand with the adulation of 'reason'. Reason had become the arbiter of belief. 'We live in such a knowing age, wherein all captivating the understanding, though it be to the obedience of faith, is made the subject of grievance,' preached Miles Barne to the King. Barne's sermon was a reply to Martin Clifford's *Treatise of Human Reason* (1674) which had urged that all individuals should be free to follow their own reason in matters of religion. Protestants took a pride in their reasonable religion as opposed to the idolatry of Rome or the superstition of sectaries, but that did not mean that everything was explicable; 'if we assent to no doctrines, but such as our reason fully comprehends, this is no longer faith but science.' Reason was how we grasped our innate ideas of the deity, 'that knowledge of God, and our duty to him, which the light of nature may lead man up to, and which is concreat[ed] with his soul.' Reason was also the first step of the journey into revealed religion: it grounds our faith by demonstrating the divine origin of scripture, but 'reason . . . before it can be available to conversion or salvation, does become faith and the gift of grace.'[68] English protestants disagreed among themselves about the degree of reason which is useful to the religious quest and about the transformation of reason by faith. But they were united in their conviction that reason complements faith, that it is an ally not an enemy of religion.[69]

Faced with those who demanded rational demonstration of the truths of Christianity, the clergy threw themselves into the work, preaching, writing and arguing, and yet the 'vicious atheists' remained unconvinced. 'We may praise God that the late godly endeavours against atheism have powerfully settled the tempted Christians in their most holy faith. But divines may write and preach their heart out, yet men whose God is in their belly and their lust, will speak and do what they list.' The doubts of the atheists grew out of their evil lives. 'It was not any strength of reason that prevailed upon you to dislike our faith, but that opposition which it now makes against your darling lusts.'[70] Behind the 'Hobbist', Epicurean, rationalist or sectary stood the atheist. This was the common enemy facing all protestants. Richard Allestree deplored the fact that 'the professors of no God begin to vie numbers with all the differing persuasions in religion, so that atheism seems to be the gulf that finally swallows up all our sects.'[71]

I

The fight against atheism and profanity should have set the agenda for English protestantism. Unfortunately many English protestants still had one foot in the past. They were trapped by a history of internecine controversy, and by the legal definitions enshrined in the 1662 Act of Uniformity and subsequent penal legislation. It was verging on the impossible for many on either side to admit that their stance was ill-founded. It would have cast doubt on their integrity for conformists to acknowledge that the Church of England imposed unnecessary terms of communion or for dissenters to admit that their own nonconformity was based on excessive scruples. There were, moreover, real denominational differences between the various protestant groups. Questions of worship, theology and church organization could matter, often profoundly, to the laity. The people of Bucklesham were apparently 'so bigoted' that they measured their assurance of salvation 'by how much they straggle from the discipline, doctrine and worship of the Church [of England]'.[72] Nonconformist churches were all by definition 'voluntary'; membership was an individual commitment often at real personal cost. Churches naturally strove to maintain the purity of their teaching and fellowship which meant keeping a strict watch on the spirituality and behaviour of members and excluding offenders from the congregation. For many dissenters, this was where the Church of England was defective. The established church was inclusive not selective: all parishioners were entitled to its sacraments. Many, both inside and outside the church, dreamed of a day when proper discipline might be exercised over the parish flock, but the reality was that the Anglican clergy never had nor would have much beyond the power of admonition. Meanwhile the parish clergy also had a pastoral obligation to preach religious unity and uniformity and so were bound to come into conflict with their dissenting brethren. This conflict was exacerbated whenever the hierarchy or the civil authorities took a hand. Protestors attributed the 1670 Conventicle Act to the bishops' pride and lamented that instead of being gospel preachers, the clergy 'must now turn state informers, and set up an inquisition to rack and torture their innocent neighbours'.[73]

The prosecution of religious minorities, whether Catholics or dissenters, was sporadic in the 1670s. It could be intense and cruel, as it was in Bristol in 1675; but it was frequently lax. Magistrates did not always enforce the laws; the King did not always want them to. Even when justices were diligent, prosecution depended on the zeal of the constable and on the evidence of neighbours. This was one reason for the rise of informers, who were often local people with mercenary motives. Informers gained a weapon to coerce reluctant justices when the 1670 Conventicle Act rendered officials who did not act on information liable to fines. The informer was a detested figure, 'bred out of the corruption of the body politic . . . he talks all law, and never troubles his head with equity or religion.' A mock elegy for one Marsh, a London informer, issues the invitation, 'Stay reader! And piss here, for it is said / Under this dirt there's an informer laid.'[74] Several informers were murdered or met untimely ends. W. S., 'the man of a very wicked life', who turns informer in Bunyan's *Life and Death of Mr Badman* (1680), and hides in trees to spy on meetings (see plate 14), is eventually struck down by the hand of God. The community often had its say on persecution: one Lincolnshire constable knew a local Quaker 'so well that he could not execute the warrant [against him] but sin against his own soul' and local people would not buy the Quaker's distrained goods 'looking upon them as the spoil of conscience'.[75] Such neighbourly involvement could, of course, work in the opposite direction, to encourage the harassment of those individuals or minorities who aroused the malice or envy of some among the community. And this harassment might range from low-level rumour all the way to prosecution at law. A classic instance of this was the 1674 case of Agnes Beaumont, a young member of Bunyan's congregation at Bedford, who suffered at the hands of her own father, local gossip, the Anglican vicar, and an avaricious former suitor, and narrowly escaped a charge of murder.[76] Ultimately, however, the persecution of religious dissidents, whether through rumour, harassment, ostracism, malicious prosecution or through the penal laws, depended upon the constant message from those in authority that dissidents were a threat.

'Papists' were the subject of a steady stream of propaganda. Some of this 'anti-popery' was directed towards the educated market. It took the guise of historical or theological tracts about the papacy, Jesuits, Counter-Reformation, Armada or Gunpowder Plot. But most anti-popery, whether it was sermons, preached or printed, engravings, ballads, the pageantry marking 5 November or even an edifice like London's Monument to the Great Fire, was aimed at the semi-literate and deeply credulous masses. So protean was popery in this version of history that the anniversary of the execution of Charles I was just as relevant as 5 November for anti-catholic rhetoric: 'we know the plot of this day's bloody tragedy was laid at Rome, and acted by the sects of their making among ourselves.' Popery, many said, was finally coming out into the open. In 1675 John Goodman claimed that 'they heretofore walked in masquerade, disguised themselves sometimes in the habit of one sect and sometimes of another; but of late they have had the confidence to lay off their disguise and play a more open game.' It was axiomatic that papists aspired to domination – 'lords paramount they must be, or else restless'.[77] A final confrontation seemed imminent.

The criticism of fellow protestants needed more careful managing. Nonconformists could complain that the Church of England had

Plate 14 A meeting or 'conventicle' of protestant dissenters is spied on by an informer. This illustration from John Bunyan, The Life and Death of Mr Badman *(1680), depicts the informer in the tree and running off to fetch a 'warrant'. Bunyan's text describes how one 'W. S.', 'a man of very wicked life', turned informer against dissenters and was subsequently 'stricken by the hand of God'.*

betrayed its principles or that it was hopelessly mired in its papal past. Many repudiated it because it was a parish-based, rather than a voluntary, church, and then concentrated their fire on Anglican intolerance. Church of England preachers often sought to accentuate the common protestant heritage with sober nonconformists and to drive a wedge between these moderates and the dangerous 'fanatics' and sectaries like the Quakers and baptists. However, they also had to point out that all dissenters were guilty of dividing protestantism and thus weakening it in the face of popery – a charge which dissenters cheerfully threw back at the church. Few Anglican polemicists could restrain themselves from denouncing dissenters as 'peevish', 'factious', 'seditious', proud and self-interested. Whenever dissenters appeared to claim that their consciences were more tender than those of conformists, or that they were the true 'godly', or that they were martyrs for the sake of religion, most Anglicans succumbed to indignation. Some lashed out at the dissenters' motives. The intemperate Samuel Parker alleged that 'some men study for impertinent scruples, to ensnare themselves, and labour to raise great doubts from little reasons, and cannot be satisfied, because they will not.'[78]

Any simple characterization of the church's 'line' towards dissenters must be regarded with caution. The Church of England was by far the largest, most sophisticated and complex institution in Restoration England, and its stance simply cannot be reduced to a pat formula. Those who tried, like Shaftesbury in 1675, produced a travesty (but then that, of course, was his intention). The church was tremendously diverse; it included such a spectrum of clergymen, who differed in theology, allegiance, education and age, and its public face was so various, that one can with relatively little effort find evidence in the pronouncements of its theologians, pastors or politicians for almost any number of characterizations.[79] However three significant aspects of the church in the 1670s which we might note here are its shaky self-confidence, its pastoral commitment and its support for the penal laws.

The Church of England did not possess the authority and self-confidence necessary to play the role which politicians were so keen to ascribe to it in the 1670s. It could not become the rallying point which Danby and Charles seemed to hope and it was certainly a long way in practice from being the handmaiden (or even stepmother) of absolutism portrayed in *A Letter from a Person of Quality*. The Anglican church saw itself as being crucified between two thieves, popery and dissent: 'the common cry is, that the Church of England must go down,' wailed Richard Allen.[80] Much of the stuffing had been knocked out of the church by Charles's betrayal in 1672 and by the failure of its gentry and other supporters to live up to their professions of loyalty. The clergy's laments about 'false friends' referred not only to the justices who would not prosecute dissenters and absentees from church, but also to those lay Anglicans who mistook outward conformity, political allegiance to the Stuarts and even an anti-puritanical lifestyle, for the substance of their religion. The Anglican ministers' profound sense of being beleaguered was exacerbated by a sharp awareness of their pastoral mission. They battled against indifference, immorality and disdain because they believed that the English were in danger of squandering their chance to placate an irate God. They felt the sins of the nation deeply, including the sin of schism committed by those who needlessly followed the nonconformist preachers. Yet they also pleaded with dissenters to 'lay aside our animosities' and unite 'lest the gravity and piety of this nation end in buffoonry' and we succumb to the fatal 'symptom of a cold clammy stupid atheism'.[81] These two characteristics were frequently accompanied by a third, a determined, sometimes combative, defence of the principle of religious uniformity and of the penal laws which underwrote it. Some mounted this defence by means of personal, pastoral, persuasion, others by long, occasionally acerbic, theological arguments, and yet others by appeal to the political principles of monarchy. As always, it is the most virulent version, the Samuel Parker version, which has attracted most attention, and there always will be individuals like Parker whose brash self-righteousness carries all before it. But throughout the 1670s neither the leaders of the church nor its clergy exude much confidence or authority. Only when it became the partner of the tories at both a national and local level in the early 1680s, did the Church of England appear to regain its self-belief.[82]

4 Religion and Politics

> 'Tis not the having several parties in religion under a state that is in itself dangerous, but 'tis the persecuting of them that makes them so . . .
>
> [Sir Charles Wolseley], *Liberty of Conscience* (1668)

> Now the way to our future happiness, has been perpetually disputed throughout the world, and must be left at last to the impression made upon every man's belief and conscience, either by natural or supernatural arguments and means; which impressions men may disguise or dissemble, but no man can resist. For belief is no more in a man's power, than his stature . . .
>
> Sir William Temple, *Observations upon the United Provinces of the Netherlands* (1673)

> There must be no opposition made between fearing God and honouring the King, but a careful discharge of both; and these precepts which God has joined together, let no man separate.
>
> William Falkner, *Christian Loyalty* (1679)

The debates on religious toleration during the 1670s were confused by imprecise terminology and contradictory aspirations among the nonconformists. Some wanted to rejoin a more loosely organized national church, others wanted to set up their own churches under the protection of the sovereign: virtually none wanted a genuine liberty of practice which would include papists. Liberty might simply mean an acknowledgement that religious uniformity was unattainable. The admission of non-Anglicans to full civil rights was a separate issue. The debate was made even more confusing because it was pursued in a haphazard series of pamphlet exchanges revolving around several different issues and written in a variety of styles. The first accompanied the moves for comprehension and indulgence bills in the late 1660s and included notable works like Samuel Parker's *Discourse of Ecclesiastical Politie* (1669) and Marvell's *Rehearsal Transpros'd* (1672). Further waves of pamphleteering surrounded the 1672 Indulgence, Clifford's *Treatise of Human Reason* (1674), and Herbert Croft's *Naked Truth* (1675).[83] Some of the most significant thinking on the issue remained unpublished or confined to Latin. Yet just because there was little systematic political philosophy published in the 1670s, that does not mean that people were not grappling with these issues.

What was a state to do about religious pluralism? Charles II offered one answer in the 1672 Declaration when he pointed out that twelve years of persecution had achieved nothing. This pragmatism was appealing to many of his subjects. Since there was a 'natural proneness' or tendency towards what was forbidden, the solution was to allow religious liberty and 'in ten years there shall not be a dissenter left to piss against the wall.'[84] Sir Charles Wolseley, an ex-Cromwellian, produced a series of cogent, but essentially pragmatic, tracts which argued that it was impossible to make someone believe and that persecution was simply creating resentment for the future. Others were more prosaic, treating the problem as one of political prudence and suggesting that manufactures, trade and population figures would all benefit from a freedom of religion. Across the North Sea was a shining example of the practical benefits, not least that no-one had 'reason to complain of oppression in conscience; and no man having hopes by advancing his religion, to form a party, or break in upon the state, the differences in opinion make none in affections.'[85] There were equally pragmatic counter-arguments. If harmony was so desirable, then the nonconformists should abandon their stubborn prejudices and defer to the established authorities. If the social consequences of religious freedom were so important, why not recognize that 'a popular religion will unavoidably introduce and end in a popular government,' or that liberty will culminate in 'a state of perfect anarchy, in which every man does what is good in his own eyes.'[86] Where was liberty to end? Surely the papists would exploit it? And, as the anti-tolerationists gleefully pointed out, the puritans themselves had been noticeably reluctant to offer freedom of religion during the 1640s and 1650s. In answer to the claim that no-one could be coerced into sincere belief, the churchmen simply replied that their aim was outward obedience, not inward assent: the church left every individual the freedom of conscience in belief.

This tit-for-tat was fruitless. There was a reluctance to claim a right of religious freedom (although that claim had been made during the puritan revolution) and many were tempted to appeal to liberty, property and religion. For example, nonconformists and their allies were keen to argue that by fining dissenters and distraining their goods in place of unpaid fines, the King was trespassing on their property rights. Every day freeborn subjects were 'divested of their liberties and birthrights, and miserably thrown out of their possessions and freeholds,' complained the Duke of Buckingham in the Lords in 1675, and 'only because they cannot agree with others in some opinions and niceties of religion.' Such facile rhetoric was easily answered by those like Sir Peter Leicester who were responsible for enforcing the law: at the Northwich Quarter Sessions in 1676, Leicester referred to Buckingham's speech and then asked, 'is it against the rule of charity to punish offenders who transgress the laws? What are laws, if not obeyed? How can obedience be constrained from offenders, without execution of the punishments?' It is not private opinion but breaking the law which leads a man to lose 'his liberty or estate'. Leicester told the 1677 grand jury,

> our monarch preserves the laws all he can; whose property or liberty does he invade of any man who lives regularly according to the law? And if he should not invade the property, liberty, lives and estates of all transgressors of the law, as traitors and felons and all other malefactors, how can he preserve the law or protect his subjects from devouring one another, wherewith he is entrusted? Which power is inherent in his authority, as a royal gem in his imperial crown given unto him by God.[87]

Responses to this argument tended to be appeals to first principles or fundamental laws: Marvell suggested that 'men ought to enjoy the same propriety and protection in their consciences, which they have in their lives, liberties and estates'; many others claimed that the penal laws against nonconformity were a breach of Magna Carta, the 'fundamental law', laws of nature and the law of God.[88]

Talk of conscience and laws of nature raises the discussion onto a different plane. Dissenters argued that 'in several things they cannot join with the public [worship of the church], without offering violence to their consciences; which is a tender part.' In reply to this essentially Pauline argument about the need to respect weak and tender consciences, the Anglicans wrote of the dissenters' erroneous conscience, of prejudice, 'fancy', 'passions and disorderly affections' masquerading as conscience.[89] Moreover this 'new gospel of private conscience' could not outweigh the obligation to obey the powers that are ordained by God. We have an obligation of conscience to obey the laws of our sovereign, otherwise our obedience would arise solely out of prudence (and that would open the way to a Hobbesian universe).[90] Many held that conscience could justify the withholding of active obedience if the conscientious were then prepared to suffer the consequences. It was also a commonplace that belief was not subject to will, that no-one, neither Sir William Temple nor the dissenters of Bristol, could 'command their consciences, nor . . . compel themselves to think otherwise of those things, than they now do'. Only argument and rational conviction could compel assent.[91] So why did the state and church continue to prosecute dissenters? The Church of England for its part was adamant that it simply presented individuals with the opportunity to reconsider their beliefs and examine all of the arguments.[92] The church had a duty to warn people against sin and no sin was more heinous than schism, the base-less separation from a true church.[93] The church also had a pastoral duty to ensure that consciences were properly informed. Mark Goldie has authoritatively demonstrated the Augustinian roots of this argument and suggested that it became more prominent in the church's ministry after 1675.[94] It was clearly a powerful weapon which gained in pertinence during the years of tory revival in the early 1680s. The Church of England's argument may not now be convincing, but it was more co-herent than that of the supporters of conscience. The argument for freedom of conscience was managed by some who took their stand on scripture and some who equated 'conscience' with the free play of human reason – and by many who muddled the two positions. All of them effectively pleaded that the sincerely conscientious should be allowed liberty. Martin Clifford argued that a man 'may now be fully a papist, and seven years hence fully a protestant, and yet his faith still remains the same, because it is all the while actuated and moved by the same soul of faith, which is conscience.'[95] Here the argument has shifted so that the scruples of the conscientious become the measure of what is permissible. Sincerity of belief matters more than being right. Although no doubt attractive to the simple-minded, this relativism would have offended most of Clifford's more thoughtful contemporaries.

The question needed to be tackled in a more fundamental way. What was at stake was the perennial problem of how to accommodate the individual's desires and society's needs. In the 1670s three different approaches were taken to this problem. One was the common-sense view that the sovereign has authority over all matters, civil and ecclesiastical, since sovereignty by definition can exist in only one person or institution. Alien to modern minds, this position nevertheless had the bible, patriarchalism, and, apparently, experience to recommend it. It assumed an autonomous morality, based on the law of nature and the revealed will of God, but sometimes found it difficult to explain how that morality could exert an influence over the sovereign. In practice, this approach could sound Erastian, as when it seemed to suggest religion and morality were subordinate to the sovereign, or even Hobbesian, if it hinted that the sovereign's will was the only rule of religion and of good and evil. The second approach can be introduced by John Shafte's *The Great Law of Nature* (1673) which asserted that toleration would lead to the collapse of government and that it was for the magistrate to decide what liberty is allowed to individuals. The reason for this is that 'our duty to God, and respect for the general good of mankind, are things inseparable from our interest, there being nothing so absolutely necessary to our well-being, as to do our duty to our creator, and to do good to our fellow-creatures, which is commanded by the law of nature, and by the example of God himself.'[96] Here the individual attains his own ends through the pursuit of the common good. The law of nature obliges us to co-operation and that puts God and natural law at the centre of the picture. This is, as Dr Parkin has shown, the result of Samuel Parker's and Richard Cumberland's critical engagement with the ideas of Hobbes. It is a position which tames Hobbes and saves God, but it also has intriguing affinities with arguments from 'interest' and with later secular utilitarianism.

The final approach is very different. It was prompted by the kind of searching question John Locke asked of Samuel Parker's book:

> The end of government being public peace 'tis no question the supreme power must have an uncontrollable right to judge and ordain all things that may conduce to it, but yet the question will be whether uniformity established by law be (as is here supposed) a necessary means to it, i.e. whether it be at all dangerous to the magistrate that, he believing free will, some of his subjects shall believe predestination, or whether it be more necessary for his government to make laws for wearing surplices than it is for wearing vests.[97]

The civil power has a right to judge all matters concerning public peace, but is religion such a matter? In various drafts and manuscript essays, Locke denied that religion was the province of the civil power. What Locke argued in his notebooks, William Penn and Charles Wolseley were prepared to assert bluntly in print: 'the civil and ecclesiastical power, are things perfectly in themselves distinct, and ought in their exercise to be kept so.'[98] As Sir William Temple told English readers in 1673, the Dutch managed very well under such a separation of church and state. Although it seems to have commanded little support, the central principle of John Locke's 1689 *Letter on Toleration* was in the public domain throughout the 1670s.

Religion and politics were not separable in the 1670s. How to treat non-conformists and what to do about popery were among the most pressing domestic political issues. In so far as the decade had ideological considerations they were generated by these issues. Yet few politicians made more than gestures; attitudinizing was their limit. But then this was not a decade that wore its heart on its sleeve: it was an age of masquerade, irony and witty detachment. The energies of political and religious debate went into unmasking opponents: revealing the vicious atheist beneath the reasoning sceptic, the Laudian wolf beneath the Anglican lamb, the seditious hypocrite beneath the conscientious dissenter. The polity was however built upon religious assumptions and institutions. Monarchy, law and parliament were committed to the defence of protestantism – even though for some that term meant simply a broad piety, while for others it signified the Church of England as re-established in 1662. So integral was the defence of protestantism to many people's political thinking that 'popery' became synonymous with all and any kind of political threat. And at the heart of this was the paradox bequeathed from 1662 of a divided English protestant community. In abstract terms, the problem of religious pluralism was reduced to the problem of reconciling the individual conscience and the demands of society. The choice was stark: either the individual was subordinated to the state or there was a separation of church and state. Which of these options individuals leaned towards in the 1670s seems to me to say much about their perception of their own society. One option reflected a fear that their society was fragile, that it teetered on the edge of moral, social and even political collapse unless authority could impose control on dissidents, rogues, cheats, papists and nonconformists. The other choice accepted that society could gain strength from its diversity, that trusting individuals to exercise their own reason, or for that matter to pursue their own interest and profit, would, like the circulation of information or the encouragement of enterprise, improve the nation.

9

1677–9: Mutinous Assemblies and Pickpocket Wars

The political options seem to narrow in the later 1670s as if the long erosion of public trust in Charles and his ministers had finally begun to undermine the whole political edifice. The spotlight increasingly fell on Whitehall and Westminster, although significant action occurred off-stage in London, Flanders and Scotland. When, in the autumn of 1678, a crisis came, it was primarily a crisis of government, not a confronta-tion between tyranny and opposition. At first the crisis was perpetuated by an irresolute monarch and the naked self-interest of his heir, his embattled minister, his long-standing parliament and those who claimed a place at the council table. The fall of Danby in 1679 created a power vacuum. A host of issues – the corruption of parliaments, the fear of popery, the control of money and troops, England's subservience to France and the aspirations of dissenters for religious liberty – were caught up in a swirl of faction as politicians attempted to force their way into office or power. Although every historian will naturally tell the tale differently, all would recognize that in the later 1670s England was enter-ing a complex political crisis not a battle of wills or principles.

After receiving reports on 14 February 1677 of journeymen and appren-tices of the cloth trade meeting in an alley near the Half Moon Tavern in Cheapside, Secretary Coventry reminded the civic authorities that the King wanted 'all such mutinous assemblies within the City' suppressed.[1] Since the riots of 1675 and Jenks's speech at the Guildhall, the govern-ment was edgy about civic disorder, but Coventry was especially nervous because parliament was due to meet the next day and trouble was certain. The previous December William Harbord heard 'that the lords are busy and preparing matters to prove the dissolution of parliament and that they will deny any conference with us [the Commons] and lay the sin of corruption to our charge and that we are unfit to represent the commons of England.'[2] The lords in question were a small group led by the Earl of Shaftesbury whose tactics were both simple and ill-judged. Over the winter Shaftesbury canvassed for a campaign for the dissolution of the present parliament and the election of a new one. Unfortunately he overestimated the likely support: if some MPs like Harbord would 'gladly be dissolved, but not by the Lords or at their pleasure', most were reluctant to vote themselves out of a job. Although in the febrile autumn of 1675 the Lords' motion for a dissolution had been lost by only two votes, now Shaftesbury could find few peers to back him: Holles dithered, Halifax, Anglesey and Winchester refused to participate, and Buckingham's enthusiasm was tempered by his ambition, while the support of York and the Catholic peers, so helpful in 1675, had all but evaporated.

The government had the upper hand. First it deployed propaganda and then it laid a parliamentary ambush – and both worked brilliantly. Marchamont Nedham's *A Pacquet of Advices* was supposed to be a reply to *A Letter from a Person of Quality* (1675), but it only appeared as parliament began to assemble in February 1677. It was a witty explosion of Shaftesbury's personality, career and motivations, and a sustained attempt to identify his methods, arguments and aims with those of the rebels of 1641, the Levellers, Ireton and other puritan traitors. It also exploited the rivalry between the dissident aristocrats. Shaftesbury, this 'Mephistopheles, the faery fiend that haunts both houses', had supposedly been compared by Buckingham to the 'will-with-a-wisp that uses to lead men out of the way, then leaves them at last in a ditch and darkness, and nimbly retreats for self-security'. Much was made of the ambition and covetousness of Shaftesbury, 'a cashiered or broken statesmen', who 'intoxicated' the nation with the fear of popery so that he could thwart Clifford in 1673 and who now sought to undermine the monarchy by attacking the episcopacy of the Church of England; 'the party is a-forming; the presbyterian hath been tickled in his own way, and other sorts of nonconformity are to be drawn in.' Shaftesbury had 'turned city merchant; and having driven a fine trade in the winter of 'seventy-five in the great corporation, he has the following summers been laying a train in the lesser corporations, in hope to blow up this parliament with the noise of a new one. The prologue to the tragedy must be, *down with the bishops.*'[3] Shaftesbury was later heard to say that this tract 'was as politically contrived and as unluckily timed to the prejudice of him as ever anything was' because sixteen of the twenty peers committed to his cause 'dropped off upon perusal and well digestion of that book'.[4] The rest then fell foul of Danby in parliament.

After Charles had opened the session on 15 February and MPs had returned to their chamber, the Duke of Buckingham rose to make a long speech which argued – on the strength of two statutes of Edward III – that the present parliament had no legal existence because of the fifteen-month prorogation. Legalistic and overblown (if these statutes did not bind then 'the whole government of England by parliaments and by law is absolutely at an end'), Buckingham's speech took a swipe at the MPs who now see themselves 'as a standing senate, and as a number of men picked out to be legislators for the rest of their whole lives'. He moved an address to the King for the remedy 'which the law requires, and which all the nation longs for, the calling of a new parliament'.[5] No sooner had the Duke sat down than Lord Frescheville, Danby's cousin, moved that he be called to the bar of the house to answer for his reflections on the parliament.

Danby's allies then led the house in parallel discussions of the two motions by Buckingham and Frescheville, and cowed all but Shaftesbury, Salisbury and Wharton from supporting Buckingham. In the Commons meanwhile 'the question [of dissolution] was more lightly touched', although even here there were some fierce exchanges: Sir Robert Howard telling Sacheverell that they were 'upon the most dangerous debate that may be' and that they would 'set the town at work and enter the lists at the coffee-house'; and Sir Richard Temple asking, 'because the legality of our meeting is questioned by libels without doors, must we therefore make it a question within doors?'[6] Yet by mid-afternoon MPs had moved on to other matters, and as soon as this was reported to Danby, he proposed that the Lords should 'consider about punishing those that argued for dissolving'. Buckingham's proposal was now laid aside and over the next two days he and his three supporters were called to the bar and, on refusing to retract their views, they were packed off to the Tower for contempt of the house. Isolated from parliament, the four lords could not even take comfort from popular support: no protests or petitions were organized, and some gentlemen at the Bear Tavern even paid for a bonfire of celebration.[7] Anyone who wished to see the four prisoners needed the House of Lords' permission and Danby could be confident that they were politically impotent until at least the end of the session.

The Commons swiftly decided to vote the King the money he needed for ships. As Sir John Reresby later saw it, 'the country party obstructed all they could the giving above £400,000,' the 'court party' were for a million or £800,000, but 'the moderate men' (of which he was one) carried the vote for £600,000 for thirty new ships.[8] Whatever the significance of this analysis by party, the Commons were definitely amenable to their monarch and his needs. On 2 March they voted to raise the sum by a land tax, despite Meres's observation that 'land tax is a melancholy thought, and should be the last for our consideration.'[9] But MPs did insist that this money be kept separately from other funds and that they be shown accounts of its expenditure. Soon after they also agreed to renew the grant of additional excises for another three years. Meres told them that "'tis money that makes a parliament considerable and nothing else,' and Powle complained that they were ignoring the convention that redress of grievances preceded supply, but the Commons happily agreed these grants before they turned to consider grievances such as the abuse of habeas corpus, the illegal exaction of money and the service of his majesty's subjects in the French army.[10] Little wonder, perhaps, that 'the people about town call this the Pump Parliament, alluding, as a little water put into a pump fetches up a great deal, so etc.'[11]

With a clear run in the House of Lords the government introduced measures to reassure the nation that protestantism would be safe under a Catholic King James. A bill provided for the education of a Catholic monarch's children as protestants. An oath against transubstantiation would be tendered to each new monarch and if declined, the education of the royal children would be deputed to three bishops of the Church of England; at the same time control of episcopal appointments would also be ceded to the bishops. For many, this was the catch. The bill seemed to create a self-perpetuating oligarchy among the bishops and give them immense influence over the heir to the throne. Another bill, supposedly 'for the better conviction of papists', effectively set up a register of existing Catholics, who would pay a weekly fine of 12 pence for absence from the parish church and suffer exclusion from all public office; the full rigour of the penal laws was redirected against converts to Catholicism.

Despite optimistic reports of public bills 'on the anvil' in both houses and a determination to avoid disputes between the chambers, the two bills to safeguard protestantism were destined to cause conflict.[12] When the first of them arrived in the Commons, Michael Mallet denounced it for setting up 'nine mitres above the crown' and, in a rare speech, the MP for Hull, Andrew Marvell, made a long and diffuse attack on this 'ill thing' which, whether it would prevent popery or not, would certainly ensure the promotion of the bishops.[13] Predictably the bill was buried in committee. No such decent interment awaited the bill for better conviction of papists when it was considered in the Commons in early April. William Sacheverell regarded this as a 'bare toleration' of popery which put only 12 pence a week 'betwixt the best protestant and the severest papist'.[14] Having rejected the bill *nem. con.*, MPs added the insulting remark that the substance of the bill contradicted its title. They countered with a resurrected and severe anti-catholic proposal of their own and, in a separate demonstration of their attitude, they expelled the convicted recusant Sir Thomas Strickland MP from his seat.[15]

MPs were as ever eager to tackle the nation's economic troubles. The veteran nonconformist John Birch brought in a bill to require every parish to grow hemp and flax, the raw materials for linen cloth, as a solution to unemployment, poverty and depopulation.[16] Meanwhile two cases seemed to reveal the ease with which the Commons' suspicions of arbitrary action could be fanned into flame and yet the reluctance of the house to take on their opponents. The Lords fined and imprisoned Nicholas Cary, an ejected nonconformist minister now earning a living as a physician, for organizing the printing of Lord Holles's anonymous *Some Considerations upon the Question, Whether the Parliament is Dissolved* (1676). When Cavendish raised Cary's case in the Commons, members like Sacheverell and Powle began to fulminate against the Lords and were told by Sir Henry Goodrick that those who pressed the matter now 'are no friends to the good of the nation' (for which remark he had to make what amounted to an apology to Cavendish). All agreed that the case had the makings of another Shirley versus Fagg and, despite their declared intentions, the Commons never found time to return to Cary's case.[17] They were soon considering an even murkier episode which Sacheverell had brought to their notice. John Harrington had been imprisoned on a charge of having suborned two Scots soldiers to complain on oath that they had been pressed, rather than volunteered, in Scotland to serve in the French army. They turned out to be utterly unreliable witnesses, and it transpired that Fonseca, the Spanish consul, also had a hand in the business, but Harrington remained in the Tower on account of his insolence towards Charles II during examination. Sacheverell, Lee and Cavendish made much of this outrageously high-handed approach by the executive, and Harrington appeared before the Commons to ask for the law and the house's protection; but he was known to be 'of Shaftesbury's crew' and, once again, the Commons let the matter drop.[18]

Over-shadowing all of this was the campaign that Louis XIV launched in early February against Flanders or the Spanish Netherlands, the Habsburg territory which provided a buffer between France and the Dutch Republic but also threatened the integrity of France's north-eastern defences. Louis took Valenciennes early in March and Cambrai before the end of the month. On 15 March parliament presented the King with an address to which he agreed 'that the conservation of Flanders is of great importance to England.' Observing that in their address the Commons were 'shy' of mentioning financial support for the war against the French to which 'their counsel tended', Sir Robert Southwell put this down to their 'fear of a pickpocket war' by which Charles would take taxes but not go to war.[19] Busy with their other business, the Commons said nothing until 29 March when they agreed an address to the King asking him to ally with the Spanish and Dutch confederates and promising that if such an alliance should lead to war with the French they would provide money. Once again members returned to other matters, mainly the detail of the land tax and excise, while awaiting Charles's response. Reresby told Danby that 'some of the discontented party' were hastening the money bill so that parliament might break up at Easter with 'the public bills' incomplete and in the hope of 'dissatisfy[ing] the nation' by creating the impression that parliament met only to vote taxes.[20] Danby was assessing his own hand at this time. In a memo for the King of 4 April he argues that 'when men's fears are grown both so general and so great as now they are by the successes of France,' Charles has to turn against Louis or risk not only the 'worst' session of parliament 'that we ever yet saw' but also alienating the hearts of the people utterly. Among the advantages of a war against France are that the responsibility would be shared with parliament: parliament must accept the costs of the war which they want and if anything goes wrong must shoulder part of the blame.[21] As if to underline the gravity of the situation, on 1 April William of Orange suffered 'a very bloody defeat' at Cassel and a few days later St Omer capitulated to the French.[22]

Charles took Danby's lead and on 11 April replied to the Commons through Williamson that the only way to secure England against danger was 'by putting his majesty timely in condition to make such fitting preparations' and to that end he proposed an adjournment until after Easter when they could meet 'to ripen this matter'. To sit after Easter to ripen things 'is, in plain English, to grant money', explained Mr Stockdale. Sir William Coventry said that the King 'seems to intimate, that he is not in a condition to do what we desire of him, and expects something from us according to our promises,' and he proposed a maximum grant of £200,000.[23] The following day MPs resolved to amend the excise bill so that the King could borrow this sum against the tax and to reimburse him for these loans. On 16 April, Good Friday, the King sent a message noting that they had enabled him to borrow £200,000 'upon a fund given him for other uses', but 'he must tell them plainly' that without £600,000 of new money 'it will not be possible for him to speak or act those things which should answer the ends of their several addresses.'[24] The Commons' reply was a delaying tactic, albeit a necessary one: many MPs had already left London for Easter and it was proposed to revisit the matter when they reassembled. The same evening Charles gave his assent to the completed money bills and adjourned parliament until 21 May. It was, however, widely understood that the King was thinking of a series of short adjournments through the summer and that parliament would only conduct business again in October.[25] The advantages of this were that parliament was available at short notice in case of emergency, that Shaftesbury could be kept in custody as the session had not technically ended, and of course that Charles had some funds voted and was not yet committed to war.

Charles rushed off to Newmarket for the racing, while Danby went to Windsor where, on 19 April, he was installed as a Knight of the Garter with 'great magnificence; duty, curiosity and friendship brought 150

coaches thither.'[26] The time was finally judged ripe for a change of guard
in Ireland and so the Earl of Essex, who had served as Lord Lieutenant
since 1672, was relieved of his post with all honour and replaced by a
previous incumbent, the Duke of Ormonde. Essex had long anticipated
his removal from office, partly because of the government's reluctance
to leave power for long in the hands of any one viceroy (save for Scottish Lauderdale), and partly because of the ceaseless intriguing of his
deputy, Ranelagh, who enjoyed the backing of Orrery, Portsmouth and,
apparently, Danby. The Lord Treasurer had wavered between the tax-
farmer Ranelagh, the pairing of Monmouth and Lord Conway, and the
old hand Ormonde.[27] At Newmarket Charles was approached on behalf
of the peers in the Tower. The elderly Wharton had already been allowed
to go into house-arrest, but the other three remained in custody. Buckingham whiled away the time with chemistry experiments and Shaftesbury amused himself by drawing up lists of 'vile' and 'worthy' members
of parliament. Their petitions for liberty, made both jointly and separately, cut little ice with Charles since they were still far from offering
the abject apology necessary to satisfy him.[28] Charles seemed in no hurry
to initiate the war expected of him. As the parliament was adjourned,
French envoys, the Duc de Crequi and Archbishop Le Tellier, arrived to
compliment the English King and Sunderland was dispatched on a re-
ciprocal mission to the French court at Calais. The public took a dim
view of such niceties, indeed the English were almost pathological in
their antipathy to things French. On 29 May the King's birthday was celebrated at Whitehall with a French opera 'pitifully done'; 'some say it
was not well contrived to entertain the English gentry, who came that
night in honour to their King, with a lamentable ill-acted French play,
when our English actors so much surpass.'[29]

By this time, parliament had met – in spite of earlier indications –
and rather than return, as Charles asked, to the issue of money, MPs
debated whether to go into committee 'that it may be scanned where
our interest lies' in foreign affairs.[30] On 23 May Charles summoned the
Commons to Whitehall to dispel the rumours that 'I had called you
together only to get money from you for other uses than you would have
it employed.' He assured them on the word of a king that they would
'not repent any trust your repose in me for the safety of my kingdoms'
and concluded by warning that 'it shall be your fault, and not mine, if
our security be not sufficiently provided for.'[31] In their over-excited
debate on Charles's speech, MPs talked wildly; Cavendish thought the
speech 'the product of ill counsel', Mallet worked in a reference to
Solomon and his vulnerability 'to strange counsels by strange women';
some wanted to trust the King, but others were queasy about that whole
approach towards their monarch, trust 'is a word of strange nature,'
remarked Howard, 'he will not be put to it, trust or not trust'; others

believed that the power of France was the ultimate issue, or that 'our interest is to keep Holland fast to us.'[32] But they agreed to draw up an address to the King and the draft brought before the house on 25 May declined further supply to Charles before his alliances were made known and beseeched him to enter into an offensive and defensive alliance with the Dutch and others of the confederates to preserve Flanders. It explained in detail why this was the opportune moment to take on the might of France. In the debate shouts of 'agree, agree' greeted those like Berkenhead who wavered. This was 'club law', complained Trelawney. The specification of an offensive alliance with the Dutch caused contention. It 'was much urged to be an entrenchment on the prerogative where the power of peace and war is singly vested. This did not receive any good answer, but that there seemed a necessity to mention Holland as most useful to us.' Harbord demurred at war on economic grounds and preferred a ban on French imports.[33] Eventually, with forty or fifty members abstaining by skulking in the Speaker's chamber, the address was approved by 182 to 142 votes. It was presented the next day and received a reply on 28 May in the Banqueting Hall. Charles told MPs that part of their address 'intrenched upon so undoubted a right of the crown, that I am confident it will appear in no age (when the sword was not drawn) that the prerogative of making peace and war hath been so dangerously invaded.' If he permitted them to trespass in this way, 'no prince or state would any longer believe that the sovereignty of England rests in the crown.' He would not part with 'so essential part of the monarchy' and so he would now continue to pursue the security of the country without parliament's help. They were to be adjourned until July, but would not sit for business until the winter. Copies, often defective, of this 'angry speech' were widely available and, in an innovation, it was printed the next day in the *Gazette*. When Speaker Seymour adjourned the house in the teeth of protests, he and his mace had to be escorted from the chamber.[34]

I

With parliament in abeyance the peers in the Tower had a chance of their liberty. Lord Oxford's lobbying won Salisbury parole and Lord Middlesex 'is the most earnest man alive' for Buckingham, who in late June was allowed to leave the Tower escorted by Sir John Robinson and go to view the building works at his house at Cliveden. That very day his former lover 'my lady Shrewsbury owned her match with Mr [George Rodney] Bridges.'[35] Shaftesbury, however, remained a prisoner. On 29 June his plea of habeas corpus was heard in King's Bench. 'The hall was never seen fuller,' and the case was handled with 'calmness' on all sides; but the judges decided that they could do nothing about the order of a superior court, the House of Lords, 'so that he is now in the Tower till his majesty shall be pleased to release him or till the House of Lords next meet.' At the end of July, Wharton was told to go and sin no more, Salisbury was released for good, and Buckingham gained a month's parole; when Shaftesbury, who was said to have sneered at Buckingham's inconstancy, asked for release because of the ill air of his prison, Charles merely promised to 'think of some other prison in a better air'.[36]

Charles was deeply engaged in diplomacy. As the Nijmegen negotiations for peace between France and the Netherlands progressed, Charles had little choice but to broker a peace in Flanders. When Louis made unreasonable demands, Charles grasped the nettle and opened discussions with William of Orange and the Dutch in the hope of forcing Louis to moderate his stance. Danby began to work towards the marriage of Orange and Mary, eldest daughter of the Duke of York; Laurence Hyde was sent over to the Hague to encourage William to visit England. All that the world knew of this was the to-ing and fro-ing of ambassadors: 'here is M. Bentinck, chief favourite to the Prince of Orange, come over yesterday to his majesty, but his business not publicly known,' reported Savile in June.[37] But as so often Charles was playing both ends against the middle. He had personally begun secret discussions with Louis and by August he had agreed to adjourn parliament until April 1678, by which time it would be too late to launch a war in that year, and to receive two million French livres for his trouble. Reluctantly Danby had sat in on these intrigues, but he only seems to have heard about the final terms of agreement from Ralph Montagu, the English ambassador in Paris. It was the rehabilitation of Buckingham that summer which kept Danby looking over his shoulder and unwilling to oppose Charles in such a delicate matter. When paroled, Buckingham had come to court, moved in with Rochester, and begun to enjoy 'merry' evenings with his monarch. On 5 August he was granted a conditional release and it was said that he might succeed Ormonde as Lord Steward.

Charles and his brother spent a fortnight sailing in August, while the young bloods of the court went further afield: 'Monmouth, Feversham, Mulgrave, Lumley, and Middleton, with some gentlemen, have gone to the French camp; Albemarle, Ossory, Plymouth and others are gone to the Prince of Orange'.[38] On his return voyage from Plymouth, Charles encountered a nasty storm, but worse awaited him at court. Danby was annoyed at the presence of Buckingham and at the final terms agreed with the French. At his urging Charles now backed out of the arrangement on the pretext that he had only now realized the true value in sterling of two million livres. While the King went off racing, arrangements were put in place for a visit from William of Orange: Secretary Coventry coyly hoped that the result would be something more than 'a bare visit', but most acknowledged that he was coming to haggle over a marriage. On 21 October William's marriage to Mary was agreed, announced to the privy council the next day, and celebrated privately by Bishop Compton on 4 November, William's birthday. The nation rejoiced with bells and bonfires; Danby was the hero of the hour, and even the Duke of York gained kudos from his willing acquiescence; the new princess danced with her husband at a splendid court ball held on the Queen's birthday, 15 November. 'A more popular thing could not have been done,' believed Bishop Morley, and he advised that 'the warmth newly kindled in the people's affections should not be suffered to cool by deferring our next meeting so long.'[39] Yet in the midst of all this Charles announced that the next session of parliament would be postponed until April, a move to which he was already secretly committed but one also intended, no doubt, to conciliate Louis. When the lieutenancy of London was also overhauled, Roger Morrice commented that 'Danby is prime minister of state, and he alone hath done all this': although the implications of all these policies were not yet evident, some anticipated a breach with France.[40]

Charles and William now put their heads together over another set of peace terms between France and the Netherlands and sent them across to Louis. They were astonished when their agent Feversham returned on 2 December with the news that his reception had been 'very cold' and Louis had declined their offer.[41] Even worse, Louis stopped the payment of his subsidy to Charles. In the face of Louis's obduracy, Charles had to huff and look big. He would now meet parliament in January 1678, not April. He listened to York and Danby who both favoured a French war as a way of defusing hostility towards the court. Williamson surveyed the nation's military and naval strength: plans were made to raise 30,000 new soldiers, and Williamson noted that 'we must have a great care of employing papists except in service abroad, not in service at home.'[42] The Foreign Affairs Committee drew up an alliance with the Dutch to force Louis to accept the last terms offered and this was signed, but not ratified, on New Year's Eve. 'Nothing is discoursed on here but a war with France, and our entering into a confederation with the Emperor, the Spaniard and the Dutch,' reported Morrice on 10 January 1678.[43] Troop movements and council meetings convinced the people that war was looming, but for many experienced observers it was implausible that Charles, with his long record of acquiescence towards France, could change his spots. MPs and peers were unsettled by the details which the confederate envoys spread about the terms that Charles and William had offered Louis. Many of the same politicians were also influenced by Barrillon, the French ambassador, who had £32,000 left on his hands after the ending of Louis's subsidy and which he now diverted into the pockets of MPs and lords in the well-founded hope of encouraging them to obstruct the King's business in the new session of parliament.

When the appointed day of 15 January 1678 arrived Charles had still not finalized the treaty with the Dutch and so Speaker Seymour announced, to much grumbling and talk of choosing another Speaker, a further adjournment until 28 January. Perhaps Charles and Louis could engineer agreement over the next fortnight; Marvell hoped for a peace, 'but those things are at present in a cloudy uncertainty.'[44] 'Our drums beat daily, and yet I think the people talk louder,' wrote Coventry. 'I hope whatsoever we have abroad we shall have peace at home, and as to my own particular a good round money vote with a nemine contradicente will please me as much as my share in a land or sea victory.'[45] On the 28th Charles told parliament that he had done what was asked of him. He had committed himself to an offensive alliance with the Dutch and promised ninety ships and 30,000 to 40,000 troops. Now it was their turn to provide him with the £1,000,000 that this would cost. The court's speakers wanted to proceed straight to supply, but Sir Thomas Lee and others proved obstructive. MPs mistrustful of the King appear to have diverted the house repeatedly: first they brought forward a debate on the irregular conduct of the Speaker in recent adjournments; then they successfully proposed an address to the King thanking him for the Orange marriage, asking him not to agree to any peace which left Louis stronger than he had been in 1659 and demanding that all the confederates cease trading with France. The house voted for the reburial with the 'solemnity of funeral rites' of Charles I's body and for a monument, but was it to be erected at Westminster, Windsor or St Paul's? MPs worried over remedies for the economy such as an export ban on wool, a requirement that all corpses be buried in woollen shrouds and action against hawkers and pedlars. When it came to foreign policy, they asked why the King still spent so much time with Barrillon? And why were new troops not being sent to Flanders immediately? 'Thus they go on,' wrote Southwell, 'contending and disputing every particular step that is made, having a great number of able and contentious speakers, though they are outdone in votes.'[46] Yet to Andrew Marvell, 'all the house seems to aim at is to see their way before them' and know to what they are committing English money.[47] As the volunteers enlisted, the Commons at last agreed, on 18 February, to provide the necessary £1,000,000, and then they began long drawn-out discussions about how this sum might be raised.[48]

Mistrust of Charles had been fostered by the appearance in February of 'a large book', supposedly published in Amsterdam in 1677, with the title of *An Account of the Growth of Popery and Arbitrary Government.* That Andrew Marvell was the author of this anonymous work seems to have been a fairly open secret. As if its title was not sufficient, the first sentence announced the book's thesis of a long hatched plot to turn the kingdom's lawful government into 'absolute tyranny' and its protestant religion into 'downright popery'. This was another salvo in Shaftesbury's campaign for the dissolution of the Cavalier Parliament. Over half of the text is a 'naked narrative' of the parliamentary sessions of 1677, the sessions which had begun so disastrously for Shaftesbury and his allies. Marvell's contextualizing of 1677 with a survey of the whole decade allows him to explain away the past records of Buckingham and Shaftesbury and to present an element in the House of Lords as the last redoubt of English freedom. The lords who opposed Danby's test 'stood up now for the English liberties with the same genius, virtue and courage, that their noble ancestors had formerly defended the great charter of England'. The Commons, on the other hand, is the subject of withering attack. One third of MPs hold office and had thus surrendered their independence, another third aspire to office and the final third are 'pensioners' of the ministers, saved only by 'a handful of salt, a sparkle of soul', those few members of true integrity and loyalty. Here Marvell was generalizing from the examples of pamphlets like *Seasonable Argument* or libels like the 'Alarum' which named names and figures, often embellishing their financial information with other lurid accusations about how MPs earned their keep. One consequence of such a tactic is, of course, to alienate likely readers in the Commons, so perhaps Marvell hoped to prick a few parliamentary consciences but mainly to appeal to wider public opinion.

Marvell certainly took care to obscure his own political stance: the author of *An Account* is loyal, for parliaments, sympathetic to religious freedom but not a partisan of dissent, anti-popish in a rather restrained way, and virulently anti-French. The pamphlet is plainly written, full of speeches, bills, parliamentary addresses and other tedious reports, and has virtually none of the characteristic brilliance, wit and wordplay to be found in his other prose. The accumulation of detail and rehashing of old grievances allows Marvell to get away with the specious claim of a continuity between the policies of the early 1670s and those of the later 1670s, between, say, the Stop of the Exchequer and Danby's Test Oath. The 'conspirators' are the shadowy deus ex machina of the whole decade. Even Marvell squirms slightly over his failure to name these conspirators; 'but if anyone delight in the chase, he is an ill woodman that knows not the size of the beast by the proportion of his excrement.'[49] A moment's serious consideration would surely suggest to contemporary readers that the only quarry who could bear responsibility for all the decade's policies is Charles II.

Even now the power and success of Marvell's book is debatable: modern scholars have argued that his facts and accusations 'were common property, and his merit is in recording them all at once', or that the book 'put into epigrammatic expression what many were clearly feeling'.[50] The government disliked it. 'There have been great rewards offered in private, and considerable in the *Gazette*, to any who could inform of the author or printer.' As many copies were 'burnt by the common hangman' from the stock of Francis Smith, book-seller, 'as would have yielded above £100'.[51] But people had been talking of the growth of popery and arbitrary government for a decade and while the publicity Marvell now gave to the quarrels of 1677 was, from the court's point of view, embarrassing, none of this was fresh news. The impact of Marvell's *Account* may have been in the implicit, but unescapable, accusation that Charles was the common link between all the steps towards absolutism and popery.

Events in Scotland surely reinforced that impression. Late in 1677, having been told that rebellion was brewing in south-west Scotland, Charles had authorized Lauderdale to take punitive action against the presbyterian landowners of Ayrshire. The most notorious part of Lauderdale's crack-down was the 'Highland Host', an army of Catholic Highlanders, who descended on Ayrshire in the first two months of 1678, lived on free quarter, extorted fines, imposed bonds for good behaviour, and disarmed and plundered the population mercilessly before withdrawing. Among the London dissenters 'great talk there is of great cruelties, outrages and persecutions of meetings in Scotland.' Morrice kept a careful record of all he discovered about 'this odd war' and concluded that 'disorders' were scarcely to be avoided 'for Highlanders must steal and are at best barbarous.'[52]

Unknown to any but James, Danby and Barrillon, in early February 1678 the irresolute Charles offered yet another deal to Louis, which substituted one Flemish town for another and suggested that if these terms were agreed they might be followed up by an Anglo-French alliance and a French subsidy of £600,000 a year to enable Charles to rule without parliament. His hopes were dashed when news arrived of Louis's attack on Ghent. The city's days were plainly numbered. On a premature report of its fall, Charles sent 1600 men under Lord Howard of Escrick to Ostend, and Monmouth followed them the next day. 'The same day the Commons upon this news grew very warm, and began to reflect on the King's ill councils, that had not advised him to this war sooner. They named no man then, but it was plain that they pointed at the Duke of York and my Lord Treasurer.'[53] It was high time for Shaftesbury to get back into the game. Despite every obstacle that Charles and Danby could throw in his path, Shaftesbury submitted to the Lords, regained his liberty, and then, on 27 February, resumed his seat in the upper chamber. Yet even now limited dialogue was possible between the court and parliament. At the King's levee, Charles told Reresby and other MPs that unless money came through soon 'it would come after the French

King had done his work.' York gloomily reported that some MPs intended to return to the question of 'ill councillors', but Reresby 'said it was not very likely, for I was told the day before by a leader of the anti-court party that it was not now a time to raise differences at home when we were in war abroad; and it proved as I said.' For several days the Commons proceeded with the poll tax, and critics of the government took their chance to add clauses banning imports from France and ensuring that money raised was spent only on the war. The attack which York and Danby anticipated finally came on 14 March when, as Marvell expressed it to his constituents, 'the progress of the French King in Flanders still threatening us, and the vigour necessary to oppose it not seeming sufficient,' the house considered the state of the nation. Cavendish wanted members to consider 'the apprehensions we are under of popery, and a standing army', but the house concentrated on the war and on evil councillors: 'several speeches were made, of jealousies and fears, and particularly of the army which was now raising, as if it were rather intended to set up absolute monarchy than to make war with France.'[54] None of the evil councillors was named and a vote to remove all those who advised the adjournment of May 1677 was defeated by five votes, but the Commons did resolve without a vote on an address to the King asking for the immediate declaration of war against France, the recall of ambassadors from Paris and Nijmegen and the expulsion of Barrillon.

II

The Commons had brought themselves to the point of stipulating precisely what they wanted – a war and a war now – because they could not trust Charles to spend money on a French war rather than simply pocketing it or spending it on troops to be used against his own subjects. When this address was debated in the Lords, Essex, Halifax, Shaftesbury, Buckingham, Holles, Clare and Wharton all spoke in favour of asking for the immediate declaration of war, but York, Finch and Danby persuaded the house on eminently practical grounds to substitute 'with all the expedition that can possibly subsist with the safety of your majesty's affairs' for 'immediately'. The Commons took exception to this and the consequent deadlock led to a request to Charles for a short adjournment until 11 April. Marvell reported to Hull that the King could not declare war until he was sure of supply and his alliances, but in the meantime commissions had been issued and officers were raising men with all speed.[55] In late March the army was being raised 'very fast in the town and in the country', a month later 'a very great army' had been created, and the Dutch were told that 17,860 men were being sent over.[56]

The earlier suggestion to the French of a treaty with England had been followed up and on 25 March a new set of proposals for peace between France and Holland and France and the Empire were sent by Danby to Ambassador Montagu with instructions to feel 'the pulse of that King'. If the peace terms were acceptable, Montagu was to suggest that Louis should pay Charles six million livres a year for three years, 'because it will probably be two or three years before the parliament will be in humour to give him any supplies after the making of any peace with France.' If the terms were unacceptable, Montagu was not to mention money at all. The whole thing was to be 'as private as is possible' and Montagu 'must not mention a syllable of the money' to Secretary Coventry.[57] This letter offers a glimpse of the secretive world of diplomacy under Charles II. It conveys, too, something of the strange hopelessness of the English position; Danby seemed to expect a refusal and truthfully there was little in the detail to entice Louis; when Montagu made the proposal he was turned down point-blank. That might have been that if this letter and its evidence of Danby's participation in Charles's secret French intrigues had not shortly returned to haunt the Lord Treasurer.

Charles used his fortnight's respite from parliament to ponder the diplomatic stalemate: Louis had rebuffed all of his offers, and the completion of the alliance with the Netherlands, Spain and Austria was delayed because their envoy had insufficient powers. Danby also needed time to marshal his strength among MPs. A little judicious spending of secret service money and the usual behind the scenes meetings of the parliamentary managers reassured Sir Richard Wiseman that two hundred and nineteen MPs could be relied upon and that thirty of them were capable speakers.[58] As an extra precaution Speaker Seymour was confined to his sickbed in the country, and Sir Robert Sawyer was proposed and accepted as his replacement: once this was done, parliament was told that since the King's alliances were 'not yet so ripe' as had been hoped, there would be a fortnight's adjournment. This 'is hard,' protested MPs. They had been itching to discuss the alarming news of popery in Monmouthshire which had only been brought to their notice on the last day of the previous sitting. All they could do was continue the committee which had been set up on 28 March to review the evidence 'concerning the danger the nation is in by the growth of popery' and prepare for the next meeting. But at least 'the popery matter is upon the anvil,' said Meres; it was as 'necessary' as the question of a standing army itself, agreed Sacheverell.[59]

So it was on 29 April that parliament met once more and was treated by Finch to a long account of recent diplomacy which culminated with the admission that, as the King had always feared, the Dutch now sought to make a separate peace and would not join any alliance against France.

The King wanted parliament's advice and would follow it. MPs showed little sign of honouring their earlier promises of aid to Charles. They simply demanded to see all the relevant treaties and in the meantime turned to the committee which had reported on the dangers of popery. That committee's 'long narrative of fact' concerning the public meetings of papists in the Welsh borders, the sacking of anti-catholic JPs and the appointment of others who were 'popishly affected', the lax treatment of recusants in the Exchequer, 'and much of the like nature' was reluctantly retailed by Marvell to the Corporation of Hull, but as this was of 'ill report' he urged the aldermen not to spread the information. The Commons offered this material to the Lords as reason for strengthening the laws against Catholic priests and laity and said that they could not 'consent to lay any farther charge upon the people, how urgent soever the occasion be that require it, till their minds be satisfied' that more effectual measures were being taken to protect the nation from papists. When court supporters protested at this, they were told by Meres that 'you cannot save the protestant religion but by this paper. Farewell parliaments and all laws and government, and the protestant religion, for they are all one.' In the Lords, Shaftesbury used this as a chance to reflect on the danger 'from those who live in this city and apply themselves to an arbitrary government and to introduce the Catholic religion entirely, and there are great personages' involved.[60] MPs were sensitive, too, to charges of corruption, ambition and influence. A remark by the flippant young court supporter, Mr Goring, that he hoped the government's opponents 'do not desire to creep into their [the ministers'] places' brought down a storm of criticism, and prompted several initiatives. MPs talked of introducing tests against office-holders and those in receipt of pensions – Mr Howe supported the latter because MPs were called 'the greatest rogues and villains, and it is said commonly "we are the greatest in nature, and that we take money to betray our county".'[61]

On returning to foreign affairs, the Commons roundly denounced the alliances made as contrary to the addresses of the house and the good and safety of the kingdom. In reply the King expressed himself as 'very much surprised' by their attitude. Reinstalling Seymour as Speaker did little to bring the Commons into line, for they now turned to the problem of evil councillors. On 7 May they resolved on one address to the King for the removal of Lauderdale and, by a majority of 154 to 139, on another for the removal of those who had advised Charles's replies to their addresses of 26 May 1677 and 31 January 1678, by which was meant Danby. Charles tried to hasten discussion of supply by sending a message on 11 May that he was on the verge of disbanding troops and laying up ships for want of money. Yet his critics span out the debate on supply and waited for his reply to their imminent address. Clarges said it was 'common fame' that MPs had been turned out of offices for voting against the court. 'Why was the army so hastily raised? Which was no good sign of good intention to the public,' remarked Powle. 'This was a work of darkness from the beginning,' lamented Birch. 'We gave money for what we see now not a word of it true.' When Samuel Pepys argued for supply by pointing out that naval supplies needed long-term investment, he was ridiculed by Sir Robert Howard. It was a long and inconclusive debate, thought Marvell, because no-one was 'willing to give a negative but neither forward to an affirmative in the uncertainty of war or peace'. When the address for removal of ministers was presented to Charles that afternoon, he angrily told them it was 'so extravagant' that he was not willing to give it the answer it deserved. On Monday, 13 May, Charles summoned the House of Lords, praised their 'dutiful behaviour', and criticized the Commons, before proroguing parliament until 23 May so MPs can 'consider better what they ought to do at their return'. In a letter to Hull Marvell remarked, a touch sententiously, that many will 'reflect upon the prorogation; but they that discourse the least and think the best of it will be the wisest men and the best subjects.'[62]

In the next few days Charles finalized the agreement with Louis to disband his forces, prorogue parliament for four months, and henceforth to maintain neutrality, in exchange for six million livres over three years. Danby would take no part in this and the treaty was now signed by Charles and Barrillon.[63] On 23 May Charles spoke to parliament 'more briskly than usually', saying he could not tell where things would end, but he was resolved 'to save Flanders, either by a war or a peace' and that in his opinion 'being armed' was 'as necessary to make peace, as war'. He left it to them to decide whether to keep up an army until peace was concluded, but reminded them of the urgency: 'I desire you will not drive me into extremity, which must end ill both for you and for me, and (which is worst of all) for the nation.' Finch began with another discourse on diplomacy, but then addressed problems closer to home. 'It has been so stale a project to undermine the government, by accusing it of endeavouring to introduce popery and arbitrary government, that a man would wonder to see it taken up again.' He explicitly referred to rebellion whose 'symptoms' had begun 'again to appear in printed libels, and in several parts of the nation', and he implicitly drew parallels with the 1640s. He urged them to trust in the 1673 Test Act, to acknowledge the moderation of Charles who daily suffers 'so much licentious and malicious talk to pass unpunished', and he chastized them for the unconstitutional tacking of one bill to another which suggests that the King and the Lords are 'so ill affected to the public' that they obstruct good laws. Copies of these speeches and their 'many remarkable passages' were soon 'cried about the streets' of London. MPs were confused. There was 'a variety of opinions' about what was going on: Marvell gathered 'by information both within and without doors' that the Dutch and Spanish had already signed a peace with France; and many other MPs assumed this too. They were 'displeased extremely' to be told that war or peace still lay in the balance.[64] And many simply did not know if Charles was lying.

In reply to their queries, Charles repeated his view that keeping up the army was the safest course of action, and so the Common promptly decided to pay off and disband all troops raised since 29 September 1677. A few days later they voted supply and on 4 June they agreed to raise £200,000 from a monthly tax and to appropriate it to paying off the army by the end of June, for fear, in Reresby's words, that 'the King should take the money and employ it to other uses'. Once secured in this way, 'the money was very willingly given, the nation (and its representatives) dreading nothing so much as a standing army.' The King appealed again for an army to be kept up until a peace was made. But 'these redcoats may fight against Magna Carta,' protested Sir John Coventry; other members complained of the 'tricks and deceits' by which the army was raised and its illegal character as 'in terrorem populi'; and some voiced their fears of 'French ministers'. Then they agreed to extend the deadline for disbanding troops in Flanders until 27 July. The Commons also decided on 11 June that they would entertain no more motions for money after 18 June. This was a practical move since many members, 'having attended now five months' in London, planned to go home shortly to see to their own affairs; but it also helped to raise the stakes in the political game between King and Commons.[65]

Parliament had not lost sight of other issues. Popery remained high on the Commons' agenda in June. They spent long hours on the threat from papists in office. The expulsion from the house of Sir Solomon Swale, an MP and a Catholic, was finally achieved, after many delays and technicalities which reflected their desire to play fair even by papists, on 19 June. They produced an old bill to hinder papists from sitting in either house of parliament, the purpose of which was to drive the noble papists from the House of Lords. It would be in vain to send it yet again to the Lords, said Sir John Trevor, 'there are so many lords papists in that house', so why not have it to apply to future lords only? But members like Littleton, Harbord and Powle clearly had present papists in their sights and the bill was committed as it stood.[66]

18 June arrived and so did Charles to ask for money. He laid before parliament his diplomacy and his likely future role as a guarantor of Flanders and then asked for an extra £300,000 a year on his peacetime income. This was a bolt out of the blue. Bennet wanted to know who had advised the King to make such an unprecedented request. Garway asked

where this sum was to come from and what it might lead to; 'this looks to me, as the House of Commons were never to come here more.' We will 'be Normans, and wear wooden shoes,' prophesied Sir John Knight. And Cavendish remarked, apparently with a straight face, that 'our liberality has brought upon us the fears of popery and arbitrary power.'[67] The usual critics, Sacheverell, Powle, Vaughan, Meres, all opposed a grant and claimed that the fate of parliament was at stake. The King's request was turned down without a vote. But he was permitted to collect customs duties on wine for another three years and to raise various sums to cover his debts and extraordinary expenses.

Charles was in danger of being overtaken by events, or at least by Louis XIV's diplomacy. The next day Charles had to tell the House of Lords that the French had stalled the peace-making at the eleventh hour by refusing to evacuate Flemish towns until their ally the Swedish King had been restored to his lost territories. Charles was furious at this 'ill usage' and the peers extended the deadline for disbandment of troops at home until 27 July and those in Flanders until 24 August. Charles wrote to the States General of the Netherlands expressing his anger and copies of this letter were soon circulating in the English counties. The Duke of York and courtiers were ready to fight: 'whoever is not now in this hot season in a drap de Berry coat with gold galoon enough to load a mule is not thought affectionate enough to the government or the army.' John Evelyn was just one of many who admired the troops encamped on Hounslow Heath.[68] The Commons, of course, was much depleted by now; 'many members go daily away and all here are weary,' wrote Marvell on 22 June. Those left were working on how to raise the money they had already voted, but they soon found themselves diverted into a quarrel with the Lords over that chamber's extension of the deadlines for disbanding the army. The deadlines were part of a vote of taxation and so the Lords had interfered in a money bill. While the two houses conferred and failed to agree, Charles's army was moderately safe. On 3 July the Commons roundly asserted that all taxes 'are the sole gift of the Commons', should start in that house, and never be altered in the Lords. The impasse was then overcome by tacking their disbanding bill to the 'grand money bill' for a total of £619,000 which became law on 8 July. As Charles would have known, this supply, along with the earlier poll tax, almost amounted to the £1,000,000 which he had asked for all those months before in January. Its work done, parliament was prorogued on 15 July, in the first instance only until 1 August, in case the European situation should require urgent consideration, but then by two further adjournments until 1 October.

Charles kept up the pressure on Louis. While hoping no doubt to avoid a fight, he continued to mobilize troops and to ship them to Flanders. On 15 July Sir William Temple had signed an agreement with the

Dutch for a declaration of war against Louis if he had not abandoned his preposterous Swedish claims within two weeks. At the very last moment, on 31 July 1678 (10 August new style), a general peace was finally signed at Nijmegen. However this was no prelude to demilitarization. News of the peace coincided with that of 'a cruel fight' near Mons between the forces of William of Orange and the Duke of Luxembourg. According to reports reaching London, thousands were killed, including many Englishmen, and Ossory was captured, but later rescued by his dashing comrades, while Monmouth was conspicuous for his bravery.[69] Until all sides ratified the peace, nothing was secure. The King continued to spend the funds voted for their disbandment on maintaining his forces: he borrowed £200,000 in the City against the recent supply and Danby obtained a down payment of £150,000 by leasing the Hearth Tax again. All August troops proceeded from London to the coast for transport to Flanders 'whither soldiers are every day going'; a council of war was established and there was talk that York would be generalissimo; 'yet for all this it's believed that we shall have peace.'[70]

III

Charles had decided to spend some time at Windsor. On 13 August 1678, the day before he left, a gentlemen of the court, Christopher Kirkby, stopped the King as he was about to go for a walk in St James's Park and told him that Jesuit assassins lay in wait to shoot him (see plate 15). Charles had heard many such tales before and continued on his stroll. But that evening Kirkby brought to Whitehall Dr Israel Tonge who produced a written narrative of a labyrinthine Jesuit plot against England's religion, government and King. Charles had no intention of altering his plans to listen to such absurd accusations and so he set off for Windsor leaving Danby to pursue the matter. Charles spent his days fishing and Sir Robert Southwell, clerk to the privy council, could not guess when the council would 'meet and fall into the track of business again, for Windsor is a charming place'. John Evelyn remarked on 'a magnificent court' kept at Windsor, which he visited as part of his tour of Thamesside gardens and villas such as the Duke of Norfolk's disappointing palace at Weybridge, Lauderdale's glorious Ham House and Sir Henry Capel's garden at Kew.[71] Others went abroad. There was much gossip about what Buckingham was up to in Paris. Was he searching for the philosopher's stone? Or chasing a woman? Or something more suspicious?[72] Meanwhile Danby was rushing between his own country mansion at Wimbledon (where he was putting the final touches to the September wedding planned for his daughter Bridget and the King's illegitimate son, Charles, Earl of Plymouth), Windsor where he could

Plate 15   A playing card showing the supposed assassination plot against Charles II while he walked in St James's Park in 1678. Thomas Pickering, a Benedictine, was later convicted and executed for this alleged plan. The popish plot was depicted on several sets of playing cards, as were other topical events. This was one of the many ways in which popular interest was maintained in the plot.

consult with the King, and Whitehall where among other matters he was dealing with Tonge's tale.

At first Danby dutifully investigated the accusation. It could, after all, be a useful way of rallying support for the King, justifying the maintenance of an army, and, of course, diverting parliament's attention from himself. It is also quite possible that he believed the story. Tonge, however, refused to say who wrote the narrative or to identify the Jesuit assassins Pickering and Grove. Interest in his charges declined. Danby went off to Oxfordshire. The letters which Tonge produced to incriminate Fr Bedingfield, the Duke of York's confessor, were obvious forgeries and the court began to lose patience. This may have been why Titus Oates, now named by Tonge as the source of the narrative, took his story outside the government and on 6 September swore to the truth of his deposed evidence before Sir Edmund Berry Godfrey, a Middlesex justice. Danby had already referred the matter to the privy council, and Charles and the Duke of York, who were spending much of their time at the races, expected the whole ludicrous story to end there. However, as Southwell wrote late at night on 28 September, what 'looked ridiculous' this morning, when alleged by Tonge, was transformed when Oates 'himself came this afternoon to tell his tale with all the particulars of it, the lords stood amazed and could do no less than send for those he upon oath accused.' The arrests that night were followed by further accusations the next day, when Oates named Edward Coleman, secretary to the Duchess of York and former secretary to the Duke, as involved in the plot. Among Coleman's seized papers were letters, dating from the mid-1670s, to Louis XIV's confessor. They alluded vaguely to schemes to promote Catholicism at the English court and included some disparaging references to Charles. Within days, 'the thing surely is become too big either for that board [the council] or the judges, and will unavoidably devolve into the cognizance of the parliament, and then God Almighty knows where the matter will stop.' The King continued to give little sign of taking the plot at all seriously; despite his brother's wish that he would take control of the investigation, Charles was intent on the October races at Newmarket. Nor was he alone in his attitude. 'There are many that slight the thing as improbable, and others who call it but a trick to get money from the parliament,' wrote Southwell, but he was not one. 'For if no conspiracy be proved, yet there will certainly appear such a growth and increase of popery as will beget a more vigorous proceeding than has hitherto ever appeared.'[73]

Rumours reached as far afield as Yorkshire and Shropshire by early October and the plot became a national issue. Some still mocked it: Barrillon told Louis XIV that the court's opponents said it was a pretence to justifying hanging on to the army and to divert parliament's attention. 'After searching over every man's sack of papers,' wrote Southwell on 15 October, 'there is but little found to corroborate Mr Oates's assertion as to the point of killing'; but the evidence against Coleman was overwhelming and had incensed the King. In passing Southwell mentioned that Sir Edmund Berry Godfrey had gone missing.[74] Godfrey had left home on 12 May, telling his servant that he would be back for dinner, and had then disappeared. His body was found in a ditch on Primrose Hill on the evening of the 17th. He had been strangled and run through with his own sword. The coroner's jury brought in verdict of wilful murder. On 31 October Godfrey's body lay in state in Old Bridewell before being carried in a funeral procession led by seventy-two clergymen to St Martins-in-the-Fields where William Lloyd, flanked by clerical bodyguards, preached on the text, 'died Abner as a fool dies?' The popish plot had acquired its first 'martyr'. And although not all were convinced that this was the work of the agents of international popery, for many the mysterious death of Justice Godfrey was 'a pattern of their way of proceeding'.[75]

When parliament met on 21 October both Charles and Lord Chancellor Finch emphasized the delicacy of foreign policy and the desperate need for money to sustain the navy and the land forces. Charles simply mentioned the plot, 'of which I shall forbear any opinion, lest I seem to say too much or too little: but I will leave the matter to the law.' Despite being a little 'thin' of members, the Commons immediately fell upon the plot and the court's insouciance. 'Many of the country gentlemen were much scandalized to see none of the other side speak a word' about this conspiracy against their own monarch and religion.[76] The court's supporters in parliament were caught in a dilemma not of their own making. For while Charles's Catholic brother and heir wanted to contain the political fallout of Oates's allegations by having the plot dealt with in the law courts, his chief minister Danby had an interest in allowing parliament its head in investigating the plot. This would reassert Danby's protestant credentials and divert attacks on his misgovernment. It was said that Danby was distancing himself from the Duke of York and was talking once more of the possibility of legitimizing Monmouth or of a royal divorce. Shaftesbury and Buckingham made little secret of their hopes that this issue would drive a wedge between York and Danby.

The Commons rapidly established committees to advise on the King's personal safety and to investigate the plot and Godfrey's murder. They revived an earlier measure to purge parliament of Catholics, which passed unopposed in a week and was ready for the Lords by 28 October. Oates appeared before the Commons on three consecutive days: he gave four hours of evidence on one day which 'was of that nature that it is impossible to be feigned without eminent contradiction'.[77] As a result the Commons asked for the arrest of five Catholic peers, Arundel of

Wardour, Bellasis, Petre, Powis and Stafford, who were committed to the Tower on the order of the House of Lords. Both houses had set up investigative committees. The Lords had a large committee meeting daily at 9.00 a.m. and 4.00 p.m., and deputed Danby, Essex, Clarendon, Shaftesbury and Bishop Compton to interrogate Coleman. William Sacheverell chaired the Commons committee which was investigating Coleman and his correspondence. Predictably 'the contents of these letters at large are now become the discourse of all, that there was great machinations in the world and much revolution intended.'[78] Together both houses asked the King to remove all papists from London, and the King agreed. They would now 'feel the weight of public indignation', wrote Southwell. Such a popular sentiment could not have been raised alone by Oates's 'loose and tottering fabric' of revelations, it required deeper roots, and Southwell blamed 'the manifest indulgence which for so many years has been extended to the [Catholic] people, and wherein some of them have so imprudently triumphed, that it became the grief and scandal of many, and turned itself into so much combustible matter against the day of wrath'.[79] This antipathy, fed by the amazingly coherent account of Oates, and the apparent confirmation of Godfrey's murder and Coleman's letters, carried the Commons along. On 1 November they passed a resolution 'that there hath been and still is a damnable and hellish plot, contrived and carried on by popish recusants' to murder the King, subvert the government and root out the protestant religion.

The 'poor Duke' meanwhile was 'surrounded with difficulties almost inextricable'. Oates had cleared James of involvement in the plot, but he was, of course, a possible beneficiary. A debate in the Lords, initiated by Shaftesbury, on the removal of the Duke of York was circumspect and inconclusive, but some observed that Danby had been ambiguous in his support of the Duke. Two days later, James appeared in the Lords to announce that he would no longer be attending the privy council. In the Commons on 4 November the discussion was more forthright. Russell was the only MP to talk of exclusion, but Sacheverell asked whether the king or parliament disposed of the succession; and on the other side, it was argued that it was unnatural to separate devoted brothers, that it might drive the papists (and James) to more desperate measures, and that matters ultimately lay in the hands of God.[80] Charles intervened on 9 November with a speech, patently the work of Danby, which although studiedly vague was a signal of his willingness to see something enacted to 'pare the nails' of a Catholic successor. He and his officials made it crystal clear that he would not countenance any interference in the succession nor any diminution of his own powers, but that he could accept a test to identify a catholic successor and various limitations on that monarch's powers. In other words, Danby was once again offering something like his 1677 scheme to secure protestantism. The subtleties were lost on many:

> It seems all the city was in bells and bonfires, the aldermen attending with wine and reporting the glad tidings of his majesty's speech that day; some reporting it to be a resolution declared of choosing a protestant successor, and in other places that the Duke of Monmouth was to succeed the King. How this dangerous mistake came about I cannot tell, but 'tis a dangerous thing for a body of people to plunge themselves into a mistake, and 'tis thought this very accident may do the Duke [of Monmouth?] as much hurt as anything else. The speech is now printed, and it is well if that may undeceive them.[81]

The Commons' test bill had been held up in the Lords by the opposition of the Catholic peers and unease about the implications of such discriminatory legislation for property rights. Then the Duke of York asked for a proviso to exempt him from the act. Eventually the bill was passed, with the proviso, and returned to the Commons. MPs were hostile to the exemption; Meres called it 'a beginning of toleration' and blamed York for parliament's past failure to pass any 'good law' against popery.[82] Danby had been absent from the Lords' debates and so unable to support York – which may have been either a simple error based on the belief that the bill would never pass or a calculated snub to York – but now he called out all his Commons' votes to ensure that the Test Act passed with the exemption of the Duke of York intact. In that and subsequent debates, a few of York's most implacable critics spoke openly of excluding papists from the succession as well as from parliament. But the real damage was plain to see and it was within the government. Neither York nor Danby could pull together. The government was in crisis and changes were inevitable. York was effectively excluded from royal councils and his co-religionists had been purged from the Lords. Shaftesbury 'is like to be at the top, and already courted by all accordingly,' observed Southwell, and Danby's situation 'is by all thought desperate'. While Danby and his wife tried to shift the blame, and apparently heaped much of it on Finch, the talk of the town and the Commons was that the Lord Treasurer had failed to investigate the plot fully in the summer and had since shielded the Duke of York.[83]

IV

From the very outset of this crisis, parliament, or at least a large majority of MPs, feared that Charles and his court did not take the popish plot seriously. Every failure to investigate the plot was proof, of course, that the culprit was part of the plot. Every doubt expressed about Oates and his tale was evidence of popish sympathies. For those who believed, the credibility of the plot was unquestionable: it lay in 'a strange coincidence of things', wrote Southwell; Oates, Coleman, Godfrey, 'then the cele-bration of 5 November, applying the present horror of things feared throughout the whole kingdom in one day to the evidence of what had formerly passed. Then comes in Bedloe . . .'. William Bedloe, the second witness, who confirmed the plot against Charles and claimed that Godfrey had been murdered in Somerset House, offered his evidence to the council and was then paraded before the Lords and Commons in early November. Bedloe's evidence was legally significant since two witnesses were needed for a felony conviction. But his contribution to the plot's credibility among the public and the political elite was inestimable. Oates and Bedloe were joined during December by Miles Prance, a Catholic silversmith who had worked at the Queen's Chapel in Somerset House, and by Stephen Dugdale, former land steward to Lord Aston, a Catholic landowner in Staffordshire.

These informants were 'rogues' with all that that word signified in the seventeenth century; several of them made no secret of a chequered past, indeed they traded on it, because it was only their ability to pass as what they were not or to inveigle themselves into the confidence and intrigues of Jesuit plotters which allowed them to discover the awful secrets that they now revealed. 'Being out of play' as a protestant min-ister, Oates 'had a mind to a dangerous experiment of knowing the intrigues of the Jesuits', so he simply joined the order and served as a go-between, for which he was suited by his 'craft under bluntness and an outward simplicity'. Thanks to his revelations Oates became the 'saviour of the nation', with a monthly allowance, lodgings in Whitehall and his own bodyguard. Bedloe, the son of a cobbler, had been one of those many small provincial traders who had 'broken' or gone bankrupt in the early 1670s. He supposedly went off to Ireland, changed his reli-gion, and fell in with the Jesuits – and in their plot he was 'to carry orders from army to army as being versed in all the roads of England'. But he also had a career as con man. According to Reresby, he 'had cheated a great many merchants abroad and gentlemen at home, by per-sonating my Lord Gerard and other men of quality, and by divers other cheats; and when he was taxed with it he made it an argument to be more credited in this matter, saying nobody but a rogue could be employed in such designs.'[84] Oates claimed to hold a 'doctorate' from Salamanca; Bedloe pretended to the military rank of captain. Yet dis-simulation was carried by these men far beyond the 'jests' and 'pranks' of the wit and rogue; when they began to inform, when they were caught up in the coils of the legal process and politics, they entered a world of mirrors in which they lost sight of the truth. Prance famously told the King that all his sworn evidence about Godfrey's murder was 'a thing invented by him and a perfect lie', but on his way back to Newgate thought better of it and retracted this recantation, incidentally disappointing those that 'were ready to catch at any twig to disbelieve the manner of that villainy'.[85]

As Southwell's description of the effect of 5 November reminds us, all of this took place against a backdrop of insistent anti-popery, a diet of propaganda dished out from the pulpit, in print and on the streets. On 5 November 1678, according to Anthony Wood, 'preachers generally in their sermons at London were bitter against the papists', as was Dr Hall at St Mary's in Oxford. Much was made of the nefarious practices of the Jesuits, while Tillotson's sermon to the Commons was a rebuttal of the papists' impudent denials of the existence of the 1605 Gunpowder Plot. Sermons like these poured off the presses and sold in huge numbers; a whole impression of 4000 copies of a Stillingfleet sermon was sold out in one day. Bonfires were even more popular and many 'costly popes' were burnt on them: at one bonfire, effigies of Coleman and Richard Langhorn 'were burnt with him as his gentlemen ushers, and a great many devils in the shape of cats and rats came tumbling out of his belly'; at St Edmund Hall, Oxford, an effigy of the pope 'was brought out in a chair, set before the fire, shot at, and then (his belly being full of crackers) was burnt'.[86] The atmosphere of fear and hysteria was heightened in many places by the searches made for priests or of papists' houses. 'No less a man than Sir Nathaniel Herne', governor of the East India Company, wrote to Southwell to ask whether to send his wife and children out of town for fear of a papist massacre of protestants.[87]

On 25 November Charles told parliament that he found it 'absolutely impossible' to finance his forces any longer, but the Spanish were begging him to keep them in place until the ratification of peace otherwise all of Flanders would, they claimed, be lost. The Commons' only reply was a resolution for the immediate disbandment of all forces. They followed this with debate on an address for the removal of the Queen from the court. Oates and Bedloe had both recently begun to implicate Queen Catherine in the plot. She was cast as that archetypal figure the foreign female Catholic poisoner and the royal physician Sir George Wakeman as her accomplice. Motivation was easily supplied; Bedloe claimed to have heard her swear that she would 'be revenged for the violation of her bed'. At the Queen's birthday, on 15 November, Evelyn had been impressed by royal sangfroid: 'I never saw the court more brave, nor the nation in more apprehension and consternation.' But Charles's fury at these allegations, his animosity towards Oates on this account, and his determination to protect the Queen ensured that the address was voted down in the Lords.[88] Edward Coleman was convicted of treason and went to the gallows at Tyburn on 3 December protesting his innocence. At the same time the new Test Act, which received the royal assent on 30 November, came into force and MPs and peers rushed to take the required oaths. The Commons drew up yet another address to the King on the dangers to the nation which included an attack on Danby's 'private council' to the King. This article had passed by 138 to 114 votes and since 'some friends of the court were for it', informed observers guessed that James might be encouraging his followers to oppose Danby, perhaps because he believed that the Lord Treasurer was floating the notion of a royal divorce once more.[89]

Danby certainly had enemies both at court and in parliament. During these weeks he sifted all the information he could gather about his opponents. One informant identified five separate groupings and many lesser cabals. Some of these were the 'friends' of a particular patron such as York or Ranelagh, others were in cahoots with the confederate ambassadors, and others were hostile simply due to an interest in the tax farms or the Exchequer. Several bore a personal grudge against the Lord Treasurer: Cavendish blamed him for turning the King against him; Lord Strafford for stopping a pension; and Birch, Meres and Powle allegedly hoped to succeed him as Treasury Commissioners.[90] Danby's tendency to advance mediocre men and to rely on backbench support, inevitably left many talented individuals excluded from the power and perks of office. Holles, Cavendish, Harbord, Littleton and Powle formed the nucleus of one of the most significant, in parliamentary terms, of the hostile groups. Secretly they had begun to meet Barrillon and to take his money, and it may have been through the French ambassador that they hatched a plan with Ralph Montagu. Montagu, former English ambassador to Paris, had lost his offices in July when he returned without authority to defuse a furious attack on him by his mistress Cleveland. His reckless personal life and his naked ambition were largely at fault, but this did not prevent him from blaming Danby for his downfall and seeking revenge. Parliament was the obvious venue. After an acrimonious by-election at Northampton, Montagu entered the Commons in November and began to lay his plans.

Among the tales 'that are whispered as great secrets' against Danby in December was 'that Mr Montagu, who is become a declared enemy to his lordship, has exposed to the view of several members (who lifted him by a very summary proceeding into the house) some letters received by him while at Paris from his lordship, which contain great matters in them – I know not what, but such as the learned in law do think contain in them matters for an impeachment of a great strain.'[91] Earlier warnings of the danger had been dismissed by Danby who had correspondence enough to implicate the former ambassador, but the Lord Treasurer now took the precaution of seizing Montagu's papers. This forced Montagu's hand and he told the Commons that he had 'letters of great consequence . . . to produce, of the designs of a great minister of state'. William Harbord brought in a box, which had been hidden from the King's Messengers, and at the house's request Montagu selected two letters to be read out by the Speaker. The first was inconclusive, but the second was Danby's letter of 25 March 1678 instructing Montagu to suggest a French subsidy. 'I wonder the house sits so silent when they see themselves sold for six millions of livres to the French,' said Bennet after this bombshell. 'Now we see who has played all this game; who has repeated all the sharp answers to our addresses, and raised an army for no war . . . I would impeach the Treasurer of high treason.' 'This agrees with Coleman's letters,' chipped in Williams. It is part of the plot 'to destroy the government and our liberties,' cried Harbord. 'I am afraid that the King will be murdered every night.'[92] A committee was deputed to draw up articles of impeachment and these were finished by 21 December: Danby was accused of usurping royal authority in the conduct of foreign policy, aiming at arbitrary government and a standing army, seeking the French subsidy to 'deprive' Charles of parliament and its 'safe and wholesome councils', being 'popishly affected', wasting money on pensions and 'secret services', and enriching himself.[93]

The Lord Treasurer was due to make his reply in the Lords on Monday 23 December. As a precaution on the Sunday he persuaded the King to write 'I approve of this letter. C[arolus] R[ex]' on the file copies of the two letters. Next day he made such a robust defence that the Lords neither asked him to withdraw from their chamber nor, despite the Commons' urging, did they agree to his imprisonment. 3 January was set as the day on which he would answer the impeachment: but would he be allowed to? Trade was already suffering and minds were 'disturbed for fear the parliament should be dissolved or prorogued for impeaching my Lord Treasurer'. On 30 December Charles prorogued parliament with complaints of being 'ill used' and assurances that he would disband the army and prosecute the plot. On this news some in London said 'it was time for them to shut up their shops, and to think of providing themselves horse and armour, lest their throats should be cut by the papists'. Charles went to the City to reassure the Mayor and Aldermen and while rumours flew that the troops from Flanders were to be quartered on London, people took comfort in the presence of their own militia, the Trained Bands. In Shropshire, the prorogation was said to please three – York, Portsmouth and the papists – and displease three – England, Scotland and Ireland.[94]

The political horse-trading now began in earnest. Shaftesbury, for instance, made overtures to the Duke of York, but at the same time his intermediaries were suggesting to Danby some kind of deal involving the replacement of York as heir by any protestant the King might name, the removal of the Duchess of Portsmouth, and 'the securing the government from the French and their mode of government'. A group led by Holles may have agreed with Danby that in exchange for disbanding the army and calling a new parliament they would organize an immediate loan to the crown, supply when parliament met, and the Lord Treasurer's retirement without further prosecution. The government meanwhile was drifting; for several days Charles was unsure what to do. On 24 January, having told his privy councillors that the 'factions' among them made it 'useless and dangerous' to consult them, the King announced that parliament was dissolved and a newly elected parliament would meet in March.[95] The Essex clergyman Ralph Josselin woke early on 26 January from a strange dream that a parliament would meet for only a morning and hear only eleven speakers. By 10.00 a.m. that day he had heard that the Cavalier Parliament was to be dissolved:

> Honest men formerly desired the dissolution thereof but now its continuance was desired in reference to the discovery of the plot. I supposed the cabal does it to gain time and to bring on the French assistance; many thought this parliament had so corrupted themselves and done so ill in the matters of the nation and were formerly so odious that God would do his work by some other and never honour them.[96]

V

Public opinion at the beginning of 1679 was volatile. Ministers were kept informed of the 'rumours of the meaner sort' by Williamson's agents. Animosity was directed against Danby, Portsmouth, York and the French; people feared the troops currently being disbanded from their regiments and the shadowy papist plotters; rumours spread of French invasion, papist massacres, arms caches, fireballs and grenadoes; Prance was reckoned to be mad, 'he confesses, unconfesses and reconfesses'; young maids were brow-beaten into admissions of arson and daggers with the legend 'Memento Godfrey, 12 October 1678' were sold for protestants' self-defence. The capital, and possibly the entire country, had reached this state of high excitement by a complex route. A significant contribution was made by print, either in the form of pamphlets and sermons, or in the more visual form of the many engravings, some in the shape of strip cartoons or playing cards, others simply broadsheets to be pinned to a wall in a tavern or coffee-house, which supplied the plot with the oxygen of publicity. But the very investigation and prosecution of the plot generated excitement. Either to save themselves or to bolster their credibility, those sucked into the maw of this fantastic tale soon found themselves accusing others. The allegations snowballed and many of those taken into custody found bail unattainable, especially after the Lord Chief Justice 'said that one positive single witness against a plotting papist was sufficient to keep them in prison'. The indefatigable priest-catcher Sir William Waller, a Middlesex justice, took to organizing bonfires of seized Catholic books and relics. Meanwhile the plot claimed its victims. On 24 January the Jesuits Ireland and Grove were executed. After they and Pickering had first been convicted in December, Charles had been reluctant to allow the sentence to be carried out, and mobs had gathered at Newgate and the Recorder of London's house demanding that justice be done; now Charles gave way, claiming that Dugdale had convinced him. Early in February Berry, Green and Hill were tried and convicted of Godfrey's murder on Dugdale's evidence and executed before the end of the month.[97]

At Whitehall Danby attempted to shore up his position. Any official who had supported the impeachment was sacked; anyone who was judged a liability was replaced. Sunderland succeeded Williamson as one secretary of state; Sir William Temple was brought back from Holland to replace the other secretary, Henry Coventry, but when Temple refused the job it went to Sir Leoline Jenkins.

February and March saw the first general election since 1661 and the first in which the clergy were enfranchised. Reresby remembered 'great disputes' across the country 'as men stood affected to the government and to the then ministers, and as men believed them well intentioned or otherways.' He found Yorkshire 'much poisoned' with the belief that Danby was 'concerned in the design to bring in popery'. At the time it seemed that anyone associated with the government would struggle to be elected: Barrillon observed a 'sharpness against the court'; Edward Seymour reported from the West Country that 'hardly a man besides my father, that served in the last parliament, will be chosen for this.' Sir John Werden 'lost his election at Reigate; not that they had any dislike to him, but they said because he was secretary to the Duke [of York] and because he voted in the last parliament for his master's continuance in the Lords' house.' Lord Norris, an ardent supporter of Danby, was 'hooted' out of Oxford with cries of 'no Lord Treasurer, no papist'.[98] In his diary for 16 February, Josselin noted:

> The nation busy about the choice of parliament. God direct them that they be not outwitted, as the former were to raise an army. Said good choices in many places and that the King says the country would choose a dog if he stood against a courtier: the peace goes on beyond the seas, and the fears of France are on this side.[99]

By 1 March the Duke of Ormonde could conclude that 'the elections are not so bad as we feared, nor so good as some hoped. I think monarchy will not be struck at the root, but I fear it will be very close lopped.'[100] One indication of what was expected of the new parliament was a petition of a group of Middlesex freeholders to their newly elected members asking them to promote the safety of the King, the maintenance of liberty and property, protestant unity and a strengthening of habeas corpus.[101] Another might be the ballad 'telling the world the papists now have no interest' in the new parliament, which 'can scarcely be printed so fast as it is sold'.[102]

As the new parliament approached, Charles persuaded Danby to accept a royal pardon for all offences committed before 27 February 1679; he attempted to quash stories about Monmouth's legitimacy by declaring that his only marriage was to the Queen; and he sent the Duke of York to Brussels. The last was to 'the surprise of all men', commented Reresby. 'Some said this my Lord Treasurer had obtained to get the King to himself.' Others said it was to protect York from 'the violence' of parliament. But Reresby believed it was 'chiefly to remove all jealousy from the parliament that his majesty was not at all influenced by popish councils, no, not his brother's'.[103] Even so when parliament did meet, the absence of York did little to diminish animosity.[104] There was 'a stumble at the threshold'[105] when Danby tried to ditch his former ally Edward Seymour as Speaker in favour of Sir Thomas Meres, a critic who would be much safer on the government's side. Seymour, however, would not go quietly. His allies stole a march on the court's spokesmen and voted him in. Seymour, believing that he had Charles's support, stuck to his guns and openly said he did not 'value the Treasurer's power of a fiddlestick'; but also at stake was the King's power to approve the choice of Speaker. The 'angry party', as Reresby called them, in the Commons would not back down, insisting on their privilege to choose their own Speaker. An embarrassing three-day prorogation was announced, while a compromise candidate, William Gregory, was arranged through the good offices of Cavendish and Russell. Offers were being made, through Monmouth, for 'money without any condition' other than the departure of Danby, who had now become, said the newsletters, 'the subject of all discourse and is made the only obstacle that stands between the King and his people'.[106]

Thus the plan to allow Danby to retire gracefully, loaded with honour and loot, came into effect: he was elevated to the rank of marquis, a pension was discussed; the King announced the formation of a Treasury Commission to take over his functions. But as Halifax scrawled to his brother on 20 March, 'the world is still jealous he may take it [i.e., office] up again in convenient time, or else keep such a station near the King as may make him the same omnipotent figure as before under the disguise of some other name.' So 'the hard-hearted Commons of England' will prevent this by continuing the impeachment which has been revived from the last parliament.[107] On that day the Lords gave him a week to answer the charges and the Commons once again asked for his committal to prison. Charles sought to nip this in the bud by appearing in his robes on 22 March to tell parliament that Danby had written to

Montagu on his orders, had never concealed the plot, and had received a full royal pardon, and the King 'would, if need required, give it him again ten times over'.[108] The next night Charles personally ordered Danby to go into hiding and on 25 March Lord Latimer surrendered his father's white staff of office to the King. Savile's epitaph on Danby's career is telling: 'he was so long tottering that he gave his friends leisure to prepare themselves; besides in the midst of his friendship now and then [were] such mortifications that, although some men may out of point of honour lament him, few besides his own family will do it out of any other reason.'[109]

For the next three weeks the Lords and Commons battled over how to proceed against Danby: the Lords produced a bill for his perpetual banishment; the Commons suggested that he should be attainted if he had not surrendered by a specified date. 'Our house is gentle,' said Lord Halifax. 'But the House of Commons, being a true representative of England, are stiff and surly in the point.' As one MP admitted 'the most violent' of them did not think he deserved death, 'even my Lord Shaftesbury's Mr Bennet himself owned as much' and confessed that banishment would be adequate. But the quarrel was now less about Danby's fate than about the legitimacy of his royal pardon and the fact that the House of Lords could shield any minister from accountability. The Commons eventually prevailed, even in the Lords 'the court party did not befriend' Danby.[110] With the situation hopeless, Charles gave him permission to end his undignified hiding. On 15 April Danby gave himself up to Black Rod and next day he entered the Tower.

10
1679–81: A Wasps' Nest

> Let his majesty (say they) once meet his parliament freely, cheerfully, and without tricks, he shall not need bespeak our purses. This the putting us off, with little tricks of court, and to gratify interests, and those who hate the nation and the religion, that we are not suffered to search things to the bottom, and which have bred this universal jealousy and alienated the hearts of a loyal and honest people . . .

This is what MPs told John Evelyn in March 1679. He was struck that so many members of such diverse backgrounds were 'inspired with the same zeal . . . against the court, popery and plots, design of introducing arbitrary government, etc'. Their 'three signal articles' were limiting the successor, unravelling the plot, and a comprehension; and they assured the sceptical Evelyn that they were 'infinitely happy under our laws, his majesty's gracious government, and present constitution'. At home Evelyn feared events could end in a republic, but abroad 'the entire protestant interest of Christendom' was in danger from France and he predicted 'sudden and inevitable confusion' unless a new political tack was taken. Roger Morrice, the nonconformist, also had hopes of 'a change of the state of the late politics that were of such an ill aspect and tendency'. Sir Robert Southwell, who on 19 April drew up a memorandum on public affairs for the Duke of Ormonde, believed that there was 'an universal demand for reformation, which the sober men limit to things moderate; but there are more who are unreasonable, and many, I fear, have no limits at all'. Fear of France and fear of popery were the two guiding lights; and the cry of 'popery' was especially dangerous because it 'is the handle of this reformation, and the arguments deduced from it are irresistible.' Southwell prescribed seven reforms: fixed meetings of parliament; protection of protestantism from a popish successor; a broader Church of England; a stronger militia to replace the standing army; a more accountable naval administration; appropriation of all public money to specific uses; and the abandonment of cabinet government.[1]

The fall of Danby, protracted though it was, perhaps represented a first step towards a new political system: the former Lord Treasurer's duties had been entrusted to a commission led by the Earl of Essex, which now set about tackling the huge debt of £2.4 million; the Earl of Sunderland had become a secretary of state in February; and Lord Halifax's claims to office were pressed hard by Sir William Temple. On Easter Monday, 21 April, Charles announced a new, smaller, privy council which was designed to embrace all factions, shades of opinion and ranks, to include office-holders and those of 'credit and sway' in parliament, and no doubt to emasculate parliamentary criticism by enticing several leading opponents, such as Powle, Capel, Holles, Russell and Cavendish, over to the court. Shaftesbury and Halifax now sat in council alongside Lauderdale, Arlington, Ormonde, Essex and Sunderland, Bishop Compton and Archbishop Sancroft. Shaftesbury, who Charles believed 'was only angry in revenge, because he was not employed', was given the title of Lord President of the Council and reportedly behaved as if he had a place as of right and 'he did grace in coming to them.'[2] One notable omission was Buckingham: as a newsletter remarked, 'the Duke of Buckingham does all this while disappear, no man knowing where he is.'[3] The declaration publicizing the new council made much of Charles's intention to 'lay aside . . . any single ministry or private advices or Foreign Committees' and presumably the King now thought that he was less vulnerable to charges of being in the hands of 'evil counsellors'. Yet there was little real hope that Charles could give up his deep-seated preference for an intimate circle of advisors; Temple seems to have been one of the brains behind the new council; and, even from the Tower, Danby continued to offer advice. Meanwhile, parliament showed no sign of turning over a new leaf, but busily continued its fossicking through past policies. 'Things are started every day that will make the world conclude we are in a more quarrelsome humour than I hope will be found,' wrote Halifax; but to the puritanical Ralph Josselin, obsessed with the plot and its ramifications at court, and fearful of 'French fraud' in the Lords, 'the parliament seems wonderful courageous not fearing prorogations or dissolutions.'[4]

Parliament had unfinished business with the Earl of Danby. On the King's orders, Danby offered his pardon in answer to the charges against him. By this, as the Earl of Burlington said, he had 'pitched upon a plea of a very great hazard', because it was tantamount to an admission and left only the pardon's validity in question. The Commons resented any pardon that seemed to thwart the process of impeachment and render ministers unaccountable to parliament: 'if this be a good pardon,' protested Maynard, 'parliaments are to little purpose.' Danby's delays and evasion also exasperated MPs like his one-time ally Edward Seymour who burst out, 'whether the pardon or plea be good or not is not the question. The justice of this nation is abused. He has turned three kingdoms into an Aceldama.'[5] On 5 May the Commons voted Danby's pardon illegal and the next day the Speaker with his mace and the MPs in a body processed to the bar of the Lords and demanded immediate judgement against the Earl. A few days later MPs agreed that any counsel who argued the validity of Danby's pardon before the Lords was a betrayer of the liberties of the commons of England. The matter was further complicated – perhaps deliberately – by two other issues: one was whether Danby should be tried before or after the five Catholic peers also languishing in the Tower; and the other was whether bishops had a right to vote in capital trials such as Danby's might well turn out to be. The Lords wished to deal with the Catholic peers first, but many MPs saw this as one more attempt to protect the disgraced minister. Danby would undeniably benefit from the bishops' votes and so, even before his surrender to custody, Shaftesbury had proposed that the bishops should not sit in 'cases of blood'. In May the issue was 'most curiously and nicely debated' and at length the Lords resolved that the bishops had 'a right to stay in court in capital cases, till such time as judgement of death comes to be pronounced'. Crucially this meant that the bishops would be able to take part in the preliminaries of Danby's trial and judge the legality of his pardon: MPs were livid and in their debates on the issue in mid-May they poured invective on the bishops and their alleged claim to judge all issues; when the decision was reaffirmed in the Lords on 27 May by sixty-five to thirty-six votes, Shaftesbury led twenty-seven peers in entering a protest.[6]

The Commons harried Danby's former allies, such as Portsmouth and Lauderdale, and inquired into his 'secret service' expenditure to identify his 'pensioners' in the Cavalier Parliament. Charles Bertie was asked to produce accounts of how the money – estimated by Sir Robert Howard as £252,467 between 1676 and 1679 – had been spent, and when he told them that he was not at liberty to reveal what he had done at the King's command, MPs assumed their darkest fears were justified. Bertie's predecessor, Sir Stephen Fox, was dragged before the house, his ledgers and papers were seized, and he was 'so violently attacked . . . and so menaced with ruin' that he finally agreed to listen while the clerk read over a list of the MPs of the previous parliament and to indicate from memory what sums had been paid to which individuals. Some of those named refuted the charge: Sir John Talbot was owed the money and disowned 'anything by way of secret service to influence my vote here'. When the committee of secrecy's report was debated, Sir Richard Wiseman was repeatedly called to the bar and interrogated by the Speaker, but he gave little away, and finally the debate was adjourned until 27 May.[7]

The popish plot had become a juggernaut which swept up the new parliament as it had the old: in March Southwell commented that 'all things pass on with a powerful stream, so that opposition is so far from being useful, that it is become dangerous. The plot will certainly have an entire and thorough prosecution, and popery be laid fast for one age.'[8] The Commons' new committee of secrecy, elected on 20 March, was dominated by old hands; Oates and Bedloe reprised their evidence for new MPs and on 15 April Oates published *A True Narrative of the Horrid Plot*. Popular animosity was unabated. When the five Catholic peers were brought by water from the Tower to Westminster to plead on 9 April, a disorderly crowd 'flocked into boats . . . showing them halters and making of gallows'.[9] Two days later the country's churches echoed to denunciations of popery on a national day of humiliation to ask for God's forgiveness, his help to defeat the nation's enemies, and his blessing on King and parliament. But this was all cant, in Anthony Wood's eyes, 'they do not care for the King; and their fast is that the preachers might rail and make the commonalty out of love with his majesty's loyal subjects.'[10] In truth, for all the sound and fury of anti-popery, little headway was being made by either house in uncovering the plot. The Lords were doing little about the five Catholic peers and the Commons had unearthed only one new informant, Sidway, who made allegations against three bishops. Dugdale was giving rather better value to the Lords' committee for examinations, developing his evidence against Lords Stafford and Aston, and, for the first time, making direct allegations against the Duke of York, who, he claimed, had promised to reintroduce Catholicism and papal authority in England. The privy council's investigations were reanimated once Shaftesbury became Lord President and orders were given, for example, that all priests convicted in the counties should be sent to the capital for interrogation.

Not content with rooting out plotters and past misgovernment, parliament had a mission to secure the country for the future. Protestant unity was essential. A first step would be the easing of legal discrimination against dissenters: the nonconformist Thomas Jolly told an American friend that 'some more hopeful members are chosen into our new parliament and (it seems) as there might be some lifting up of the yoke.'[11] The Lords, however, went off in the opposite direction when they prepared a bill to expel all papists from London that would have applied equally to all protestant dissenters. A proviso was added in the Commons to allow dissenters to nullify any proceedings against them under this legislation by taking the 1678 Test Act's anti-catholic declaration. In other areas reform was attempted. The bill to regulate elections, which was introduced on 26 March and received a second reading a fortnight later, sought to prevent the 'treating' of electors, the payment of wages to MPs, and abuses by returning officers, but it also went on to propose substantial franchise reform and a maximum duration of two years for any parliament.[12] This was obviously a response to the 'corruption' of parliament under Danby, as was the Richard Hampden's bill providing for the automatic replacement of any MP preferred to a place of profit under the crown and the parallel measure in the upper chamber to forbid ministers from offering gifts and pensions to individuals. The rights of the individual were not neglected. Since 1674 parliament had been considering bills designed to close loopholes in the procedure of habeas corpus which gave the subject legal protection against arbitrary imprisonment. In 1679 yet another bill was proposed and once again it had become bogged down in minor amendments between the two houses. Although it was widely recognized that MPs would only consider voting money for the King once all their other grievances had been addressed, the existence of an army, said to cost £1100 a day, and always a potential threat to English liberties, spurred them on to vote £206,000 for its disbandment and to appropriate that sum to paying off the troops. Important as all these issues were, however, the great problem in securing the country's future lay in the succession to the throne.

As an authoritarian Catholic, the current heir to the throne was not only a threat in himself, but an incitement to every papist assassin to do away with the protestant Charles. In 1679 the range of possible solutions was much as it always had been. 'Limitations' could be imposed upon a popish successor, preventing him from subverting the Church of England, suppressing parliament or perpetuating popery through his children; in the most extreme form of 'limitation', a Catholic king might rule in name only while a regent exercised real authority. Alternatively, a new heir to the throne could be found by, for example, legitimizing Monmouth or a royal divorce and remarriage. A third option was to 'disable' the Duke of York from succeeding to the throne. This would require an act of parliament to exclude him from the line of succession and to allow the crown to 'skip a generation'. In the cold light of day, none of these options was particularly feasible. Could an act of parliament really be expected to restrain a monarch from exercising his full powers should he wish? Could a parliament curb royal powers or interfere with the line of succession without endangering the whole balance of the constitution? And, as always in the Stuarts' dual monarchy, the reaction of their other kingdom, Scotland, was a dangerously unpredictable factor. More importantly, while Charles had talked vaguely of paring the nails of a successor the previous November, he had categorically refused to entertain any bills tending 'to impeach the right of succession'.

It was only on 27 April that the Commons directly raised the issue of the succession. Stoked up by all manner of allegations about Catholic conspiracies, the house began to debate the 'preservation' of the King, but soon launched into a frank discussion of the Duke of York and unanimously concluded that his Catholicism and his position as heir to the throne gave encouragement to popish plotters. Of course, such a vote was impossible to challenge since it accused York of nothing. The house then instructed the committee of secrecy to draw up an abstract of 'such matters as concern the Duke of York, relating to the plot', which was meant to include all the references to York in Coleman's letters. Before the committee could report, Charles summoned Lords and Commons ('we were all in amaze', fearing prorogation, recorded one MP), and reminded them of the urgency of disbanding the army, supplying the fleet and investigating the plot. Then Lord Chancellor Finch told members that while the King would not agree to alteration of the succession, he could accept legislation to differentiate between a protestant and papist successor, to provide for parliament's automatic sitting on his own death, to transfer powers of ecclesiastical, judicial and military appointment to parliament during the reign of a Catholic monarch, and to recognize that parliament enjoyed the sole right to raise money. This endorsement of 'limitations' had been agreed by the privy council in extraordinary meetings the previous evening and that very morning. Only Shaftesbury demurred, apparently arguing that the limitations were 'too like a republic', but his attitude and motives were significant. Since Shaftesbury was to be the great standard-bearer for exclusion in 1680 and 1681, historians have been ready to see him as committed to that policy in 1679 and to portray him as orchestrating developments to that end in the Commons, the committee of secrecy and elsewhere. Yet there is a plausible case that in April 1679 Shaftesbury was still casting around for weapons in what was primarily a struggle for influence at court; now he had a toe-hold in the council, he needed to advance his claim to office and to distinguish his policy from that of his rival and nephew, Halifax. Shaftesbury took up exclusion, therefore, as a disruptive tactic rather than out of constitutional principle.[13]

The immediate response among MPs to the King's offer was mixed. Southwell detected three attitudes: one favoured limitations and would enact them; another, prevalent among York's enemies or those who doubted that laws could restrain him, 'would, by a law, step over his head and entitle the Princess of Orange and her issue to succeed immediately upon the King's death'. But the third is perhaps the most intriguing. 'Others do mutter that his majesty is so backward in agreeing to the execution of Pickering and the priests who have been condemned . . . that they are for present laws of defence against popery, and that the model laid down in the speech should even presently [i.e., immediately] be put in practice'; in other words, they would have limitations imposed on Charles II.[14] Although they did not vote their thanks to the King for his speech, neither did MPs give credence to Sacheverell's arguments that limitations were intended to delude the people; instead the debate was adjourned while parliament pursued the vendettas against Danby and Lauderdale. In Essex Josselin heard that 'the King and parliament seem to be on good terms.' The Earl of Longford wrote on 6 May that 'the debate concerning the succession lies without a day, and by some very understanding men of the house I am told much of the heat of that matter is blown over.'[15] Four days later, William Leveson Gower MP argued that the Commons was losing sight of the need to secure the King's person and protestantism, and he suggested a Sunday sitting:

> this speech set many's zealous tinder on fire. Some guided theirs against the evil ministers, others against the evil principles imbibed at court. Others excused both in comparison of the ill ones of the other sex, urging Samson's being betrayed by his Delilah, and Solomon outwitted by strange women, and that no good can be expected whilst the French interest and the popish both were centred in the one person (which some did not stick to name), and she admitted a place in the King's bosom.[16]

So on Sunday, 11 May, the Commons began to consider the material produced by the committee of secrecy, and heard many professions of concern about York. 'Something must be done,' claimed Sir John Knight, 'but I dare not venture to propose what'; others proposed that York should not return to England without parliament's approval, that he suffer an 'eternal banishment', or that he be impeached for high treason. Many of those like Powle, Cavendish, Capel, Littleton, and even Sir William Coventry, who had in the past been so critical of the government, were now heard counselling caution, while the radical suggestions came from men like Hugh Boscawen or Sir Thomas Player. Player proposed a bill to exclude York and all papists from the succession, and eventually, late at night, the house took a vote on the motion to being in a bill to disable York from inheriting the crown. When it became clear that the noes would lose badly they abruptly left their seats and yielded the vote. But before the house broke up, MPs resolved *nem. con.* to stand by his majesty with their lives and fortunes in defence of the King's person and the protestant religion and 'if his majesty shall come by any violent death (which God forbid!) that they will revenge it to the utmost upon the papists'.

The exclusion vote was 'so bitter a bill that all the gilding and sweeting that followed' about preserving Charles and protestantism 'will not make it to be swallowable either by the King or House of Lords,' wrote Edward Cooke.[17] Elements in London relished the bill however. Its proposer Sir Thomas Player also presided over the Green Ribbon Club at the King's Head tavern by the Temple, and the next evening the club celebrated with a bonfire which they defended with drawn swords when the servants of the Temple were sent to put it out. Player took a leading part too in the petition presented to London's court of aldermen on 20 May that in its original form praised parliament and snubbed Charles and seemed sympathetic towards nonconformism. Its purpose was to indicate to undecided MPs that large numbers of Londoners approved of exclusion and would welcome measures to help protestant dissenters.[18] Others, like Danby, saw petitioning and the 11 May resolution to defend the King as preludes to popular unrest and even republicanism. Once prepared, the bill had a first reading on 15 May, despite 'the thinness of the house, occasioned by a dog match at Hampton Court and a horse race at Banstead Downs.' Doubtless some MPs were taking refuge at the races from agonizing decisions in parliament, but by 21 May a large number had steeled themselves to vote in favour of the exclusion bill which passed its second reading by 207 to 128. Scholars disagree about the chances of the exclusion bill at this stage, but Charles II was sufficiently alarmed to heed the advice of Temple, Danby, and three ministers who were increasingly coming to dominate his counsels, Sunderland, Essex and Halifax, that he should prorogue parliament. He did not – for all his earlier professions – feel the need to consult his full privy council about the decision.

A prorogation was justified because of 'the vast difference' between the two houses over the trials of Danby and the five popish lords. After the Commons' appearance in the Lords on 6 May, the Lords had refused to discuss impeachment procedures with the lower house, and the government had been able to use its majority, and the contentious side-issue of the bishops' right to sit in capital cases, to draw out business, and finally to set 27 May as the trial date for the five lords (rather than Danby) – much to the fury of MPs. On the 27th the five lords were brought to Westminster Hall, 'environed with spectators of both sexes and all qualities', and left to wait for the peers to finish their other business. The House of Lords was busy with a request from the Commons for a conference on the habeas corpus bill, to which in an apparent fit of absence of mind they agreed, and with voting once more on the rights of bishops in capital trials. Having dealt with this, they found the King waiting to address both houses. Charles told them that 'he had promised himself great good from this session' but their disagreements had frustrated his hopes, he therefore prorogued parliament until 14 August. One of the few pieces of finished legislation, the Habeas Corpus Amendment Act, received the royal assent; the five lords were remanded to the Tower; the Speaker's mace was packed off to Whitehall; and 'thus all parted in a mist of surprise'.[19] The city guard was doubled in case Londoners protested, but public attention was soon diverted by events in Scotland.

The unease felt about Charles's government of his Scottish kingdom, and particularly about the methods of Lauderdale, was a constant factor in English politics. Whether it was Burnet's revelations about Lauderdale in 1674 or the use of the Highland host in 1677, there was much fuel to feed the incendiary claims of Shaftesbury that the fate of Scotland was linked to that of England: 'in England, popery was to have brought in slavery; in Scotland, slavery went before, and popery was to follow,' he told the Lords on 25 March. Now presbyterian Scotland rose in rebellion. On 3 May Archbishop Sharp of St Andrews was dragged from his coach and murdered; on 29 May a protest (in which the records of the abjuration of the covenant were burned) turned into a proclamation of the covenant; and a subsequent successful confrontation with the royal army under Graham of Claverhouse left Glasgow at the mercy of the rebels, '8000 of the desperatest and worst sort of fanatics'. Although some cynics still thought it 'a trick to get an army together, and then have no more need of parliaments,' the Duke of Monmouth was confidently dispatched with about 10,000 men to put down the rising. He defeated the ill-armed and undisciplined rebels on 22 June at Bothwell Bridge on the Clyde: 'common fame says [he killed] 2000, took 1000 prisoner, and lost only six men.' It was Monmouth's success and the reaction to it which 'alters the whole face of affairs', according to some contemporaries. He was hailed as a military hero, a good protestant for his clemency towards the defeated Scots, and as a potential successor to his father.[20]

In England fears of popery and the prosecution of the plot continued throughout the summer. In May there were suspicious fires in London, including one at a prison in Clerkenwell where Catholic priests were held, and the Earl of Burlington maintained that there were attempts by alleged Catholics to fire houses 'almost every second night' which 'infinitely enrages the people here against the papists.' In June 'our judges are very busy upon the trial' of popish plotters such as Richard Langhorn and the five Jesuits who were convicted of high treason; while out in the shires, Catholic priests began to go to the gallows for the crime of being priests.[21] Philip Henry noted that in mid-July 'were executed two priests, condemned at the last assize by Sir Job Charlton, the one at Denbigh, the other at Chester – they were hanged, drawn and quartered – as were also several others in other counties.'[22] But there were also significant reversals for those prosecuting the plot. On 9 July Lord Chief Justice Scroggs gave bail to Samuel Pepys and Sir Anthony Dean, who had been committed by the Commons in May. More dramatically, on 18 July Sir George Wakeman, the Queen's physician, along with Marshall, Romney and Corker, was acquitted of high treason; 'which I hear was not disliked by the court,' wrote William Fall. 'All people judge Wakeman guilty,' observed John Verney, 'although the evidence could not so positively make it appear so.'[23] For many, the political reality of the plot was what mattered. As Halifax told his brother, 'I hope the notoriety of the fact, as our lawyers call it, is evidence enough of the plot'; but Sir William Temple reported that Halifax had brazenly asserted that 'the plot must be handled as if it were true, whether it were so or not, in those points which were so generally believed by the city or country, as well as both houses.'[24]

'We are full of jealousies, libels and iniquities,' complained Henry Coventry in the spring of 1679. One reason was simply because 'never was there as great a licence taken in dispersing such scandalous libels and pamphlets as now.' When parliament ended, the Licensing Act lapsed, and press censorship, never easy at the best of times, became virtually impossible. With only nugatory restraint, the pamphleteers, propagandists, satirists and newsmongers had a field day.

> Men may prate and may write, but 'tis not their rhymes,
> That can any ways change or alter the times,
> It is now grown an epidemical disease,
> For people to talk and to write what they please.[25]

As Anthony Wood records, 'many pamphlets come out now against popery and papists, and some old ones with new titles put to them; great rascallity and thieving from other books merely to get money or cheat.' Pieces which had circulated in manuscript, like the 1673 libel *Advice to a Painter to Draw the Duke By*, 'now by the liberty of the press is made public', and while some feared the consequences, others argued 'that such old stuff is so long forgot that I do not think it will have any effect.'[26] Other reprints included Francis Jenks's speech in the Guildhall and works on constitutional monarchy dating back to the early 1640s, which suggest an element of ideological continuity between 1679 and earlier crises. Personalities, however, were also a prominent theme in the contemporary publications. Vitriolic personal attacks were published against the court and ministers, the Duchess of Portsmouth and even the King. One acerbic 'vision' described 'the lewd palace' of Charles II, 'the fountain of our woe, / From whence our vices and our ruins flow ... Cease, cease, o'Charles, thus to pollute our isle; / Return, return to thy long-wished exile.'[27] Tracts like the notorious *An Appeal from the Country to the City*, often attributed to Charles Blount, were naked propaganda, designed to play upon fears of popery with stomach-churning visions of popish massacre, rape and plunder, and to promote exclusion of the Catholic heir. 'When he (as all other popish kings do) governs by an army, what will all your laws signify? You will not then have parliaments to appeal to; he ... will levy his arbitrary taxes and his army shall gather them.'[28]

I

In July it was announced that the parliament was dissolved and that a new one would meet on 7 October. According to Edmund Verney, this was 'very unwelcome news to the country, for it was a parliament according to the people's mind.'[29] The dissolution was the work of Temple and the triumvirate of ministers, who feared the increased popularity of Monmouth and the use which Shaftesbury and a recalled parliament might make of it. Clumsily handled in the privy council, where most opposed it, the calling of a new parliament promised no advantage to the government; indeed many believed that the same members would be returned, 'but they will not be in much better humour for having spent a great deal of money for the same place they had most of them paid dear for before.' Sir Robert Howard predicted that they might demand a Triennial Act, while Henry Coventry concluded from the elections that the new parliament 'will be much the same as to the persons, but more the same as to the humour'.[30]

In most areas the elections were held during August and naturally the only talking point became 'who is like to carry it, and who to lose it': there were in fact contested elections in sixteen county seats and sixty-one borough seats. William Harbord did 'not find any great gall in the new elections, but even that not only men in places, but long parliament men, and even my Lord Danby's pensioners, come in promiscuously. So that I trust in God the same calmness in the house will answer that of the kingdom'.[31] However Mark Knights's analysis of the election campaign and its printed propaganda reveals that the principal slogan in contests was 'no courtier'. An honest country man was to be preferred before a courtier, 'a pernicious piece of luxury, a drone, a two-faced Janus,' as he was described by *The Countries Vindication*.[32] The struggle for influence and local precedence between patrons was often the most significant factor in contested elections, closely followed by conflicts between 'country' and 'court', and then – and too a far lesser extent than had previously been thought – questions about the prosecution of the plot or support for the exclusion bill. In several cases exclusionist candidates were paired with anti-exclusionists. There were 'great factions' at the York assizes when it came to choosing the knights of the shire, noted Reresby, a disappointed candidate himself at Aldborough. Two of the three candidates, Lords Clifford and Fairfax had sat in the previous parliament and voted for exclusion, and they enjoyed the support of 'the entire dissenting party in matter of religion'; Sir John Kaye set himself up as Clifford's rival and tried to engage 'the help of the gentry and their interest', but rather than force an expensive poll, Kaye withdrew and allowed the two lords to take their seats uncontested. The only national political issue even implied in Reresby's account of this election is that of nonconformity.[33]

Late in August, in the middle of the election campaign, the King fell ill with a fever, 'occasioned (it's thought) by staying too late in the evening a-hawking after having played at tennis in the morning'.[34] The Duke of York rushed back in disguise from Brussels, only to find that Charles was already on the mend. This illness 'and the consequence at such a critical time did so strike men that they were not left at liberty to judge of it with indifference,' as Halifax delicately expressed it.[35] Not only was the succession once again brought to the forefront of public consciousness, but York succeeded in facing down his nephew Monmouth who was relieved of his offices and ordered into exile. On 24 September Monmouth left for Holland; the next day York departed for Brussels, but this was merely to gather his wife and household as he now had permission to 'withdraw' to Scotland. In October the Duke and Duchess of York set out from London, progressing in easy stages and being greeted by the loyal gentry at each place of note. They were received 'but very coldly' at York and soon after Sunderland wrote to the Lord Mayor of that city expressing the King's 'surprise' and 'dissatisfaction' at this lack of respect.[36] Shaftesbury took advantage of the improvement in the Duke of York's position to engineer his own dismissal from the privy council and a return to overt opposition.

In September the most vocal opposition to the court was in London, among the civic radicals like Sir Thomas Player and Francis Jenks whose support came from nonconformity and the lower orders. John Verney believed that 'the city is now strangely divided between mad separatists and the Church of England men.' Ossory commented acidly on how Monmouth had portrayed his loss of office there: 'you may imagine that whoever pretends to suffer upon the score of religion will not want friends. I am told that in the town great rancour and partiality does appear.'[37] When Jenks made an unsuccessful bid for election as sheriff in September, Player supported him with a speech which hammered home the threat of a popish successor and emphasized the danger from those who doubted the popish plot or even worse those 'deservedly styled protestants in masquerade' who suggested it was all the work of protestants. That same month, the bookseller Matthew Taylor had been sent to Newgate for printing and publishing *The Compendium of the Plot*, a satire on the plot and the witnesses. The authorities were anxious about the populism of the radicals because London had still not elected its MPs, but on 9 October, 'although there was very violent opposition made against them (and the eyes of the nation much fixed therein as the criterion of interests)', the former members were returned without dispute or disorder.[38] Eight days later it was announced that parliament would be further prorogued. This decision, influenced by York, convinced many onlookers that the survival of parliament was in doubt: Josselin already suspected that 'the court's design is to make parliaments useless or rid the crown of them'; and John Verney believed that it left England open to French invasion.[39]

Popery remained the centre of popular attention, thanks in large part to propagandists and plot investigators. Just before he left for Scotland, James had dined with the Artillery Company at Merchant Taylor's Hall where papers had been stuck on the doors and stairs denouncing those who dined with him as 'papists in masquerade'.[40] Another plot was revealed when Thomas Dangerfield, alias Willoughby, was arrested on 20 October. Dangerfield led the authorities to papers that seemed to show that Sir Robert Peyton and various Green Ribbon Club members and presbyterians had planned armed mass resistance to York's succession. Yet it turned out that Dangerfield was the agent of a Catholic midwife, Elizabeth Cellier, and when evidence was found hidden in her meal tub that this was indeed a Catholic plot designed to sow confusion among protestants, the whole popish plot hysteria gained a new lease of life. By November the council were 'frequently employed' in investigating 'this second plot of the papists'; and popular feeling found a release in two great 'pope-burnings' on 5 November and 17 November. The 'chief' of the bonfires on the 17th, Elizabeth I's accession day,

> was at Temple Bar, over which gate Queen Elizabeth was decked up with a magna carta and the protestant religion; there was a devil in a pageant and four boys in surplices under him, six Jesuits, four bishops, four archbishops, two patriarchs of Jerusalem and Constantinople, several cardinals, besides Franciscans, black and grey friars in all habits; there was also a great crucifix, wax candles and a bell, and 200 porters . . . to carry lights along with the show . . . [and] Sir Edmund Godfrey, on horseback, murdered, in a black wig and pale-faced, and behind him rode one of the murderers.[41]

These were massive popular entertainments in which the procession, a parody of a papal coronation, wound its way around the streets before the effigies, including on this occasion an effigy of Peyton and 'a pope . . . in pontificalibus that cost above £100' were thrown on the bonfire. There were said to be 100,000 spectators on 17 November 1679, including the King himself. Even the French ambassador was smuggled into the city in disguise to witness the spectacle, and he marveled that 'no manner of mischief was done, not so much as a head broke, but in three or four hours the streets were all quiet as at other times. It would not have been so at Paris.'[42]

The Duke of Monmouth suddenly reappeared in London on 28 November. His unauthorized return from exile was greeted with rapture in the city, 'the acclamation of the rabble as to bonfires have been very great and not a little disorderly'; but his reception at court when he asked to kiss the King's hand was very different, Charles 'in great fury' told him 'to begone again'.[43] By remaining in London, Monmouth was openly defying his father. Meanwhile Shaftesbury, disappointed once more in his effort to force his way into government, had decided to resort to 'the weight of the nation', to employ popular opinion to force Charles to call parliament. But first a gesture was needed. On 7 December Shaftesbury and fifteen other peers stopped the King on his way to chapel and presented a petition for the sitting of parliament. The immediate royal response was to postpone the next parliament until November 1680 and issue a proclamation against petitioning which immediately became the talk of the town: "'tis now believed the parliament will never sit.'[44]

Although several counties were eager to follow Shaftesbury's lead, the petitioning campaign of the winter of 1679–80 was not a success. It enjoyed some central co-ordination: blank petitions were distributed and were available in different wordings; the 'monster petition' signed by 60,000 people in London was a striking achievement; but overall, as the Countess of Sunderland concluded, 'the petitions fell flat to what was expected.' When Sir Gilbert Gerrard presented the London petition to Charles on 13 January 1680, 'the King, as is said, told Sir Gilbert, he thought he had been a more prudent person than to appear in the head of such a faction, who answered he had an English spirit and a loyal heart and what he did he did with that, etc. The King granted not their request then.'[45] The King was similarly scathing about the six provincial petitions that were eventually presented, and he dismissed any office-holders involved in the petitioning. He was adamant that he would meet parliament when he decided. As Mark Knights has argued the political significance of this campaign was two-fold. First, it showed that Charles was the problem, that the present King, not his heir, was wilfully obstructing the meeting of parliament. And, secondly, the resort to popular, mass politics, with all its overtones of the 1640s, convinced many hitherto quiescent supporters of the monarchy that it was time to stand up and be counted.

At Whitehall they were playing musical chairs. Late in January 1680 Cavendish, Russell, Capel and Powle, the one-time critics who had become privy councillors the previous April, came to the King and asked to be dismissed. 'Their entry and their exit have been both very remarkable, and neither very well comprehended by men of my small talent,' commented Henry Coventry. 'We are full of fear and jealousies and the effects of those passions.'[46] Essex had resigned from the Treasury Commission in November. The work of government was now shouldered by Sunderland, Sidney Godolphin and Laurence Hyde, who were known derisively as 'the chits'. The capable but melancholy Halifax was stuck in

London, dreaming of planting cabbages and carrots at home in Rufford. 'Our world here is so overrun with the politics,' he wrote to his brother, and 'the fools' heads so heated, and the knaves so busy, that a wasps' nest is a quieter place to sleep in than this town is to live in.'[47]

II

Charles's ministers had to find a foreign policy and, ideally, score a diplomatic success that might reassure parliament when it eventually met that the King and his government were not enslaved to the French and popish interests. In 1679 the goal was to reach some kind of agreement with the Dutch and another with the French while preventing a French–Dutch rapprochement which might leave Charles II diplomatically isolated and looking more than a little foolish. Stalemate ensued. Secret talks with the French produced terms which might buy Charles a temporary respite from parliaments and a degree of international security but only at the cost of huge domestic unpopularity and restricted freedom of manoeuvre in foreign affairs. More was hoped for from the Dutch, and especially from a planned Anglo-Dutch treaty to guarantee the peace of Nijmegen. Not only should this be popular in England, it might also exert some leverage on France. Yet there were many obstacles, not least of which was that no-one was eager to sign treaties with Charles II while he was locked in a domestic political crisis. Henry Savile, the English envoy at Paris, claimed that he was repeatedly asked whether rebellion had broken out or if Charles was besieged in Whitehall. Meanwhile the Dutch and French seemed to be moving closer together; only an intense flurry of English diplomacy prevented the conclusion of an alliance over New Year 1680. In 1680 English diplomacy's only tangible achievement was the treaty signed with the Spanish in June to defend Flanders against any future French attack.

In England monarchical authority was being vigorously asserted in the spring of 1680. Charles frowned on the petitions for the sitting of parliament; he sacked judges like Sir Robert Atkins who had countenanced the petitioning; he purged JPs and other officers; he insisted on the enforcement of the Corporation Act; he encouraged the local authorities to act against popish recusants and looked more coldly upon nonconformity; and he approved of attempts to curb the press such as the conviction of Benjamin Harris for publishing *An Appeal from the City to the Country*.[48] In February he recalled the Duke of York from Scotland and on 8 March they both attended a great entertainment at the house of the Lord Mayor Sir Robert Clayton, 'where the bonfires, bells and loud acclamations of the multitude testified the joy and loyalty of the citizens of London.' Two days later Charles, York and the Duchess of Portsmouth went to the races at Newmarket. When Cavendish turned up there and pointedly ignored the Duke, Charles banned him from the court. The royal brothers lived 'very privately' at Windsor during April and May, only paying a weekly visit to Whitehall for council meetings. As a wave of addresses from the loyal provincial gentry abhorring the late petitioning campaign arrived at Whitehall, they were printed in the *Gazette*. Despite the 'cabals' of Monmouth, Shaftesbury, Russell, Cavendish and 'other persons dissatisfied with the court', the chits allowed themselves a little optimism. Bishop Carleton of Chichester found things much better than they had been: 'the dissenting party in all parts of this country are more crestfallen since his majesty began to act like himself, like a king, and to let the people know they are but subjects.'[49]

Even the popish plot was 'pretty well asleep'.[50] Although this was not for want of effort by Shaftesbury, who appeared before the privy council on 24 March with a lurid tale of a popish plot in Ireland. A few days later, commented Gilbert Burnet, the coffee-houses which had been languishing for lack of rumour were 'in heart again'.[51] Anti-popery was momentarily inflamed the following month by the attack on John Arnold, JP and informant on Monmouthshire popery, in Jackanapes Lane. 'A nice hubbub among the prentices' of London planned for the 29 May holiday caused some consternation before it was put down to their 'dear delights of bonfires and ale'.[52] But by May, it was alleged, most of the population, even in London, thought 'the plot was only a piece of state pageantry, and no real thing, and that mischief, if true, was fully satisfied in the death of those few miscreant martyrs.'[53] At York assizes that summer 'several persons of quality' were accused of high treason on the evidence of popish plot informants: 'though some had been found guilty in London on this or the like evidence, yet it found so little credit in this county that three of the four were acquitted'; only the priest Thomas Thwing was convicted, 'a priest being more his guilt than the plot'.[54] People were becoming disenchanted. There had been too much double-dealing and too much masquerade: writer after writer claimed to 'unmask' (from their own position naturally) popish politics or false justice, to reveal the truth behind the deceptive exterior. One of the most comprehensive examples is the broadsheet engraving *The Committee, or Popery in Masquerade* (1680) (see plate 16) in which the royalist propagandist L'Estrange depicts a conglomeration of rebels, sectaries and dissenters, whose factious and seditious activities had led to civil war in the past and could provoke disorder in the present. These so-called protestants are doing the work of the papists (they are urged on by the pope from the top-right) because they are introducing the tyranny which will pave the way for popery. This, as Tim Harris has shown, is what was to become the tory version of anti-popery.[55]

Plate 16 The Committee, or Popery in Masquerade *(1680) is royalist propaganda which depicts the collusion of dissenters and papists in a conspiracy to subvert English liberty, property and religion.*

The succession issue still loomed, of course, but even in this Charles was taking the offensive wherever possible. He was irritated by the persistent stories that he had married Lucy Walter, the mother of Monmouth, in Paris in 1650 and a copy of the wedding contract had been left in a mysterious black box. At 'an extraordinary council' on 26 April Charles denied this before the Duke of York and the judges, and had this reported in the *Gazette*. Charles pursued those who had spread the story; and when 'a pamphlet lately printed by stealth' repeated the canard, he ordered witnessed copies of his declaration to the privy council to be printed.[56] Charles might have felt that he was taking the fight to his enemies, but his success in dispelling suspicion is debatable. People assumed that York was behind the King's declaration and Burnet remarked that 'it was generally thought that the Duke has lost more than he has gained by procuring the declaration.' Philip Henry hinted at doubts about Charles's sincerity when he referred in his diary to this 'manifesto wherein he [the King] avows again and again as before, that he was never married to any woman but Queen Catherine. At this the papists sing Io paean, but God sees.'[57]

A strange calm seemed to descend on England during the summer months: the government restrained their propagandists and discouraged the prosecution of nonconformists; and even the newsletters contained little of interest.[58] In order to keep the issue of a popish successor before the public, Shaftesbury and his allies employed several tactics, some no more than stunts. In June one of the three Middlesex grand juries was persuaded to petition for parliament to sit. An attempt to present the Duke of York as a popish recusant and the Duchess of Portsmouth as a common whore to the same grand jury was only thwarted by Sir William Scroggs's quick thinking. At mid-summer Henry Cornish and Slingsby Bethel, both radicals and exclusionists, were elected as London's sheriffs, but then disqualified because they had not taken the Anglican sacrament. They rapidly qualified themselves and successfully stood again at a disorderly meeting in July; 'there was a world of insolencies committed in the hall that day; one of the sheriffs was taken by the throat, and punched in the breast, and all this by the fanatic party.'[59] Monmouth triumphantly progressed through the West Country, stopping at Bristol, Bath and Exeter where he was led into the city by a throng of more than 10,000 well-wishers. On his return to London in October he took up residence in the City. Increasingly Monmouth adopted not only the role of 'protestant duke' as opposed to James, the Catholic duke, but also the air of a rightful prince and claimant to the succession. He enjoyed being called 'your highness'; and it was noticed that the 'baton sinister', denoting his illegitimacy, had been erased from the coat of arms on his coach. According to his supporters, Monmouth had even managed quite inadvertently to cure a girl of the king's evil near Yeovil that summer.[60]

On 26 August a proclamation announced that parliament would meet in October. Having already failed to win the active help of Halifax, Sunderland formed an alliance with the Duchess of Portsmouth and against York. Portsmouth had been so badly rattled by the attacks on her in the summer that she had already begun to talk to Shaftesbury, and had even relayed to the King Shaftesbury's offer of £600,000 in return for allowing parliament to name his successor. In September Sunderland was negotiating with Shaftesbury and some thought him ready to abandon York and accept exclusion, and possibly take Shaftesbury and Monmouth into office, in return for a well-managed and generous parliament.[61] Much of this depended upon Sunderland's conviction that Charles would not defend his brother to the last: the minister suspected that Charles wanted to be forced into exclusion as an easy way out of his dilemma. No wonder that when Halifax returned to London in September, he found 'a new scene in state matters' and that 'there is now as much anger against York at court as at Westminster.'[62] When Charles returned to Whitehall in early October, he was persuaded by

Portsmouth, Sunderland and Essex that the Duke of York must be sent to Scotland before parliament met. So on 20 October, the day before parliament sat, the Duke set off for Edinburgh and that evening the King was observed to be in a particularly good humour at the Duchess of Portsmouth's. On the same day Monmouth, Shaftesbury and a hundred members of parliament had dined at the Sun tavern in the City and, in a dramatic gesture, a group had been sent to search parliament's cellars for explosives.

Untroubled by explosions, the King's speech at the opening of parliament on 21 October 1680 touched on the alliance with Spain, further investigation of the popish plot, the cost of defending Tangier, and his readiness to concur in any bill to protect protestantism that was consistent 'with preserving the succession of the crown in its due and legal course of descent'. But MPs had their own agenda. Some were angry, others fearful, and yet others were ambitious. This headstrong Commons chose their own speaker, William Williams, rather than wait for royal guidance and later decided to print each day's votes. Shaftesbury brought a long parade of popish plot witnesses before the Lords and Dangerfield appeared in the Commons to say that York had suggested to him that he kill the King. This presented a natural opportunity for debate of the dangers posed by a popish successor, a debate that encompassed all the grievances of the past eighteen months. MPs were quick to assert the subject's right to petition and to censure those who had either thwarted petitions or had been involved in the addresses of abhorrence. On 2 November Lord Russell revived the motion of 27 April 1679, that the Duke of York's religion and position as heir encouraged popish plotters, and William Harbord argued that everything they had heard from the plot witnesses demonstrated that 'till the papists see that the Duke cannot be King, the King's life will be in danger.' The Commons agreed that a bill excluding James from the succession should be brought in and two days later Russell presented the bill. In a debate on 8 November a proviso was added that the crown should pass as if James was dead, a significant political compromise which disappointed Monmouth's pretensions but stopped short of naming Princess Mary and William of Orange as heirs, and so maintained unity in the exclusionist camp. The King then intervened and in effect told MPs to go on with the plot, but not to meddle with the succession. In reply the Commons pointed to what had been achieved in prosecuting the plotters, to the difficulties caused by the King's evil advisors – principally those who advised the dissolution of the last parliament and the 'many and long prorogations' of this one – and said absolutely nothing about the succession. Meanwhile the exclusion bill passed its third reading on 11 November and Russell was instructed to carry it up to the House of Lords.

Now it was necessary to play for time. The King's attitude was plain, but Shaftesbury, and perhaps Sunderland, hoped that the Lords and even the King might yet be persuaded that the demand for exclusion was irresistible. Behind the scenes negotiations continued, London's common council asked the King to take parliament's advice, and on the morning that the bill arrived in the Lords, Dangerfield was wheeled on to repeat his allegations in front of the peers. These desperate tactics were to no avail. On 15 November, with the King standing by the fire, the House of Lords debated exclusion and, for all the arguments of Shaftesbury and Essex, they voted it down by sixty-three votes to thirty. Contemporaries made much of the effect of Halifax's oratory against exclusion, but in reality the vote was a foregone conclusion – it had indeed been predicted very accurately a week before – and owed most to political calculation and Charles's clear wishes. The purpose of Halifax's oratory was to impress the King with his indispensability as a minister and to humiliate Sunderland whose gamble in backing exclusion had so spectacularly misfired.

What was the Commons to do now? There was still hope of saving something from the wreckage. When MPs considered the plight of Tangier, Hampden spoke of 'coming to a plain bargain', in other words, extorting some measure on the succession from Charles by their control of supply. But first they would exact their revenge, 'all those who are looked upon as friends to him [the Duke of York] will be struck at.'[63] The Commons 'fall upon Lord Halifax, who I hear defies them,' wrote Dr Denton; 'The house has started many hares, but catched very few.' An address for Halifax's removal was ignored by Charles, but that still left Halifax more hated than even Danby had been.[64] The Commons impeached Edward Seymour for malversation of finances, Sir Francis North for drawing up the proclamation against petitioning, and three other judges, Jones, Weston and Scroggs, on various charges. More productively members continued to work on a proposal 'for uniting his majesty's protestant subjects' which had emerged from a committee chaired by Daniel Finch as two bills, one for the 'comprehension' of moderate nonconformists within a broader Church of England and the other for a toleration of the remaining protestant dissenters. Both bills received their second reading before Christmas and disappeared into the committee stage.

The day after rejecting the exclusion bill, the House of Lords turned to 'expedients' for the succession problem. Halifax proposed a five-year banishment for York, Shaftesbury suggested a royal divorce and remarriage but lost interest in the idea a few days later, and Essex came up with an Association modelled on that of 1585 to protect Elizabeth I from Catholic assassination. The house soon became caught up in the trial of Lord Stafford, one of the five popish lords still languishing in the Tower.

Charles had exhorted parliament to bring them to trial and the evidence seemed to be strongest against Stafford. The elderly peer was a feeble defendant, unable to mount a coherent or even audible response to the tissue of lies alleged against him. On 7 December the peers found him guilty by fifty-five votes to thirty-one. Charles, who was convinced of his innocence, could not afford politically to help Stafford beyond commuting the sentence of hanging, drawing and quartering to one of beheading. Some of the peers who convicted Stafford probably hoped to regain credit that they had lost by voting against exclusion, but most of the hostile lords and observers were more concerned to reassert the reality of the popish plot. A few days after Stafford's execution, and having been presented with the evidence collected by their own committee over the last weeks, the House of Lords voted that for several years there had been a plot in Ireland to massacre the English and subvert the protestant religion.

Charles was growing impatient. On 15 December he asked parliament what it intended to do to help him defend Tangier and maintain his alliances – and he took care to mention once more that he would not be moved on exclusion. The Commons made no rush to answer, but got on with debating Cavendish's suggestion of an Association in support of a protestant heir and the exclusion from office of any who refused to join it. This blatant attempt at a backdoor form of exclusion appealed to members like Sir Gilbert Gerrard, who believed 'the popish plot goes on as much as ever', and the house agreed to prepare an Association bill which also explicitly excluded James, Duke of York, or any other papist from succeeding to the crown. The Commons' committee on securing the kingdom against popery and arbitrary government agreed on bills to ensure frequent parliaments, to give judges security of tenure, and to make the illegal exaction of money from the subject high treason. When on 20 December – 'a critical day' believed Secretary Jenkins – the Commons replied to the King's speech of 15 December, they offered money for Tangier, the fleet, and the maintenance of alliances in exchange for bills to exclude the Duke of York, create an Association, and guarantee frequent parliaments.[65] While Charles was digesting this, the town was 'very full of some proposals made in private' to the King. Russell, Montagu, Monmouth and others of the opposition had apparently offered to engineer a vote of money and allow Charles to name his own successor if he took into office and agreed to an exclusion bill. But the scheme seems to have foundered on Shaftesbury's refusal to participate despite the prospect of becoming Lord Treasurer. Charles officially refused the Commons' Address on 4 January and MPs, either in hope of intimidating the King or out of simple frustration, lashed out against Halifax and Hyde and passed votes against courtiers like Feversham, Clarendon and Worcester. 'I am at this hour threatened with more thunder from the House of Commons tomorrow,' Halifax wrote to his brother on 6 January. 'Where all this will end, either in relation to myself or to the public, God in heaven only knows.'[66] The end came on 10 January. The Commons had wind of a prorogation and met early to pass 'several angry votes', denouncing those who advised a prorogation as traitors, demanding the recall of Monmouth, thanking London for its support and criticising the persecution of dissenters. Parliament stood prorogued until 20 January and for all their misgivings Londoners did not rise in protest. Some suggested that Charles would accede to a new exclusion bill which could be offered when parliament reconvened in a new session; others that this was a prelude to a dissolution. On 18 January, without taking advice, the King dissolved parliament and called another to meet at Oxford in March.

III

There was neither time nor money nor, one suspects, the stomach to fight elections on the scale of 1679. Before the dissolution the MPs for North Allerton were told that their voters were resolved 'to continue you both as our representatives' and they should not go to the trouble or expense of a journey to the constituency: a stance which 'may serve for a good precedent' elsewhere. Only nine counties saw contests, involving fifteen seats, and forty-five boroughs, where sixty-three seats were disputed. There were sixty new members in an eventual Commons of 502. From Halifax's point of view at court, 'the elections generally speaking are very naught', for good or bad most of the old faces would be returning. Morrice learned that 'of the elections already made the persons are generally the same, and where there is any change, persons of the same sentiment are still chosen.'[67] This continuity of members should not be taken to imply an absence of politicking, propaganda and controversy in the weeks before the Oxford parliament met.

No sooner had the dissolution been announced than petitioning began in Warwickshire and London. On 25 January the Earl of Essex presented Charles with a petition from sixteen peers, including Monmouth and Shaftesbury, which remarked that since Henry II onwards parliaments held at Oxford 'have proved very fatal' to kings. Playing to the gallery, the petition claimed that parliament would not be able to speak its mind there and that Charles would be dangerously exposed to 'the swords of the papists' many of who had infiltrated his guard. A subsequent torrent of propaganda pushed all the right opposition buttons, playing on the dangers of electing pensioners and courtiers, printing lists of those who had voted against exclusion in the past, expatiating on the hardships of protestant nonconformists and worrying at the popish plot. Monmouth attracted cheering crowds wherever he went. In February Shaftesbury even succeeded in finally presenting York as a popish recusant to a Middlesex grand jury.

In the midst of this, however, there were signs of a reaction, of a resurgence of 'loyalty' towards the Church of England, monarchy and the Stuarts. At the Bristol election, one of the most bitterly fought, the contest turned on religion, indeed exclusion was not even mentioned, and the candidates backed by the dissenting interest were narrowly beaten by two loyalists to church and state.[68] Where poll books survive for these and previous elections, they indicate a high turnover of voters and shifting loyalties. Voices were now heard to question the tactics and direction of the two previous parliaments: Anthony Wood opined that parliament was dissolved in January for 'acting high and doing little', and Sir Edward Dering also remarked on MPs' pretensions; Edmund Warcup suggested to Jenkins that the new parliament had lost its freedom of action, that MPs were already in thrall to their radical leaders and constituents.[69]

None of this was of much help to Charles II who was committed to facing a parliament which was largely of the same humour as its predecessor. Since the King had set his face against exclusion, ministers like Essex and Sunderland, and his mistress Portsmouth, were politically washed up; dismissing Sunderland, Essex and Temple, Charles now put his parliamentary business in the hands of Halifax and Edward Seymour, an uneasy pairing which was strained by Seymour's growing association with Hyde and the Duke of York. Halifax and Seymour decided to offer parliament a regency as the solution to the succession problem and finally, after toying for a week with excluding James in favour of Monmouth, Charles agreed. Hyde meanwhile had been entrusted with secret negotiations with the French ambassador Barrillon. Late in 1680, fearing that exclusion might succeed, Barrillon began to make overtures to Charles. By January he was offering £200,000 if Charles abandoned his Spanish alliance and his attempts to work with parliament; by March he and Hyde were meeting in the Queen's apartments and then at Oxford, where, three days before parliament sat, they reached a verbal agreement. Charles was to receive £385,000 over three years provided he did not help Spain against France or call a parliament for that purpose; he retained the right to meet parliament for other reasons and Louis undertook not to attack Flanders.

Charles, accompanied by his guards and court, arrived in Oxford to an elaborate welcome, a week before parliament was due to meet. MPs arrived, often with cavalcades of supporters, some armed and some wearing ribbons reading 'no popery, no slavery' in their hats, and Shaftesbury turned up on horseback, 'with holsters and pistols before him, attended with a great many horsemen well armed and [with] coaches'. This was gesture politics, underlining the popish danger, rather than serious preparation for resistance or rebellion – although it was later open to a more sinister interpretation. Meanwhile parliament settled into its unfamiliar and awkward accommodation and on Monday 21 March, heard their monarch's speech. Charles recalled his treatment by the last parliament, and neatly turned the rhetorical tables on his critics: 'I, who will never use arbitrary government myself, am resolved not to suffer it in others,' he told them; yet 'no irregularities in parliament shall make me out of love with them.' He urged parliament to tackle the plot and popery, but reminded them to be ruled by the laws of the land and that 'without the safety and dignity of the monarchy, neither religion nor property can be preserved.' Ruling out exclusion, the King was happy to consider any expedient by which 'the administration of the government may remain in protestant hands' under a Catholic monarch. Charles made no request for money from his parliament.[70]

After a few days spent swearing members according to the Test Act, naming committees, and agreeing to print their votes, the Commons moved on to serious business: Sir Nicholas Carew's motion for an exclusion bill was debated and postponed, and the house then considered the case of Edward Fitzharris, the latest in the long line of disreputable popish plot witnesses, who had offered evidence against the Duke of York, the Queen and the Duchess of Portsmouth. Charles had imprisoned Fitzharris in the Tower, so the Commons tried to bring his evidence out into the open by impeaching him in parliament. On Saturday morning, in the stuffy, crowded, Convocation House, the Commons returned to exclusion and for the first time heard the details of the King's proposal for a regency: Princess Mary was to be named as regent during the reign of her father. Debate raged until about 4.00 p.m. when MPs voted to bring in an exclusion bill. Charles's expedient had been unacceptable. An hour later MPs reassembled to learn that the Lords had rejected Fitzharris's impeachment. They angrily voted this refusal a denial of justice, a hindrance of the plot investigation, and a violation of the constitution of parliament. That evening the talk was all of another dissolution, even though Charles was busying himself preparing a more commodious chamber for the Commons in the Sheldonian Theatre. On Monday morning, as MPs gave the exclusion bill its first reading, they were interrupted by a summons to Christ Church hall where the King dissolved parliament, 'and that so suddenly, that only his majesty was in his robes, but not any one of the lords, nor was the sword of state there'. After his lunch, the King drove off in his carriage to Windsor, leaving MPs to pack their bags for home.

Charles II never met another parliament and in due course his brother James succeeded to the throne. In hindsight, then, a great constitutional struggle over exclusion came to an end with the dissolution of the Oxford parliament. But contemporaries did not possess hindsight. They did not know that the parliamentary storms around exclusion that began in November 1680 had blown themselves out by March 1681. All they saw was that Charles had failed to reach an agreement with this parliament and that he was soon talking about calling another. The parliamentary crisis was rooted in a political failure. And that failure was due to Charles's own political style and personality. Often lazy, slow to reach a decision and poor at keeping to it, Charles seemed a fickle politician, whose intentions and preferences were deliberately obscure. Masquerading in this way may have kept his options open, but, as Halifax observed, 'the King's changeableness and silence in affairs at that time made people in fear to serve him.' If Charles was to command excellent ministers and to succeed in his goals, he must establish and follow a single line of policy: 'it would ruin all if his majesty continued to advise with those of one interest this day, and hearken to those of another tomorrow, nor could his ministers be safe under such uncertainties; and if he would be advised, it was in the King's power to make all his opponents' tremble.'[71] Lacking a dominant minister since the fall of Danby, Charles had no protection against the incessant jealousies of his insecure councillors, the aristocratic feuds and the avid hunt for influence and office, which not only ruled at Whitehall, but increasingly stirred up public opinion in London and the provinces.

If there were parliamentary and political crises between 1679 and 1681, was there also a national upheaval, an 'exclusion crisis'? If there was, it deserves to be renamed. This was not a narrow crisis about exclusion, but more a controversy over the succession problem and the political and constitutional implications of all the various expedients offered to solve it.[72] It was not, in truth, merely a succession crisis either, but rather a collapse of political confidence. This collapse can be traced to anxieties about the whole range of Charles II's misgovernment, his toadying to France, the corruption of parliament, the creation of standing armies, the abuse of the law, and the persecution of dissenters, and to even wider concerns about public and private interest, integrity and honour. The erosion of political trust had produced parliamentary deadlock by 1681, but it had not yet begun to effect ordinary people in their daily lives. It was the loyalist resurgence, based first on a revulsion against extreme tactics and rebellious principles, then gathering strength as royal policy and propaganda supplied party labels and slogans, which in the months and years to come was to carry partisan political strife into virtually every parish vestry and every urban corporation, every conventicle, church and manor house in the kingdom.

Epilogue: Remnants of the Old

Oxford is now the public theatre,
And you both audience are, and actors here.
The gazing world on the new scene attend,
Admire the turns, and wish a prosperous end. . . .
Our ark that has in tempests long been tossed
Could never land on so secure a coast.
From hence you may look back on civil rage,
And view the ruins of the former age.
Here a new world its glories may unfold,
And here be saved the remnants of the old.

Dryden, *The Epilogue – Spoken to the King at the*
opening the playhouse at Oxford on Saturday last,
being March the nineteenth 1681

Devouring time swallows us whole.

Rochester, *Seneca's Troas*, Act 2. *Chorus*

As John Dryden prophesied on the eve of the Oxford parliament, England did move towards 'a new world' when the 'civil rage' of 1678–81 was succeeded by the often carefully staged quarrels of whigs and tories in the 1680s. Dryden himself was to provide much of the script for the 1680s by transmuting older images and language into new political weapons, resolving some of the difficulties which loyalists had experienced over Charles's sexuality and indulgence, and rewriting the past just as powerfully as Marvell had done, but this time to pin the blame for past discord firmly on the Absaloms, Zimris and Achitophels, on a 'headstrong, murmuring race', and even on their over-indulgent David. Charles II contributed to the refashioning of the recent past with the royal declaration of 8 April 1681, to be read in all parish churches, which attributed the political chaos of the past winter to 'the restless malice of ill men who are labouring to poison our people, some out of fondness for their old beloved Commonwealth principles, and some out of anger at their being disappointed in the particular designs they had for the accomplishment of their own ambition and greatness.'[1] Every age rewrites its own past, and does so in part from the remnants of its predecessor. The personalities and politics, language and topoi of the 1670s would be quarried by all later accounts of that decade, and just as inevitably these materials would be transformed to serve new purposes. Nothing and no-one was safe. Rochester, that irredeemable sinner, Rochester, the poet who intoned with Seneca that 'after death nothing is, and nothing, death', no heaven, no hell, no eternal soul, even Rochester was rewritten as the rake reclaimed. Redeemed for Christianity on his deathbed in 1680 by the ministrations of Gilbert Burnet, Rochester's last mask, his death mask for public display, was that of the penitent sinner.[2]

Much else that was characteristic of the 1670s could not survive in the harsh political environment of the early 1680s. The burgeoning tolerance of religious diversity, the openness to wit, irony and emotional experimentation, were temporarily set back, while other traits, such as commercialism or political trimming, advanced, but more cautiously than before. These and others characteristics of the 1670s discussed in this book are, of course, ones which I have chosen to isolate and emphasize; and I readily acknowledge that my account cannot avoid recasting the past in the process of telling it, nor is it immune to the dangers of hindsight. But this book has at least attempted to show that the 1670s had wide-ranging political concerns which are not easily reduced to the glib slogan of the fear of 'popery and arbitrary government'; and it has suggested that these concerns were deeply informed by broader currents of thought about such things as the reconciliation of opposing needs and interests, the role of consumption, the drives of commerce, the power of information and public opinion, the feasibility of intolerance, the implications of sexuality, and the nature of public and private virtue. Although these issues still speak to us in the twenty-first century, my purpose has been to bring to light concerns from the 1670s. It is enough if the vitality, passions and fears of the English people in these turbulent years have not been forgotten; if they have not returned to 'that mass of matter . . . where things destroyed with things unborn are kept'; if they have not been swallowed whole by time.[3]

Notes

PREFACE AND ACKNOWLEDGEMENTS

1 Dering, *Diaries*, pp. 125–6.
2 For a guide to work published before 1969 see W. L. Sachse, *Restoration England 1660–1689* (Cambridge, 1971). More recent work can be approached through T. Harris, P. Seaward and M. Goldie (eds), *The Politics of Religion in Restoration England* (Oxford, 1990); P. Seaward, *The Restoration, 1660–1689* (1991); L. K. J. Glassey (ed.), *The Reigns of Charles II and James VII and II* (1997). There is a spirited attempt to 'rethink' the period and generate some controversy, mainly about the terms 'radical' and 'party', by the various contributors to 'Order and Authority: Creating Party in Restoration England', a special issue of the journal *Albion* 25: 4 (1993).
3 J. Miller, *Charles II* (1991); R. Hutton, *Charles II* (1989); Browning, *Danby*; Haley.
4 See T. Harris, *London Crowds in the Reign of Charles II* (Cambridge, 1987); J. Scott, *Algernon Sidney and the English Republic 1623–1677* (Cambridge, 1988) and *Algernon Sidney and the Restoration Crisis 1677–1683* (Cambridge, 1991); S. C. A. Pincus, *Protestantism and Patriotism: Ideology and the Making of English Foreign Policy 1650–1688* (Cambridge, 1996); A. Marshall, *Intelligence and Espionage in the Reign of Charles II, 1660–1685* (Cambridge, 1994); M. Knights, *Politics and Opinion in Crisis, 1678–81* (Cambridge, 1994).

PROLOGUE

1 D. Roberts, *The Ladies – Female Patronage of Restoration Drama* (Oxford, 1989), p. 27; Dryden, *Poems*, p. 246; 'Epilogue' to unidentified play, *Covent Garden Drollery* (1672), pp. 33–4.
2 *CSPVen 1673–5*, p. 68.
3 Joseph Arrowsmith, *The Reformation* (1672: Augustan Reprint Society Publications, 237–8, Los Angeles, 1986), p. 26; *The Plays of Sir George Etherege*, ed. M. Cordner (Cambridge, 1982), pp. 289–90; Wycherley, pp. 130–1; *The Complete Works of Thomas Shadwell*, ed. M. Summers (5 vols, 1927), III. 170–1.

4   Aphra Behn, *Oroonoko, The Rover and Other Works* (Penguin, 1992), p. 174.
5   Buckingham, p. 97.
6   *CSPVen 1671–2*, pp. 54–73.
7   Edward Chamberlayne, *Angliae Notitia* (1669; 2nd part 1671: quoting 5th edition, parts 1 and 2, 1671), sig. A6, ch. 2.
8   BL Add MS 32681, fol. 127.
9   [Thomas Lambert], *Sad Memorials of the Royal Martyr* (1670), sig. A2v.
10   *England's Imminent Danger* (1671), p. 24.
11   *England's Imminent Danger*, p. 161.
12   *The Letters of King Charles II*, ed. A. Bryant (1935), p. 242.
13   *CSPD 1670*, pp, 69–70; W. D. Christie, *The Life of Anthony Ashley Cooper, First Earl of Shaftesbury* (2 vols, 1871), II. appendix I; cf. Haley, pp. 256–8.
14   BL Stowe MS 186, fol. 21.
15   Richard Lingard, *A Letter of Advice to a Young Gentleman* (1670), p. 29.
16   *England's Imminent Danger*, p. 295; Chamberlayne, *Angliae Notitia*, ch. 2.
17   [Slingsby Bethel], *The Present Interest of England Stated* (1670), p. 6.

1   1670–2: SO BEWITCHED A TIME

1   Marvell, *Letters*, p. 315; Josselin, p. 551; Henry, *Diaries*, p. 226; PRO SP 104/176, fol. 223v.
2   BL Add MS 36916, fol. 182; *CSPD 1670*, p. 240. Also see A. Marshall, 'The Westminster Magistrate and the Irish Stroker: Sir Edmund Godfrey and Valentine Greatrakes, Some Unpublished Correspondence' *Historical Journal* 40 (1997), 504.
3   Marvell, *Letters*, p. 314; Bulstrode, p. 132; BL, Verney Microfilms M636, reel 23, Sir Ralph Verney to Edward Verney, 23 February 1670 (I am grateful to Major R. B. Verney for permission to cite these letters). The main sources for the politics of these years include Grey; *PH*; Dering; Marvell, *Letters*; and newletters such as BL Add MS 36916 (Starkey's newsletters), Bulstrode, and *HMC Verney*. Indispensable secondary works include Haley; J. Miller, *Charles II* (1991); R. Hutton, *Charles II* (Oxford, 1989); D. T. Witcombe, *Charles II and the Cavalier House of Commons 1663–74* (Manchester, 1966).
4   W. Westergaard, *The First Triple Alliance: The Letters of Christopher Lindenov Danish Envoy to London 1668–1672* (New Haven, 1947), p. 312; Marvell, *Letters*, p. 316. On the background to the Roos case see F. Clifford, *A History of Private Bill Legislation* (2 vols, 1885), I. 394–8; A. Fraser, *The Weaker Vessel* (1984), pp. 298–308; F. R. Harris, *The Life of Edward Mountagu KG, First Earl of Sandwich* (2 vols, 1912), appendices H and I; Grey, I. 251–3.
5   *HMC Various Collections (serial number 55)*, II. 134; Marvell, *Letters*, p. 315; PRO SP 104/176, fol. 231.
6   Marvell, *Letters*, p. 317. For the secret treaty see C. H. Hartmann, *Charles II and Madame* (1934), pp. 307–16; R. Hutton, 'The Making of the Secret Treaty of Dover 1668–1670', *Historical Journal* 29 (1986).
7   *The Journal of George Fox*, ed. N. Penney (Letchworth, 1924), pp. 254–5; 'P. Christian', *The Copy of a Letter sent to . . . Sir Samuel Starling* (1670); *The Christian Conventicle* (1670), p. 52; Henry, *Diaries*, p. 226.
8   BL Add MS 36916, fol. 181.

9   Henry, *Diaries*, p. 227; BL Add MS 36916, fol. 184.
10 *CSPD 1670*, pp. 370, 384, 433, 401–2, 418, 448, 309.
11 Marvell, *Letters*, p. 318; C. W. Horle, *The Quakers and the English Legal System 1660–1688* (Philadelphia, 1988), pp. 116–17; Henry, *Diaries*, p. 233.
12 Marvell, *Letters*, pp. 318, 117, 228; Grey, I. 294–6; BL Verney Microfilms, reel 24, Denton to Sir Ralph Verney, 24 November 1670.
13 BL Add MS 36916, fol. 185; Bulstrode, p. 144; *The Right Honourable the Earl of Arlington's Letters*, ed. T. Bebington (2 vols, 1701), I. 437.
14 BL Add MS 36916, fol. 187.
15 See Westergaard, *First Triple Alliance*, pp. 254–5; BL Add MS 36916, fol. 187; Bulstrode, p. 146.
16 Bedfordshire Record Office, HSA W 1670, fols 83, 76, 88–9.
17 *CSPD 1670*, pp. 39–40, 510.
18 *CSPD 1670*, pp. 49–50, 187; Danchin, I. 2. 523; Bulstrode, p. 150. Carleton, who is discussed in chapter 4 below, was transported to Jamaica in 1671 but returned and was executed in 1673.
19 Marvell, *Letters*, p. 318.
20 Dering, pp. 23, 8–9, 27.
21 Bulstrode, pp. 152, 155, 157; Dering, p. 28; Westergaard, *First Triple Alliance*, p. 314; Marvell, *Letters*, p. 318.
22 Henry, *Diaries*, p. 235.
23 T. Carte, *The Life of James Duke of Ormonde* (6 vols, Oxford, 1851), IV. 441–3; *HMC Verney*, p. 489; Marvell, *Letters*, p. 121; Bulstrode, pp. 162, 165; *CSPD 1670*, pp. 574, 576; BL Add MS 36916, fol. 200.
24 Marvell, *Letters*, p. 321; BL Add MS 36916, fol. 203.
25 Dering, pp. 4–7; *Arlington Letters*, II. 318.
26 Dering, p. 49; Grey, I. 349–50.
27 BL Add MS 36916, fol. 207.
28 BL Add MS 36916, fol. 212.
29 Witcombe, *Charles II and Cavalier Commons*, p. 121.
30 Harris, *Sandwich*, II. 336; A. Swatland, *The House of Lords in the Reign of Charles II* (Cambridge, 1996), p. 134.
31 Harris, *Sandwich*, II. 335; Marvell, *Letters*, p. 140.
32 Miller, *Charles II*, p. 185.
33 *CSPVen 1671–2*, p. 67.
34 Marvell, *Letters*, p. 322.
35 Marvell, *Letters*, p. 326; Evelyn, III. 576. Also see A. Marshall, *Intelligence and Espionage in the Reign of Charles II, 1660–1685* (Cambridge, 1994).
36 *HMC Verney*, p. 464.
37 BL Add MS 36916, fol. 208.
38 *CSPD 1671*, p. 179.
39 Bulstrode, pp. 183, 186–7; Evelyn, III. 575, 577; *CSPD 1671*, p. 237; BL Verney Microfilms, reel 24, Denton to Verney, 18 May 1671.
40 *CSPD 1671*, pp. 18–19, 124.
41 *CSPD 1671*, pp. 15, 65–6, 309–10, 426, 438, 464, 545, 591.
42 *CSPD 1671*, p. 368.
43 BL Add MS 36916, fol. 227.
44 *CSPD 1671*, pp. 335, 356–7, 385–6.

45 *HMC Verney*, p. 489; Evelyn, III. 589–90.
46 The volumes of *CSPD* are bursting with information about the navy; and for an account of naval tensions see J. D. Davies, *Gentlemen and Tarpaulins: the Officers and Men of the Restoration Navy* (Oxford, 1991).
47 *HMC Verney*, p. 489; K. Feiling, *British Foreign Policy 1660–1672* (1930), p. 315; Westergaard, *First Triple Alliance*, p. 468.
48 *CSPD 1671*, pp. 464, 554, 562–3.
49 *CSPD 1671*, p. 291.
50 Bod. MS don b. 8, p. 265; Henry, *Diaries*, p. 248.
51 *Arlington Letters*, II. 437, 348–9.
52 BL Add MS 28040, fol. 16.
53 *Calendar of the Correspondence of Richard Baxter*, ed. N. H. Keeble and G. F. Nuttall (2 vols, Oxford, 1991), II. 146; *CSPD 1671–2*, p. 72; also see J. K. Horsefield, 'The "Stop of the Exchequer" Revisited', *Economic History Review* 35 (1982).
54 Bulstrode, p. 216.
55 *Arlington Letters*, II. 352; BL Add MS 40860, fol. 23v.
56 This reconstruction is based on PRO SP 104/177, especially fols 12, 14, 16, 17v.
57 Miller, *Charles II*, p. 189.
58 P. Fraser, *The Intelligence of the Secretaries of State and their Monopoly of Licensed News 1660–1688* (Cambridge, 1956), p. 97; cf. Evelyn, III. 605–6. My account of the war draws on *Journals and Narratives of the Third Dutch War*, ed. R. C. Anderson (Navy Record Society Publications, LXXXVI, 1946); *CSPD*; Harris, *Sandwich*; Davies, *Gentlemen and Tarpaulins*; C. R. Boxer, 'Some Second Thoughts on the Third Anglo-Dutch War', *Transactions of the Royal Historical Society* XIX (1969); J. R. Jones, *The Anglo-Dutch Wars of the Seventeenth Century* (1996).
59 *CSPD 1672–3*, p. 251; *Particular Friends: The Correspondence of Samuel Pepys and John Evelyn*, ed. G. de la Bédoyère (Woodbridge, 1997), p. 80; Evelyn, III. 609–11; S. Pincus, 'From Butterboxes to Wooden Shoes: The Shift in English Popular Sentiment from Anti-Dutch to Anti-French in the 1670s', *Historical Journal* 38 (1995), 343.
60 Evelyn, III. 614–15.
61 *CSPD 1672*, p. 110.
62 Evelyn, III. 616; *CSPD 1672*, pp. 558–9; *Particular Friends*, pp. 79–81.
63 Evelyn, III. 617–19; Harris, *Sandwich*, II. 248–9; R. Ollard, *Cromwell's Earl* (1994).
64 Evelyn, III. 610.

2 1672–4: AFFAIRS BEGIN TO ALTER

1 Marvell, *Letters*, p. 327; Josselin, p. 564; Bulstrode, p. 238.
2 Bulstrode, pp. 239–40, 242, 246, 248.
3 P. Fraser, *The Intelligence of the Secretaries of State and their Monopoly of Licensed News 1660–1688* (Cambridge, 1956), p. 118; Bulstrode, pp. 221–2.
4 C. R. Boxer, 'Some Second Thoughts on the Third Anglo-Dutch War', *Transactions of the Royal Historical Society* XIX (1969), p. 76.

5 Dryden, *Poems*, p. 272; Henry, *Diaries*, pp. 250–1; *CSPD 1672–3*, pp. 148, 341 (cf. D. A. Winn, *John Dryden and his World* (New Haven, 1987), p. 239 and note); Thomas Jordan, *London Triumphant* (1672); *Defiance to the Dutch* (1672), Luttrell III. 83; *The Grand Abuses* (1672), Luttrell III. 79.

6 J. Miller, *Charles II* (1991), p. 197; *The Right Honourable the Earl of Arlington's Letters*, ed. T. Bebington (2 vols, 1701), II. 389.

7 J. Spurr, *The Restoration Church of England, 1646–1689* (New Haven, 1991), p. 61; Henry, *Diaries*, p. 250.

8 Henry, *Diaries*, p. 253.

9 Spurr, *Restoration Church*, p. 62; BL Add MS 40860, fol. 25v.

10 *The English Ballance* (1672), p. 51.

11 This and all other speeches can be found in Grey and *PH* from which the political narrative is drawn, supplemented by Dering, pp. 103–49; Williamson; and the authorities mentioned in chapter 1.

12 Dering, p. 111.

13 BL Add MS 40860, fol. 44.

14 Dering, pp. 116, 119.

15 Miller, *Charles II*, p. 201.

16 Dering, p. 136; Miller, *Charles II*, pp. 202–3; *HMC Verney*, p. 490.

17 BL Add MS 17012, fol. 37.

18 E. Legh (Lady Newton), *Lyme Letters 1660–1760* (1925), pp. 85–92.

19 *English Ballance*, pp. 61–2.

20 See S. C. A. Pincus, *Protestantism and Patriotism – Ideologies and the Making of English Foreign Policy, 1650–1668* (Cambridge, 1996).

21 J. Miller, *James II* (1978: 1989 edn), p. 65.

22 Evelyn, IV. 7.

23 Williamson, I. 24.

24 *HMC Verney*, p. 490.

25 Williamson, I. 6, 24, 41.

26 Williamson, I. 51, also 44, 47–8, 63.

27 *POAS*, I. 217.

28 Spurr, *Restoration Church*, p. 64; Henry, *Diaries*, p. 262.

29 Henry, *Diaries*, pp. 262–3; BL Add MS 70012, fol. 63; Williamson, I. 42, 31–4, 25.

30 Williamson, I. 91, 89.

31 Williamson, I. 55–6, 60, 63.

32 *HMC Verney*, p. 491; Williamson, I. 75.

33 Williamson, I. 69; also see Evelyn, IV. 13; *News from the Camp* (1673), Luttrell, II. 144.

34 *Journals and Narratives of the Third Dutch War*, ed. R. C. Anderson (Navy Records Society Publications, LXXXVI, 1946), p. 36.

35 Williamson, I. 17–20, 36, 39.

36 *Journals*, ed. Anderson, pp. 393, 47–53.

37 *HMC Verney*, p. 491; *Journals*, ed. Anderson, pp. 54–5, 390–4; Williamson, I. 162, 168–9, 174–5, 185–6.

38 Williamson, I. 137–8; *HMC Verney*, p. 491.

39 Williamson, I. 143.

40 Williamson, I. 165; II. 31, 35–6.

41   Dering, p. 150; *Essex Papers*, I. 130; Williamson, II. 49.
42   *POAS*, I. 219.
43   *The Burning of the Whore of Babylon* (1673), pp. 2–4; Evelyn, IV. 26; Williamson, II. 63; *Essex Papers*, I. 145.
44   Williamson, I. 81, 84, 88, 99, 102–3, 107, 108.
45   Williamson, I. 77.
46   Williamson, II. 29; *Essex Papers*, I. 131–2; *CSPVen 1673–5*, p. 155.
47   Williamson, II. 62.
48   Grey, II. 212–13; Dering, p. 158; Williamson, II. 69; D. T. Witcombe, *Charles II and the Cavalier House of Commons* (Manchester, 1966), p. 147.
49   *Essex Papers*, I. 140, 146, 155, 152.
50   Williamson, II. 105–6.
51   *CSPVen 1673–5*, p. 187.
52   *Essex Papers*, I. 155.
53   *Essex Papers*, I. 1659; Evelyn, IV. 30.
54   K. H. D. Haley, *William of Orange and the English Opposition 1672–4* (Oxford, 1953), pp. 166–7.
55   *CSPD 1673–5*, pp. 128–32.
56   *Essex Papers*, I. 159.
57   Haley, *William of Orange*, p. 159.
58   Rochester, pp. 30, 328.
59   *Essex Papers*, I. 161; Haley, *William of Orange*, p. 161.
60   Williamson, II. 29.
61   Williamson, II. 106, 107; *HMC 9th Report, Appendix Part 2 (House of Lords MSS)*, pp. 35–7; A. Pritchard, 'A Defense of His Private Life by the Second Duke of Buckingham', *Huntington Library Quarterly* 44 (1980–1).
62   Haley, p. 357.
63   Haley, *William of Orange*, p. 167.
64   Grey, II. 227.
65   Grey, II. 252; Buckingham, p. 98; Williamson, II. 115, 119; Pritchard, 'Defense of Private Life'.
66   *PH*, 646.
67   Grey, II. 270; Williamson, II. 115; BL Add MS 70012, fol. 115v.
68   Williamson, II. 135, 138, 152.
69   Williamson, II. 128–9, 130.
70   *Essex Papers*, I. 168.
71   Haley, *William of Orange*, p. 181.
72   *Essex Papers*, I. 168; Williamson, II. 133, 147.
73   Williamson, II. 130.
74   *Essex Papers*, I. 174; Grey, II. 415.
75   *The Lauderdale Papers: III 1673–1679*, ed. O. Airy (Camden Society, XXXVIII, 1885), pp. 32–3; Haley, p. 360.
76   *Essex Papers*, II. 179–80; Williamson, II. 154.
77   Williamson, II. 156.
78   Haley, *William of Orange*, p. 192.
79   Josselin, p. 573.
80   *Essex Papers*, I. 180.

3 1674–6: NOTHING IS TO BE TRUSTED TO GOOD NATURE

1 Williamson, II. 142; Browning, *Danby*, II. 63–4.
2 *Essex Papers*, II. 187; Josselin, p. 574; Marvell, *Letters*, p. 282.
3 Bod. Carte MS 72, fol. 177; BL Add MS 40860, fol. 66v; *Essex Papers*, II. 197, 199, 228, 241–2, 258, 260.
4 *Essex Papers*, II. 260; Bod. Carte MS 72, fol. 188.
5 Marvell, *Letters*, pp. 332, 143–4; Browning, *Danby*, I. 141–5.
6 See Marvell, *Letters*, p. 333; Bulstrode, p. 311; M. Priestley, 'Anglo-French Trade and the "Unfavourable Balance" Controversy, 1660–1685', *Economic History Review* IV (1951); M. Priestley, 'London Merchants and Opposition Politics in Charles II's Reign', *Bulletin of the Institute of Historical Research* XXIX (1956).
7 *Essex Papers*, I. 218, 259; Bulstrode, p. 271.
8 Josselin, p. 581.
9 Bod. Tanner MS 42, fols 119, 75.
10 Bod. Carte MS 72, fol. 229; Marvell, *Letters*, pp. 331, 336, 338.
11 Bod. Carte MS 72, fols 253, 264–5; BL Add MS 25124, fol. 14; BL Add MS 70012, fol. 172; *CSPD 1673–5*, pp. 548–9; Josselin, p. 582.
12 BL Add MS 70012, fol. 180; *The Records of a Church of Christ Meeting in Broadmead Bristol, 1640–1687*, ed. E. B. Underhill (1847), p. 225; Thomas Hobson, *The Bristol Narrative* (1675); *A Reply to the Bristol Narrative* (1675).
13 BL Add MS 70012, fol. 188; BL Add MS 25124, fols 16, 33.
14 BL Add MS 70012, fols 164, 165, 183, 185, 186; *Calendar of the Correspondence of Richard Baxter*, ed. N. H. Keeble and G. F. Nuttall (Oxford, 2 vols, 1991), II. 173–4; John Spurr, 'The Church of England, Comprehension and the Toleration Act of 1689', *English Historical Review* CIV (1989), 935–6 and sources cited there.
15 Bod. Carte MS 72, fols 257, 255.
16 Haley, pp. 369–71.
17 *HOP*, III. 53.
18 BL Harleian MS 7377, fol. 58; BL Add MS 25124, fols 25, 26, 27, 28,
19 Bulstrode, p. 283.
20 The most informative sources for this session include not only Grey and *PH*, but Marvell's *Letters*, pp. 144–63; Bulstrode, pp. 283–301; Dering, *Diaries*, pp. 57–103. Shaftesbury's *Letter from a Person of Quality* (1675) is an indispensable, but partisan, account of debates in the Lords.
21 *HMC Verney*, p. 492; Bulstrode, p. 284; Dering, *Diaries*, p. 59; *PH*, 678.
22 Bulstrode, p. 285; cf. Dering, *Diaries*, pp. 60, 68.
23 Dering, *Diaries*, pp. 61–2, 63–4, 70.
24 Marvell, *Letters*, p. 150; *HMC Verney*, p. 492; Bulstrode, pp. 286, 287.
25 Marvell, *Letters*, p. 149; Bulstrode, pp. 286, 291.
26 Dering, *Diaries*, pp. 64–5; Grey, III. 17; *HOP*, III. 54.
27 Dering, *Diaries*, pp. 80–2; Marvell, *Letters*, pp. 154–5.
28 Bulstrode, p. 295; Dering, *Diaries*, p. 89.
29 Dering, *Diaries*, pp. 73–4; Grey, III. 54, 55, 57; *HMC Verney*, p. 492.

308 *Notes to pp. 67–78*

30 *Essex Papers*, II. 4. On Carr see C. Holmes, *Seventeenth-century Lincolnshire* (Lincoln, 1980), p. 239.
31 Marvell, *Letters*, pp. 157, 158; Bulstrode, p. 297. Also see Browning, *Danby*, I. 162, for an explanation of why Danby supported the Commons, and Haley, pp. 382–4, for Shaftesbury's part.
32 Bulstrode, p. 301.
33 Marvell, *Letters*, p. 343; John Miller, 'A Moderate in the First Age of Party: The Dilemmas of Sir John Holland, 1675–85', *English Historical Review*, CXIV (1999), 860; Bod. Tanner MS 42, fol. 148.
34 *CSPD 1673–5*, pp. 548–9; *The Voice of the Nation* (1675), also see *CSPD 1673–5*, pp. 88–90.
35 See Bulstrode, p. 312; *HMC Verney*, p. 465.
36 Bulstrode, p. 320; Marvell, *Letters*, p. 342; Evelyn, IV. 75.
37 Rochester, *Letters*, pp. 27, 106; Bulstrode, pp. 308, 313; Haley, p. 387.
38 *The Bloody Murtherers Executed* (1675), p. 5; *Blood Justly Revenged* (1675).
39 *News from Sea* (1674); Bulstrode, p. 274
40 BL Thynne MS 41, fol. 142 (on microfilm); Bulstrode, p. 310; *HMC Verney*, p. 493.
41 See P. J. Norrey, 'The Restoration Regime in Action: The Relationship between Central and Local Government in Dorset, Somerset and Wiltshire, 1660–1678', *Historical Journal* 31 (1988), 800–1.
42 BL Add MS 25124, fols 50, 43. Also see T. Harris, *London Crowds in the Reign of Charles II* (Cambridge, 1987), pp. 191–204; R. M. Dunn, 'The London Weavers' Riot of 1675', *Guildhall Studies in London History* I (1973–5); Bulstrode, pp. 310–11, 314; *HMC Verney*, pp. 465, 466; *A True Narrative of all the Proceedings against the Weavers* (1675).
43 *A True and Faithful Relation of the Late Dreadful Fire at Northampton* (1675); Simon Ford, *The Fall and Funeral of Northampton* (1677); *A Sad Relation of the Dreadful Fire at Cottenham* (1676).
44 Josselin, pp. 587–8.
45 Bulstrode, p. 302; *HMC Buckinghamshire, Lindsey etc*, p. 377; Haley, p. 285;
46 Bulstrode, pp. 307–9; Browning, *Danby*, I. 166.
47 Browning, *Danby*, I. 167–73, III. 44–50, 56–71.
48 Bulstrode, pp. 314, 316.
49 Bulstrode, p. 320.
50 Grey, III. 323, 341, 345.
51 Bulstrode, 316, 317; *PH*, 758–61, 770–2; Reresby, pp. 101–2; *HMC Verney*, p. 466; BL Add MS 32094, fol. 389.
52 Marvell, *Letters*, p. 392; *CSPD 1675–6*, pp. 445–5; Josselin, p. 588.
53 Bulstrode, p. 324; Marvell, *Letters*, p. 344; Josselin, pp. 588, 589.
54 Bulstrode, p. 322; also see Marvell, *Letters*, p. 172; Haley, p. 399; *CSPD 1675–6*, p. 393.
55 *A Letter from a Person of Quality, to his Friend in the Country* (1675), pp. 1–2, 34, 4, 19, 31. There are echoes of the *Letter* in several of Shaftesbury's speeches and in Locke's manuscripts, see *Locke – Political Essays*, ed. M. Goldie (Cambridge, 1997), pp. 230–5, 360–1.
56 *Letter from a Person of Quality*, pp. 34, 32.
57 *Two Speeches* (Amsterdam, 1675); also see Buckingham, pp. 102–3; B.

Yardley, 'George Villiers, Second Duke of Buckingham, and the Politics of Toleration', *Huntington Library Quarterly* 55 (1992).

58 *Two Seasonable Discourses*, pp. 4, 9–10.

59 T. E., *A Letter from a Parliament-Man* (1675).

60 On the proclamation against coffee-houses see chapter 6 below. For Leicester and Turner see Sir Peter Leicester, *Charges to the Grand Jury at Quarter Sessions, 1660–1677*, ed. E. M. Halcrow (Manchester, Chetham Society, V, 1953), pp. 77–8, 82–3; M. Goldie, 'Restoration Political Thought', in L. K. J. Glassey (ed.), *The Reigns of Charles II and James VII and II* (1997), p. 19. I have outlined the doubts about the Church of England's pre-eminence in 'Religion in Restoration England' in Glassey (ed.), *Reigns of Charles II*, pp. 97–104, and at greater length and more subtly in my *The Restoration Church of England, 1646–1689* (New Haven, 1991).

61 See E. A. O. Whiteman (ed.), *The Compton Census of 1676* (1986); Spurr, *Restoration Church*, p. 72; BL Harleian MS 7377, fol. 62; *CSPD 1675–6*, p. 568.

62 See *Account of the Barbarous Attempt of the Jesuits upon Mr de Luzancy* (1675); *PH*, 780–3; *CSPD 1675–6*, pp. 389–93; Marvell, *Letters*, pp. 171, 173–4, 175; Bulstrode, pp. 322–3; Reresby, pp. 100–2; *HMC Verney*, pp. 466, 493; J. P. Kenyon, *The Popish Plot* (Penguin, 1974), pp. 21–2.

63 *HMC Verney*, pp. 467, 493.

64 Josselin, p. 591; *CSPD 1675–6*, p. xiii.

65 *An Account of the Proceedings at Guildhall . . . 24th of June 1676* (1676), pp. 2, 3, 4, 9; Marvell, *Letters*, pp. 345, 348; M. Knights, 'London Petitions and Parliamentary Politics in 1679', *Parliamentary History* 12 (1993), 41–2; Haley, pp. 409–10.

66 Marvell, *Letters*, p. 345; *CSPD 1676–7*, pp. 145, 194, 207, 293.

67 *An Impartial Account of the Trial of the Lord Cornwallis* (1679).

68 Marvell, *Letters*, pp. 344–5; *HMC Verney*, p. 467; Rochester, *Letters*, pp. 27–8.

69 *Essex Papers*, II. 86.

4 GREAT SOULS: HEROISM, WIT AND MASQUERADE

1 *Journals and Narratives of the Third Dutch War*, ed. R. C. Anderson (Navy Records Society Publications, LXXXVI, 1946), p. 167; Evelyn, III. 160.

2 F. R. Harris, *The Life of Edward Mountagu KG, First Earl of Sandwich* (2 vols, 1912), p. 298; C. F., *Wit at a Venture* (1674), pp. 89, 90.

3 *New Advice to a Painter; A Poetical Essay describing the last Sea-Engagement with the Dutch: May the 28th 1673*, Luttrell III. 81; J. W. *English Illiads* (1674).

4 *The Glory of Dying in War* (1672), Luttrell I. 138.

5 *The Critical Works of Thomas Rymer*, ed. C. A. Zimansky (New Haven, 1956), p. 42; cf. Richard Perrinchief, *The Syracusan Tyrant* (1676), p. 193.

6 *On His Royal Highness His Expedition against the Dutch* (1672), Luttrell III. 98.

7 *Englands Lamentation* (1679?), Luttrell I. 94.

8 Dryden, X. 107.

9 Francis Sandford, *The Order Used at the Solemn Interment of George, Duke of Albemarle* (1670); Seth Ward, *The Christian's Victory over Death* (1670), p. 19;

The Cloud Opened; or the English Hero (1670) in *HM*, IV, 145; *Georgio Monck . . . Epitaphium* (1670), Luttrell I. 99; *A Great Cry and Little Wool* (n.d.), Luttrell, I. 98.

10   *Honour's Invitation* in *HM*, I. 347.

11   *Remarks upon Remarques* (1673), pp. 19–20.

12   *Remarques on the Humours and Conversations of the Gallants of the Town* (1673: 2nd enlarged edn, 1673), p. 17.

13   *Reflexions on Marriage and the Poetick Discipline* (1673), p. 93.

14   Dryden, *Poems*, p. 43; *Remarques*, p. 53.

15   BL Add MS 17017, fols 33v–34, where Henry Coventry warns Sir Thomas Chichley against 'L[or]d R[ochester], H[enry] Savill and the rest of our Westminster heroes'.

16   Rochester, p. 57.

17   [Richard Head], *Proteus Redivivus* (1675), pp. 198–9.

18   *The Confession of the Four High-way-men* (1674), p. 4. An anonymous pamphlet, *A True and Perfect Relation of a Robbery and Murder Committed by Five Notorious Highwaymen, on Wednesday the 18th of Instant March, near Col[n]brook* (1674) is about the gang, but does not name them.

19   *HMC Verney*, p. 475.

20   *The Memoirs of Monsieur Du Val* (1670) in *HM*, III. 295, 298, 300; *The Life of Deval* (1669).

21   *CSPD 1670*, pp. 39–40, 49–50.

22   *Bloody News from Yorkshire* (1674), pp. 6, 7.

23   *Groans from Newgate* (1677), Luttrell I. 134.

24   *Three Burlesque Plays of Thomas Duffett*, ed. R. E. DiLorenzo (Iowa City, 1972), p. 209.

25   D. Hughes, *English Drama 1660–1700* (Oxford, 1996), p. 135.

26   *The French Rogue* (1672), 'To the Reader'.

27   See L. Faller, *Turned to Account* (Cambridge, 1987), p. 10.

28   *The Lives of Sundry Notorious Villains* (1678), p. 19.

29   BL Add MS 36916, fol. 163; *Savile Correspondence*, p. 58; Rochester, *Letters*, pp. 157, 103.

30   *An Elegie upon the Death and in Commemoration of Truly Honourable and Truly Learned John Lord Wilmot, Earl of Rochester* (1680?), Luttrell II. 124.

31   Rochester, pp. 195–6.

32   *Elegie upon . . . Rochester.*

33   *Lives of Sundry Notorious Villains*, sig. A3.

34   Rochester, *Letters*, p. 99.

35   On the background see M. West, 'Dryden and the Disintegration of Renaissance Heroic Ideals', *Costerus* VII (Amsterdam, 1973); D. Hughes, *Dryden's Heroic Plays* (1981); Dryden, XI. 411–35.

36   Thomas Traherne, *Christian Ethicks* (1675), p. 441.

37   Ward, *Christian's Victory*, pp. 18, 4.

38   *Paradise Lost*, IX, ll. 25–33; *Paradise Regained*, III, lines 188–9, 194–6, in J. Carey (ed.), *John Milton – Complete Shorter Poems* (1968), pp. 477–6.

39   *Samson Agonistes*, lines 1279–80, 1287–96, in *Complete Shorter Poems*, pp. 385–6.

40   Pepys, V. 235; William Penn, *No Cross, No Crown* (1669); and much can be

learned from N. H. Keeble, *The Literary Culture of Nonconformity in Later Seventeenth-century England* (Leicester, 1987), pp. 184–94; J. R. Knott, *Discourses of Martyrdom in English Literature 1563–1694* (Cambridge, 1993).

41 John Bunyan, *The Pilgrim's Progress* (1678), pp. 64, 264.
42 Rymer, *Critical Works*, p. 8.
43 Thomas Hobbes' answer to Davenant's preface to Gondibert, 1650, in J. E. Springarn (ed.), *Critical Essays of the Seventeenth Century* (3 vols, Oxford, 1908), II. 55.
44 *Apology for Heroic Poetry and Poetic Licence* (1677), Dryden, XII. 88
45 Dryden, XIII. 39.
46 P. D. Cannan, 'New Directions in Serious Drama on the London Stage, 1675–1678', *Philological Quarterly* 73 (1994); on rhyme see R. D. Hume, *The Development of English Drama in the Late Seventeenth Century* (Oxford, 1976), pp. 310–11.
47 Dryden, XVII. 35; Hume, *Development*, pp. 150–61.
48 Dryden, XI. 6, 31.
49 Hughes, *Dryden's Heroic Plays*, p. 21.
50 Dryden, XIII. 28.
51 Dryden, XI. 3.
52 Dryden, XII. 5.
53 Dryden, IX. 411.
54 *Remarques*, p. 61.
55 John Downes, *Roscius Anglicus*, ed. J. Milhous and R. D. Hume (1987), pp. 41, 75.
56 Danchin, I. 2. 501.
57 George Villiers, Duke of Buckingham, *The Rehearsal*, ed. D. E. L. Crane (Durham, 1976), pp. 45, 48, 49; Dryden, XI. 134.
58 Rochester, p. 60.
59 Joseph Arrowsmith, *The Reformation* (1672: Augustan Reprint Society Publications 237–8, Los Angeles, 1986) pp. 47–8.
60 *Remarques*, p. 57.
61 *To the Right Honourable Thomas Earl of Ossory* (1673), Luttrell I. 110.
62 *An Encomium* (1675), Luttrell I. 65, also see 66 (*On the death of that most noble knight Sir John Harman*).
63 Dryden, XI. 30.
64 Rochester, pp. 72–7.
65 *The Dramatic Works of John Crowne*, ed. J. Maidment and W. H. Logan (1874), III. 44.
66 *The Poems of John Oldham*, ed. H. F. Brooks with R. Selden (Oxford, 1987), pp. 56–70.
67 *POAS*, I. 175–6.
68 C. F., *Wit at A Venture*, p. 89.
69 Quoted in H. Weber, 'Rakes, Rogues, and the Empire of Misrule', *Huntington Library Quarterly* 47 (1984), 19.
70 Crowne, *Works*, I. 128.
71 Rymer, *Critical Works*, pp. 9–10.
72 Crowne, *Works*, III. 11; Dryden IX. 7; Danchin I. 2. 352, 373.

73 *The Complete Works of Thomas Shadwell*, ed. M. Summers (5 vols, 1927), II. 111; Crowne, *Works*, III. 14.
74 *POAS*, I. 327 ff.
75 S. N. Zwicker, *Lines of Authority – Politics and English Literary Culture 1649–1689* (Ithaca, 1993), pp. 22, 25.
76 Aphra Behn, *The Rover and Other Works* (Penguin, 1992), p. 248. Two fine recent works discuss the emergence of the professional writer: B. S. Hammond, *Professional Imaginative Writing in England, 1670–1740* (Oxford, 1997); P. Kewes, *Authorship and Appropriation: Writing for the Stage in England, 1660–1710* (Oxford, 1998).
77 Dryden, XII. 97.
78 See the discussion in J. A. Winn, *John Dryden and His World* (New Haven, 1987), pp. 262–7.
79 Rochester, p. 60.
80 Walter Charleton, *Two Discourses* (1669: 1675 edn), p. 18.
81 Joseph Glanvil, *An Essay Concerning Preaching* (1678: 1703 edn), p. 71.
82 Thomas Hobbes, preface to *Homer's Odysses* (1675) in Springarn, *Critical Essays*, II. 70.
83 Obadiah Walker, *Of Education* (1673), pp. 133, 130.
84 Dryden, *Poems*, p. 119.
85 [Thomas Culpeper], *Essayes or Moral Discourses on Several Subjects* (1671), p. 112.
86 *Coffee-Houses Vindicated* (1675), p. 1.
87 *Three Restoration Divines*, ed. I. Simon (2 vols, Paris, 1967, 1976), II. 427.
88 Crowne, *Works*, III. 12.
89 J. H. Wilson, *Court Satires of the Restoration* (Columbus, Ohio, 1976), p. xiv; *POAS*, I. 327ff, 368.
90 Dryden, X. 209.
91 Dryden, *Poems*, p. 244.
92 *The Works of George Savile Marquis of Halifax*, ed. M. N. Brown (3 vols, Oxford, 1989), II. 496.
93 Quoted in E. N. Hooker (ed.), *Essays on Wit* (Augustan Reprint Society Publications, 4, Los Angeles, 1946), p. 1.
94 Dryden, XI. 221.
95 Dryden, XI. 320–1.
96 Evelyn, III. 565.
97 Pepys, IX. 219.
98 Halifax, *Works*, II. 495.
99 *Raillerie a la Mode* (1673), p. 3.
100 Dryden, XI. 221–2.
101 Wycherley, p. 378.
102 See J. Hayman, 'Raillery in Restoration Satire', *Huntington Library Quarterly* XXXI (1967–8); C. D. Cecil, 'Raillery in Restoration Comedy', *Huntington Library Quarterly* XXIX (1965–6).
103 'Frank Careless', *The Floating Island* (1673), p. 10; Wycherley, p. 254; the same is said of John Eachard, see *A Vindication of the Clergy from the Contempt Imposed* (1672), sig. A8.
104 *The Character of a Coffee House* (1673), p. 4.

105 Edward Stillingfleet, *Works*, [ed. by R. Bentley], 6 vols (1710), I, 245.

106 *Remarques*, p. 69; Goodman, *Serious Inquiry*, p. 225.

107 *Remarques*, p. 79; S. Wintle, 'Libertinism and Sexual Politics', in J. Treglown (ed.), *The Spirit of Wit – Recollections of Rochester* (Oxford, 1992); J. G. Turner, 'The Libertine Sublime: Love and Death in Restoration England', in *Studies in Eighteenth-century Culture: Volume 19*, ed. L. E. Brown and P. Craddock (Michigan, 1989).

108 Rochester, p. 35; *POAS*, II. 242; Rochester, *Letters*, pp. 75, 99. On female voices and male impersonations, see *Female Poems on Several Occasions. Written by Ephelia* (1679); John Dryden's *Ovid's Epistles. Translated by Several Hand* (1680) in Dryden, *Poems*, pp. 376–412.

109 Rochester, p. 192.

110 A. Andrews, *The Royal Whore* (1971), p. 151.

111 Margaret Cavendish, *Sociable Letters* (1664) in *The Life of the Duke of Newcastle and Other Writings* (Everyman edition, no date), p. 268.

112 Rochester, *Letters*, p. 67.

113 Sir Robert Howard and George Villiers, Duke of Buckingham, *The Country Gentleman* (1976), pp. 24–6; Burnet, II. 3–4; Buckingham, p. 39.

114 *Clarendon – Selections*, ed. G. Huehns (Oxford, 1955; repr. 1978), p. 431.

115 Marvell, *Letters*, p. 343; [Shaftesbury], *A Letter from a Person of Quality* (1675), p. 31.

116 Grey, II. 257.

117 A. Pritchard, 'A Defense of His Private Life by the Second Duke of Buckingham', *Huntington Library Quarterly* 44 (1980–1), 164.

118 R. D. Hume, 'The Myth of the Rake in "Restoration" Comedy', *Studies in the Literary Imagination* 10 (1977).

119 *Character of Coffee-House*, p. 4.

120 See Robert Markley, *Two-edg'd Weapons: Style and Ideology in the Comedies of Etherege, Wycherley and Congreve* (Oxford, 1988); H. Love, *Scribal Publication in Seventeenth-century England* (Oxford, 1993), p. 175; S. Staves, *Players' Scepters – Fictions of Authority in the Restoration* (Lincoln, Nebraska, 1979); R. Zimbardo, 'At Zero Point: Discourse, Politics and Satire in Restoration England', *E[nglish] L[iterary] H[istory]* 59 (1992).

121 *An Elegie on the Famous and Renowned Lady, for Eloquence and Wit, Madam Mary Carlton* (1673), Luttrell I. 20.

122 Head, *Jackson's Recantation*, sig. A2.

123 Head, *Proteus Redivivus*, pp. 7–8.

124 Pepys, IV. 181. On the mask see J. L. Styan, *Restoration Comedy in Performance* (Cambridge, 1986), pp 112–18; D. Roberts, *The Ladies – The Female Patronage of Restoration Drama* (Oxford, 1989), pp. 41, 84–7; A. R. Botica, 'Audience, Playhouse and Play in the Restoration Theatre' (Oxford University D.Phil. thesis, 1985), p. 211. On the development of the masquerade, especially in the eighteenth century, see T. Castle, *Masquerade and Civilization* (1986).

125 Danchin, I. 2. 510.

126 BL Add MS 36916, fols 198, 199, 208; Bulstrode, pp. 169, 312; *HMC Verney*, p. 488; Roberts, *Ladies*, pp. 103, 107; Burnet, I. 473.

127 Dryden, XI. 281.

128 Danchin, I. 2. 460.
129 BL Add MS 70011, fol. 219.
130 BL Add MS 36916, fol. 213; *POAS*, I. 172–5; Dryden IX. 493–5.
131 *The English Rogue* (1679), p. 9.
132 Pepys, VIII. 71–2.
133 Dryden, *Poems*, p. 242; Wycherley, p. 270; Shadwell, *Works*, II. 116.
134 *The Plays of Sir George Etherege*, ed. M. Cordner (Cambridge, 1982), p. 131.
135 Wycherley, p. 330.
136 Etherege, *Plays*, pp. 284–5.
137 E. Howe, *The First English Actresses – Women and Drama 1660–1700* (Cambridge, 1992), pp. 55–62.
138 Dryden, XI. 552; *An Elegy on the Worthy and Famous Actor, Mr Charles Hart* (1683), Luttrell I. 62.
139 Howe, *First English Actresses*, p. 57; Pepys, IX. 189.
140 Pepys, IX. 415.
141 Marvell, *Letters*, p. 356.
142 Hume, *Development of English Drama*, p. 91.
143 L. J. Rosenthal, ' "Counterfeit Scrubbado": Women Actors in the Restoration', *The Eighteenth Century* 34 (1993), 10, 11.
144 *The English Rogue* (1679), pp. 1, 31, 'To the reader'; *HMC Ormonde*, IV. 388; *The Lives of Sundry Notorious Villains* (1678), pp. 27–9.
145 *Life and Death of Major Clancie*, p. 11.
146 J. Todd and E. Spearing (eds), *Counterfeit Ladies* (1994), pp. xliii, xlvii; Pepys, V. 124.
147 Rochester, p. 93.
148 See [George Jones] *Jones of Hatton Garden . . . His Book of Cures* (no date: versions internally dated 1671 and 1673).
149 Rochester, p. 94.
150 Head, *Jackson's Recantation*, sigs. B2–3.
151 Rochester, pp. 72, 38, 48.

5 ENGLAND'S INTEREST AND IMPROVEMENT

1 Hooke bought a copy on 18 July 1673 for six pence: Hooke, pp. 51, 353.
2 Thomas Sprat, *The History of the Royal Society* (1667: ed. J. I. Cope and H. W. Jones, 1959), p. 423. On the earlier history of 'improvement' see C. Webster, *The Great Instauration: Science, Medicine and Reform, 1626–1660* (1975) and M. Leslie and T. Raylor (eds), *Culture and Cultivation in Early Modern England* (Leicester, 1992).
3 *The Present State of Christendom* (1677), *HM*, I. 243; [Slingsby Bethel], *The Interest of Princes and States* (1680), sig. A3. Of help in approaching the notion of interest are: J. A. W. Gunn, *Politics and the Public Interest in the Seventeenth Century* (1969); J. Scott, *Algernon Sidney and the English Republic, 1623–1677* (Cambridge, 1988); D. Wootton (ed.), *Divine Right and Democracy* (1986), pp. 58–77.
4 Sprat, *History*, p. 419.
5 Rochester, *Letters*, p. 207.
6 [Joseph Hill], *The Interest of these United Provinces* (Amsterdam, 1673), sig. B2.

7   Fortrey's tract and William Petyt's *Britannia Languens* (1680) are conveniently reprinted in J. R. McCulloch, *Early English Tracts on Commerce* (1856: reprinted Cambridge, 1970), see pp. 218, 219, 287; Sprat, *History*, p. 426.

8   Dering, p. 36.

9   T&C, p. 72; M. Priestley, 'Anglo-French Trade and the "Unfavourable Balance" Controversy, 1660–1685', *Economic History Review* IV (1951); J. M. Sosin, *English America and the Restoration Monarchy of Charles II* (Lincoln, Nebraska, 1988), pp. 171, 177.

10 *Troia Rediviva* (1674) in R. A. Aubin (ed.), *London in Flames, London in Glory: Poems on the Fire and Rebuilding of London, 1666–1709* (New Brunswick, 1943), p. 215.

11 T&C, pp. 73, 79.

12 J. Thirsk, 'Agricultural Conditions in England, circa 1680', in R. Dunn and M. Dunn (eds), *The World of William Penn* (Philadelphia, 1986), p. 94; P. Jenkins, *The Making of a Ruling Class: The Glamorgan Gentry 1640–1790* (Cambridge, 1983), p. 49; *AH*, p. 77.

13 George Clarke, *A Treatise of Wool and Cattel* (1677), p. 4.

14 F. T. Melton, *Sir Robert Clayton, and the Origins of English Deposit Banking, 1658–1685* (Cambridge, 1986), p. 177.

15 *The Ancient Trades Decayed; Repaired Again* (1678), p. 2.

16 *AH*, pp. 329–31, 239, also see 41–2, 829.

17 Clarke, *Treatise*, pp. 6, 11; T&C, p. 179.

18 *CSPD 1673–5*, p. 319.

19 P. Earle, *The Making of the English Middle Class* (1989), p. 47.

20 T&C, p. 393; Earle, *Making of Middle Class*, pp. 131, 112; R. Grassby, 'The Personal Wealth of the Business Community in Seventeenth-century England', *Economic History Review* XXIII (1970), p. 223.

21 See J. Thirsk, *Economic Policy and Projects* (Oxford, 1978); L. Weatherill, *Consumer Behaviour and Material Culture in Britain, 1660–1760* (1988); M. Spufford, *The Great Reclothing of Rural England: Petty Chapmen and their Wares in the Seventeenth Century* (1984); and C. Shammas, *The Pre-Industrial Consumer in England and America* (Oxford, 1990).

22 *The Grand Concern of England* (1673), in *HM*, VIII. 533.

23 *AH*, p. 288.

24 T&C, p. 82.

25 Melton, *Clayton*, p. 192.

26 T&C, p. 85; *AH*, p. 354.

27 T&C, p. 79.

28 T&C, p. 85: but note that in 1676 Dering sold land for 'about the same I had paid about twenty years before'; Dering, *Diaries*, p. 114.

29 Clarke, *Treatise*, pp. 6, 27, 33.

30 T&C, p. 82; Grey, II. 336.

31 T&C, p. 97.

32 R[ichard] H[aines], *The Prevention of Poverty* (1674), pp. 12–13; Sir William Temple, *Observations upon the United Provinces*, ed. G. Clark (Oxford, 1972), p. 120. A typical lament of consumption is John Hodge's broadsheet *The True and Only Causes of the Want of Money* (1666; 1673), also reprinted in 1673 as *How to Revive the Golden Age*.

33 *CSPD 1675–6*, p. 374.
34 [William Carter], *A Brief Advertisement to the Merchant and Clothier* (1672); W[illiam] C[arter], *Englands Interest by Trade Asserted* (2nd impression, 1671).
35 *AH*, p. 364.
36 Joseph Trevers, *An Essay to the Restoring of our Decayed Trades* (1675), p. 3.
37 *CSPD 1675–6*, pp. 373–5. Also see Carter, *Englands Interest by Trade*; G[eorge] C[arew], *Severall Considerations, offered to the Parliament concerning the Improvement of Trade, Navigation and Commerce, more especially of the Old Draperies and other Woollen Manufactures of England* (1675).
38 *Ancient Trades*, p. 16.
39 Trevers, *Essay*, title page.
40 *CSPD 1675–6*, p. 375.
41 T&C, p. 83.
42 Haines, *Prevention of Poverty*, p. 15.
43 J. O. Appleby, *Economic Thought and Ideology in Seventeenth-century England* (Princeton, 1978), pp. 211, 216.
44 T&C, pp. 70, 71; T. Keirn and F. T. Melton, 'Thomas Manley and the Rate-of-Interest Debate, 1668–1673', *Journal of British Studies* 29 (1990).
45 See *The Diary of John Milward*, ed. C. Robbins (Cambridge, 1938), p. 270.
46 T&C, pp. 83, 70.
47 T&C, p. 84; Melton, *Clayton*, p. 108 and passim.
48 See H. G. Roseveare, *The Financial Revolution 1660–1760* (1991), pp. 19–20.
49 T&C, pp. 83–4.
50 Grey, I. 271–2.
51 Dryden, *Poems*, p. 271.
52 Evelyn, III. 625–6; IV. 185; Melton, *Clayton*, appendices 1 and 2, p. 228.
53 H. J. Habakkuk, 'The Rate of Interest and the Debate on Land Prices', *Economic History Review* V (1952), 40, quoting Philpot, *Reasons and Proposals for a Registry of Deeds* (1671).
54 Bethel, *Interest of Princes*, p. 13; Andrew Yarranton, *Englands Improvements by Sea and Land* (1677), pp. 26–7, 15.
55 W. D. Christie, *The Life of Anthony Ashley Cooper, First Earl of Shaftesbury* (2 vols, 1871), II. appendix I; cf. Haley, pp. 256–8.
56 T&C, p. 80.
57 Carew Reynell, *The True English Interest* (1674), sigs A7–A7v, p. 59; D. Statt, *Foreigners and Englishmen. The Controversy over Immigration and Population, 1660–1760* (Newark, New Jersey, 1995), p. 73.
58 T&C, p. 79.
59 T&C, pp. 71, 535.
60 McCulloch, *Early English Tracts*, p. 234; Haines, *Prevention of Poverty*, p. 2; Priestley, 'Anglo-French Trade', 39.
61 Reynell, *True English Interest*, p. 9.
62 Roger Coke, *A Discourse of Trade* (1670), p. 76; Bethel, *Interest of Princes*, p. 2; Buckingham, p. 94.
63 McCulloch, *Early English Tracts*, p. 237.
64 *Certain Considerations Relating to the Royal African Company of England* (1680), quoted in Appleby, *Economic Thought*, p. 161.

65 Coke, *Discourse of Trade*, sig. Bv; John Evelyn, *Navigation and Commerce* (1674), p. 61; Hill, *Interest of United Provinces*, sig. G2v.
66 Buckingham, p. 91.
67 C. H. Hartmann, *Charles II and Madame* (1934), p. 268.
68 T&C, p. 69.
69 Priestley, 'Anglo-French Trade'.
70 G. Jackson, 'Trade and Shipping', in J. R. Jones (ed.), *The Restored Monarchy* (1979), pp. 143–4.
71 T&C, pp. 532–3, 542, 534, 535.
72 T&C, p. 548.
73 Jackson, 'Trade and Shipping', p. 152.
74 Roger Coke, *England's Improvement* (1675), preface; Evelyn, *Navigation and Commerce*, p. 11; see p. 10 marginal reference to Coke.
75 Hooke, p. 77.
76 Hooke, p. 19.
77 Yarranton, *Englands Improvement*, dedication; Trevers, *Essay*, p. 1; Smith, *Treatise*, dedication.
78 See Roger Coke's *Discourse of Trade* for a particularly unreadable example.
79 W. Letwin, *The Origins of Scientific Economics* (1963), pp. 105–13; Evelyn, IV. 56–61.
80 Letwin, *Origins*, p. 134; C. H. Wilson, *England's Apprenticeship 1603–1763* (1965), p. 168.
81 Reynell, *True English Interest*, pp. 44ff.
82 *AH*, pp. 341–3.
83 Haines, *Prevention of Poverty*, p. 5; *AH*, pp. 339–40; T&C, p. 302.
84 M. Hunter, *Science and Society in Restoration England* (Cambridge, 1981), pp. 95–6; also see F. Willmoth, *Sir Jonas Moore: Practical Mathematics and Restoration Science* (1993) and H. W. Dickinson, *Sir Samuel Morland* (Cambridge, 1970).
85 T&C, p. 177; Wilson, *England's Apprenticeship*, p. 145.
86 Jenkins, *Making of Ruling Class*, p. 52; *AH*, p. 235.
87 T&C, pp. 180–1.
88 T&C, pp. 164–5.
89 *AH*, p. 236.
90 Smith, *England's Improvement*, p. 7; Haines, *Prevention of Poverty*, pp. 8–10.
91 See *AH*, pp. 374–6; Hunter, *Science and Society*, p. 93; R. G. Albion, *Forests and Sea Power: The Timber Problem of the Royal Navy 1652–1862* (Cambridge, Mass., 1926), pp. 130–2, 217–28; Melton, *Clayton*, pp. 174–6.
92 Albion, *Forests and Sea Power*, p. 57.
93 Robert Thoroton, *Antiquities of Nottinghamshire*, ed. J. Throsby (3 vols, 1790–6; reprinted 1972), II. 161.
94 Henry, *Diaries*, p. 242; Aubin, *London in Flames*, p. 210. Also see R. Porter, *London – A Social History* (1994); and chapter 6 below.
95 Aubin, *London in Flames*, p. 172.
96 Appleby, *Economic Thought*, p. 164.
97 McCulloch, *Early English Tracts*, p. 262.
98 Temple, *Observations*, p. 118.
99 Thoroton, *Antiquities*, I. xvii.

100 *Particular Friends: The Correspondence of Samuel Pepys and John Evelyn*, ed. G. de la Bédoyère (Woodbridge, 1997), pp. 111–12, cf. p. 140.

6 SURVEYING AND COMMUNICATION

1 R. A. Skelton, *County Atlases of the British Isles 1579–1850* (1970), pp. 151–2, 153–4.
2 Barber, 'Necessary and Ornament: Map Use in England under the Later Stuarts, 1660–1714', *Eighteenth-century Life*, 14 (1990), 18; S. Tyacke, *London Map-Sellers 1660–1720* (Tring, 1978), p. 10.
3 Tyacke, *London Map-Sellers*, p. i ; Barber, 'Necessary and Ornament', 1–2.
4 Sir William Temple, *Observations upon the United Provinces*, ed. G. Clark (Oxford, 1972), p. 2; Edward Chamberlayne, *Angliae Notitia* (1671 edn), sig. A6.
5 *Aubrey's Brief Lives*, ed. O. L. Dick (Penguin, 1976), pp. 124–5.
6 F. Willmoth, *Sir Jonas Moore: Practical Mathematics and Restoration Science* (1993), p. 148.
7 S. L. Clapp, 'The Subscription Enterprises of John Ogilby and Richard Blome', *Modern Philology* 30 (1932–3), 368. On Ogilby see K. S. van Eerde, *John Ogilby and the Taste of his Times* (Folkestone, 1976); *Ogilby's Road Maps of England and Wales [A Facsimile of Ogilby's 'Britannia' of 1675]* (Reading, 1971); H. M. Wallis and A. H. Robinson (eds), *Cartographical Innovations* (1987), esp. pp. 21, 58, 64.
8 B. Tyson, 'John Adams's Cartographic Correspondence to Sir Daniel Fleming of Rydal Hall, Cumbria 1676–1687', *Geographical Journal* 151 (1985), 29.
9 *CSPD 1672*, p. 332.
10 For instance T. Chubb, *The Printed Maps in the Atlases of Great Britain* (1927; reprinted 1977) p. 81, describes a rival publication, Richard Blome's *Britannia* (1673) as consisting of 'fifty poorly drawn and sketchy maps'.
11 *The A–Z of Restoration London*, ed. R. Hyde, J. Fisher and R. Cline (1992), pp. viii–ix; A. Powell, *John Aubrey and his Friends* (1948: 1963 edn), pp. 149–51, 278–81.
12 Plot, *Natural History*, p. 62.
13 Tyson, 'John Adams', 28.
14 Tyson, 'John Adams', 23.
15 Powell, *Aubrey*, p. 108.
16 See F. T. Melton, *Sir Robert Clayton and the Origins of English Deposit Banking, 1658–1685* (Cambridge, 1986), pp. 170–2.
17 A. W. Richeson, *English Land Measuring to 1800: Instruments and Practices* (Cambridge, Mass., 1966), p. 126.
18 *A–Z*, ed. Hyde, p. x.
19 Ogilby, *Britannia* (1675), preface.
20 Birds-eye views remained popular and reached ever higher standards, especially in the hands of the engraver David Loggan, see his *Oxonia Illustrata* (1675); cf. Wood, II. 313.
21 Tyson, 'John Adams', 31.

22 It is not clear whether Fleming was omitted from the preface or the map itself: Tyson, 'John Adams', 32; Barber, 'Necessary and Ornament', 3.

23 D. Chambers, *The Reinvention of the World – English Writing 1650–1750* (1996), p. 40.

24 Henry, *Diaries*, p. 240–1; *CSPD 1670*, p. 521; cf. *CSPD 1671*, p. 549.

25 *CSPD 1672–3*, p. 346.

26 Henry, *Diaries*, pp. 291, 292; Wood, II. 220, 221, 223, 242, 243, 245; T&C, pp. 379–86.

27 See T&C, pp. 379–86.

28 George Clarke, *A Treatise of Wool and Cattle* (1677), p. 33.

29 Melton, *Clayton*, pp. 13–14; Powell, *Aubrey*, pp. 157, 137; also see *Savile Correspondence*, p. 161.

30 On the Post Office see A. Marshall, *Intelligence and Espionage in the Reign of Charles II, 1660–1685* (Cambridge, 1994), ch. 2; J. Sutherland, *The Restoration Newspaper and its Development* (Cambridge, 1986), pp. 91–2, 116–17; P. Fraser, *The Intelligence of the Secretaries of State and their Monopoly of Licensed News* (Cambridge, 1956), *passim*; M. Knights, *Politics and Opinion in Crisis, 1678–1681* (Cambridge, 1994), p. 173.

31 BL Add MS 77011, fol. 226v.

32 N. Penney (ed.), *The Household Account Book of Sarah Fell of Swarthmoor Hall 1673–78* (Cambridge, 1920), introduction, pp. 443, 459.

33 Tyson, 'John Adams', 32.

34 See M. Spufford, *The Great Reclothing of Rural England: Petty Chapmen and their Wares in the Seventeenth Century* (1984); L. Weatherill, *Consumer Behaviour and Material Culture in Britain, 1660–1760* (1988).

35 R. A. Aubin, *London in Flames, London in Glory: Poems on the Fire and Rebuilding of London, 1666–1709* (New Brunswick, 1943), pp. 159, 217; Thomas Jordan, *London in Splendor* (1673), p. 7.

36 Rochester, *Letters*, p. 134.

37 S. E. Whyman, 'Land and Trade Revisited: The Case of John Verney, London Merchant and Baronet, 1660–1720', *London Journal* 22 (1997), 19; Aubin, *London in Flames*, p. 214.

38 J. L. Howgego, *Printed Maps of London* (1964), pp. 55, 61; also see P. Glanville, *London in Maps* (1972).

39 *A–Z*, ed. Hyde et al., pp. vi–vii.

40 See *Lorenzo Magalotti at the Court of Charles II*, ed. W. E. K. Middleton (Ontario, 1980), pp. 123–9.

41 Quoted in E. Jones, 'The First West End Comedy', *Proceedings of the British Academy* 68 (1982), 226.

42 Dering, *Diaries*, pp. 113, 114, 16.

43 T. F. Reddaway, *The Rebuilding of London after the Great Fire* (1940), p. 302. On the development of the West End see N. G. Brett-James, *The Growth of Stuart London* (1935); L. Stone, 'The Residential Development of the West End of London in the Seventeenth Century', in B. Malament (ed.), *After the Reformation* (Manchester, 1980).

44 Wycherley, p. 248.

45 B. Lillywhite, *London Coffee Houses* (1963), pp. 97, 95.

46 Bathsua Makin, *An Essay to Revive the Ancient Education of Gentlewomen* (1673), p. 43.
47 Marvell, *Letters*, p. 342; cf. Evelyn, IV. 75.
48 Rochester, *Letters*, p. 126; Wycherley, p. 282; *The Complete Works of Thomas Shadwell*, ed. M. Summers (5 vols, 1927), II. 121.
49 Marvell, *Letters*, p. 344.
50 18 January 1681, quoted in Sutherland, *Restoration Newspaper*, pp. 103–4.
51 Shadwell, *Works*, II. 110.
52 *HMC, 13th Report, Appendix, Pt II (Portland MSS)*, II. 270.
53 P. Borsay, 'The London Connection: Cultural Diffusion and the Eighteenth-century Provincial Town', *London Journal* 19 (1994), 24, 27.
54 *Savile Correspondence*, p. 157.
55 *AH*, pp. 568–9.
56 *Raillerie a la Mode* (1673), p. 4.
57 Andrew Marvell, *Mr Smirke: Or the Divine in Mode* (1676) in *The Complete Works of Andrew Marvell*, ed. A. B. Grosart (4 vols, 1872–5), IV. 60–1.
58 Whyman, 'John Verney', 19.
59 Sutherland, *Restoration Newspaper*, p. 97.
60 Williamson, II. 68; P. Seaward, *The Cavalier Parliament and the Reconstruction of the Old Regime, 1661–1667* (Cambridge, 1989), p. 73; H. Love, *Scribal Publication in Seventeenth-century England* (Oxford, 1993), p. 204; S. Pincus, ' "Coffee Politicians Does Create": Coffeehouses and Restoration Political Culture', *Journal of Modern History* 67 (1995), 813. Also relevant is C. J. Sommerville, *The News Revolution in England* (Oxford, 1996).
61 BL Microfilm M904, Thynne MS 42, fol. 164; W. Westergaard, *The First Triple Alliance: The Letters of Christopher Lindenov Danish Envoy to London 1668–1672* (New Haven, 1947), p. 291; Bulstrode, p. 139.
62 Hooke, pp. 221, 222.
63 Rochester, *Letters*, p. 125.
64 Marshall, *Intelligence*, p. 39.
65 Morrice P, fol. 317; Sutherland, *Restoration Newspaper*, p. 74.
66 Quoted in M. Knights, *Politics and Opinion in Crisis, 1678–81* (Cambridge, 1994), p. 170.
67 See R. B. Walker, 'Advertising in London Newspapers, 1650–1750', *Business History* XV (1973), 114–15; C. Nelson and M. Seccombe (eds), *British Newspapers and Periodicals 1641–1700* (New York, 1987).
68 Sutherland, *Restoration Newspaper*, pp. 15–16.
69 *CSPD 1678*, p. 304.
70 *CSPD 1672–3*, p. 585.
71 J. G. Muddiman, *The King's Journalist 1659–1689* (1923), p. 205.
72 Browning, *Danby*, III. 2–3.
73 Fraser, *Intelligence*, pp. 119–20.
74 Marvell, *Mr Smirke*, p. 19.
75 Bod. Tanner MS 38, fol. 14.
76 *HMC Verney*, p. 486.
77 Marvell, *Letters*, p. 111.
78 [Marchamont Nedham], *A Pacquet of Advices* (1675), p. 7.
79 See chapter 3 above for Howard; the 'Alarum' is PRO SP 29/266, fol. 152.

80 *HMC Verney*, p. 479.

81 Knights, *Politics and Opinion*, p. 171; J. Walker, 'Censorship of the Press under Charles II', *History* XXXV (1950), 229.

82 T. J. Crist, 'Francis Smith and the Opposition Press in England, 1660–1688', (Cambridge University Ph.D. thesis, 1977), p. x. It is likely, but not certain, that Bohun was distinguishing between manuscript libels and printed replies.

83 Love, *Scribal Publication*, pp. 257–8; cf. the reference in *Timon*, Rochester, p. 56..

84 BL MS Add 28043, fol. 19v; Sutherland, *Restoration Newspaper*, p. 18.

85 See L. Schwoerer, 'Liberty of the Press and Public Opinion, 1660–1695', in J. R. Jones (ed.), *Liberty Secured?* (1992).

86 See J. Hetet, 'A Literary Underground in Restoration England: Printers and Dissenters in the Context of Constraints 1660–1689' (Cambridge University Ph.D. thesis, 1987), pp. 44, 64–5, 79–80.

87 See Hetet, 'Literary Underground', pp. 175–6; for Lucas see ch. 8 below; *CSPD 1677–78*, p. 449.

88 *CSPD 1676–7*, p. 51.

89 Crist, 'Francis Smith', pp. 48–9, 86–7; Hetet, 'Literary Underground', p. 176; Morrice P, fol. 57; cf. Marvell, *Letters*, p. 345. On Cary see A. G. Matthews, *Calamy Revised* (Oxford, 1934); and on the King's interest in the case, BL Add MS 28043, fols 5–7; BL Add MS 25124, fol. 121.

90 Hetet, 'Literary Underground', pp. 79–80.

91 Crist, 'Francis Smith'; Hetet, 'Literary Underground'; Adrian John, *The Nature of the Book: Print and Knowledge in the Making* (Chicago, 1998).

92 Crist, 'Francis Smith', pp. 87–9.

93 Love, *Scribal Publication*, p. 74.

94 Love, *Scribal Publication*, p. 86.

95 Bod. MS don. b 8, p. 235.

96 Marvell, *Letters*, pp. 349–50; also see F. H. Ellis, 'John Freke and *The History of Insipids*', *Philological Quarterly* 44 (1965).

97 *CSPD 1675–6*, p. 490; *CSPD 1676–7*, pp. 182, 334.

98 Morrice P, fols 59, 53, 58, 61; Haley, pp. 424–6.

99 Pincus, 'Coffee Does Politicians Create', 813.

100 Morrice P, fol. 58.

101 BL Stowe MS 186, fol. 21.

102 Morrice P, fol. 317; *CSPD 1675–6*, p. 563.

103 Williamson, I. 194, II. 24.

104 Knights, *Politics and Opinion*, p. 155.

105 *CSPD 1675–6*, pp. 456–7.

106 Williamson, I. 133.

107 Pepys, X. 71.

108 Browning, *Danby*, I. 194–5; Hooke, pp. 204, 210; Love, *Scribal Publication*, pp. 241–2.

109 Bod. MS don. b 8, p. 557.

110 *CSPD 1676–7*, p. 368; Lillywhite, *London Coffee Houses*, p. 323; BL Add MS 32095, fol. 38 (*POAS*, I. xxxviii).

7 TYRANNIC LOVE: SEX, MARRIAGE AND POLITICS

1   Dryden, *Poems*, pp. 227–8; also see Dryden, X. 192; R. D. Hume, *The Development of English Drama in the late Seventeenth Century* (Oxford, 1976), pp. 271, 191; P. Holland, *The Ornament of Action* (Cambridge, 1979), p. ix; E. Howe, *The First English Actresses – Woman and Drama 1660–1700* (Cambridge, 1992), pp. 72, 98.

2   T. Harris, *London Crowds in the Reign of Charles II* (Cambridge, 1987), pp. 82–91.

3   Pepys, IX. 81.

4   Pepys, IX. 410.

5   A. L., *The Woman as Good as the Man* (1677), translator to reader.

6   BL Add MS 40860, fol. 6.

7   Hooke, p. 3 for the relevant symbol, and see *passim*, but especially pp. 268, 273, 299, for his niece Grace.

8   Rochester, *Letters*, p. 175; H. G. Roseveare, 'Prejudice and Policy: Sir George Downing as Parliamentary Entrepreneur', in D. C. Coleman and P. Mathias (eds), *Enterprise and History* (Cambridge, 1984), p. 146.

9   Rochester, p. 31.

10   Evelyn, III. 465–6; *Angliae Speculum Morale* (1670), pp. 14–15.

11   Dryden, XIV. 5; *Angliae Speculum Morale*, p. 29.

12   *Savile Correspondence*, p. 62; Rochester, *Letters*, pp. 172–3.

13   Pepys, IX. 218; E. Legh [Lady Newton], *Lyme Letters 1600–1760* (1925), p. 36.

14   *Lorenzo Magalotti at the Court of Charles II*, ed. W. E. K. Middleton (Ontario, 1980), p. 125.

15   See Danchin I. 2. 698–701; *The Gyldenstolpe Manuscript Miscellany of Poems by John Wilmot, Earl of Rochester and Other Restoration Authors*, ed. B. Danielsson and D. M. Vieth (Stockholm, 1967), pp. 115, 98, 63; H. Love (ed.), *The Penguin Book of Restoration Verse* (1968), pp. 138–9; Rochester, *Letters*, p. 259; Wycherley, pp. 347–53; Pepys, IX. 218–19; *HMC Verney*, p. 477.

16   Dryden, XIV. 60–1.

17   Rochester, p. 255; and see R. Thompson, *Unfit for Modest Ears* (1979).

18   *The Character of the Town Gallant* (1675), p. 2; Pepys, IX. 21–2; *CSPD 1676–7*, pp. 492–3. Also see J. G. Turner, 'Pepys and the Private Parts of Monarchy', in G. Maclean (ed.), *Culture and Society in the Stuart Restoration* (Cambridge, 1996).

19   Rochester, *Letters*, pp. 62–3; for the poem see Rochester, pp. 40–2; and on its dissemination the little noticed letter by Armorer in *CSPD 1673–5*, p. 108, the related letter in Williamson, II. 132; and H. Love's two articles in *Studies in Bibliography*, 46 (1993) and 49 (1996).

20   Pepys, IV. 209–10.

21   Rochester, pp. 89, 35.

22   See R. Trumbach, 'The Birth of the Queen', in V. Duberman and J. Chauncey (eds), *Hidden from History: Reclaiming the Gay and Lesbian Past* (Penguin, 1991); J. Kenyon, *The Popish Plot* (1972: 1974 Penguin edn.), pp. 54–5.

23   Howe, *First English Actresses*, p. 42.

24 Dryden, X. 176.
25 Dryden, *Poems*, pp. 248–9.
26 Quoted in M. Novak, 'Margery Pinchwife's "London Disease": Restoration Comedy and the Libertine Offensive of the 1670s', *Studies in the Literary Imagination*, X (1977), 21.
27 Wycherley, p. 348–9. The identification of the maids of honour as Wycherley's target in D. Roberts, *The Ladies – Female Patronage of Restoration Drama* (Oxford, 1989), pp. 107–9, seems a little forced.
28 Joseph Arrowsmith, *The Reformation* (1672: Augustan Reprint Society Publications 237–8, Los Angeles, 1986), p. 48.
29 See Hume, *Development of English Drama*, pp. 97–104, 280–99.
30 *The Works of Thomas Shadwell*, ed. M. Summer (5 vols, 1927), III. 139, 179.
31 *The Muse of Newmarket* (1680), pp. 2, 17.
32 *HMC Rutland MSS*, II. 36.
33 Dryden, *Poems*, p. 368.
34 Sir William Temple, *Observations upon the United Provinces of the Netherlands*, ed. G. Clark (Oxford, 1972), p. 89.
35 Dryden, XI. 110.
36 Dryden, XIII. 89, 39, 88, 110.
37 Aphra Behn, *The Rover and Other Works* (Penguin, 1992), p. 347.
38 *The Plays of Sir George Etherege*, ed. M. Cordner (Cambridge, 1982), pp. 288–9.
39 Roberts, *Ladies*, p. 104.
40 Dering, *Diaries*, pp. 112, 113.
41 R. Grassby, *The English Gentleman in Trade – The Life and Works of Sir Dudley North 1641–1691* (Oxford, 1991), p. 209.
42 F. T. Melton, *Sir Robert Clayton and the Origins of English Deposit Banking 1658–1685* (Cambridge, 1986), p. 48.
43 Josselin, pp. 593, 596, 597, 600.
44 *The Commonplace Book of Sir Edward Bayntun of Bromham*, ed. J. Freeman (Wiltshire Record Society, XLIII, 1988), pp. 20–1.
45 Marvell, *Letters*, p. 150. The best account is by David Allen, 'Bridget Hyde and Lord Treasurer Danby's Alliance with Lord Mayor Vyner', *Guildhall Studies in London History*, 2 (1975).
46 Browning, *Danby*, I. 288–9; *HMC Verney*, p. 470; F. R. Harris, *The Life of Edward Mountagu KG, First Earl of Sandwich* (2 vols, 1912), II. 234–5; also see Marvell, *Letters*, p. 340; and a very funny account of Mrs Colombine's 'abduction', in *Savile Correspondence*, pp. 48–9.
47 BL Add MS 27447, fol. 331.
48 Josselin, p. 626; BL Add MS 70012, fol. 21r.
49 *Lyme Letters*, p. 36.
50 Quoted in R. Houlbrooke, *Religion, Death and the Family in England 1480–1750* (Oxford, 1998), p. 147.
51 BL Add MS 40860, fols 58v, 77v, cf. fols 69, 71v; G. E. C[okayne], *The Complete Peerage* (13 vols, 1910–59), IX. 27.
52 Richard Leigh, *Poems*, ed. H. Macdonald (Oxford, 1947), p. 50.
53 R. Ollard, *Cromwell's Earl – A Life of Edward Montagu, First Earl of Sandwich* (1994), pp. 250–1.

54 Buckingham, p. 129.
55 Pepys, VIII. 17.
56 Henry, *Diaries*, p. 257; T. H., *A Treatise of Marriage* (1673), sig. A3.
57 *CSPD 1672*, pp. 456–7; *The Confession and Execution of Elizabeth Lillyman* (1675).
58 *Remarks upon Remarques* (1673), p. 60.
59 *Character of Town Gallant*, p. 2; *Remarques on the Humours and Conversation of the Gallants of the Town* (1673, 1st edn.), p. 81; *The Town Misses Declaration* (1675); *A Broad-Side against Marriage* (1675), Luttrell II. 137; William Seymar, *Conjugium Conjurgum, Or, Some Serious Considerations on Marriage* (1673), p. 12, sig. a10v; *Gyldenstolpe Miscellany*, p. 59; also see W.P. *The Flying Post* (1678), pp. 10–13, 43–5.
60 *London Drollery* (1673), p. 54.
61 *A Vindication of Marriage [sic] Life* (1675), Luttrell II. 138; *Reflexions on Marriage and the Poetic Discipline* (1673), p. 15.
62 A. B., *Learn to Lye Warm* (1672), p. 38.
63 Harris, *Sandwich*, II. 326.
64 *Reflexions*, pp. 55, 27–8.
65 *Reflexions*, pp. 6–7, 23.
66 *Reflexions*, pp. 118–20.
67 Dryden, XI. 135.
68 Aphra Behn, *Love Letters between a Nobleman and his Sister* (Penguin, 1996), p. 16.
69 Novak, 'Margery Pinchwife's "London Disease"'.
70 Pepys, VIII. 368.
71 Rochester, *Letters*, p. 189; Rochester, p. 30.
72 *The Works of George Savile Marquis of Halifax*, ed. M. N. Brown (3 vols, Oxford, 1989), II. 490.
73 *POAS*, I. 244.
74 G. E. C., *Complete Peerage*, VI. appendix F.
75 Pepys, VIII. 286; IX. 515.
76 Bulstrode, p. 311.
77 See C. Price, *Cold Caleb – The Scandalous Life of Ford Grey* (1956) and Behn, *Love Letters*.
78 J. H. Wilson, *Court Satires of the Restoration* (Columbus, Ohio, 1976), p. 236.
79 Rochester, *Letters*, p. 93.
80 O. Millar, *Sir Peter Lely 1618–80* (1978), p. 63.
81 Rochester, pp. 195, 61, 194; also see W. Chernaik, *Sexual Freedom in Restoration Literature* (Cambridge, 1995).
82 See Wilson, *Court Satires*, p. 38 and *passim.*
83 See note 19 above.
84 Wilson, *Court Satires*, p. xvi.
85 Rochester, p. 80.
86 Rochester, *Letters*, p. 198.
87 Bulstrode, p. 305.
88 Wilson, *Court Satires*, pp. 26–7; Rochester, p. 241.
89 Bulstrode, p. 303.
90 Bulstrode, pp. 304–5; *Gyldenstolpe Miscellany*, pp. 227–35; Marvell, *Letters*, p. 340.

91 Love, *Penguin Book of Restoration Verse*, p, 224; Wilson, *Court Satires*, pp. 38–9.
92 Ollard, *Cromwell's Earl*, p. 251.
93 H[enry] C[are], *Galliae Speculum, or, A New Survey of the French Court and Camp* (1673), p. 14.
94 Evelyn, III. 596; I. Sinclair (ed.), *The Pyramid and the Urn: The Life in Letters of a Restoration Squire William Lawrence of Shurdington (1636–1697)* (Far Thrupp, 1994), letter 12, which is misdated.
95 Pepys, IV. 191.
96 B. Sharp, 'Popular Political Opinion in England 1660–1685', *Journal of the History of European Ideas*, 10 (1989), 19; K. H. D. Haley, *William of Orange and the English Opposition 1672–4* (Oxford, 1953), p. 71; also see Harris, *London Crowds*; P. Hammond, 'The King's Two Bodies', in J. Black and J. Gregory (eds), *Culture, Politics and Society in Britain 1660–1800* (Manchester, 1991).
97 Pepys, VIII. 362; J. Spurr, *The Restoration Church of England, 1646–1689* (New Haven, 1991), p. 248.
98 *The English Ballance* (1972), p. 21.
99 Evelyn, III. 589–90, 592–3.
100 Behn, *Love Letters*, p. 11.
101 Marvell, *Letters*, p. 317.
102 Dryden, *Poems*, p. 455.
103 See M. A. Goldie, 'Contextualizing Dryden's Absalom: William Lawrence, the laws of marriage, and the case for King Monmouth', in D. B. Hamilton and R. Strier (eds), *Religion, Literature and Politics in Post-Reformation England 1540–1688* (Cambridge, 1996).
104 *POAS*, I. 427.
105 BL Add MS 36916, fol. 221; Evelyn, IV. 74.
106 Marvell, *Letters*, p. 325.
107 *HMC Verney*, p. 467.
108 Reresby, p. 149.
109 BL Add MS 70012, fol. 228; *CSPD 1675–6*, pp. 473–5.
110 Halifax, *Works*, II. 490–1; Rochester, *Letters*, p. 232.
111 Rochester, *Letters*, p. 187.
112 Rochester, *Letters*, pp. 200–1; A. Andrews, *The Royal Whore* (1971), pp. 201–10.
113 By Rachel Weil in 'Sometimes a Scepter is only a Scepter: Pornography and Politics in Restoration England', in L. Hunt (ed.), *The Invention of Pornography* (New York, 1993), p. 142. Weil is one of several excellent commentators on these questions: see R. Elias, 'Political Satire in *Sodom*', *S[tudies in] E[nglish] L[iterature]* 18 (1978); Hammond, 'King's Two Bodies'; H. Love, *Scribal Publication in Seventeenth-century England* (Oxford, 1993), ch. 6; H. M. Weber, *Paper Bullets: Print and Kingship under Charles II* (Lexington, Kentucky, 1996), ch. 3; S. N. Zwicker, *Lines of Authority – Politics and English Literary Culture 1649–1689* (Ithaca, 1993), ch. 4. For the comparison with France see R. Darnton, *The Forbidden Best-sellers of Pre-Revolutionary France* (1996), ch. 8.
114 Bod. MS don. b 8, pp. 452–5; *Lyme Letters*, pp. 85–9.
115 Bod. MS don. b 8, pp. 562, 184, 185.
116 *POAS*, I. 232.

117 *POAS*, I. 250–1.
118 Rochester, p. 30.
119 On *Sodom* see Weber, *Paper Bullets*, pp. 112–37; Thompson, *Unfit for Modest Ears*, pp. 125–7; Weil, 'Scepter', p. 143; cf. Richard Perrinchief, *The Syracusan Tyrant* (1676), p. 266, for another reference to buggery and tyranny.
120 Pepys, IV. 136–7.
121 Rochester, p. 30.
122 *POAS*, I. 161; cf. *A New Ballad of King Edward and Jane Shore* (1671).
123 *POAS*, I. 152, 426.
124 Williamson, II. 35.
125 *POAS*, I. 169–71.
126 *POAS*, I. 233.
127 Pepys, VIII. 181.
128 *POAS*, I. 427–8.
129 *POAS*, I. 152.
130 Sinclair (ed.), *Pyramid and Urn*, letter 12.
131 *POAS*, I. 281.
132 Pepys, VIII. 183.
133 *The Poems of John Oldham*, ed. H. F. Brooks with R. Selden (Oxford, 1987), p. 345.
134 *POAS*, I. 146.
135 *Gyldenstolpe Miscellany*, p. 302.
136 Rochester, p. 68; Weil, 'Scepter', pp. 148–9.
137 The term is Love's, see *Scribal Publication*, p. 175.
138 A. Bryson, *From Courtesy to Civility* (Oxford, 1998), p. 273.
139 Rochester, *Letters*, p. 151.
140 Oldham, *Poems*, introduction, p. xliv and note.
141 Weil, 'Scepter', p. 138.
142 Weil, 'Scepter', p. 146.
143 *Annals of Love* (1672), sig. A2–A2v.
144 R. Braverman, *Plots and Counterplots: Sexual Politics and the Body Politic in English Literature 1660–1730* (Cambridge, 1993), p. 100 and pp. 98–113 *passim*; Weber, *Paper Bullets*, p. 111.
145 Dryden, XIII. 27–8.
146 Dryden, X. 156, 158–9; Care, *Galliae Speculum*, p. 23.

8 POLITICS, PIETY AND TOLERATION

1 See T. Harris, ' "Lives, Liberties and Estates" ': Rhetorics of Liberty in the Reign of Charles II', in T. Harris, P. Seaward and M. Goldie (eds), *The Politics of Religion in Restoration England* (Oxford, 1990); J. R. Jones (ed.), *Liberty Secured? Britain Before and After 1688* (Stanford, California, 1992); cf. Carew's comments in *HMC Verney*, p. 492.
2 [Marchamont Nedham?] *Truth and Honesty in Plain English* (1679), p. 14.
3 H. Nenner, 'Liberty, Law and Property: The Constitution in Retrospect from 1689', in Jones (ed.), *Liberty Secured?*, p. 89.
4 *CSPD 1670*, p. 322.
5 Bulstrode, p. 282.

6   Harris, 'Lives . . .', p. 220.
7   [Andrew Marvell], *An Account of the Growth of Popery and Arbitrary Government in England* ('Amsterdam', 1677), p. 4.
8   Nenner, 'Liberty, Law and Property', p. 98.
9   Nenner, 'Liberty, Law and Property', p. 98.
10 See T. A. Green, *Verdict According to Conscience* (Chicago, 1985), ch. 6; A. F. Havinghurst, 'The Judiciary and Politics in the Reign of Charles II', *Law Quarterly Review* 66 (1950), esp. pp. 76, 230: even on Havinghurst's own estimation, it cannot be said that a case has been established that Charles interfered with the judiciary for political ends.
11 Sir Philip Warwick, *A Discourse of Government* (1694), p. 41; [Marchamont Nedham], *A Pacquet of Advices* (1676), p. 10.
12 Sir Peter Leicester, *Charges to the Grand Jury at Quarter Sessions 1660–1677*, ed. E. M. Halcrow (Chetham Society, V, 1953), p. 66.
13 Nenner, 'Liberty, Law and Property', p. 111.
14 Dering, *Diaries*, p. 175.
15 Warwick, *Discourse*, pp. 41, 45; Nedham, *Truth and Honesty*, p. 2.
16 W. D. Christie, *The Life of Anthony Ashley Cooper, First Earl of Shaftesbury* (2 vols, 1871), appendix VI, p. xcii.
17 Lord Keeper Finch's speech to parliament, 7 January 1674: PH, 617–18; Grey, II. 25.
18 Reresby, p. 177, note; John Miller, 'A Moderate in the First Age of Party: The Dilemmas of Sir John Holland, 1675–85', *English Historical Review*, CXIV (1999), 878.
19 Marvell, *Letters*, p. 177.
20 *A Seasonable Question* (1676), quoted by J. M. Wallace, *Destiny His Choice – The Loyalism of Andrew Marvell* (Cambridge, 1968: 1980 edition), p. 222.
21 Christie, *Life of Shaftesbury*, appendix VI, p. xcii.
22 Bod. Carte MS 72, fol. 255.
23 BL Add MS 40860, fols 12, 50.
24 Reresby, pp. 111–12.
25 *Savile Correspondence*, p. 45.
26 *Essex Papers*, I. 72, 238.
27 HMC *Ormonde*, IV. 454; Bod. MS don. b 8, pp. 259, 257; *A Seasonable Argument* (1677), pp. 10, 16.
28 Dering, *Diaries*, pp. 111, 112, 115.
29 HMC *Buckinghamshire, Lindsey etc*, pp. 386–7.
30 Grey, II. 334.
31 *Savile Correspondence*, p. 25.
32 HOP, I. 306, 368, 328, 303.
33 HOP, I. 289–90 (strictly, the backing for Lane was from the ministers at court).
34 HOP, I. 325; P. Gauci, *Politics and Society in Great Yarmouth, 1660–1722* (Oxford, 1996), ch. 4.
35 See chapter 3 above.
36 Sir Thomas Meres in Grey, III. 136, cf. 17; II. 202.
37 PRO, SP 104/176, fol. 289.

38 BL Add MS 36926, fols 215, 216; also see Marvell, *Letters*, 322–3; Josselin, pp. 558–9.
39 There are several manuscript versions of the speech and two printed ones, *My Lord Lucas His Speech . . . London. Printed in the Year 1670* dates from 1673, as does the version with the imprint 'Middleburgh, 1673'. The MS in the State Papers is printed in *CSPD 1671*, pp. 93–4; BL Stowe MS 182, fols 96–7, and Bod. MS don. b 8, pp. 198–201, have only minor verbal differences to the printed versions; as does the text printed in *Sitwell Letters*, pp. 85–7. The version in *PH*, 473–6, is taken from the printed version. On the details of the speech and its dispersal, see *CSPD 1671*, pp. 137, 154, 166; Marvell, *Letters*, pp. 322–3; and for Lucas see *DNB* under Charles Lucas.
40 *My Lord Lucas His Speech*, pp. 4, 5.
41 BL Add MS 36916, fol. 212.
42 *The English Ballance* (1672), p. 100.
43 The denunciation is a Stationers' Company Hall MS quoted by J. Hetet 'A Literary Underground in Restoration England' (Cambridge University Ph.D. thesis, 1987), p. 113; also see K. H. D. Haley, *William of Orange and the English Opposition* (Oxford, 1953), p. 166.
44 J. Godwin, 'Basil Feilding, the second earl of Denbigh and the Test Act', *Historical Journal* 111–15.
45 Holland's speech is at Grey, III. 294–5 and PH, 746–7. The original, in Bod. MS Tanner 238, is to be edited by Dr Paul Seaward. For a discussion see Miller, 'Moderate in First Age of Party', 861–2.
46 Marvell, *Account*, pp. 55–6.
47 For examples of the term see *HOP*, I. 336, 431, 468; Grey, II. 334.
48 *HMC Buckinghamshire, Lindsey etc*, p. 384.
49 *HOP*, II. 36; *A Relation* (1673), pp. 9, 11.
50 Grey, II. 335.
51 *HOP*, II. 271.
52 Dering, pp. 128–9, also see Grey, II. 52–3.
53 See Grey, II. 52–3; F. R. Harris, *The Life of Edward Mountagu KG, First Earl of Sandwich* (2 vols, 1912), II. 334–5; *CSPD 1678*, p. 170; Reresby, p. 111; BL Add MS 36916, fol. 166.
54 Bulstrode, p. 316; Williamson, II. 150.
55 Nedham, *Pacquet*, p. 4.
56 See Anglesey's diary, BL Add MS 40860; and for Harley, J. Spurr, *English Puritanism, 1603–1689* (1998), p. 144 and ch. 9 for the broader context.
57 Henry, *Diaries*, p. 234.
58 Bod. Tanner MS 40, fols 18–19.
59 BL Add MS 40860, fols 11v, 23v, 27, 28v; Bedfordshire Record Office, Lucas MSS, L30/20/19; BL Add MS 70011, fols 226, 152.
60 [Rober]T [Boyl]E, *Some Considerations about the Reasonableness of Reason and Religion* (1675), p. i; BL Add MS 19333, fol. 2v; BL Add MS 17012, fol. 22; John Fell, *The Character of the Last Daies* (Oxford, 1675), p. 19.
61 Wood, II. 334, 429, 332, 240.
62 Clement Ellis, *The Vanity of Scoffing* (1674), p. 7.

63 George Herbert, *A Priest to the Temple* (1671), preface by Barnabas Oley, sig. a verso.

64 Reresby, p. 208.

65 See, for example, Walter Charleton's *Natural History of the Passions* (1674).

66 *Locke – Political Essays*, ed. M. Goldie (Cambridge, 1997), pp. xxiii, 237–45.

67 A. Le Grand, *The Man without Passion; or the Wise Stoick* (1675).

68 Miles Barne, *A Sermon Preached before the King at Whitehall, October 17 1675* (1675), pp. 21–2; Matthew Barker, *Natural Religion* (1674), p. 4; Meric Casaubon, *Of Credulity and Incredulity* (1670), p. 13.

69 See J. Spurr, ' "Rational Religion" in Restoration England', *Journal of the History of Ideas* XLIX (1988).

70 *The Voice of the Nation* (1675); Ellis, *Vanity of Scoffing*, p. 30; also see M. Hunter, 'The Problem of "Atheism" in Early Modern England', *Transactions of the Royal Historical Society* 35 (1985); J. Spurr, *The Restoration Church of England, 1646–1689* (New Haven, 1991), pp. 249–75.

71 [Richard Allestree], *The Government of the Tongue* (1674) in *Works of the Author of the Whole Duty of Man* (Oxford, 1684), part II, p. 109.

72 Bod. Tanner MS 41, fol. 49.

73 *The Act of Parliament against religious meetings proved to be the Bishops act* (1670), p. 6.

74 *The Character of an Informer* (1675), pp. 1, 3; *An Elegy upon Marsh* (1675), Luttrell I. 83. Also see Josselin, p. 554; M. Goldie, 'The Hilton Gang and the Purge of London in the 1680s', in H. Nenner (ed.), *Politics and the Political Imagination in Later Stuart Britain* (Rochester NY, 1997), p. 45.

75 C. Holmes, *Seventeenth-century Lincolnshire* (Lincoln, 1980), p. 230.

76 *The Narrative of the Persecutions of Agnes Beaumont*, ed. V. J. Camden (East Lansing, Michigan, 1992).

77 John Cave, *A Sermon preached in a Country-Audience* (1679), p. 5; John Goodman, *A Serious and Compassionate Inquiry* (1675), p. 235; William Denton, *The Burnt Child* (1675), p. 115.

78 Samuel Parker, *A Discourse of Ecclesiastical Politie* (1669: 3rd edn 1671), p. 277.

79 I have attempted a full-scale characterization in *Restoration Church*. For a very different interpretation see the various writings of Mark Goldie, especially his 'Priestcraft and the birth of Whiggism', in N. Phillipson and Q. Skinner (eds), *Political Discourse in Early Modern Britain* (Cambridge, 1993), pp. 212–13 and 'The Theory of Religious Intolerance in Restoration England', in O. Grell, N. Tyacke and J. Israel (eds), *From Persecution to Toleration: the Glorious Revolution and Religion in England* (Oxford, 1991), pp. 334, 345, 368. As Dr Goldie points out in 'Priestcraft', his interpretation rests heavily on whig perceptions; mine, on the other hand, tends to take the Anglican clergy at their own estimation with all the dangers that that entails.

80 R[ichard] A[llen], *England's Distempers* (1677), dedication to Charles II.

81 Goodman, *Serious . . . Inquiry*, p. 233.

82 See M. Goldie and J. Spurr, 'Politics and the Restoration Parish: Edward Fowler and the Struggle for St Giles Cripplegate', *English Historical Review* CIII (1994).

83 See the following for an introduction and further references: G. De Krey, 'Rethinking the Restoration: Dissenting Cases for Conscience, 1667–1672', *Historical Journal* 38 (1995); G. Schochet, 'Samuel Parker, religious diversity, and the ideology of persecution', in R. Lund (ed.), *The Margins of Orthodoxy* (Cambridge, 1995); Spurr, *Restoration Church*, pp. 70–2.

84 *An Expedient* (1672), p. 6.

85 William Temple, *Observations upon the United Provinces*, ed. G. Clark (Oxford, 1972), p. 106. Also see W[illiam] A[glionby], *The Present State of the United Provinces* (1669: 1671 edn), p. 351.

86 *Representation*, p. 22; Parker, *Discourse*, p. 7.

87 Buckingham, pp. 102–3; Leicester, *Charges*, pp. 78–9, 82.

88 Marvell, *Account*, p. 33; Harris, 'Lives . . .', p. 230.

89 *Some Reasons Briefly Suggested, Which have prevail'd with the Dissenters in Bristol to Continue Their Open Meetings However Persecuted or Disturb'd* (1675), p. 1; Falkner, *Christian Loyalty*, ch. VIII, section 1.

90 Robert Conold, *The Notion of Schism* (1676; 2nd edn, 1677), p. 65; John Meriton, *The Obligation of a Good Conscience to Civil Obedience* (1670), pp. 8–10.

91 See epigraph from Temple above; *Some Reasons*, p. 2, which also cites Jeremy Taylor and Samuel Parker in its own support.

92 William Starkey, *An Apology for the Laws Ecclesiastical Established* (1675), pp. 169–70.

93 J. Spurr, 'Schism and the Restoration Church', *Journal of Ecclesiastical History* 41 (1990).

94 Goldie, 'Intolerance'.

95 Clifford, *Treatise*, p. 19.

96 See J. Parkin, *Science, Religion and Politics in Restoration England – Richard Cumberland's De Legibus Naturae* (Woodbridge, 1999), p. 48. I owe my knowledge and understanding of this 'second approach' to Dr Parkin's stimulating book.

97 *Locke – Political Essays*, p. 213.

98 See *Locke – Political Essays*, pp. 216–21, 230–5, 246–8; Wolseley, *Liberty*, p. 25.

9 1677–9: MUTINOUS ASSEMBLIES AND PICKPOCKET WARS

1 BL Add MS 25124, fols 119, 120.

2 *Essex Papers*, II. 86.

3 [Marchamont Nedham], *A Pacquet of Advices* (1676), pp. 2, 8, 15, 36.

4 Browning, *Danby*, I. 218 note 3.

5 Buckingham, pp. 105, 107, 111. The parliamentary narrative of this chapter is based primarily on Grey and *PH*, but Haley's *Shaftesbury* and Browning's *Danby* have been indispensable guides.

6 *Essex Papers*, II. 101–2; Grey, IV. 63, 71.

7 *HMC Verney*, p. 468.

8 Reresby, p. 111.

9 Grey, IV. 150.

10 Grey, IV. 138.

11   *HMC Verney,* p. 469.
12   *Essex Papers,* II. 105.
13   *PH,* 855–7.
14   *PH,* 861.
15   Grey, IV. 188.
16   Grey, IV. 160–4.
17   Marvell, *Letters,* p. 183; on Cary see chapter 6 above.
18   Haley, pp. 424–6; *HMC Verney,* p. 469.
19   *Essex Papers,* II. 109–10.
20   Reresby, p. 116.
21   Browning, *Danby,* II. 66–9, I. 225.
22   *Essex Papers,* II. 118.
23   *PH,* 864, 866–7.
24   *PH,* 868–9.
25   *Essex Papers,* II. 121.
26   *Essex Papers,* II. 122; Reresby, p. 117. Both sources imply that the King was
      at Newmarket while Danby was installed at Windsor.
27   See *Essex Papers,* II. 49, 125–6.
28   *HMC Verney,* p. 469, which includes letters from Wharton; *Savile Corre-*
      spondence, p. 50; Haley, p. 427.
29   *HMC Verney,* p. 469.
30   *PH,* 871.
31   *PH,* 873.
32   *PH,* 876, 874, 878.
33   *PH,* 884, 888; *Essex Papers,* II. 142; cf. Reresby, p. 124.
34   *PH,* 889–91; *HMC Verney,* p. 469.
35   *Savile Correspondence,* pp. 58, 61, 62.
36   Morrice P, fol. 57; *Savile Correspondence,* pp. 63, 66; Haley, pp. 432–3; PRO
      SP 104/180, fol. 87.
37   *Savile Correspondence,* p. 59.
38   *HMC Verney,* p. 494.
39   BL Add MS 17017, fol. 55; *HMC Ormonde,* IV. 38, 45, 47–8, 376.
40   Morrice P, fol. 58.
41   *HMC Ormonde,* IV. 385, 387, 388.
42   J. Childs, *The Army of Charles II* (1976), p. 186; *HMC Ormonde,* IV. 389–90.
43   Morrice P, fol. 60.
44   Browning, *Danby,* II. 332; Marvell, *Letters,* 209.
45   BL Add MS 25125, fol. 44.
46   Miller, *Charles II,* p. 275.
47   Marvell, *Letters,* p. 213.
48   See Henry, *Diaries,* p. 274; Marvell, *Letters,* p. 217.
49   *Account,* p. 155.
50   J. M. Wallace, *Destiny His Choice – The Loyalism of Andrew Marvell* (Cam-
      bridge, 1968), p. 210; Haley, p. 438.
51   Marvell, *Letters,* p. 357; T. J. Crist, 'Francis Smith and the Opposition Press
      in England, 1660–1688' (Cambridge University Ph.D. thesis, 1983), p. 49;
      CSPD 1678, pp. 69–70, 281, 305–6.
52   *CSPD 1678,* p. 66; Morrice P, fol. 66, and see fols 60, 66–8, 73, 75.

53 Reresby, p. 134.
54 Marvell, *Letters*, p. 224; *PH*, 953; Reresby, p. 136.
55 Marvell, *Letters*, p. 226.
56 Morrice P, fols 73, 80; Childs, *Army of Charles II*, p. 187.
57 Browning, *Danby*, II. 346–9.
58 Browning, *Danby*, III. 111–20.
59 *PH*, 958, 961; Reresby, p. 131; Marvell, *Letters*, pp. 227–8, 229.
60 Marvell, *Letters*, p. 230; *PH*, 966; Haley, pp. 447, 448.
61 *PH*, 966–9.
62 *PH*, 973, 974, 977; Marvell, *Letters*, pp. 233, 234.
63 Browning, *Danby*, I. 278.
64 Morrice P, fol. 83; Marvell, *Letters*, pp. 235–6; Reresby, p. 144, 143; *PH*, 978, 980.
65 Reresby, p. 147; Haley, p. 449; *PH*, pp. 987–90; Marvell, *Letters*, p. 240.
66 *PH*, 986, 1003, 990.
67 *PH*, 997; Marvell, *Letters*, p. 242.
68 *HMC Verney*, p. 470; *HMC Bath*, II. 164; Evelyn, IV. 136–7.
69 *HMC Ormonde*, IV. 186, 446–7; *HMC Verney*, p. 494; and for the downbeat reality see Childs, *Army of Charles II*, p. 190.
70 *HMC Verney*, pp. 494, 470–1.
71 *HMC Ormonde*, IV. 448; Evelyn, IV. 140–4.
72 *Savile Correspondence*, pp. 73, 69–70; *HMC Ormonde*, IV. 448.
73 *HMC Ormonde*, IV. 454–5, 458, 457.
74 Browning, *Danby*, I. 291, note 2; *HMC Ormonde*, IV. 458–9.
75 *HMC Verney*, p. 494; *HMC Ormonde*, IV. 460; *POAS*, II. 3–16. Dr Marshall has uncovered new evidence on Godfrey's earlier career, see 'The Westminster Magistrate and the Irish Stroker', *Historical Journal* 40 (1997).
76 *PH*, 1016; Reresby, p. 152; *HMC Ormonde*, IV. 453, 460–1.
77 *HMC Verney*, p. 494.
78 *HMC Ormonde*, IV. 465.
79 *HMC Ormonde*, IV. 462.
80 *HMC Ormonde*, IV. 465; see *PH*, 1026–34; Dering, *Diaries*, pp. 183–4.
81 *HMC Ormonde*, IV. 470.
82 *HOP*, III. 56.
83 *HMC Ormonde*, IV. 470; *HMC Verney*, p. 471.
84 *HMC Ormonde*, IV. 455, 468; Reresby, p. 157.
85 *HMC Ormonde*, IV. 494.
86 Wood, II. 422; *HMC Verney*, p. 471; *HMC Ormonde*, IV. 472.
87 *HMC Ormonde*, IV. 473.
88 *HMC Ormonde*, IV. 480, 483–4; Evelyn, IV. 157.
89 Reresby, p, 161.
90 See Browning, *Danby*, I. 300, II. 371–2, III. 6–9; Reresby, p. 167; M. Knights, *Politics and Opinion in Crisis, 1678–1681* (Cambridge, 1994), pp. 26–7.
91 *HMC Ormonde*, IV. 490.
92 *PH*, 1061.
93 Articles printed in Browning, *Danby*, II. 74–5.

94   *PH*, 1074; Knights, *Politics and Opinion*, p. 204, note; M. Knights, 'London Petitions and Parliamentary Politics in 1679', *Parliamentary History* 12 (1993), 30; *CSPD 1679–80*, p. 19; Henry, *Diaries*, p. 278.
95   Knights, *Politics and Opinion*, pp. 43, 42.
96   Josselin, p. 618.
97   *CSPD 1679–80*, pp. 21, 24, 81, 83 and 19–26 *passim*; Morrice P, fols 103–6, 135–6.
98   Reresby, pp. 169, 170; Browning, *Danby*, I. 315, note 7; *CSPD 1679–80*, p. 77; M. A. Kishlansky, *Parliamentary Selection* (Cambridge, 1986), p. 173.
99   Josselin, p. 619.
100 *HMC Ormonde*, IV. 340, cf. 335 for Coventry's view.
101 Knights, 'London Petitions', 31.
102 Morrice P, fol. 135.
103 Reresby, p. 171.
104 *HMC Ormonde*, IV. 499.
105 Henry, *Diaries*, p. 279.
106 Reresby, p. 171; Browning, *Danby*, I. 320, II. 112; Knights, *Politics and Opinion*, p. 45.
107 *Savile Correspondence*, p. 76.
108 Reresby, p. 173.
109 *Savile Correspondence*, p. 78.
110 *Savile Correspondence*, p. 80; *HMC Ormonde*, V. 38, 48.

10   1679–81: A WASPS' NEST

1   BL, Evelyn Letter Book, Letter CCCC (I am grateful to Mark Knights for his generosity in giving me a copy of his transcription of this letter and to the trustees of the will of Major Peter George Evelyn for permission to quote from the manuscript); D. R. Lacey, *Dissent and Parliamentary Politics in England 1661–1689* (New Brunswick, 1969), p. 121; *HMC Ormonde*, IV. xviii. This chapter's political and parliamentary narrative is drawn from Grey, *PH*, Southwell's letters in *HMC Ormonde*, and other sources; but it is deeply indebted to M. Knights, *Politics and Opinion in Crisis, 1678–81* (Cambridge, 1994); J. R. Jones, *The First Whigs* (Oxford, 1961), and Haley.
2   Haley, p. 513; *HMC Ormonde*, V. 55.
3   *HMC Ormonde*, IV. 504.
4   *Savile Correspondence*, pp. 89–90; Josselin, pp. 621, 620.
5   *HMC Ormonde*, V. 93; Grey, VII. 180; Browning, *Danby*, I. 336.
6   *HMC Ormonde*, V. 99; the best account is Mark Goldie, 'Danby, the Bishops and the Whigs', in T. Harris, P. Seaward and M. Goldie (eds), *The Politics of Religion in Restoration England* (Oxford, 1990).
7   *HOP*, I. 641; *HMC Ormonde*, IV. 517; Morrice P, fols 188–9; Grey, VII. 228–9, 231–6, 329–30, 333–6.
8   *HMC Ormonde*, IV. 501.
9   *HMC Ormonde*, IV. xx.
10 Wood, II. 448.
11 Quoted by Lacey, *Dissent and Parliamentary Politics*, p. 121.
12 Knights, *Politics and Opinion*, pp. 197–8; Jones, *First Whigs*, pp. 53–4.

13 Compare Haley, p. 517 and Knights, *Politics and Opinion*, pp. 49–50.
14 *HMC Ormonde*, IV. 508.
15 *HMC Ormonde*, V. 84.
16 *HMC Ormonde*, V. 89.
17 *HMC Ormonde*, V. 97–8.
18 *HMC Ormonde*, IV. 514; and see M. Knights, 'London Petitions and Parliamentary Politics in 1679', *Parliamentary History* 12 (1993).
19 *HMC Ormonde*, V. 116; also see 118; *Savile Correspondence*, p. 102.
20 W. D. Christie, *The Life of Anthony Ashley Cooper, First Earl of Shaftesbury* (2 vols, 1871), II. appendix VI; Morrice P, fols 179, 195, 196, 197; *HMC Verney*, pp. 472, 473.
21 *HMC Ormonde*, V. 91, 93.
22 Henry, *Diaries*, p. 279.
23 *HMC Verney*, p. 474; Morrice P, fol. 208.
24 *Savile Correspondence*, p. 98; H. C. Foxcroft, *A Character of the Trimmer* (Cambridge, 1946), p. 76.
25 *A New Satyricall Ballad* (1679); Luttrell II. 116, stanza xxi. See also T. Crist, 'Government Control of the Press after the Expiration of the Licensing Act in 1679', *Publishing History* V (1979).
26 Wood, II. 429; *POAS*, I. 213; *Savile Correspondence*, pp. 107, 108–9.
27 *POAS*, II. 145–53.
28 See *PH*, appendix IX; Morrice P, fol. 211.
29 Knights, *Politics and Opinion*, p. 206.
30 *HMC Ormonde*, V. 157, 156, 166. Also see *HMC Verney*, p. 473; Morrice P, fols 207, 208.
31 R. Blencowe (ed.), *Diary of Henry Sidney* (1843), I. 94–5, 81.
32 Knights, *Politics and Opinion*, pp. 206–19.
33 Reresby, pp. 185–8, 190.
34 *HMC Ormonde*, V. 191.
35 *Savile Correspondence*, p. 119.
36 Reresby, p. 91; *CSPD 1678–9*, p. 278.
37 *HMC Verney*, p. 475; *HMC Ormonde*, V. 204.
38 Narcissus Luttrell, *A Brief Historical Relation* (Oxford, 1857), p. 22; Morrice P, fol. 209.
39 Josselin, p. 625; *HMC Verney*, p. 476.
40 Bod. MS don. b 8, p. 597; *HMC Verney*, p. 476.
41 *HMC Verney*, p. 477. For a modern account with illustrations and further references see T. Harris, *London Crowds in the Reign of Charles II* (Cambridge, 1987), pp. 103–6, 120–1.
42 J. Miller, *James II* (1978: 1989 edn), p. 96.
43 *HMC Verney*, pp. 477–8; Morrice P, fols 237–8, 240.
44 *HMC Verney*, p. 478.
45 Morrice P, fol. 241; Henry, *Diaries*, p. 283; and Knights, *Politics and Opinion*, ch. 8.
46 *HMC Ormonde*, V. 271.
47 *Savile Correspondence*, p. 134.
48 See Knights, *Politics and Opinion*, pp. 260–3.
49 *HMC Ormonde*, V. 288, 290, 301; Reresby, pp. 193–4; J. P. Kenyon, *Robert*

Spencer, Earl of Sunderland (1958), p. 43; Knights, *Politics and Opinion,* p. 265.

50 Knights, *Politics and Opinion,* p. 265.
51 *Some Unpublished Letters of Gilbert Burnet,* ed. H. C. Foxcroft (Camden Society, XI, 1907), p. 39; and on the Irish plot, Haley, pp. 569–72.
52 *HMC Ormonde,* V. 295, 296; Morrice P, fol. 255. For a full analysis see Harris, *London Crowds,* p. 166.
53 Knights, *Politics and Opinion,* p. 265.
54 Reresby, pp. 197–9.
55 See Harris, *London Crowds,* pp. 139–40 on this engraving. For other examples of the masquerade topos see *POAS,* II. 284–8, 380–90.
56 *HMC Ormonde,* V. 310–11, 314, 315, 329.
57 *Letters of Burnet,* p. 35; Henry, *Diaries,* p. 289; cf. I. Sinclair (ed.), *The Pyramid and the Urn* (Farr Thrupp, 1994), p. 50 (letter possibly misdated).
58 Knights, *Politics and Opinion,* pp. 274–5.
59 *HMC Ormonde,* V. 349; cf. Morrice P, fol. 264.
60 *CSPD 1680–1,* p. 31; Morrice P, fol. 264; *POAS,* II. 273–9, for a 1681 satire mocking the cure.
61 Haley, pp. 589–90.
62 Foxcroft, *Character of Trimmer,* p. 113.
63 Haley, p. 605; *HMC Ormonde,* V. 489.
64 *HMC Verney,* p. 496; Foxcroft, *Character of Trimmer,* p. 119.
65 *HMC Ormonde,* V. 530.
66 *Savile Correspondence,* p. 173. A dissolution was widely anticipated by 1 January: Morrice P, fol. 289.
67 *CSPD 1680–1,* p. 138; *HOP,* I. 480; Morrice P, fol. 298.
68 *HOP,* I. 238–9; Knights, *Politics and Opinion,* p. 287.
69 Wood, II. 513; Dering, *Diaries,* p. 120; Knights, *Politics and Opinion,* pp. 306–7.
70 *PH,* 1303–5; and see Haley, pp. 623–4, 632–1; for the Oxford Parliament see Haley, ch. xxvii; Dering, *Diaries,* pp. 122–5.
71 Reresby, pp. 211, 215.
72 The most comprehensive account of the issues involved in this 'succession crisis' is Knights, *Politics and Opinion.* Also see J. Scott, *Algernon Sidney and the Restoration Crisis, 1677–1683* (Cambridge, 1991) which stresses the international dimension and the republican perspective; T. Harris, *Politics under the Later Stuarts* (1993), ch. 4, is a broader view of party conflict.

EPILOGUE

1 *The Letters of King Charles II,* ed. A. Bryant (1935), p. 321; P. Harth, *Pen for a Party – Dryden's Tory Propaganda in Its Contexts* (Princeton, 1993), ch. 3.
2 Gilbert Burnet, *Some Passages of the Life and Death of . . . John Earl of Rochester* (1680), p. 1.
3 Rochester, p. 39.

Index